THE COSTA RICANS

RICHARD BIESANZ

KAREN ZUBRIS BIESANZ

MAVIS HILTUNEN BIESANZ

Prentice-Hall, Inc., Englewood Cliffs, New Jersey 07632

Library of Congress Cataloging in Publication Data

BIESANZ, RICHARD.
    The Costa Ricans.

    Includes bibliographical references and index.
    1. Costa Rica. I. Biesanz, Karen Zubris.
II. Biesanz, Mavis Hiltunen.   III. Title.
F1543.B57   972.86   81-7380
ISBN 0-13-179606-2   AACR2

Cover painting by Fausto Pacheco.

*Special Costa Rican editions by Editorial
Universidad Estatal a Distancia,
(EUNED), San José, 1983 and 1987.*

CONTENTS

Preface / *vii*

1
LAND AND PEOPLE / 1

2
HISTORY / 14

3
COMMUNITY / 33

4

CLASS AND RACE / 47

5

HOUSING, HEALTH, AND EVERYDAY LIVING / 71

6

THE FAMILY AND THE LIFE CYCLE / 88

7

EDUCATION / 114

8

RELIGION / 137

9

LEISURE AND THE ARTS / 158

10

POLITICS AND GOVERNMENT / 177

11

CHANGE A LA TICA:
SUMMARY AND CONCLUSION / 207

12

TOWARD THE YEAR 2000
(Update, October 1987) / 215

Notes / 223
Index / 245

Pejibayes for sale on the Atlantic slope (Miguel Salguero)

Sunset on Manuel Antonio Beach (Mavis Biesanz)

Coffee picker (Miguel Salguero)

Central Avenue, San José (Miguel Callaci)

The "corner grocery" and bar (Katherine Lambert)

A cowboy herding cattle in Guanacaste (Katherine Lambert)

A housewife in San Antonio de Escazú (Mavis Biesanz)

A school fiesta in Acosta (Miguel Salguero)

A family returning from Sunday mass (Mavis Biesanz)

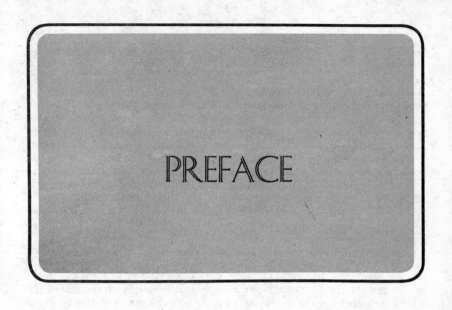

PREFACE

This book examines the institutions through which one society functions, how they evolved and how they are changing. These institutions are found in one form or another in every society. Costa Rican institutions in many ways resemble those in the rest of Spanish America. As in other societies in the so-called *Third World,* they are undergoing the stresses of that complex of trends usually labeled—though not always accurately—"development" or "modernization." To some extent, then, Costa Rica presents a case study of a developing Spanish American society.

At the same time, every society is in many ways unique, and Costa Rica is indeed a very special society. Costa Ricans are self-consciously and even proudly "different." The nation's respect for democracy, its lack of an army, its widespread education, its honest elections, and its atmosphere of liberty are proverbial in Latin America. Its two million people are proud of their heritage. But many of them also feel that this pride, while justified, has tended to blind them to serious social problems. And many are concerned lest their society fall prey to social, economic, and political trends that endanger Costa Rican democracy.[1] They often say that changes should

---

[1] In 1981, these concerns were intensified when civil war in El Salvador lost Costa Rica a major market and provoked a large influx of Salvadorean refugees. This compounded a political and economic crisis which arose when the colon was sharply devalued in 1980 in response to rapid increases in the costs of oil—all of it imported—and a sharp decline in coffee earnings. Characteristically, Costa Rican officials responded by announcing plans for development of alternative energy sources and diversified exports, appealing to the International Monetary Fund for a major loan, and attempting to promote a nonmilitary solution to the Salvadorean conflict.

occur only *a la tica*—according to their "idiosyncrasy," or particular norms and values.

We are dealing here, then, not only with universal and with Spanish American patterns, but also with those of a specific culture. Occasionally we spell out similarities and contrasts with other societies, but on the whole they remain implicit. One pitfall of this treatment is that some generalizations may seem unduly harsh. Let us emphasize that we could often have added "as in many other societies," "as in much of Latin America," or, in many instances, "but this problem is far less serious than elsewhere." If we had made all the possible qualifications and comparisons the book would have run to many volumes. In any case, the Costa Ricans themselves are extremely self-critical as individuals and as a society, and their own indictments are on the whole much more severe than those of foreigners, who often say that Costa Ricans are not fully aware of the special graces and virtues of their own land and people.

The Costa Ricans have a strong self-image that orients much of their behavior as individuals and as a nation. However "false" this insiders' point of view may be from some stand-points, it cannot be doubted that a people's self-image affects their relations with one another and with the rest of the world, though not always in ways of which they are aware. Any description of them and their society must take this self-image into account. Outsiders, on the other hand, may see aspects of a culture that insiders miss. It must be added that outsiders are not likely to be more "objective" about a society in every respect. Theirs, too, is a perspective, not a dispassionate description, and different analysts of a society are likely to use different conceptual schemes. Such similarities as exist among these schemes are largely due to similarities in the cultural backgrounds of the analysts.

Costa Rica offers several advantages to students of human societies. Among nation-states, it is relatively small and cohesive, yet has many different groups and categories. There is a relatively free press in which problems and policies are openly and often vehemently discussed, and in which thoughtful and informative essays frequently appear. And Costa Ricans are generally tolerant of and cooperative with (though often amused by) social anthropologists and their innumerable questions. We appreciated their cooperation and the freedom they allowed us to investigate the way they live.

ACKNOWLEDGMENTS

Many people have helped make this book possible. We are particularly indebted to John Biesanz, Theodore Creedman and Carlos Meléndez Ch. for their advice and unfailing encouragement. Among those who read the manuscript in various stages and offered valuable suggestions, we would especially like to thank John Biesanz, Antonio Picado, Odilie de Picado and Marco Tulio Salazar. We are grateful to Jimmy Socash for his maps and graphs, and to Sylvia Boxley de Sassone, La Verne Coleman, Francisco González, Katherine Lambert, Rodrigo Montenegro, Miguel Salguero, Jim Theologos, Sergio Méndez, Jorge Ramírez, Miguel Callaci, Luis Ferrero, Hector Gamboa, and the staffs of *La Nación* and *Tico Times* for photographs. Many thanks to June Groves and Brenda Wilson for typing the manuscript, and to Jeanne Hoeting of Prentice-Hall for her editorial skills. Finally, we wish to express our affection and gratitude to the many Costa Ricans who helped us learn about them and their compatriots.

A METHODOLOGICAL NOTE

The fieldwork on which this book is chiefly based includes periods of varying length beginning in 1968. During that year we (Richard and Karen) spent seven months in San José, Costa Rica's economic and political capital, where many social trends affecting the entire society first appear. For seven more months we lived with the fourteen-member family of a telegraph operator in their rented house on the central plaza of San Isidro de Heredia in a coffee-growing *cantón* (county) of about 4,500 people. We devoted three more months to research in other parts of the country. We made month-long return visits in 1970, 1973, 1974, 1977, 1978, and 1979. Mavis Biesanz, a resident of Costa Rica since 1971 and coauthor of *Costa Rican Life,* with John Biesanz, spent considerable time from 1974 to 1979 tracing changes in the major social institutions and collaborating in editing and revising the manuscript.

Our primary emphasis is descriptive rather than theoretical. Admittedly, all description involves numerous theoretical implications, many of which must remain implicit. Our descriptions and attempted interpretations of Costa Rican society are not cast in any single theoretical framework, and whether or not the reader finds them adequate will depend in large part on personal interests and theoretical perspectives. Anthropologists realize that it is impossible to describe completely even a slowly changing "primitive" society. This is certainly true of Costa Rica, which is neither.

Our primary research methods were participant observation and informal open-ended interviews with approximately a thousand people, some of whom we saw many times and came to know well. By taking part in many different kinds of social situations, we tried to alternate between the perspectives of cultural outsiders and those of Costa Ricans themselves. We observed interaction in a wide variety of natural settings and noted the different contexts in which various kinds of behavior occurred. We recorded our observations in a daily log and checked the consistency of our observations with each other as a way of increasing their reliability. We also made constant use of documentary sources such as newspapers, books, stories, and scholarly theses and journals.

R.B., K.Z.B.

A FURTHER NOTE

When I first knew Costa Rica it was sleepy and provincial. In *Costa Rican Life* John and I described a country that had only begun to take tentative steps toward modernization. In spite of great poverty and growing unrest, we did not foresee the turmoil that would erupt later in the decade and would mark a watershed in Costa Rican history.

The unpredictable twists of life brought me back to Costa Rica in 1971 as the wife of a retired professor. We see ourselves as we were thirty-five years ago, a serious and enthusiastic young couple deeply immersed in the life of the country, now reflected in our son and daughter-in-law. It has been a privilege to collaborate with them on this book concerning the tremendous changes since the 1940s. Also, this is a book about the strength of cultural patterns that persist even as people bemoan the loss of old ways. My share began with a promise to spend several months helping to edit and update their manuscript, a task which turned out to last five years. I therefore accept the honor of being listed as coauthor.

This task forced me to learn a great deal about the country I now call home, and to take a solemn vow henceforth to leave the exhausting labor of social anthropological research on such a large topic to the younger generation. Even in a tiny country facts are elusive and much time and thought must be spent on efforts to bring the assemblage of facts into perspective. The interpretations of my coauthors have been challenging. We have not always agreed. Sometimes I have bowed to the insights they gained from deeper immersion in the daily life of village and countryside. Sometimes they have recognized that added years, at least when combined with thought and work, lend perspectives denied the young, just as John and I look back and see how today's hindsight and maturity would have made *Costa Rican Life* quite a different book.

This book adds one more personal tie to this very special country. Perhaps another generation, which includes two Tica granddaughters, will feel impelled in turn to record the changes between today and the year 2000. My share of this work is dedicated to the younger generation.

M. H. B.

Our special thanks to our United States publishers, Prentice-Hall, Inc., for permission to bring out this special edition in Costa Rica, thus making it more readily available locally. We are also grateful to Carlos Arce and the staff of EUNED for bringing out this edition, which is a condensed and slightly updated version of LOS COSTARRICENSES, published by the same institution.

R. B., K.Z.B., and M.H.B.

1

LAND AND PEOPLE

Costa Ricans call themselves Ticos. This name is said to stem from the colonial saying "We are all *hermaniticos* (little brothers)." It also reflects their custom of referring to many things in the diminutive, ending in *-ito*, as in other Spanish-speaking countries, and more characteristically in *-ico*. They even combine the two into a super-diminutive. Thus something small may be not simply *chico* or *chiquito*, but *chiquitico*.

In some respects the land itself suggests diminutives. With roughly 51,000 square kilometers or 19,965 square miles, about the same area as West Virginia, it is the second smallest country in mainland America; only El Salvador is smaller. (See Map 1) Costa Rica's maximum length from the Nicaraguan border to the Panamanian border is 484 kilometers; its minimum width from the Pacific Ocean to the Caribbean Sea, 119 kilometers. Not until 1976 did the population pass the two million mark. Only 10 degrees north of the equator, Costa Rica experiences little variation in the hours of sunrise and sunset. Dawn and twilight are beautiful but brief.

But in other respects, descriptions of Costa Rica by both Ticos and visitors have long abounded in superlatives: The most peaceful country in Latin America—the only one with no army. The most democratic. The friendliest people. The prettiest women. The highest literacy rate in Central America. An ideal climate. Scenery so beautiful it is called "the Switzerland of Central America." Writers of travel books and tourist pamphlets, as well as promoters of land development projects, parrot these and other clichés. Some are quite true. But newcomers who expect to find Costa Rica the last idyllic tropical retreat from world problems may find themselves a bit disillusioned,

1

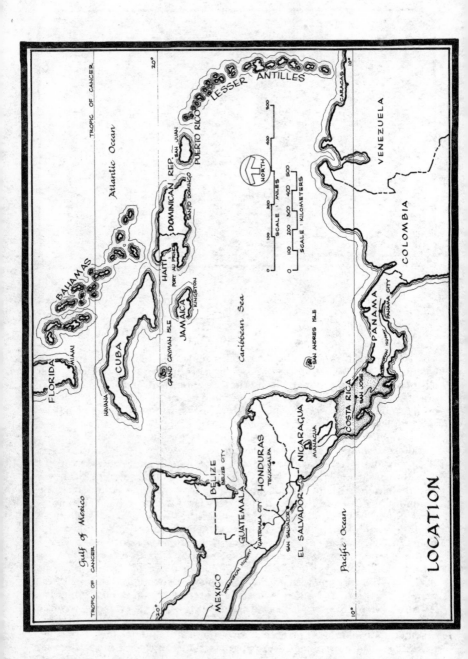

LOCATION

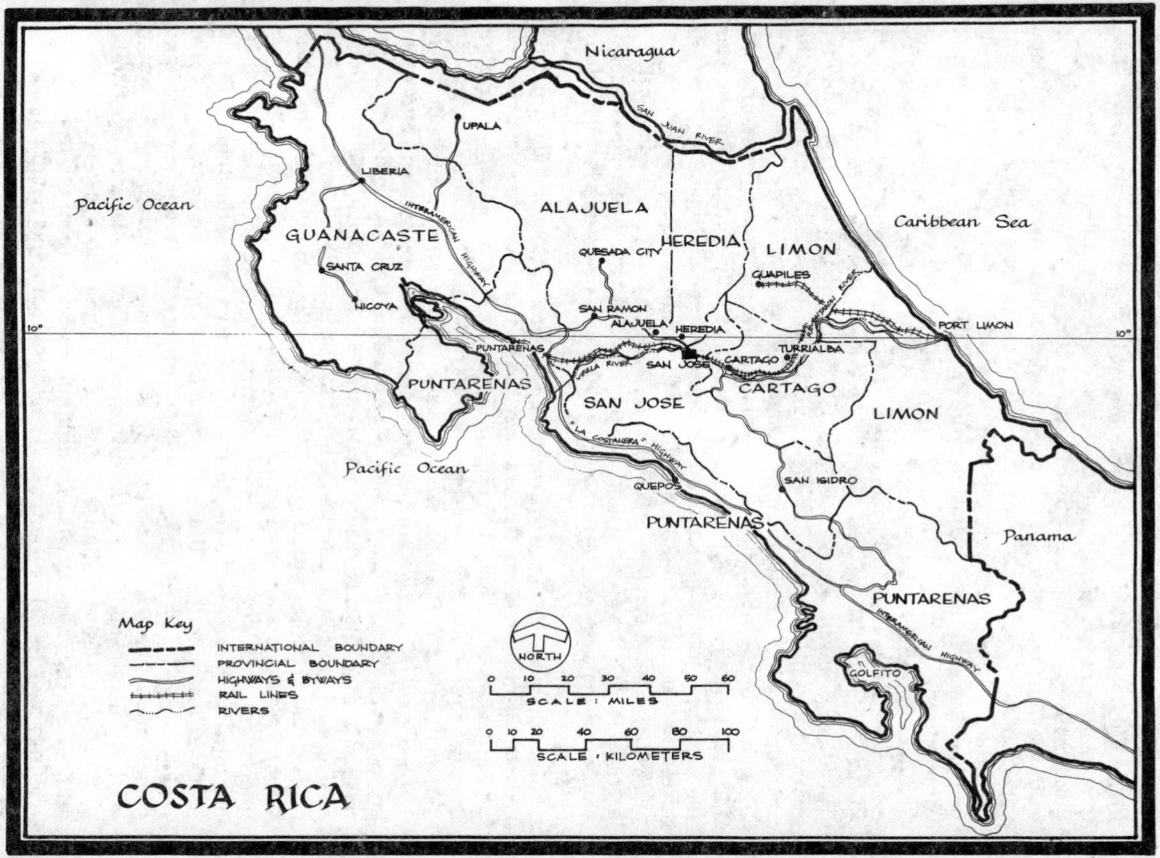
Nicaragua
SAN JUAN RIVER
UPALA
LIBERIA
Pacific Ocean
ALAJUELA
Caribbean Sea
INTERAMERICAN HIGHWAY
GUANACASTE
HEREDIA
LIMON
QUESADA CITY
SANTA CRUZ
GUAPILES
NICOYA
SAN RAMON
10°
ALAJUELA
HEREDIA
PORT LIMON
PUNTARENAS
TURRIALBA
SAN JOSE
CARTAGO
PUNTARENAS
CARTAGO
SAN JOSE
LIMON
"LA COSTANERA" HIGHWAY
Pacific Ocean
QUEPOS
SAN ISIDRO
PUNTARENAS
Panama
PUNTARENAS
Map Key
INTERNATIONAL BOUNDARY
PROVINCIAL BOUNDARY
HIGHWAYS & BYWAYS
RAIL LINES
RIVERS
NORTH
0 10 20 30 40 50 60
SCALE : MILES
0 10 20 40 60 80 100
SCALE : KILOMETERS
GOLFITO
COSTA RICA

MAP 2

while Costa Rican social critics attack many accepted generalizations as cultural myths or consoling fallacies.

Yet superlatives are tempting when one describes the enormous variety of topography, climate, and plant and animal life in this small country. The temperature drops greatly as one climbs from coastal lowlands to treeless mountaintops. Rainfall and humidity vary with nearness to oceans as well as to mountains, and with the direction of prevailing winds. These climatic variations help explain the great diversity of Costa Rica's flora and fauna, as does the country's "strategic position near the junction of two great continents, biologically quite different, from each of which it has received large contributions."[1]

Mountain ranges run the length of the country from northwest to southeast and separate the Caribbean and Pacific coastal areas. A volcanic range, the Cordillera de Guanacaste, begins near Nicaragua and meets the volcanic Cordillera Central, which ends near the center of the country. A higher nonvolcanic range, the Cordillera de Talamanca, runs from the center to the southeastern border and on into Panama and Colombia.

As in all of Central America, the Atlantic slope is mostly broad, gradual, and gentle; the Pacific slope, narrow, steep, and hilly. In the northeast near the Caribbean and in the southwest lowlands on the Pacific side are the rain forests that still cover about a quarter of the country's area,[2] despite extensive cultivation of bananas and African palm. By contrast, the tropical dry forest of the northwest has a long and severe dry season; it is largely flatland, with great expanses of cotton and rice fields and of grassy savannas where cattle graze.

More than half the Ticos live in the *Valle Central* or Central Valley, and are especially concentrated in the relatively flat section called the *Meseta Central* or Central Plateau. The Central Valley is formed where the two chief mountain ranges nearly meet, and runs from San Ramón in the west to Turrialba in the east. Altitudes on the valley floors range from about 800 to 1,500 meters, averaging about 1,000 meters. While sugarcane and other crops are also common here, much of the Central Valley is planted in coffee, the crop that "paradoxically has contributed as much to the underdevelopment as to the development of Costa Rica."[3]

The *Valle Central* is not, strictly speaking, a valley any more than the *Meseta Central* is a plateau, but both terms are traditional and, in everyday speech, interchangeable. The *Meseta* is really two small sections of the Central Valley, between Turrúcares and Tres Ríos on the western side of the mountains and around Cartago and Paraíso to the east. In and near the Central Valley, as well as the Valley of El General to the southeast, the terrain is rugged and fragmented. The slopes of hills and mountains are a patchwork of woodland, cropland, and pasture; the lush green valleys are laced with streams.

Weather varies with altitude, time of year, and exposure to ocean winds. In the Central Valley, daytime temperatures range from 60° to 85°F., averaging about 70°(21°C.), and writers of tourist pamphlets rhapsodize about "The Land of Eternal Spring." But many evenings are so chilly that sweaters and warm blankets are welcome.

Costa Rica has a modified version of a monsoon climate. There are two

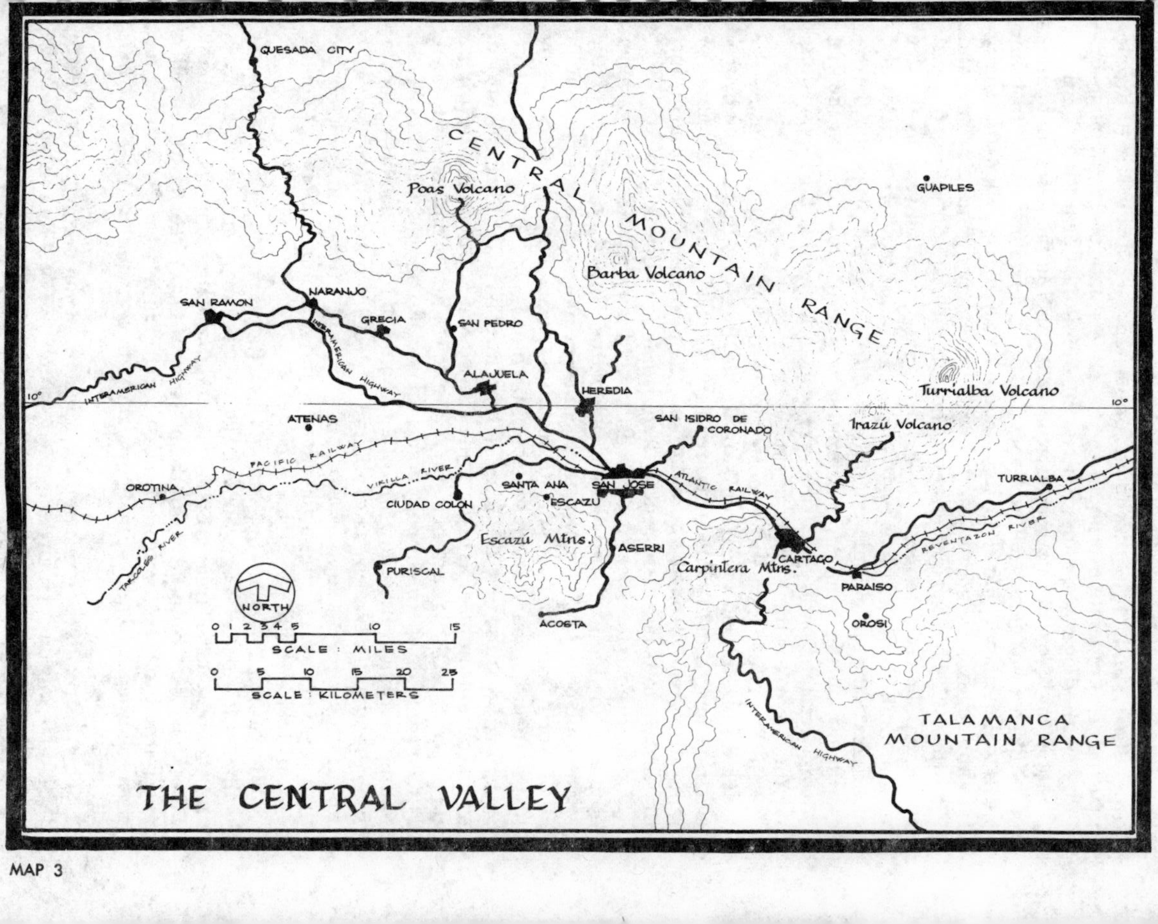
THE CENTRAL VALLEY
CENTRAL MOUNTAIN RANGE
TALAMANCA MOUNTAIN RANGE
QUESADA CITY
Poas Volcano
Barba Volcano
Turrialba Volcano
Irazú Volcano
GUAPILES
NARANJO
SAN RAMON
GRECIA
SAN PEDRO
ALAJUELA
HEREDIA
ATENAS
SAN ISIDRO DE CORONADO
SAN JOSE
SANTA ANA
ESCAZU
CIUDAD COLON
OROTINA
PURISCAL
Escazú Mtns.
ASERRI
ACOSTA
CARTAGO
Carpintera Mtns.
PARAISO
OROSI
TURRIALBA
REVENTAZON RIVER
VIRILLA RIVER
TARCOLES RIVER
PACIFIC RAILWAY
ATLANTIC RAILWAY
INTERAMERICAN HIGHWAY
INTERAMERICAN HIGHWAY
INTERAMERICAN HIGHWAY
10°
10°
NORTH
0 1 2 3 4 5 10 15
SCALE : MILES
0 5 10 15 20 25
SCALE : KILOMETERS

MAP 3

fairly distinct seasons, called *invierno* and *verano*; the usual English translations as "winter" and "summer" are misleading. *Invierno*, the rainy season, lasts from May to November. Cloudless mornings are usually followed by overcast skies and a brief downpour, or perhaps by a steady rain or drizzle that may continue all afternoon. In the rainiest months, September and October, there are sometimes periods of several days of unceasing rain.

About mid-November strong north winds usher in the first cool months of the dry season for the Central Valley and the Pacific slope (but bring rainy spells to the Atlantic side of the mountain watershed). Dispelling the dreary rain and fog of *invierno*, the winds herald the gaiety of coffee picking and Christmas. Early *verano* is often chilly and may include a number of overcast and damp days. While most wooded areas stay green all year, as the dry season continues grass turns toasty brown and dust blows from fields and dirt roads in the center and west of the country. Many people prefer the dry season, but during its final warm months, they become as eager for the first downpour as the parakeets flying overhead in screeching flocks, pleading, say the Ticos, for the rains to begin.

Rain is one of Costa Rica's most valuable resources. It replenishes the water supply, irrigates the crops, and feeds the rivers that supply hydroelectric energy and in some areas are the only travel routes. The amount of rain varies greatly from the humid Atlantic slopes, where there is no distinct dry season, to Guanacaste, where there is a long and severe one.

Costa Rica has long been a naturalist's paradise. There are more varieties of plants in this tiny land than in all of the United States east of the Mississippi: over 1,500 distinct species of trees, more kinds of ferns than in all of North America north of Mexico, and over 6,000 kinds of flowering plants, including a thousand species of orchids.[4]

Animal life is also profuse. Some 760 species of birds have been identified, about the same number as in the entire United States. But unlike the tropical forests of the Old World, here there are few animals dangerous to man. Fifteen common species of poisonous snakes inflict about 2,000 bites a year, but the mortality rate is now almost nil, thanks to the availability of serum. Insects and water creatures also abound, especially in the rain forests. Acre for acre these forests support a greater variety of animal and vegetable life than any other area of the earth's surface, and the interrelationships among various forms of life are highly complex.

But naturalists lament the fact that Costa Rica is no longer the paradise it seemed a few decades ago. Some large stretches of virgin forest still exist, and some extensive areas are now preserved as national parks.[5] But many others have been reduced to shreds and patches. Giant trees have been felled and burned to make cropland and pasture; in hilly areas, soil erosion has soon followed. Bird and animal populations have dwindled along with their shelter.

This destruction of much of the original beauty and ecological balance of the land is only one of many man-made problems Costa Rica shares with the rest of the world. Some of these problems are common to many countries of the Third World: unequal and inefficient distribution of arable land; dependence on world markets for one or two main export products; dependence on large industrial nations for trade—in the case of Latin America, the United States in particular; and relative powerlessness to affect the terms of that trade. With a steady rate of economic growth and a per capita income that has passed the $1,500 mark, Costa Rica now is classed in the middle range of development, and these problems are less severe than in many other countries. Nonetheless, many of its people still live in poverty. Although some efforts have been made to redistribute farmland, and although population growth has slowed down considerably, unemployment and consequent migration to an already overcrowded capital remain pressing concerns.

Like many peoples, Costa Ricans are eager for the benefits of "development" but uncertain of how to achieve them without sacrificing older values and institutions. Although many changes seem inevitable, Costa Rican decision-makers and social observers are concerned with guiding and promoting change in ways that will not violate their national identity, and rejecting changes that threaten to do so.

THE PEOPLE OF COSTA RICA

In comparison with the people of most other Latin American countries, Costa Ricans are physically and culturally homogeneous. About 95 percent of Ticos inherit varying mixtures of the *mestizo* blend of Spanish conquerors and colonists with Indians, including some African heritage in many cases.

Most Ticos share similar ways of thinking, acting, and feeling. Their cultural homogeneity is apparent in religion, language, and many other shared values and customs. Roman Catholicism is the official religion and, to varying degrees, that of nine out of ten Ticos. Almost everyone speaks a

Rural village couple at home (Miguel Salguero)

non-Castilian Spanish rich in archaic words and expressions, including the use of the word *vos* rather than *tu* as the familiar form of address. Although town-dwellers joke about the peasant dialect and some writers employ it to amusing effect, the language has few regional variations. The Ticos have, of course, modified various elements of Spanish culture, integrating them with foreign influences and Indian folkways[6] into a distinctively Costa Rican way of life.

Homogeneity is also fostered by the fact that the capital, San José, and the national government control or influence almost all aspects of life even in remote areas: education, health services, the mass media, political administration, religion, the fine arts, provisions for water and electricity, and commerce.

The homogeneity of Costa Rica can be overstated. People of many other nationalities and cultures have come as immigrants or permanent residents and have usually found a warm welcome or at least acceptance and tolerance. From 1870 to 1920 between 20 and 25 percent of population growth could be attributed to immigration; since 1920 its effect has been minor.[7] Anthropologist Richard Adams distinguishes six separate cultural traditions in Costa Rica: (1) Spanish-American, (2) Meso-American (Indian), (3) South American (Indian), (4) Africo-European American (Caribbean Blacks), (5) Euro-American, and (6) Chinese-American.[8]

Although many minority group members are also Costa Ricans, when we refer to "Ticos" or "most Ticos" we will generally have in mind the dominant Spanish-American majority, which is also divided in several important ways, the chief of which are social class and rural-urban differences.

CULTURAL VALUES AND THE NATIONAL SELF-IMAGE

Costa Ricans believe they have a unique way of life and a distinctive national character. People of all classes, political parties, and regions share a sense of national identity and define themselves as Ticos. They sometimes explain an action by saying "We Latins are like that," but far more frequently they say "We Ticos are like that." They feel set apart from their Central American neighbors in particular, not only by the "whiter" appearance of the average Costa Rican but also by sharp differences in culture and personality. Their strong self-image is reflected in frequent comments that something is *muy tico*—very Costa Rican—and in the proud assertion that one is as Tico as *gallo pinto*, referring to a favorite dish of rice and beans. In discussing proposed innovations, decisionmakers and social critics constantly measure things according to how well they express or fit in with their "idiosyncrasy" and "the national reality."

Throughout the book we often use the concept of "myth" in the sense not of falsehood but of a pervasive complex of cultural values and beliefs. In a time of rapid social change many myths are questioned. They may be denounced as blinders that obscure reality. They may, on the other hand, be recognized as worthy goals. Myths about education and class structure, for example, have long lulled most Costa Ricans into complacency; now they are increasingly dismissed as falsehoods on the one hand and held up on the other as guides to help them bring reality closer to the ideal.

Democracy is perhaps the most cherished value of Costa Ricans. Surrounded as they have been by military dictatorships, they are most keenly aware of their democratic myth and apprehensive of threats to its validity. As it has evolved it has come to include a deep-rooted belief in a free press and fair elections and in the rule of law.

Among Costa Ricans the sense of individual liberty is very strong, and freedom is often mentioned as their greatest blessing. They also profess the essential equality and dignity of all human beings. Ticos loath arrogance and expect people in high places to act *humilde*. There is an easy give-and-take between boss and employee. Except when the occasion definitely calls for coat and tie, presidents typically go about in sports clothes or at least in shirtsleeves, and are referred to by their first names or nicknames.

The values of liberty, dignity, and equality include a belief that Costa Rica, though small, is a sovereign and independent nation with the right to make its own decisions free of foreign domination, whether military, economic, or cultural. This nationalist theme has been expressed in various ways throughout its history. One manifestation is great concern for the nation's image abroad. But nationalist sentiments seldom take the form of xenophobia. "There are few peoples as willing as ours to receive a foreigner without prejudices, and to treat him on a truly fraternal level."[9]

Peace is one of Costa Ricans' dearest values, although, as their national hymn says and as their history has shown, they will exchange their tools for arms if national freedom is threatened. They consider Costa Rica a tranquil haven in a violent world, and their hackles rise when anything smacking of militarism occurs. They speak slightingly of their Nicaraguan neighbors as being prone to violence, and smile at the fact that presidents visiting Costa Rica are greeted, to be sure, with a twenty-one-gun salute—but with the only cannon in the country! Raised voices are seldom heard, fights rarely seen, and Ticos will nod or say *"Sí"* even when they don't mean it, simply to avoid conflict.

Most Ticos consider the family the cornerstone of society, a belief reflected in the constitution. They spend much of their leisure time with relatives, and many confine intimate friendship to kinfolk. The extended family group often functions as a unit in politics and business.

Masculine and feminine roles are clearly defined in the family culture complex, which includes *machismo*. As superior beings, men are to be deferred to; their masculinity is expressed in amorous conquests, daring feats, and freedom to do as they please. Women, by contrast, must be soft and submissive, willing to sacrifice their own pleasures for their families.

Formal education is highly valued. It is seen not only as the best means of ensuring progress toward a higher material level of living (both socially and individually) but also as a guarantee of a more perfect democracy. "We have more teachers than soldiers," the Ticos boasted while they still had an army. Schoolchildren rather than guardsmen parade on patriotic holidays and line the streets to welcome visiting dignitaries. Framed school diplomas hang on the walls of humble homes, and parents urge children to show visitors their

school notebooks. Many Ticos distinguish, however, between formal training in skills and knowledge, on the one hand, and actual behavior on the
other. A rude or graceless person is considered "badly educated," no matter
how much schooling he or she may have had.

Ticos themselves—social analysts and critics as well as laymen—see these
dominant values as the basis of their common behavior patterns and traits.
The value of peace, for example, is expressed in the habit of moderation and
compromise, both in political life and in group relations in general. Few
Ticos express great hatreds or passions. Many say of their religion, for
instance, "I am a Catholic but not a fanatic." According to anthropologist
María Bozzoli de Wille:

> The Costa Rican is a fence sitter. He says, *"Quién sabe?"* (Who knows?), *"Tal vez"*
> (Maybe), *"Más ó menos"* (More or less). He does not want to commit himself.[10]

This *Sí pero no* (yes but no) attitude allows Ticos to find ways out of
difficult situations by means of compromise. Says one observer:

> Every Costa Rican avoids extremes and, at the hour of truth, seeks a way of
> getting along with others. . . . Solving problems *a la tica* means preventing
> blood running down to the river. And this, in a continent bathed in blood, in
> which a concrete individual life is worth hardly anything, is something ex-
> traordinary.[11]

Decision-making *a la tica* means constant bargaining in an effort to avoid
conflict, even when the problem is not really resolved. Their saying "Each in
his own house and God in all" indicates the high value Ticos place on
convivencia, or peaceful living side by side. They often refer to their nation as
a family.

At the same time, freedom and individualism are highly valued. Some
critics see this as a "negative attitude toward all forms of association and
collective enterprise," except for the circus aspect of politics and the similarly
superficial emotions aroused by soccer.[12] And even so, "The Tico is such an
individualist that he plays soccer only by a miracle." As social critics see it,
individualism often takes the form of a selfish concentration on personal
and familial affairs and an unwillingness to work with others or to cooperate
and sacrifice for the common good.[13] Except among relatives and close
friends, they say, Ticos tend to be wary, mistrustful, and suspicious even
when they act friendly.

Much as they like to think of themselves as individuals, Ticos are to
varying degrees, like all of us, conformists. The strongest social control
among Costa Ricans is fear of what others will say. They are quick to gossip
about and ridicule others but are afraid to become the object of ridicule or
gossip. Mockery or *choteo* keeps people in line without violence. "We don't
chop off heads," Ticos say, "we lower the floor." *Choteo* ranges from friendly
irony to rancorous attacks. If it is done with humor it is very effective and
may even be appreciated by its targets. The destructiveness of much *choteo*,
however, discourages ambition and imagination. Costa Ricans, say writers

and critics, want to keep everyone on the same mediocre level; they envy someone who excels.

Along with conformity go conservatism and caution. "Few societies," wrote a historian in 1942, "are more fearful of innovation than that of Costa Rica."[14] Ticos have long tended to be extremely suspicious of change. Mario Echandi, president from 1958 to 1962, was said to be popular "simply because he didn't move the Cathedral to another corner."

The ubiquitous small general store, the *pulpería*, lends itself to other evaluations of Costa Rican character. "The psychology of the *pulpería*" is Eugenio Rodríguez Vega's term for the tendency to think small and go slow in business and government. History has been a succession of small happenings with few crises. Changes are accepted only *poco a poco*, little by little, with a great suspicion of large-scale organized planning.[15] A folk proverb indicates a preference for "muddling through" rather than planning: *"En el camino se arreglan las cargas"* (The load can be arranged along the way).

Costa Ricans tend to be formalistic and legalistic as well as conservative. They do not want the form of an institution changed even though its content may undergo radical changes. Rodríguez sees this as a virtue; the form keeps change within bounds and prevents dangerous experimentation.[16] Similarly, Ticos pass laws, create agencies and institutions, and hold meetings and symposiums to "solve" problems—often only symbolically. "Saying is more important than doing, announcing than acting."[17]

At the same time, there is a strong strain of resistance to law, an anarchic, anti-authoritarian tendency that goes along with the belief in individual liberty. For example, the workers and peasants on an interurban bus hissed at a policeman who was trying to make a long-haired ("hippie") youth get off; finally, the embarrassed policeman himself left the bus. But this tendency also reflects the belief that one can get away with breaking laws. Either "godfathers" (patrons in high positions) or a pretty smile will work, especially if one is clearly of high social standing.

Closely allied with this tendency is localism. Most Ticos are oriented primarily to their families, villages, and neighborhoods rather than to the larger society and the world. "There is no bread like that baked at home" goes an old saying. Conservatism is supported both by this localism and by a strong fatalist streak. Many Ticos believe they must be resigned to the will of God, and habitually add the phrase *"Si Diós quiere"* (God willing) to any mention of plans, even something as simple as "I'll see you tomorrow." Death, they believe, comes only at the preordained moment, and therefore one must be *conforme*—accepting and resigned—in the face of death or bereavement. Old sayings indicate a strong belief in luck: "Nothing will ever straighten out a tree that grew twisted."

Personalism characterizes small societies such as Costa Rica. Where "everyone is everyone else's cousin," political parties tend to form around personalities rather than programs, employment is sought through connections more than on merit and, as we have noted, legal sanctions such as fines and imprisonment may not be impartially applied to those who have *padrinos* (godfathers) in strategic positions.

In their relations with others, Ticos want above all to *quedar bien*, to get along and make a good impression in an encounter, to appear amiable. Their use of diminutives is often an attempt to *quedar bien* by expressing affection or softening a word or assertion. "I will get your *facturita* [little bill]," says a salesperson. The desire to *quedar bien* often wins out over other values, such as keeping one's word. It is easier to promise to have something ready *ahorita* or *mañana* and thus avoid possible friction at the moment than it is to tell someone that it cannot be done soon, or tomorrow, or perhaps ever.[18]

One corollary of the desire to *quedar bien* is the great value Costa Ricans place on courtesy and social ritual, such as the proper ways of greeting and leavetaking. Men shake hands, pat shoulders, and often embrace; women embrace and pat shoulders, perhaps touch cheeks and kiss the air. They ask after one's health and that of the entire family (even the dog, jokes one Tico). There is a specific thing to say in almost every situation. Upon first seeing another member of the household early in the day, the standard question is "*¿Cómo amaneció?*" (How did you awaken?) and the standard reply, "*Bien, por dicha*" (Well, fortunately). Upon entering a house, the visitor asks permission, "*Con permiso,*" just as one does when passing someone in a crowded room or bus. Even going on errands, one is wished a good journey. Flowery language and compliments are common even in business letters. These rituals both ease interaction and act as barriers to an unwanted degree of intimacy. They also give Ticos their reputation for courtesy and friendliness.

Emphasis on dignity and courtesy often takes the form of saving face for others as well as oneself. Despite their penchant for sarcastic humor, Ticos usually take care not to embarrass another, especially in public. A question that might be taken as criticism or reproof is not phrased directly, such as "Have you finished it yet?" but indirectly and in the negative—"You haven't finished it yet, no?" in a very matter-of-fact tone, hardly questioning at all.[19]

Though "irreverent by nature"[20] and extremely fond of jokes, including jokes about national shortcomings, Ticos very seldom tell jokes on themselves as individuals. They are *delicados*—easily offended. The criminal code provides a prison sentence of from ten to fifty days for one who by word or deed offends a person's "dignity or honor" whether in that person's presence or by a written or spoken message. The value placed on face-saving is indicated by the fact that the sentence is far heavier if the slander is committed in public.[21]

Although these generalizations about Costa Rican culture and personality are subject to many qualifications and exceptions, we shall see common values and behavior patterns reflected over and over again in such institutions as the family, government, and religion, and in such social structures as the class system. Nowhere are they more apparent than in behavior on the road.

In 1955, there were 9,000 motor vehicles in circulation in the country; in 1978, more than 207,000, or one for every nine inhabitants. By several indices Costa Rica is said to have the highest traffic death rate in the Western hemisphere, and possibly in the world. Per number of vehicles, the rate is four times that of the United States, and only 15 percent of fatalities are due to bad road conditions or to vehicle defects such as brake failure, while 85 percent are attributed to the actions of drivers and pedestrians.[22]

These figures appear to reflect, first of all, lack of planning and order. But other values and patterns are also involved. The stress on individual liberty allows drivers to feel they can drive as they please without formal training or fear of punishment. Anonymous behind the wheel, they do not show their usual concern with getting along with others. Fatalism and *machismo* appear to condition the behavior of male drivers, who take all kinds of chances, and of male pedestrians, who make a game of dodging cars by a hair's breadth. Personalism shows up in the confidence that somebody in government or politics will help one avoid a traffic fine or other punishment—up to now a rare occurrence except for such relatively innocuous infractions as parking violations. Only recently have attempts been made to bring some order to the massive traffic snarl. But these go against the grain for the "naturally undisciplined" Ticos,[23] who are culturally conditioned to resent authority and to think there are always ways of evading punishment (pull, a smile, a bribe). They also believe that imported solutions to problems won't work. An editorial writer comments on the traffic problem in terms we have heard in many other connections: "We have not studied the social psychology involved, so we cannot apply foreign experience to our reality."[24]

Such deep-seated patterns clash with what some Ticos see as the traits of a "developed" society. In the minds of tradition-oriented Ticos, individualism and liberty are threatened by the tyranny of the job and the clock. *Hora tica* means perhaps an hour or two after the appointed time; *hora americana* or *hora exacta* means punctually. But industrialization, radio and television, and expanded formal schooling appear to be making the Ticos more time-conscious. Some observers also see a far greater emphasis on work, planning, and enterprise, especially among the middle class, since the 1940s, and cooperation is evident in many associations and community projects. Competence and efficiency are slow of achievement, however, especially in the mazes of government bureaucracy. As the society grows more complex and new subcultures emerge, old social rituals no longer apply in many situations, and confusion follows.

Even as Ticos lament the disappearance of old ways, many cultural patterns persist. Despite all the changes of the past three decades, numerous observations made in the 1940s—and even in the 1850s—still apply today. In the next chapter we discuss the origins of today's Costa Rican culture, both its changes and its continuities with the past.

2

HISTORY

Many writers seek in history the explanation for the Costa Rican way of life. They see colonial conditions as fostering democracy, individualism, and love of liberty. In the republican era they note a growing emphasis on education and popular suffrage. Throughout the country's history they trace the weakness of Church and army as compared to other Latin American societies, and the great strength of family ties.

For nearly four centuries after the Spaniards settled there, Costa Rica remained isolated, its few people concentrated on the *Meseta*. The twentieth century has seen a dramatic growth in population and settlement of most outlying areas. At the same time, modern communications and transportation have expanded the horizons of Costa Ricans within their own country and in the world as a whole. The tiny nation has become deeply involved with and affected by trends in other societies, in ways that go far beyond the impact of the two chief export crops, coffee and bananas, and many believe these influences threaten their cherished values and traditions.

PRE-COLUMBIAN CULTURE

From an archeologist's perspective, all of these changes are very recent. Humans have lived in what is now Costa Rica for at least 10,000 years. Before the Spaniards arrived, the region served as both a bridge and a filter for human cultures as well as for biological species from north and south. It contained two main culture areas, one largely Mesoamerican, the other reflecting South American influence.[1]

Archeological data show that the Mesoamerican culture, strongly influenced by Mexican and Mayan tribes, reached into western Costa Rica through trade, migration, and conquest. The people of *la Gran Nicoya*, the northwestern area that includes modern Guanacaste, lived in towns with central plazas and practiced a Mesoamerican type of agriculture based on corn, beans, and sunflowers as well as squash, gourds, and cotton. Like that of the Aztecs and Mayas, their society was rigidly stratified. A *cacique* or chief governed with a council of elders and shared high status with priests and nobles; the lower strata were peasants, artisans, slaves, and prisoners of war. Religious rites resembled those farther north, although there was less human sacrifice. The calendar, writing, and games showed strong Mexican and Mayan influences, which were also evident in ceramic objects, three-legged rimless *metates* or corn-grinding stones, jewels and religious artifacts of jade, and stone sculptures.

While the Nicoyan culture included some South American traits, these were far more pronounced among eastern and southern peoples, who raised tubers, used corn mostly for drinks, both fermented and non-alcoholic, and chewed coca, a custom usually associated with Andean cultures. On river banks they erected large stockaded dwellings where hammocks were hung for two dozen or more families. Some South American motifs appear in their stone statuary and monochromatic ceramics, much decorated with incisions and holes. The graves in which they laid embalmed bodies have yielded elaborate gold and jade objects.

To build up such a rich heritage of artifacts the aboriginal civilization must have had a food surplus and occupational specialization. Why then did they apparently not build great ceremonial centers such as those at Tikal and Chichen-Itzá? Systematic research has only begun. Many of the treasures of the National Museum and other collections have been acquired from grave robbers. Some archeologists suspect that vegetation and volcanic ash still cover many ceremonial centers similar to El Guayabo on the slopes of Turrialba. Although only a tiny fraction of the area has been investigated, excavation already indicates that aboriginal culture was more complex and sophisticated than many had believed.[2] Yet it evidently lacked the cities and formal laws of the Aztecs, Mayas, and Incas, and the first Spanish explorers found the area still populated by several autonomous tribes, each headed by a chief.[3]

EUROPEAN DISCOVERY AND CONQUEST

On September 18, 1502, on his fourth voyage to the New World, Christopher Columbus landed at Cariay, now Limón, and stayed eighteen days to repair his ships. He established friendly relations with the "Indians," who offered him gifts of gold.

For nearly sixty years Spanish expeditions stayed close to the seashore. Rain, heavy jungle, and the steep climb from the coastal plain made the rugged highlands almost inaccessible. In 1522 Captain Gil González, exploring the Nicoya Peninsula, was given so much gold that the Spaniards came to think of this area as "the rich coast," and by 1539 the territory between

Panama and Nicaragua had become officially known as Costa Rica. But little gold was ever found, and mineral-rich Guatemala became Spain's administrative center for Central America.

Several coastal settlements established after González's exploration were destroyed by pirate raids and by rivalries among the Spaniards. By 1560 many thriving cities had been founded in the New World, and the royal representatives in Guatemala thought it high time to explore and colonize the interior of Costa Rica. Philip II of Spain had insisted in 1559 that the area be populated—well inland to be safe from pirates—in order to Christianize the inhabitants. To this end he promised any future conquerors that they could divide the Indians among themselves as serfs. In 1561 an expedition founded Garcimuñoz in the western Central Valley.

The following year Juan Vázquez de Coronado, considered the true conquistador of Costa Rica, was named Alcalde Mayor (head of the governing council). With his companions he explored the Central Valley, befriended many of the Indians, and, in 1564, moved the residents of windswept and sterile Garcimuñoz to Cartago, the first permanent settlement.

THE COLONIAL PERIOD

Costa Rica has been called the Cinderella of Spanish colonies, for it was taxed, scolded, ignored, and kept miserably poor. It was a minor and

Pre-Columbian polychrome vessel with plumed serpent motif (Hector P. Gamboa)

neglected province of the Captaincy General of Guatemala and its clergy were subordinate to the Bishop of León in Nicaragua. Partly because of this very subordination, neglect, and isolation, during two and a half centuries of colonialism a distinct society concentrated in the Central Valley slowly evolved, and became the nucleus of the Costa Rican nation.

Indians in many Spanish colonies were obligated to work as serfs for the colonists a certain number of days a year, or pay taxes. The colonists in turn offered to protect and Christianize them. The system did not work well in Costa Rica, where so many Indians fled to the forests that by the middle of the seventeenth century the colonists, sometimes including the governor himself, had to work the soil with their own hands in order to eat. With the failure of the feudal system, a pattern of family farms became the norm. When Irazú erupted and covered Cartago with a layer of ashes in 1723, the town still consisted of only seventy houses of adobe and thatch, a main church, a parish church, and two chapels. There was no doctor, no druggist, no sale of food. Most "Cartagans" lived in isolation on their own farms and came to town only on festival days; poorer and lower-status colonists, who had by then settled farther west in the Central Valley, seldom came even then.

The poverty and isolation of the colonists worried civil authorities because taxes were hard to collect. Religious authorities were concerned because the colonists did not fulfill their obligations as Catholics. In 1711 the Bishop of León, dismayed by low attendance at mass, commanded the colonists to form settlements around churches, and five years later decreed excommunication for all who had failed to do so; but the edict went unenforced.

Under such pressures the colonists eventually built churches, and very slowly towns grew around them. But the landowning farmers continued to prefer their own *fincas*. Each was, by one writer's account:

> a small world in which the family was born and raised, far from other farms. Their simple life, without ambitions or desires, gave the inhabitants a rude, mistrustful, very individualistic character. They were without exception peasants who had to till the soil for their food; as a result Costa Rica became a rural democracy. Unlike other Spanish colonies, Costa Rica had no social classes or castes, no despotic functionaries who looked down on others, no powerful creoles owning land and slaves and hating the Spaniards, no oppressed *mestizo* class resentful of the maltreatment and scorn of the creoles.[4]

Thus historian Carlos Monge Alfaro—ignoring the distinctions of wealth and power that we examine later—sees in the *labrador* or working farmer, with his love of liberty and autonomy, the foundation of Costa Rican democracy.

The same conditions that kept Costa Rica poor may help account for its tranquility. Mineral wealth—often a bone of contention—remained undiscovered. Land was readily available, but there was only family labor to work it. The few settlers were isolated from one another by heavy rains, broken terrain, and lack of roads. Finally, Costa Rica was remote from other colonies, which were often the scene of raging disputes. In 1809 Governor Tomás de Acosta used almost the same phrases to describe the condition of

Costa Rica as his predecessors had employed since 1648. Everyone still lived near a subsistence level: farming methods and crops were little different from those of pre-Columbian aborigines.

THE EMERGENCE OF A NATION

Despite Spain's neglect, few Costa Ricans actively sought independence. Though aware of the independence movement in neighboring colonies, Costa Ricans were taken by surprise when in October 1821 they learned that the independence of all Central America had been proclaimed in Guatemala on September 15. The councils of the four *Meseta* towns met separately, and each declared its independence from Spain.

The first few years of the republican era were marked by division and conflict. Nicaragua, Guatemala, and Mexico all sought to dominate the new nation. Each of its four main cities felt as independent as the city-states of ancient Greece, and claimed the right to be the capital. On other questions they formed two factions that were to clash for years. The conservative and aristocratic leaders of Cartago and Heredia joined forces against the republican and progressive leaders of San José and Alajuela, and their differences sometimes erupted into armed confrontations.[5] Victorious in a battle in the Ochomogo Hills, the republicans moved the capital to San José in 1823.

Costa Rica joined the Central American Federation that same year. In 1824, when Guanacaste asked to be annexed to Costa Rica rather than remain part of strife-torn Nicaragua, the Federation approved, but sporadic disputes over the province flared up between the neighboring countries. By 1838 the Federation existed in little more than name. Costa Rica withdrew and proclaimed itself a sovereign state, which would nonetheless continue to "belong to the Central American family." The dream of union persists to this day, and so do some of the old obstacles, as we shall see in Chapter Ten.

Many years before the Federation was dissolved, Costa Ricans organized their own government. In 1824 an elected Congress chose Juan Mora Fernández[6] as the first chief of state. Mora tried to dispel the rancors of division and localism, and offered rewards to anyone who would open up roads and ports or other means of promoting industry and commerce. Shortly after Mora's reelection in 1829, the first newspaper appeared.

Costa Rica was not yet a unified nation but "a group of villages separated by narrow regionalisms."[7] Braulio Carrillo, who ruled as a heavy-handed dictator from 1835 to 1842, is given credit for defeating the opponents of national unity and integration. He established an orderly public administration without lining his own pockets, and replaced the anachronistic Spanish laws with new legal codes. His other great accomplishment, which had lasting repercussions on the nation's economic, social, and political history, was to promote coffee production.

When coffee was first cultivated in Costa Rica, coffee plants were little more than botanical curiosities, allowed to reach their full height of twelve to fourteen feet in the patios of urban houses. Because coffee was becoming a modish drink in Europe, the municipalities, and later the republican government, encouraged its cultivation by gifts of plants to the poor, decrees that every homeowner plant a few trees near his house, exemptions from tithes, and land grants. These efforts were rewarded in the 1840s, when a system of export and marketing, based on British shipping and credit, was established.

Costa Rica had several advantages over its isthmian neighbors in building up a large-scale coffee export business. There were no rival products to claim time, energy, and investment, nor Indians to claim coveted lands. The *Meseta Central*, where most Costa Ricans lived, offered the ideal combination of altitude, temperature, rainfall, and volcanic soil for producing prime coffee. The dry season made harvest and transport easy.

By the end of the century the heart of Costa Rica was almost entirely given over to coffee, except for enough pasture and cane to feed the oxen. For about a hundred years the large planters and exporters were the leaders— and in some ways the owners—of the country.[8]

Despite Carrillo's political and economic achievements, opposition to his autocratic methods was bitter, especially outside San José. In 1842 his enemies invited General Francisco Morazán of Honduras, ex-president of the Central American Federation, to use Costa Rica as a base for fulfilling his dream of restoring union. Morazán accepted, and exiled Carrillo. But a military draft and direct taxes made him even less popular than Carrillo had been. Five months after the general entered the country there was an uprising during which he was captured and executed.

In 1847 Congress named as the first President (rather than simply Chief of State) José María Castro, a twenty-nine-year-old doctor of laws from the University of León. In the interim administration of his predecessor, José María Alfaro, Castro had inaugurated the University of Santo Tomás and established a newspaper; one of his first acts as president was to found a high school for girls. He believed that ignorance is the root of all evil and that freedom of the press is a sacred right—risky stands to take in a land "moved by personal and family interests and passions."[9] In 1849 the powerful coffee barons used the army to force his resignation.

From 1849 to 1859 Juan Rafael Mora, a coffee planter, was president of the young nation. In his first term, with his popularity slipping, he dissolved the rebellious Congress and rigged new elections in his own favor. If it had not been for an American adventurer named William Walker he would probably not have been allowed to finish his second term. Walker was responsible for "the most transcendent event" in Central American history—more important than independence.[10]

Like many other Americans, Walker believed it was his nation's "manifest destiny" to control other peoples. Soon after his arrival in 1855 with his private army, he dominated Nicaragua and took command of its armed forces. Cornelius Vanderbilt, who owned various enterprises in the country, threatened to oust him. Just when Walker was becoming desperate, a group of Southern slaveholders offered him men, arms, and money on condition that he institute slavery in Nicaragua. Although once an abolitionist, Walker accepted. He dreamed of handing over the weak nations of Central America to his supporters as part of a "Confederacy of Southern American States." Leading his *filibusteros*, he invaded Guanacaste in March 1856.

The Costa Rican envoy to Washington had informed President Mora of Walker's designs, and in February the legislative assembly authorized an invasion of Nicaragua. People of all social classes responded enthusiastically when Mora called up an army of 9,000 men, which he led in ousting Walker from Costa Rica. Pursuing Walker's men into Nicaragua, Mora forced their further retreat in the battle of Rivas. Half of the Costa Rican soldiers fell there, including private Juan Santamaría, who set fire to a *filibustero* stronghold before he was gunned down. He is now the national hero.

Although Walker did not again invade Costa Rica, he threatened other parts of the isthmus until 1860, when he was executed by a Honduran firing squad. His inadvertent role in Costa Rican history was to unite its people. For the first time Costa Ricans felt a sense of nationalism transcending old localist interests and grudges.

National unity did not mean equality, however. In the mid-nineteenth century the pattern of "coffee power" was already apparent. Leading families struggled among themselves for political office. Political enemies and allies alike were often relatives or in-laws and nearly always members of the coffee-growing elite.[11] During the 1860s even the military men who helped make and topple presidents, or assumed the office themselves, were members of this elite or subordinate to it.

But after a successful coup in 1871, Colonel Tomás Guardia curbed the power of the upper-class coffee barons. In doing so he sometimes ignored the legislature and took harsh measures against his critics. He levied high taxes and spent tax revenues on education, public health, and transportation, including the Atlantic railroad.

This railroad, built to transport coffee from the *Meseta* to the Caribbean coast, led to the development of another product even more dependent on foreign investment and markets—bananas. Guardia negotiated a contract with John Meiggs, an American who had built railroads in the Andes. In 1876 Meiggs's nephew Minor Cooper Keith gradually assumed control and contracted for one stretch after another of the railroad.[12]

Malaria, yellow fever, and dysentery, lack of fresh food, and the difficulty of securing laborers all slowed progress. Costa Ricans would not or could not work in the lowlands. Keith imported Chinese and Italians and finally completed the job with the aid of thousands of West Indians, and, when financing proved difficult, with lucrative contracts to transport bananas, using the stretch of railroad already built near the Atlantic. The banana venture quickly attracted foreign capital. Exports increased from 100,000 stems in 1883 to over a million seven years later, when the railroad was finished. No export tax was levied until 1909.

The coffee oligarchy that ran the nation thus helped create the country's other leading agricultural export—"a curious embrace, for both [crops] were destined to produce, in addition to juicy profits for their financial leaders, deep social and economic problems," says a Costa Rican sociologist.[13] The railroad continued the transformation of the old subsistence economy to a specialized commercial-agricultural one largely dependent on powerful foreign nations—increasingly the United States rather than Britain.

Large investments were needed to make malarial swamps and tropical jungles habitable. But Costa Rican coffee producers were reluctant or unable to invest in an enterprise that demanded a huge capital outlay: transportation systems, drainage, a dependable labor supply, and facilities for housing, schooling, and health care in the virgin lowlands. Nor, declares another Costa Rican sociologist, were the coffee barons concerned about protecting Costa Rican banana producers, who might have formed a second agrarian bourgeoisie competing for power.[14] The banana-producing areas of Limón Province, therefore, began as isolated enclaves under foreign control, and remained so for decades.

THE UNEVEN TREND TOWARD ELECTORAL DEMOCRACY

During Guardia's dictatorship, a group of young men banded together to study and discuss republican principles and liberal ideas. After Guardia's death in 1882 this "generation of 1889"[15] ushered in a new stage in Costa Rican history, a shift from "patriarchal" to "liberal" democracy. They believed that Church and state should be separate, with the state dominant, and that formal education would solve the problems of individuals and the nation. The parties that formed around prominent members of this group were based on personal appeal rather than on programs and ideologies. Violence, the monopoly of power by the elite, and electoral fraud by no means disappeared during the decades of their influence, nor did the lower classes have any power over the political process or much interest in it. But a free press increasingly guided public opinion, and Costa Ricans became accustomed to listening to educated people speak in the name of ideas and reason.

In the 1880s, liberal governments secularized the cemeteries, expelled the Jesuits, and prohibited the establishment of religious communities. They proclaimed that primary education should be not only free and obligatory, as provided in the 1869 constitution, but also secular. Santo Tomás University was closed in 1888 on the grounds that it was too academic and too closely tied to the Church. Only a college of law remained, and for many decades most young men who wanted higher education but could not go abroad studied there.

In 1889, for the first time, the election was not rigged by the government, and both presidential candidates sought the popular vote. Propagandists for both parties went to rural villages, speaking to people as they left church. As election day neared, however, the president imposed his own candidate. Angry peasants marched on San José with sticks and knives, and the candidate withdrew. For the first time a large number of Costa Ricans had insisted on their right to choose their leader.

But their choice, José Joaquín Rodríguez, turned dictatorial in the face of bitter conflict between the liberals and the Catholic Union Party headed by Bishop Thiel. His handpicked successor, Rafael Iglesias, wanted to achieve great material progress for Costa Rica; he opened the National Theater in 1897 and began construction of a railroad to the Pacific. He ignored public opinion and even had his enemies flogged in public. When accused of tyranny, he declared that the violently critical newspapers had turned the people against him. Toward the end of his term, his enemies united behind Bernardo Soto as choice for president. Nonetheless, when Iglesias suggested a compromise candidate, Ascensión Esquivel, the opposing faction of the oligarchy capitulated in one of the agreements or "transactions" so frequent in Costa Rica even today.

Despite general rejoicing when he took office in May 1902, Esquivel was hampered by an economic crisis. The price of coffee had dropped sharply, and it was necessary to import corn and beans for the fast-growing population, which had nearly tripled in fifty years and numbered 342,000 in 1906. A heated campaign for the next term included five contenders, three of whom joined forces against the front runner in the primaries, Cleto González Víquez, for the final election. Believing the public order to be in danger, Esquivel exiled all three. González Víquez took office on May 8, 1906, amid great political unrest because he had been "imposed" on the people.

"Don Cleto," however, soon pacified them with his respect for law and public opinion and his promotion of public works and public health; he is now revered as one of the country's greatest presidents. He was succeeded by Ricardo Jiménez, who also won the hearts of the Ticos over many years of public service. "Don Ricardo" changed the electoral system so that the voters chose the president directly instead of merely choosing electors. If no candidate had an absolute majority, Congress was to choose between the two with the largest share of votes. But this system was not followed in the next elections. Although the campaign and the election were conducted in a spirit of freedom, two of the three candidates resigned; instead of naming the third, Congress declared him ineligible and chose Vice-President Alfredo González Flores to serve as president, though he had not been a candidate at all. Costa Ricans believed in honest popular elections, but they had not yet achieved them.

After his inauguration in 1914, González Flores faced a decline in exports and a rise in debts because of World War I. He considered the tax system the root of the government's financial problems; taxes were indirect and regressive, and since they affected the well-to-do very little, revenues were negligible. Unwilling to follow the usual practice of taking out foreign loans, he proposed an income tax. The large planters and businessmen as well as the liberals attacked him as a radical, and worked to defeat him in the next election. Before it could be held, he was ousted in a coup, early in 1917, by his Minister of War, Federico Tinoco, and the latter's brother Joaquín.

The Tinocos tolerated no criticism and, once entrenched, they filled the jails with political prisoners and clamped rigid controls on the press. The Costa Ricans might have tolerated an ineffective government, but they repudiated one that overtly mistreated them and restricted liberties they had come to expect. School teachers, mostly women, and high-school students organized a demonstration. Wearing bits of green, the color of the opposition, they set fire to the pro-Tinoco newspaper's plant. When the government sent troops against them and fired into the United States consulate where some had taken refuge, the public was thoroughly alienated. On August 9, 1918, when a coup seemed imminent, Congress gave President Tinoco permission to resign and go into exile in Europe.

The immediate postwar years saw three presidents come and go, trying to bring normality and peace to a country in financial chaos, with shaky international relations and little domestic order. Then Ricardo Jiménez was elected for a second term beginning in 1924. He had defeated the first candidate of an ideological party in Costa Rican history—General Jorge Volio, whose Reformist program included some "Christian socialist" ideas he had acquired in Europe.[16]

Don Cleto and don Ricardo between them occupied the presidency for twenty of the years between 1906 and 1936. Except for the Tinoco era, these years are now widely considered more democratic and tranquil than any previous period. But tranquility also meant perpetuation of the status quo[17] and lack of concern for the underprivileged; these presidents limited the state's economic role primarily to the building of roads and schools. Depression, the exploitation of workers on banana plantations, and the influence of fascist and communist ideas rudely disturbed this apparent tranquility in the 1930s and resulted in violent conflict over the distribution of power and privilege in the 1940s.

Leon Cortés, who succeeded Ricardo Jiménez in 1936, was less protective of civil liberties. In the midterm elections a Communist organization, the Bloc of Workers and Peasants headed by the young lawyer Manuel Mora, won a seat in Congress. Cortés, whose sympathies (like those of many other Costa Ricans) were with the Nazis, dissolved the Electoral Tribunal and did not allow the congressman to be seated.

Though Jorge Volio had been defeated in 1924, he had made many Ticos more receptive to socialist ideas. Costa Rica's abysmal poverty in the 1930s and 1940s was all too apparent in low pay, unemployment and underemployment, inadequate housing, deficient transporation, malnutrition and ill health, all of which were compounded by a 27 percent increase in population (from 516,000 to 655,000) between 1930 and 1940. Growing awareness of such social ills put great pressure on government to find new solutions to the problems left unsolved by old-fashioned liberals.[18]

THE 1940S: A DECADE OF TURMOIL

These problems, as well as government attempts to solve them, led in the 1940s to events that divided the nation, eroded the power of the old elite, and started Costa Rica on the path toward social democracy and welfarism as well as toward attempts to industrialize. The decade and its climax, the civil war of 1948, mark a major turning point in Costa Rican history.[19]

Dr. Rafael Angel Calderón Guardia, elected in 1940, and supported by Archbishop Víctor Sanabria, instituted a program of social security (mainly health insurance) patterned after the Chilean system, and brought about enactment of a labor code that provided for a ministry of labor, guaranteed workers the right to organize and a minimum wage, protected them against arbitrary dismissal, and made collective bargaining mandatory in labor-management disputes. He also secured passage of a law allowing the landless to acquire title to unused land by cultivating it.

Such measures won the strong support of workers and some members of the heterogeneous and growing middle class (who had benefited most from the University of Costa Rica established in 1940). The president aroused their fervent admiration, even adoration, but landlords and big businessmen were strongly opposed to his reforms, and many small businessmen and professionals felt that these programs improved the workers' lot at their expense. Fiscal disorder and widespread graft at all levels of public office increased their opposition.

Calderón defended his reforms as checks on the growing power of the Communists, who opposed his measures as merely palliative and advocated government control of the economy. Nonetheless, most members of the elite followed former president Cortés, who had defected from Calderón's National Republicans to form his own rightist Democratic Party. With his popularity slipping, Calderón agreed in 1942 to an alliance with Mora's Bloc of Workers and Peasants. In 1943 the Bloc changed its name to Vanguardia Popular and ostensibly accepted Calderón's social-Christian program. The fact that the Soviet Union, toward which it was clearly oriented, was now an ally in the Second World War lent the party some respectability.

While this alliance won Calderón support in some sectors, it alienated others, particularly independent farmers who felt it threatened their traditional way of life. Modernization, says historian John Patrick Bell, was the real threat to the individualistic and conservative farmers and peasants, including coffee planters, but the Communists served as a visible scapegoat.[20]

Another source of persistent attacks on *calderonismo* was the Center for the Study of National Problems. Founded in 1940 by a small group of law students, the Center attracted idealistic young middle- and upper-class professionals, students, and white-collar workers. Their ideology included a government program to foster economic and social development; but, being largely of the elite, they were unsympathetic to Calderón's labor and social reforms. They were also alienated by Calderón's "personality cult," by alleged corruption in his administration, and above all, by fraud in elections. "Electoral purity," though rarely a reality, had long been held sacred in Costa Rica, and Center members saw their group as a major defender of this value. Like other anti-Calderón Ticos, they were angered by deceptive measures used to assure the victory of the government candidate, Teodoro Picado, in the 1944 election.

Largely a puppet of Calderón, whose immediate reelection was prohibited by the Constitution, Picado maintained the National Republicans' alliance with the Communists despite their gradually waning appeal. Calderón hoped to regain the presidency in 1948, and Picado's term was one long electoral campaign, made more intense by a strange new coalition called simply "The Opposition."

In 1945 the Center merged with Acción Demócrata, a group of young men, largely middle-class, to form the Social Democratic party. The Center contributed the ideological element and Acción Demócrata the practical know-how of political contests and fiscal matters. The Social Democrats entered an electoral coalition with Cortés's personalist party, which was committed to a reactionary economic program, and with another personalist party clustering around Otilio Ulate, publisher of the daily *Diario de Costa Rica*. One purpose—the defeat of Calderón—united oligarchic elites, idealistic reformers, and ambitious activists.

The Opposition made honest elections the central issue of the campaign. Though they charged the government with tyranny and oppression, actually the press remained free "to the point of license; newspapers were permitted to print even outrageous personal attacks against the President."[21] Freedom of assembly and the independence of the courts were respected under Picado, and the tiny army, led by nonprofessional officers, could not have upheld an oppressive government.

A man who favored armed rebellion proved to be the nemesis of those in power. Coffee planter José ("Pepe") Figueres, seized in 1942 during a radio broadcast bitterly attacking Calderón, became Costa Rica's first political exile since the Tinoco era.[22] During two years abroad, mostly in Mexico, he formed an alliance with other Caribbean exiles and vowed to use military means to end dictatorship throughout the region, to promote social justice and electoral purity, and to reestablish a Central American Union. After his return in 1944 he preached military rebellion.

Figueres's exile had made him a charismatic symbol of resistance. He was a key figure in Acción Demócrata, and the organization of the Social Democratic Party in 1945 gave him a solid political base as well as potential soldiers. He won further sympathy at home and in the "Cold War"-obsessed United States by charging links between Calderonism and international communism. His ally, Otilio Ulate, served as the chief spokesman for the Opposition, mainly through his newspaper.

In February 1947 an Opposition convention chose Ulate to run against Calderón. Amid a climate of sabotage, assassination attempts, and fights between police and armed youth groups, the Opposition called for a general strike in July 1947; many businesses, including banks, supported it by closing their doors. Government leaders sent police and military forces to patrol the streets, reinforced by the workers' militia of the Vanguardia. "San José appeared to be a city besieged by its own security forces."[23] Ulate asked the government to guarantee open elections in return for an end to the strike.

An August 2 demonstration by thousands of women led the government to promise electoral guarantees, and the strike ended under the mediation of the archbishop. An Electoral Tribunal including members of the Opposition was to be in complete charge of the electoral process during the last week before the election, and would count the votes.

Though compromise was a time-honored Costa Rican way of keeping the peace, Figueres scorned it and insisted on a fight to the finish. He also acted contrary to the nation's historic isolationism. To overthrow the government, organization and help from abroad were necessary, and late in 1947, hoping to get arms from President Arévalo of Guatemala, Figueres signed the Pact of the Caribbean, an agreement to cooperate in ending dictatorships in the

The leaders of the forties. Above: Manuel Mora, Archbishop Sanabria, Teodoro Picado, and President Calderón Guardia *(Libertad)*. Below: Figueres and Ulate *(La Nación)*.

Caribbean area. Meanwhile, Social Democrats contributed to the general unrest by making people suspicious of government promises of free elections; many *ulatistas* declared they were denied the registration cards necessary at the polls.

Both sides charged electoral fraud after the February 8, 1948, election. On February 28 the Electoral Tribunal issued a provisional count showing Ulate in the lead. In a tumultuous session of Congress the following day, twenty-seven of the forty-five congressmen voted to annul the presidential election. They intended to have the newly elected Congress vote Calderón into the presidency when it convened May 1.

Neither coalition, obviously, would settle for anything less than seeing its candidate as president. Atrocities on both sides aroused fear and hatred, and pushed people to commit themselves. Answering Figueres's radio appeals for more men to join him in "overthrowing Communists and dictators" and reestablishing free suffrage, young middle-class Ticos daily slipped out of town in trucks that took them to his farm, La Lucha.

On March 10, 1948, the forces based at La Lucha began the "War of National Liberation" by attacking several strategic places far from the capital. President Picado, still wanting to avoid civil war and unaware of Figueres's strength, failed to respond decisively. Since the army consisted of only about 300 poorly trained and equipped men, he accepted Mora's suggestion that they be supplemented by the militia, made up largely of machete-wielding banana workers. The officers were reluctant to train these irregulars; the United States publicly refused to ship small arms; and Somoza of Nicaragua offered armed men but no arms. The rebels, by contrast, were trained, led, and supplemented by skilled fighters of the Caribbean Legion, and supported by arms and men brought from Guatemala in captured DC-3s.

During the first month of hostilities several bloody battles occurred, and on April 10 the rebels began a well-planned offensive directed at San José. Picado had little heart for the conflict; "Many of the revolutionaries were sons of relatives or personal friends and some were even his former students."[24] He no longer had control over Mora, who had continually strengthened his position in San José and held in reserve 1,500 disciplined workers with whom he declared he would fight to the last.

After rebel forces took the Cartago barracks, Figueres warned that if the Communists continued to resist, National Liberation forces would have to march on the capital. Already there were at least 2,000 dead, and savage fighting complicated by foreign intervention seemed imminent. A Nicaraguan expeditionary force had already invaded northern Costa Rica, and rumor had it that United States forces stationed in the Canal Zone were ready to step in. On April 13 a cease-fire was arranged and peace negotiations began.

On April 18 Picado and Padre Benjamín Nuñez, emissary of the victorious Figueres, signed a negotiated peace treaty, which guaranteed a general amnesty and provided for indemnities to all victims regardless of their affiliation. Mora's influence was responsible for a clause stating that "the social rights and guarantees of all employees and workers will be respected and extended."

In Bell's judgment the treaty prevented far worse bloodshed, followed the customary Costa Rican pattern of pacification and compromise, and provided a basis for continuity. But Figueres, though pledged to honor Ulate's election, wanted a sharp break with the past. He believed that if Ulate took office little would change. Only he himself should be the architect of a "Second Republic," which would benefit from the same careful planning that distinguished the revolutionary movement. On May 1 he and Ulate signed an agreement by which a revolutionary junta headed by Figueres would govern for eighteen months, during which time a duly called constitutional congress would ratify Ulate's election as the first president of the Second Republic.

The junta violated the peace terms by taking reprisals against the losers. Calderón was exiled to Mexico. Many members of the two losing parties were imprisoned or sent into exile for speaking out against the junta, and their goods were confiscated by courts outside the regular judicial system.[25] Critics and political opponents were fired from both government and private positions and prevented from teaching in or graduating from the university.

During its eighteen months the junta issued 834 decree-laws which, Figueres still insisted thirty years later, "transformed everything." Two of them permanently alienated "establishment" elements of the former Opposition—nationalization of the banking system and a forced contribution of 10 percent of their wealth by owners of more than ₡50,000 worth of private property (a levy successfully applied only to bank deposits).

The constitutional congress, which counted only four *figueristas* among its forty-four members, would not even discuss the draft of a new constitution presented by a junta-appointed committee. The congress modified the constitution of 1871 under which government had been carried on for over half a century. But it also incorporated changes prompted by the events of the 1940s. It abolished the army; it outlawed the Communist Party;[26] and it provided that no one could be reelected president for eight years after leaving office.[27] It provided for civil service rather than a spoils system for government employees. It gave the executive less power and the legislature more than is usual in Latin America. It established the Supreme Electoral Tribunal as a completely independent agency to oversee all details of elections and guarantee their impartiality. Not only did it extend the franchise to women and illiterates, but it also conferred full citizenship rights on the children of West Indian immigrants by providing that anyone born in Costa Rica was automatically a citizen. Finally, it provided for some of the first of what is now a large number of "autonomous institutions" (public corporations resembling the TVA) to take over basic services.

An important consequence of the period of junta rule was general acceptance of Calderón's reforms, which no longer seemed radical when compared with Figueres's proposals for sweeping change. They soon came to be regarded as part of Costa Rica's heritage, just as happened with many New Deal measures in the United States.

Calderón, who retained many supporters, continued to work for a return to power. The junta quashed an attempted armed coup and an invasion from Nicaragua headed by Calderón with Somoza's support. A similar attempt in 1955 was repelled by an army of 6,000 volunteers, including high-school youths, with the aid of the Organization of American States. Calderón was allowed to return to Costa Rica and ran unsuccessfully for president in 1962; he died in 1970.

THE LEGACY OF THE FORTIES

Idealists on both sides during this decade of turmoil were convinced that they were fighting for electoral purity. *Calderonistas* thought they were also fighting to preserve social reforms; *figueristas*, that they were also fighting corruption and communism. Both committed atrocities on the grounds that the end justifies the means, and hundreds of lives were lost on both sides.

This bloodiest event in Costa Rican history left deep wounds that are still not entirely healed. It broke up many families and alienated friends, relatives, and neighbors. Although the coalitions forming the opposing sides have broken up and re-formed in shifting patterns, for three decades political campaigns played upon the old loyalties and antagonisms.[28]

What did the fratricide of 1948 really accomplish? It restored (some say it established) the honesty of elections. No administration has come to power by force since 1948. On November 9, 1949, Ulate peacefully assumed the presidency. It is generally agreed that elections since then have been free and fair. Until 1974 the "outs" won every presidential election, so that presidential power alternated between Figueres's National Liberation Party (PLN, formed in 1951) and a constantly changing coalition of other parties. Bell sees as the most important result of the conflict

> a rededication to the maintenance of civil government, the peaceful transfer of power from one popularly elected candidate to another, and a perfecting of the electoral process. . . . The bitterness engendered by the whole process of the revolution proved anew to the Costa Rican people that, even though representative government can be slow and at times unresponsive, it is an effective safeguard against government excess.[29]

Victory made Figueres and his supporters, who call themselves "the generation of 1948," largely responsible for the direction of Costa Rican society during the next three decades. "The revolution and the junta consolidated the reform program of the previous eight years by moving the center of controversy farther to the left."[30] Power clearly shifted from the coffee planters and merchants who had long dominated the scene to a political bureaucracy committed to the welfare state.[31] The PLN adopted a program of modernization guided by university-trained professionals.

SOCIAL CHANGE IN RECENT DECADES

Recent changes—profound though uneven—are largely a legacy of the 1940s. Among them are commitment to government-guided "development" and social justice achieved by a welfare state. Even when the more conservative opposition parties have gained control of the executive branch, they have been unable to reverse these tendencies. The state has become bigger, more powerful, and more expensive. At least one person out of five in the labor force is a government employee. By some estimates, in 1979 the government, including the autonomous institutions, accounted for half the Gross National Product; by official figures, about a fourth.

Mass production industry has emerged, financed largely by foreign capital, including multinational corporations. The services sector grows while the number of workers engaged in agriculture declines. And although population doubled between 1954 and 1974, per capita income more than doubled, reaching $1,514 in 1978 in current dollars and rising faster than inflation. Even so, many material demands of the rapidly growing and consumption-oriented population remain unsatisfied.

Costa Rica's economic problems have been less acute than those of most Latin American countries. Nevertheless, it shares to some degree many conditions common to Latin America and to the Third World in general. It is forced to sell cheap and buy dear. It has a rapidly growing population with a high proportion of young dependents; a heavy reliance on a few agricultural products vulnerable to world price swings, as well as on foreign aid, loans, and investment; great economic inequality along with rising expectations; and increasing involvement of the government in the economy.

Latin American social scientists usually interpret much of this situation in terms of dependency theory.[32] Wrote economist Rodrigo Facio in 1941: "Our production has developed primarily with regard to the needs of the great international markets, our ideologies with reference to problems alien to us, and our culture within a system of meanings unrelated to the reality that surrounds us."[33]

Dependency is a major source of friction in international relations, and, like the other conditions mentioned, it generates ideological differences within the nation. Controversy over the proper means of overcoming these conditions and achieving all-around development is chronic and often bitter.

"Social benefits"—toward which the Calderón administration took the first steps in the 1940s—now amount to 35 to 45 percent of the basic payroll, the highest in Central America. They include health insurance, pensions, compulsory risk insurance, vacations with pay, severance pay, and a yearly pre-Christmas bonus. Workers and many politicians exert pressure for ever greater benefits, while employers protest that high payroll taxes discourage production. The old paternalistic pattern of *patrones* and *peones* has largely given way to impersonal relationships, and many employees as well as employers regret the change.

In the 1960s and early 1970s, policy-makers encouraged industry to the neglect of agriculture. In 1950 agriculture generated 45 percent of the Gross National Product while industry contributed 12 percent; in 1978 industry accounted for 24 percent and agriculture for 20 percent. Because many products of *campesinos* never enter the market, however, these figures minimize the continuing importance of agriculture. It is still the largest single source of jobs, and agricultural exports still buy well over half of all foreign exchange.

Coffee and bananas continue as the major exports. Both are subject to fluctuations on the international market. Coffee production is often blamed for the unbalanced economy that led to a shortage of basic foods by 1900. Nonetheless, it is the crop closest to Costa Rican hearts and pocketbooks, and is surrounded by a cultural mystique and folklore that invest it with an aura of romance and national pride.

No such mystique surrounds the banana industry. On the contrary, many Ticos still accept the image of exploitation and Yankee imperialism depicted in Carlos Luís Fallas's novel, *Mamita Yunai*. Although multinational corporations still retain much control over banana operations, conditions have changed enormously. Costa Ricans rather than Americans occupy most managerial and supervisory posts. The endemic conflict between the government and the banana companies was largely resolved in the late 1970s by expropriation of the companies' reserve lands and the imposition of an export tax that in effect made the government a working partner in the banana industry. Labor conditions have improved greatly; year-round employment, high wages, and numerous fringe benefits make banana workers by far the highest paid manual laborers in the country. But their relative concentration in small areas makes them a handy target for union leaders of the extreme left, who frequently call strikes. The companies have responded by switching some of their lands from bananas to African palm nut oil, which requires a small fraction of the labor force demanded by bananas. In 1980 numerous strikes were threatening Costa Rica's position as one of the leading exporters of bananas, second only to Ecuador, and even posing the possibility that the entire banana industry, which has often served as a bulwark of the economy that takes up the slack when the coffee market declines, will be destroyed.

The first large-scale attempt at diversification—explained by the government as a remedy for the vulnerability of a country heavily dependent on two export crops—is now seen as unwise by many Costa Ricans. In the 1950s and 1960s, encouraged by foreign markets and foreign investment, as well as by government aid with infrastructure and credit, many Ticos (and others as well) invested heavily in beef cattle. A boom in the late 1960s and early 1970s appeared to justify their optimism. The glow has faded as profits have fallen and as ranching is seen to be bad for employment (four *peones* can work the same area of cattle pasture as a hundred *peones* in cultivated crops), and an inefficient as well as very destructive use of Costa Rican land. More than 70 percent of all farmland is in pasture as compared to 2.5 percent in coffee and 1.1 percent in bananas. The trend toward ever more pasture land has brought about deforestation and erosion. In 1950, 72 percent of the nation's territory was covered with forests; by 1979, only 34 percent. One consequence is depletion of water resources which could provide abundant and exportable hydroelectric power as well as irrigation.

Costa Rica has had an unfavorable balance of trade since 1936, aggravated in recent years by worldwide inflation. For a decade or more after the country joined the Central American Common Market in 1963, the economy was bolstered by trade with other isthmian countries, which encouraged the development of industry. Political turmoil in neighboring countries, however, cut deeply into this source of income, and by 1980 the country was experiencing a severe economic crisis.

At the same time, Ticos have come to demand more educational and health facilities. Formal education, long held in high esteem, has come to be regarded as the birthright of all Costa Ricans. The demand for publicly supported high schools and universities has resulted in an expensive system of mass education. Efforts to orient courses and students toward technical, scientific, and vocational occupations are hampered by the traditional admiration for professional titles and white-collar jobs.

Typical of "developing" societies is a transition from an era when both birth and death rates are high, to another during which death rates drop sharply (thanks to modern medicine and public health measures) while birth rates remain high and population grows rapidly, to a third stage during which birth rates decline. Within a relatively short period Costa Rica has experienced all these stages.

These and other changes challenge religious belief and observance. The Church, never strong or rich in Costa Rica, experiences ups and downs of influence, and divisions among traditionalist and reform-minded clergymen.

Extended kin networks are still much stronger than in most modern societies, and their strength may serve as a buffer against the shock of change. But industrialization and urbanization have somewhat eroded them, and as the family loses some traditional functions, other institutions do not always emerge to fulfill them. The "decline of the family" is often lamented by Ticos, who see it as the central problem of the society. Some also say that the society is fragmented into interest groups, and that its members have lost the awareness of belonging to a people with a common destiny. Traditional beliefs, values, and norms seem to be vanishing, they say, without being replaced by clear new standards and patterns for behavior.

In the following pages we will be concerned with all these changes, real and imagined. The fact of change itself is perhaps overemphasized and unnecessarily feared by the Costa Ricans. Many cultural patterns are so deep-seated that on closer analysis some changes appear relatively superficial. Ticos' strong self-image contributes to the fact that the society is experiencing change *a la tica*, choosing, guiding, rejecting, and fitting new ways as much as possible, consciously or unconsciously, to what they are fond of calling "our idiosyncrasy."

3
COMMUNITY

Most Costa Ricans are greatly attached to home and community. Nearly everyone's dream is to have a house of one's own with a little garden. Many still spend their entire lives in one community and even in the same neighborhood or house. Local pride, as we have noted, is strong, especially outside the San José area. When in one village we saw a drunken woman being taken to jail, residents hastened to assure us that she was from another community. Ticos who move away from their birthplace feel a continuing attachment to the place where they "left the umbilical cord." But community and neighborhood ties are increasingly strained or broken as San José encroaches on surrounding towns and villages, and as people leave outlying areas in hope of a better life in the city.

Ticos living in the peripheral areas are overwhelmingly agricultural. They are also extremely poor. A 1973 IFAM study showed that family heads on the *Meseta* earned more than five times the income of those in peripheral regions. In the Northern Plains, average income was scarcely one-seventh of that in the metropolitan area.[1]

The distribution of many services, public and private, is also very unequal. Of *Meseta* communities sampled in the 1973 survey, 57 percent had a doctor, but only one of the 85 peripheral communities did. All the *Meseta* communities had electricity and piped water; none in the Northern Plains did.

Only primary schools were widely distributed; more than 92 percent of the outlying communities had primary schools.[2] But there were no high schools in the sampled communities on the Atlantic Slope and the Northern Plains, and very few in other areas. Most peripheral communities had no

One of over 9,000 *pulperías* (Katherine Lambert)

business establishments aside from a *pulpería*, the general store which serves in many rural communities not only as the social center, but also as a crop storage facility, post office, poolhall, restaurant, bar, and town hall.

LAND USE AND LAND OWNERSHIP

The lush vegetation of Costa Rica leads the casual observer to believe the frequent claim that the soil is so fertile you can plant a stick and watch it grow. But to the trained eye, the very lushness and variety of vegetation indicate a wide variety of soils and growing conditions and a fragile ecological balance. Tropical soils are seldom fertile. Heavy rains wash away the most important nutrients in many plains and hills, particularly deforested ones. Mountain soils are even poorer. Coastal plains would be fairly fertile if they could be properly drained, but they are very difficult to work, and clay lies near the surface. About half of Costa Rica's soil is red clay.

Only two kinds of soils provide the right combination of texture, minerals, and rich organic materials for highly productive farming. These are the alluvial soils found mostly in the valleys, especially in the eastern part of the Central Valley, and the volcanic soils of the Central Cordillera and the Cordillera of Guanacaste. The combination of black volcanic ash and organic material on the Meseta Central makes the soil perfect for coffee, which must have humus and good drainage.[3] Although coffee occupies little more than 2 percent of agricultural land, 40 percent of all Costa Ricans live in coffee-growing regions.

Fernando Zumbado, Minister of Planning in 1977–1978, studied land use in relation to economic trends and to prospects for employment and for regional development in the face of population pressure. Only a fourth of the nation's territory is suited to intensive cultivation, he reports, while another fourth permits extensive agriculture, such as rice fields or cattle grazing. Over half is suited to forests or should be off-limits to farming and ranching, such as the endangered rain forests.[4] The population, which will double in thirty years at the present rate of growth, is already crowding the available land.

Optimal use of land would dictate an increase in cultivation and in forests rather than in pasture. But the trend is in the opposite direction. Forest is rapidly being turned into pasture. If this trend is allowed to continue, not only will forests disappear and soils be ruined for crops, but water tables will drop disastrously, rural unemployment will drive more Ticos cityward, and available jobs will fall far short of demand. If, on the contrary, land were used more carefully according to its potential, Zumbado believes there would be "greater agricultural diversification, a much more dispersed population, and the development of an important agroindustrial sector integrated with the production of the various regions." As world population grows, food-producing nations will gain advantage on world markets, and exports of agricultural products may well continue to be the "motor of the development process."[5]

The one crop closest to Costa Rican hearts and pocketbooks is coffee. Coffee is surrounded by a cultural mystique and is the core of a romanticized history and folklore. It is still largely an enterprise of small growers who live on and work their own land, thus supporting the myth that Costa Rica is "a small democracy of small landowners."

Almost half of Costa Rican farmers may fit that description. Some 47 percent of farmland owners, according to the 1973 census, have farms between five and 100 hectares in size, and these include 31 percent of farmland. Another 6 percent of farm proprietors with 100 to 500 hectares apiece own 31 percent more of all farmland. The smaller *fincas* are typically family enterprises with a few regularly employed *peones* and some seasonal workers, and they raise labor-intensive crops that commonly yield a cash surplus for the owners. Many of these are dairy farms or truck farms, or both. In some areas, fertilizer and other technical aids help farmers make a decent living from farms of five to fifty hectares, which constitute 39 percent of all holdings. "These are the ragged *campesinos* with ₡100,000 checking accounts," says one observer.

When we look at the way the rest of Costa Rica's farmland is distributed, however, the myth is seen as a half-truth, if not a falsehood. Nearly half the nation's landowning farmers—46 percent—own parcels smaller than five hectares, and together these include only 2 percent of all farmland. These *minifundios* are too small to satisfy the minimum needs of a family or to employ all family members the year round. Even more significant is the fact that 37 percent of all landholding farmers have less than three hectares, and *all their holdings put together include only one percent of the land in agricultural production.*

While parcels under five hectares are *minifundios* by Costa Rican standards, those over 500 hectares are *latifundios.*[6] In 1973 only one percent of all landholdings were over 500 hectares in size, but they occupied 36 percent of

Hired peons planting potatoes (Jim Theologos, Studio 1)

all privately owned land. Put another way, 3.5 percent of all landowners held more than half the land—54.5 percent. Marshall Seligson declares that among fifty-four countries on which data are available, Costa Rica ranks as the sixth "most unequal" in land distribution.[7]

Among "farmers" must also be included thousands of agricultural workers who own no land at all. Many *minifundistas* join them in working for landowning farmers, a pattern Seligson said was already evident over a century ago. The 1864 census found only 46 percent of the labor force employed in agriculture; half of them were primarily wage laborers, although many also owned a small piece of land. A hundred years later, while the same percentage worked in agriculture, the proportion who were primarily wage laborers had risen to 73 percent.[8]

The agricultural *peón* is the most poorly paid and insecure member of the labor force. Between 1963 and 1973 the rural population grew by about 27 percent, but the number of jobs in agriculture increased by only 9.7 percent. The shift from a shortage of hands to a shortage of jobs has accompanied other changes. One is a sharp drop in the number of employers. In the 1950 census, 10 percent of farmers were listed as employers; by 1973, less than one percent. The average size of farms has grown, and fewer workers are employed per unit of land. These data reflect the trend toward cattle ranching, the impact of the capital-intensive "Green Revolution," and the introduction of new crops (such as African palm in place of bananas) or new varieties of traditional crops (such as coffee) that demand less hand labor.

In 1950, only 9 percent of all those in agriculture were self-employed; by 1973 the figure had risen to 27.5 percent. This reflects two kinds of migration prompted by landlessness and unemployment. First, a shift away from the *Meseta* into new, mostly lowland, regions, including the pioneering of a new "subsistence sector" that is called "spontaneous colonization," a trend that has declined as the supply of public land has disappeared. Some landless migrants, nonetheless, continue to "squat" on idle, privately owned lands or even on some that are being worked by large landowners. Like the original colonists, they have experienced dire poverty and virtual isolation; they are the Costa Ricans most seriously affected by regional inequalities. Second, the increase in self-employed farmers reflects the cityward migration of unemployed rural *peones*, who have "transferred rural misery to urban misery," as one economist puts it.

URBAN-RURAL DISTRIBUTION OF THE POPULATION

Although data from different census years are not strictly comparable because of changes in criteria, it is clear that there has been a marked urban trend in the last fifty years. In 1927 only 19 percent of the population was labelled urban—the same as in 1864—while in 1973, 40 percent was urban.[9] And in the decade from 1963 to 1973, urban areas absorbed 62 percent of the growth in population.

Over a third of all Ticos live in sparsely settled rural areas, in communities with fewer than 500 people. At the opposite extreme, one out of four lives in the San José Metropolitan Area (SJMA), which in 1973 accounted for two-thirds of the urban population.

The San José area continues to attract those in search of greater opportunities for education, employment, and diversion. And the boundaries of the city have expanded into surrounding areas, enveloped whole villages such as Guadalupe and Tibás, and turned towns like Heredia into suburbs or dormitory towns, from which many people commute daily to the metropolitan area to work, shop, and amuse themselves.

Ticos have always preferred to live in the Central Valley, with its healthful climate and fertile soil. In 1844, 92 percent lived on the *Meseta*. By 1936, six years after all the land on the *Meseta* had passed into private hands, the figure had dropped to 76.5 percent.[10] Most of the shift was due to migration, some to a higher rural birth rate. As health conditions in the lowlands improved and as roads and other means of transportation and communication opened up new areas, migration continued. By 1963, residents of the Central Valley constituted only 54 percent of the population. But fifteen years later, the percentage had risen to 61, reflecting a stream of cityward migration from impoverished rural areas such as Guanacaste, where expanding cattle ranches and the Green Revolution have reduced the demand

MAP 4

for labor. Some migrants try their luck in the banana-producing regions of the Atlantic and the South Pacific, while others follow the harvests of such seasonal crops as coffee, rice, sugar, and cotton. But many, particularly women, swell the supply of cheap labor in urban centers in the highlands. Migration into peripheral areas, usually to pioneer virgin lands, has decreased considerably, as almost all arable land has been claimed.

The rural-urban division is at best a rough classification for many Costa Rican communities. San José, the towns, and most villages are further subdivided by unofficial agreement into neighborhoods called *barrios*, while villages may include several small clusters of houses called *caseríos*. Communities do not necessarily coincide with any political boundaries. They may center around a church or school, and be delimited by natural boundaries such as rivers or simply by custom. The census lists 4,872 "localities," each recognized as such by consensus of its inhabitants.

Anthropologist Victor Goldkind distinguishes three urban and two rural types of communities according to size and cultural traits: the metropolis, towns, and villages; and rural hamlets and caseríos.[11]

María Bozzoli de Wille, also an anthropologist, finds these distinctions somewhat arbitrary. San Antonio de Escazú, for example, on the fringes of the SJMA, has always been classified in the census as rural and so considered by outsiders and residents alike. Yet she found among its 6,000 people in 1969 a mixture of rural and urban characteristics, with the rural ones predominant.

Rural traits include dependence on an urban center (Escazú) for government and commercial services; a predominance of farmers and scarcity or absence of resident priests, teachers, doctors, lawyers, and engineers; low population density but large households; few roads, and these in bad condition; space between one house and the next rather than the wall-to-wall construction of urban centers; and traditional culture elements that have almost vanished from the rest of the country.

Its urban traits include closeness to the capital; a number of residents with urban occupations; motorized transport; *pulperías* and *cantinas* (saloons) with pool tables and juke boxes; a dance hall, a church, and a school, all close together; some expensive houses owned by city people; a sports ground elsewhere than in front of the school or church; telephones; and television and other electrical appliances.

This mixture, similar to that of many localities, indicates that urban-rural differences are gradual and relative, and the decision to label a community urban or rural depends on the relative concentration of contrasting traits.[12]

MOBILITY AND COMMUNICATION

The 1973 census found 85 percent of all Costa Ricans living in the canton in which they were born. To members of many modern societies this is a remarkable phenomenon; to Costa Ricans it seems so natural, so much the proper order of things, that they stress instead the fact that as many as 15 percent today live in a *different* canton from the one in which they were born.

New means of transportation have made it easier to leave one's birthplace—and to go back. Whenever politicians visit a remote area, the first request is a road. The interurban bus is the lifeline of the countryside. In rural areas, packages and oral or written messages may be entrusted to bus drivers, who pass them along to bystanders in the recipient's neighborhood.[13] Both coasts are also linked by rail with the capital, while networks of tracks and canals crisscross much of Limón province. Commercial and private planes fly between the major airport near Alajuela and landing strips throughout the country, many in regions difficult to reach by other means.

Better transportation has been accompanied by improved communication. Few villages are far from a government telegraph office, whose services, though often slow, are very inexpensive. Letters sent via the government postal system are usually delivered within one to four days, and many rural Ticos write their faraway relatives occasionally, sometimes with the help of the local schoolteacher. But few Ticos communicate regularly by letter; even bills are usually paid on the spot or to a collector who comes to the house.

Many communities have some subscribers to the three major newspapers published in the capital and, in Heredia, to that province's new monthly. But reading matter of any kind is scarce in remote rural areas. Most Ticos prefer the spoken word, preferably face to face.

Almost everyone has a transistor radio, and some stations broadcast messages from distant relatives, announce deaths and funerals, and in other ways take the place of telephones, which are only now reaching many rural communities. Telephone service has improved markedly since the mid-1960s, when an efficient dial system was instituted. It connects most Central Valley communities, and even remote communities usually have a public phone, often an outdoor booth. The number of telephones continues to increase—from 35,000 in 1970 to 182,000 in 1978.

In 1977, 82 percent of SJMA homes and more than half the homes in the rest of the country had television. People who don't have a set frequently watch at relatives' or neighbors' houses or in a neighborhood *pulpería* or *cantina*. Now that three out of four homes have electricity, television is high on the list of desired items.

THE METROPOLIS

At the same time as television relieves the monotony of rural and small-town life, it adds to the appeal of the capital city as a locus of interesting events and desirable goods and services. Like many other Latin American capitals, San José dominates national life. Roughly a quarter of all Ticos and alien residents, as noted above, live in its metropolitan area. Many commute to work in San José not only from the suburbs but from elsewhere in the Central Valley. The national government, far overshadowing provincial and local governments, is centered there.

Diplomats and multinational corporations, as well as industry and agribusiness, make San José their headquarters. Many material necessities and almost all luxuries are available only in San José. Most good hospitals and doctors, the main university, the big libraries, the National Theater, and the most prestigious private schools are found in the SJMA. Painters, writers, and musicians gravitate to the city. Good restaurants and night clubs, prestigious country clubs, modern department stores and shopping centers, imported specialties in supermarkets and boutiques are found almost exclusively in or near the capital.

In the early 1940s San José had only 70,000 residents, a mere tenth of the country's population, and what are now its suburbs were still separate villages. When its population began to mushroom after World War II, the city grew haphazardly, encroaching on surrounding villages and coffee groves with neither planning nor zoning. The infrastructure of streets, water supply, and sewage disposal—even of cemeteries—was totally inadequate for future growth. Residential areas have sprung up on the fringes of the city and in the suburbs, including not only fashionable modern neighborhoods but also housing projects for low- and middle-income groups, and squalid slums and shanty towns. It is in the old central part of town that traffic, both motor and pedestrian, is most snarled, streets and sidewalks most inadequate, diesel and gasoline fumes most noxious, crowding, noise, and contrasts most apparent. Here long lines of people wait for buses, Social Security papers, stamps, and their turn at the government bureaucrat's or bank teller's window.

Many streets in the older part of San José are still lined with one- or two-story houses of wood, even adobe, often flush with one another and abutting on the sidewalk, their rooms opening on secluded inner patios. The stroller finds such surprises as "Moorish castles," stained-glass bay windows, and ornamental grillwork in these old neighborhoods. But one is also likely to see wreckers tearing down old buildings to make way for high-rise offices and apartment buildings, such as the sixteen-to-twenty-one story ones now going up on main avenues.

Just as many urban Americans have, since colonial times, tended to think of cities as necessarily unpleasant places to live, it is possible that most *josefinos* are not urbanites at heart. "Great, disorderly, deformed, San José is sick," said a presidential candidate in 1977, echoing these words written in 1833:

> People [in San José] were beginning to complain about billiards and gambling houses that encouraged vagrancy; of prostitution which degraded youth; of liquor that brutalized the people; of liberal doctrines that undermined social order. Already there was talk about the traps in which laborers were caught, of stolen coffee, of false money and forbidden loves.[14]

Today even long-term residents still speak of the city as a breeding place for problems and bad influences, even as they admit it is the wellspring of great projects and new ideas. Municipal government is badly organized and

Most travel to and from San José's center is by bus (Jorge Ramírez)

financed; broken sidewalks, haphazard construction, and polluted air testify to its weakness.

Few residents identify primarily with the city. The well-to-do feel they are citizens of the nation and even of the world. The majority, though, are more likely to feel they live in and are part of *barrios* or neighborhoods rather than the city itself. Each of these unofficial communities is a social grouping that, in the past if not currently, has conveyed to its members a much-needed sense of belonging.

Constant razing and rebuilding, and the mobility afforded by rising income, all contribute to decreased identification with one's *barrio*. Although a resident of the capital still runs into many acquaintances during a brief stroll, *josefinos* frequently say that they hardly know their nearest neighbors, and that their friends are widely scattered. Says a San José grocer, "Neighbors used to chat in here all the time until not so long ago. But now I hardly know anything about my customers." San José's suburbs, once tightly knit villages where even a passing stranger was greeted with an *"Adiós!"* have become as impersonal as the capital itself.

San José's working- and lower-class *barrios* are, according to Tito Prudencio Quirós, the most unified in the capital. Low incomes, he says, often make mutual aid especially necessary. Although the poor move often, it is within the same area or to a similar neighborhood, and, once there, they confine most activities to the neighborhood. Then, too, many are migrants from rural areas and have a strong sense of neighboring. Quirós describes solidarity in one *barrio* in the city's slum-infested south side:

> When someone dies, a neighbor generally collects money to help the bereaved family pay for the wake and funeral. Small cash loans between neighbors are also common, and serve to fill pressing needs for food and medicine. Earnings from the community clothing sale go chiefly toward the neighborhood children's Christmas party.[15]

A study of poor urban women, by contrast, found no such sense of community. Eugenia López de Piza concluded that the urban slum is an example of "social atomism"; the women mistrust their neighbors, are anxious and complain of "nerves," fear theft and rape, and mention among their problems bureaucratic red tape and inefficient public services such as the poor water supply. Their social relationships are limited to their families and food vendors, except for superficial contacts with work partners and the staff of medical institutions. Almost all are migrants who have lived in three or more places, hoping each move would improve their situation.[16]

TOWNS

There is, we have suggested, a wide political and cultural gap between the capital city and all other settlements, including the towns: the six provincial capitals and seven other population centers of 10,000 or more inhabitants. The contrast in size is also great; Cartago, the largest town, with 34,500 residents, is only a tenth the size of metropolitan San José. Cartago, Heredia, and Alajuela are part of the metropolitan region in which the daily influence of San José is powerful.

The capitals of the three lowland provinces are, by Costa Rican standards, so far away that most Central Valley residents go there only as tourists: Puntarenas, on the Pacific, a port town of 26,000 people; Liberia, the inland capital of Guanacaste province with nearly 11,000 residents; and Limón, on the Caribbean, which has 30,000 residents and, even more than Puntarenas, belies the literal meaning of "Costa Rica"—rich coast. The nation's wealth is concentrated in the highlands, and such towns are neglected poor relations.

Highland towns, like San José, typically follow a grid pattern and center around a plaza that contains benches, a fountain, and a bandshell among colorful shrubs, flowers, and towering trees. Although most churches stand on the eastern edge of the plaza, they are built to no standard pattern.

On the streets near the plaza are schools, stores, offices, restaurants, and hotels, as well as a bus station and a roofed market place that typically covers an entire block. A general hospital and a social security clinic are located not far from the center.

Not so long ago, the choicest location for a house was in the center of town, and many of the more affluent still live there. But gradually the well-to-do have built new homes farther out, even at the edge of town or in the country. Most towns today consist of a hodgepodge of attractive new or remodeled homes juxtaposed with rundown old ones and with *pulperías, cantinas,* small churches, and parks. Filling stations mark the few highways leading out of

The Sunday afternoon scene in Santa Ana still looks much the same as twenty years ago (Mavis Biesanz, 1963)

town, while most streets trail off into dirt roads at the edge of coffee *fincas* or cane fields.

There is still some cooperation within the *barrios* of *Meseta* towns, and some community spirit is evident during such events as Holy Week processions, but Ticos say that both community and neighborhood solidarity have declined. A Heredia professor's wife says:

> We used to chat with the neighbors whenever we met on the street, and to visit one another's homes frequently. Now we just wave and say, "How are you?" Most of us around here have cars now, so we run to San José even on minor errands, and often go to the countryside for a picnic. We just don't have time to talk.

Similarly, an Alajuela cabinetmaker remarks: "Thirty years ago neighbors didn't wait until someone died to pay a call. Now one may not know his next-door neighbor's name."

A few decades ago Ticos talked of the differences in personality among the residents of the *Meseta* towns. Comparative isolation over generations gave each city a distinctive stamp. Heredians were said to be withdrawn and pious, Alajuelans open and merry, Cartagans as proud and cold as their old town. Although today one still hears cities characterized as liberal or conservative, such differences have largely vanished because of the homogenizing effects of easy travel and communication among cities, of the mass media, and of sheer growth in numbers. Not only do Heredians, for example, work and shop in the capital, their town is invaded daily by thousands of students attending the National University.

THE VILLAGE

The typical seat of a rural canton is a village of fewer than 10,000 people. There are perhaps 180 villages in Costa Rica, not all of them cantonal capitals. They are urban, in Goldkind's scheme, for several reasons. They serve as marketing and trade centers for the surrounding rural districts, and the buying and selling of goods and services is more important than agricultural, craft, or industrial production. There is also a city-like concentration of shops, offices, and houses near the central plaza and for several blocks in each direction. Finally, national government offices at the lowest level are located in the village, and their personnel are far more urban than rural in educational background, outlook, values, and relationships. And, in Central Valley villages, at least, villagers in nonagricultural occupations—store clerks, for example—earn several times as much as agricultural *peones*.

The church may have a resident priest who says mass daily. The school is staffed by teachers trained in larger urban centers. The municipal building is the administrative center of the canton; its personnel are typically much more interested in beautifying and improving the village than in providing paved roads and other services to the rural districts.

San Isidro de Heredia will serve as our example of a *Meseta* village. It counted 4,300 residents in the central district and 2,000 more in the outlying areas of the canton in 1968–69. Like a number of other highland urban villages, San Isidro boasts an elaborate church on the east side of the grassy plaza. Next to the church is the priest's house, constructed with funds raised at village fairs. The primary school and the new secondary school share a building on another side of the plaza. Several businesses and local government buildings, as well as private houses, also border it. Butchers, bakers, barbers, tailors, shoemakers, greengrocers, furniture makers, and mechanics have shops near the plaza. Like many small communities, San Isidro boasts a health center staffed by trained nurses and visited several times a week by a physician.

Wooden-wheeled carts drawn by a pair of yoked oxen still rumble through the streets of San Isidro, carrying coffee and firewood. But these old-fashioned vehicles are being replaced by jeeps and trucks.

Most streets, except those near the village plaza, are unpaved, and are lined with the homes of small farmers, merchants, artisans, and residents who commute to work in larger towns, as well as with *pulperías* and *cantinas*. There is a pool hall and a movie theater where American and Mexican films, often more than a decade old, are shown. Not far from the plaza are several dance halls attached to *cantinas*. On a slope above the village is the water reservoir, a metal-covered spring. On a hillside below is the iron-fenced cemetery.

Coffee warehouses and processing plants stand near the edges of some Central Valley villages, although many are out on large farms. On the fringes of some villages are small diesel-powered mills (and even an occasional one still run by oxen) where cane is processed into raw sugar. Smithies and leather shops are numerous in Guanacaste, where horses and oxcarts still outnumber jeeps and tractors.

Sometimes identification with one neighborhood is so great that villagers distinguish, say, between San Rafael Arriba (upper San Rafael) and San Rafael Abajo (lower San Rafael). Still, rivalries among *Meseta* villages appear to create a feeling of community within each one. The residents of San Isidro feel the urge to keep ahead of the rival villages of San Rafael and San Pablo—in soccer above all, but also in the success of church fairs and in such signs of progress as new health centers. Residents of one village may taunt those of another because their soccer field lacks night lights or their church needs painting. Villages muster up far more enthusiasm and cooperation for their patron saints' festivals than do towns.

THE HAMLET AND THE CASERÍO

About a third of Costa Ricans, as we have mentioned, live in rural communities of fewer than 500 people, either hamlets or the little clusters of houses called *caseríos,* outside the central district of a canton. The widely scattered wooden or adobe houses of a hamlet surround a central plaza, which is usually a grassy square used for soccer. Near the plaza are a school, a *pulpería,* and a tiny wooden church where mass is said by a visiting priest at most once or twice a month. In some communities the school does double duty as a church.

Hamlets have no buildings devoted exclusively to government functions.

Typically, the only government employees in a hamlet are a policeman (who may be forced to operate without a jail) and a teacher (who is often responsible for all six primary grades). Nearly all other residents, perhaps even the *pulpería* owner, are farmers. Houses, especially in peripheral regions, still frequently lack running water, electricity, and sanitary facilities, though all of this is rapidly changing.

Caseríos are made up mostly of peasant farmers or of *peones* working for landowners. Some are so remote even from a hamlet that if their children are to go to school they must ride horseback or walk an hour or two, or in some areas go by boat. Many lack all urban amenities except transistor radios.

COOPERATION AND ORGANIZATION IN THE COMMUNITY

In 1935 Chester Lloyd Jones noted that "community activities are poorly developed except for those centering around the church, the schools, and the recently introduced sports, the chief of which is soccer."[17]

As we saw in Chapter 1, Costa Ricans often describe their compatriots as self-centered and uncooperative. But it would seem that Ticos have always been more cooperative, especially in the most remote areas, than they are given credit for. There has been a long tradition of neighborhood working bees, whether to build a house or school or to harvest a crop. Each provincial capital long had a Board of Social Protection to administer the local hospital, and a number of church and charity organizations. This cooperative tendency is now being expressed in formal community development organizations. Mireya de Padilla, former director of DINADECO, a central government agency established in 1968 to promote and advise such associations, says that despite Ticos' proverbial self-centeredness, common problems have proved to be "a marvelous unifying factor."[18]

It was in the most remote areas that we most often saw locally organized efforts to build schools, roads, and health units. Although, as in highland settlements, the same persons were usually involved in directing several projects, community decisions were almost always arrived at by formal and informal discussion, leading to a tacit consensus. Such a procedure avoids confrontation and open conflict and permits people to *quedar bien*, to get along and keep their dignity.[19]

Community organization, according to a government survey, is stronger and involves a greater number of projects in communities of 500 to 3,000 people than in larger or smaller ones. The main impulse toward organization comes from lack of such basic services as water supply and electricity (and from such conditions as exist among neglected minority groups, for example, the blacks in Limón province).[20] Compared to the metropolitan area, heads of families in peripheral areas are twice as likely to be involved in communal projects—and *three* times as likely in the Northern Plains. Concluded the directors of the survey: "It is in the least central parts of Costa Rica that the greatest potential exists for an investment of time and effort on the part of the people."[21]

4

CLASS AND RACE

"If there is one thing that describes the political and human atmosphere that prevails in Costa Rica, and distinguishes us from other nations of the hemisphere and the rest of the world, it is that here any man, any woman, or any child is 'somebody.'" A columnist was moved to write these words after President Oduber, about to enter the National Theater to address a meeting of the Organization of American States in 1975, stopped to greet "Chaplin," a ragged street character. "'Chaplin' is 'somebody' in Costa Rica. Similarly, any workman, peasant, public employee, artisan, or domestic servant is 'somebody.'"[1]

This stress on the importance of each person and on everyone's right to a feeling of worth and dignity leads many Ticos to insist that their country is a "classless democracy." Their myth of classlessness arose from interpretations of colonial and early republican times by liberal democratic politicians and historians. It is perpetuated in schools and mass media and accepted as gospel by many Ticos, rich and poor.

But wealth, power, and prestige *are* unevenly distributed, and some people have an advantage from birth. In short, Costa Rica has a class system. Samuel Stone believes this system differs from those in other Latin American societies in one fundamental respect—the delicate balance between "elitism" and egalitarianism that originated in colonial days and has characterized Costa Rican society ever since.[2] This is also true to some extent of "race"[3] and ethnicity, but for purposes of analysis, we will touch upon "racial" and ethnic stratification only where necessary until we come to the last part of this chapter.

Because there were few Indians to conquer or enslave and little gold or silver to exploit, a feudal aristocracy buttressed by a strong army and a wealthy Church could not arise in colonial Costa Rica. Extremes of wealth and poverty were far less pronounced and land far more evenly distributed than in most other colonies. Accepted myth has it that this rural classless democracy served as a foundation for today's democratic society.

The Spanish population was small. A census in 1700 enumerated 19,293 inhabitants, of whom only 2,416 were classified as "Spaniards."[4] The colonists were divided from the start into *hidalgos* (nobles) and *plebeyos* (common people). The wealthier Spaniards headed for the most promising territories in the New World, those with the largest numbers of aborigines and rich mines. The *hidalgos* who came to Costa Rica, by contrast, were largely from the poorer petty nobility of the Spanish provinces.

The Spanish Crown conferred certain rights and privileges on *hidalgos*. Not only were they exempt from imprisonment for debt, they were also the only settlers who could serve on the municipal council or *cabildo*. Thus the founders of Cartago formed the colonial government and controlled the territory from the start.[5] As other towns were founded this small nucleus of nobles named their sons and sons-in-law to municipal office.

The *hidalgos* jealously guarded their status. They insisted on being addressed as "Don" and snubbed anyone they suspected of plebeian origin. A dozen families of the highest nobility among the colonists intermarried closely and formed a "great family" that monopolized power and governed for four centuries, according to Stone. Three out of four congressmen between 1821 and 1970 were descended from this "dynasty of the conquistadores," and many could trace their ancestry to two or more of the dozen families. Just three families, Stone says, have produced thirty-five of the nation's forty-six presidents.[6]

Early in the colonial era, distinctions of wealth as well as of ancestry and power were sharp, with few intermediate gradations between rich and poor. The wealthier settlers had slaves[7] and servants, signs of high social status. They were able to invest in cacao production and trade with neighboring colonies.[8]

Very few Spanish women came in the early colonial period and there were many unions between male Spaniards and Indian women. Soon after the conquest about fifty Indian chiefs were given the status of *hidalgos*, with the title of "Don." The children of Indian princesses and Spanish nobles were also nobles, called *mestizos-hidalgos*.

Neighborhoods in Cartago were segregated by racial classifications, which were the basis of a sort of caste system: Spaniards or whites, *mestizos*, Indians, *pardos* (people of mixed black and mestizo or Indian ancestry), mulattoes, and blacks, in descending order of status. Nonetheless, the "fusion of bloods" went on continually, according to Victor Sanabria.[9] American historian Lowell Gudmundson says interracial mixing was "impressively rapid."[10] Poor white girls, whether or not they could claim noble ancestry, were often given in marriage to somewhat wealthier persons of "mixed" ancestry or to illegitimate sons of *hidalgos*. Children of slaves or servants by their masters were often given tacit recognition as part of the master's family and went on to marry people of similar status in other families. Immigration added to the complexities of status. Both mulattoes and "people of distinction," in Sanabria's phrase, migrated from Panama, and many mixed-bloods also came from Nicaragua.

Toward the end of the colonial era poverty and miscegenation had levelled status to a great extent and blurred the sharp economic and racial distinctions of the early years. Nevertheless, in 1800 about 20 percent of the "Spanish" population of the four main cities were *hidalgos*, most of whom resided in Cartago and Heredia. (San José had been settled largely by Spaniards and creole smugglers who, having rebelled against the royal monopoly of commerce by resorting to contraband, were punished by being "exiled" from Cartago.) Despite miscegenation, the old elite families kept political power and continued to do so after independence from Spain.

INDEPENDENCE AND COFFEE POWER—1821–1940

The signers of the Act of Independence were the most influential members of a homogeneous and tightly knit elite—in fact, twenty-three of the twenty-eight were close relatives. "It could almost be said that the new nation was handed over to a single family."[11]

From 1821 on, political struggles were largely confined to different factions of this traditional elite, which retained its power largely through control of the vital coffee trade. Although many sources give the impression that the coffee boom changed Costa Rica from a rural democracy of small landowners into a semifeudal society of *latifundistas*,[12] distribution of "coffee power" was more complicated. It involved not only ownership of coffee-producing lands but also—and more significantly—ownership of *beneficios* or processing plants, access to credit and export markets, and political power. Although wealthy families consolidated their holdings through intermarriage and through foreclosure on loans to small farmers, turning some peasants into *peones*, small- and medium-size growers remained numerous, as they are today.[13] The wealthy *cafetaleros* monopolized processing, export, and credit rather than land. Paid in advance by their British and European customers, exporters in turn contracted with growers for their harvests and loaned them part of the agreed-upon price, at high interest rates, for their expenses.[14]

Rich *cafetaleros* dominated government for over a century. Although power struggles occurred among them, they usually united to further their own interests by controlling taxes, granting themselves exemptions and subsidies, spending government revenues on roads and railroads that would facilitate shipping, and, at one time, arranging for a government-guaranteed minimum price.

In spite of their economic and political power, Costa Rican *cafetaleros* have typically run their *fincas* and processing plants themselves, and have had direct contact with their laborers. Stone believes this contact made them far more adaptable to political and social change than was the Peruvian oligarchy of absentee owners, for example.[15] The paternalistic relationship that long prevailed between *patrón* and *peón* somewhat softened the disparities of power, wealth, and prestige. Especially in the first decades of coffee export, *patrones* and *peones* mingled at cockfights, baptisms, and harvest feasts. Later, the tastes and life styles of many of the more affluent coffee planters diverged toward urban and contemporary European ways.

Inheritance customs and occupational differences further diversified the class structure. The 120,000 Ticos of wartime 1856 could be divided fairly easily into elite *cafetaleros*, small farmers, and *peones*, plus a few merchants of different degrees of prosperity. But when the first rich *cafetaleros* died, their most capable sons or sons-in-law usually inherited their holdings, and the others had to seek wealth and prestige elsewhere. Many studied for the professions, especially law and medicine. They tended to be less conservative than those who stayed on the land. Stone sees this as a third breach in the ranks of the dynasty of the conquistadores; the first had been racial inter-breeding and the second the breaking off of contraband runners—the founders of San José—from conservative Cartago in the colonial period.[16]

Another complication was nineteenth-century immigration, especially of Germans and Englishmen, as well as some Spaniards and Frenchmen. Some of those who made their fortunes in Costa Rica stayed, and they or their children married into elite families, often converting to Catholicism as a necessary step toward acceptance. The elite have always been more open to marriage with well-to-do foreigners than with Costa Ricans of lesser ancestry than their own. This openness may also be interpreted as a means of absorbing possible competitors for status—first economic and eventually political—and hence as one reason why the same "families" have retained power for so long.[17]

Despite the reluctance of the elite to "marry down," many Costa Ricans did "climb." A few went from rags to riches by beginning with a small farm and perhaps an oxcart transport business, and investing in more farms and eventually in processing plants.[18] Their mobility feeds the myth of classless democracy. But only after their children acquired foreign diplomas and upper-class life styles were they accepted by the elite.

As the needs of government and commercial interests for well-trained employees grew, educated white-collar workers joined the older middle class of small businessmen and such nonelite professionals as teachers. At the same time, an urban lower class composed of urban workers and craftsmen also grew. Their low status in national society was reinforced by a traditional attitude of condescension toward manual laborers.[19] Yet it was much higher than that of the landless rural *peones*, whose numbers were also growing.

At the height of coffee power during the second half of the nineteenth century and as late as the 1940s, two distinct social classes were evident in the Central Valley's rural areas, small provincial towns, and provincial capitals. The *clase social* was composed of well-to-do planters, businessmen and professionals, teachers and white-collar workers, while the *clase obrera* (working class), also called *el pueblo* (the people), consisted of rural and urban *peones*, artisans, vendors, servants, and other manual workers. A 1968 interview with a sixty-year-old upper-class woman produced this comment: "No worker was allowed inside the *club social* at San Ramón when I was a girl. The workers had their own club and their own gatherings, which no one in the *clase social* would have dreamed of attending." This status division was not directly correlated with income, for an artisan might earn more than a higher-ranking teacher. It *was* related to occupation, educational attainment, and life style. Money was not, however, irrelevant to one's position *within* the *clase social*. Wealth brought political power and acceptance by San José's upper class.[20]

A three-class system was evident in San José, where no broad *clase social* existed, and where members of the upper class—typically set apart by both lineage and wealth—had comparatively little intercourse with the small businessmen, intellectuals, and white-collar workers of the middle class, and even less with the lower class. The urbanized *patrones* traveled to Europe and educated their sons abroad; they embraced European literature and other fine arts. Anyone with pretensions to "culture" spoke French. Upper-class men were more likely to take their wives and daughters to formal dances and concerts than to join their *peones* at cockfights.

Influential peasants or *gamonales* did not aspire to European life styles, nor put on city airs. The *gamonal* played a very important role in small towns and villages until quite recently. Typically the wealthiest farmer in the community, he worked as hard and lived almost as simply as his *peones*, who respected him not only for his wealth but also for his maturity, honesty and common sense. Because his workers voted as he did, he was much courted by politicians from the capital, beginning with the 1909 election, when two descendants of Vázquez de Coronado vied for the presidency, and one of them, Ricardo Jiménez, went to all the *gamonales* on the *Meseta* with promises to restore local self-government and thus enhance their power.

Like the paternalistic *patrón-peón* relationship, the *gamonal* as a social type was on the decline by the 1940s. Stone recounts, however, that some friends who wanted to sell a *finca* in 1950 were asking ₡60,000 (almost $10,000 at the rate of exchange then in effect), and "a client appeared, barefoot, dressed like a *peón*, with a denim apron, guiding oxen pulling a cart. Learning the price, he paid it on the spot in cash. He was a *gamonal*."[21] One *gamonal* we know still works all morning with his *peones* at age eighty-seven. He cannot read or write, except to sign his name.

When we consider the nation as a whole rather than just the Central Valley, class structure looks more complex. Just as the coffee barons had to share economic power with British financiers, so the banana trade and the Atlantic railway also diluted the power of the old elite, who relinquished much of it, willy-nilly, to American enterprise around the turn of the century. At the same time, at the other end of the social scale, a new and alien proletariat of Afro-Caribbean immigrants was growing, but its members were long confined to the Caribbean coastal enclave of the United Fruit Company.

Early in the 1940s, social anthropologists observed that the myth of equality existed along with sharp class distinctions. Although family background was still important—especially in choosing a marital partner—wealth, occupation, and education also weighed heavily. Social clubs and clothing were much clearer signs of status than they are now, and perhaps half the Ticos went barefoot all or much of the time.

The two-class system was still common outside the capital. Although in San José a middle class of small businessmen, professionals, and white-collar workers had existed for nearly a century, the boundaries between it and the upper class were already somewhat blurred by social and physical mobility, by the fact that degrees of wealth, power, and prestige did not always coincide, and by middle-class spending on status symbols such as clothing. The myth of classlessness still dampened resentment of class differences.[22]

Some resentment did exist, however, and was largely responsible for the events of 1948. By the 1930s, as we noted, wealthy descendants of the early coffee barons no longer wished to risk investing in new enterprises, as had earlier generations.[23] The middle class, which was already larger than in other Latin American societies and far less identified with the oligarchy—indeed often antagonistic toward it—had very little political power and saw little hope of advancement unless the country began to industrialize. Professionals in particular felt condemned to "the service of some businessman, coffee baron, or the United Fruit Company, in which they would vegetate with their salaries until the day they died."[24] *Calderonistas* and Communists were also eager to break the status quo, but they stressed more equal distribution rather than increased production of wealth. The clash between these groups may be seen in part as a class struggle, in which members of the old elite vacillated between the two main coalitions both during and after the 1940s.

Leaders of the National Liberation Party (PLN)—the 1948 victors over *calderonismo*—claim that they have achieved both aims: modernization and social justice. Their party, they say, democratized the society by giving more people a share of both wealth and political power.

Both Stone and political scientist Oscar Arias Sanchez believe that the old coffee oligarchy has had to share its power with an emerging industrial elite, but each sees this change quite differently. Stone insists that although the hereditary elite are far from ideological unity and have lost some control over political decision-making, they still exert considerable control over many important new sectors of the economy and social order.[25]

Although Arias discerns a clear system of five levels of stratification, he does not believe that a traditional aristocracy governs, or even exists, and insists that in no era of Costa Rican history has one social sector held absolute power. The "politico-mercantile oligarchy" that dominated the political, social, and economic life of the nation for much of the nineteenth century was divided into warring factions, he says. Arias studied the class backgrounds of the 461 Costa Ricans who served as presidents, cabinet ministers, legislators, and Supreme Court justices between 1948 and 1974. He found little evidence of a monolithic elite. But neither did his findings support his own (PLN) party's claims to have made power more accessible to young, poor, and rural Costa Ricans. Almost all the ministers and three out of five legislators were already in the upper class when they got their first political post. Although many legislators did come from the middle classes, only three—one percent—came from the lower classes. The proportion from the various classes in high places, moreover, had not changed since 1948—not even, other data suggest, since 1920.[26]

But PLN's claim that wealth is now more equitably distributed than it was before 1948 appears to be supported by the universally acknowledged increase in the size, power, and wealth of the middle class.

The growth of the middle class is generally considered beneficial for a society. Some Costa Ricans now question that assumption. Their reasons will become clear as we examine today's class structure more closely.

CLASS TODAY

Fragmentary studies of Costa Rican class structure, and our own observations, suggest that a five-stratum scheme is a fairly useful, though arbitrary, abstraction from reality. Most Costa Ricans, from a well-to-do cabinet minister with a distinguished surname to a barefoot rural *peón*, fit into it somewhere. The upper class, the upper-middle and lower-middle classes, the working class, and the lower class—all these terms are common parlance among Costa Rican social scientists and, increasingly, among other Ticos. They emerge no matter what criteria of class are used.[27]

Income statistics show a broad-based "pyramid" tapering off to a high narrow peak (see p. 99). Half of the people get only a fifth of the national income, while over a third of the income goes to only a tenth of the people. The income of this top tenth is well over double that of the next tenth. The richest 5 percent of the population receives nearly a fourth of all income; the richest one percent, a tenth. In a general way, the national class structure corresponds to this pyramid.

The elite includes most of the one percent (about 20,000 people) who receive 10 percent of the national income, and who almost without exception are also of *la sociedad* or the "principal families." (Some of the latter belong to the elite despite lack of riches.) The lower-upper class includes the newly-rich who often interact with the elite but have no "old family" connections—perhaps another 20,000 people.

An upper-middle class of about 5 percent (100,000 people) includes well-to-do professionals, industrialists, and landowners who lack the wealth and family background to claim elite status.

The lower-middle class includes perhaps 15 percent of Ticos, about 300,000 people who have white-collar jobs, small businesses, or poorly paid professional jobs such as nursing. Some teachers fall into this category, but family connections or a spouse's status would place others at a higher level. Fairly prosperous small farmers also belong here.

These classes account for some 22 percent of present-day Costa Ricans. The rest, then, belong to what many higher-status Ticos call "the working class" or "the lower class," lumping together unskilled urban workers and poor peasants and rural *peones*. It is useful, however, to distinguish between "the working class" and "the lower class." The first includes more than half of all Costa Ricans, the second, between 20 and 25 percent.

Though monetary income is an imprecise measure, it seems safe to say that about three quarters of all Ticos are either working or lower class. The 1973 census reports that 70 percent of all remunerated workers over age twelve earned less than ₡700 ($82) a month, and 42 percent earned less than ₡400 (about $47).[28] Statistics like these lend credence to statements that a fourth of all Costa Ricans are *marginados*, so poor that they remain outside the mainstream of progress and development. These would include at least the lowest fifth on the table of income distribution (see p. 99). Rural laborers, domestic workers, gardeners, janitors, and vendors are the steadier, more "respectable" members of this lower class. At the bottom are bootblacks, beggars (whose numbers have greatly diminished since the 1940s), thieves (widely believed to have multiplied), and prostitutes.

Wealth alone is not a reliable criterion of any one person's status. Although many middle- and working-class Ticos, who make no distinction between *los ricos* and *la sociedad*, believe that wealth is the only requisite for membership in the upper-class Union Club and the Costa Rica Country Club, for instance, money is not enough to open their doors. Prospective members must be proposed by two established members and voted on by the board of directors. (Robert Vesco's bid to join the Union Club was denied.)

While "family" is still very important to upper-class Ticos, many people whom Stone would class as members of the hereditary elite are not even aware of their noble ancestry—and if they are, they tend to play it down. Overt pride in blue blood is now ridiculed. "Twenty-five years ago," recalled a university professor in 1968, "people used to stop and say, 'Look! There goes a Montealegre!' Now they hardly notice." Social pages in the newspapers no longer accord special treatment to upper-class families. Today such family mottoes as *"Despúes de Diós, la casa de Quirós"* (after God, the house of Quirós) are rarely heard except in jest.[29] And descendants of the *conquistadores* are found at all levels of the social spectrum.

In 1970 a team of investigators headed by sociologist Eugenio Fonseca found education, income, consumption patterns, and family life highly correlated with occupational status.[30] Likewise, Arias used occupation as the criterion of class standing in his study because it is easiest to measure and because it correlates closely with other criteria such as wealth, education, and social participation.

Still, boundaries between classes are far from clear. "Since the 1940s," says a professor who has twice served in the cabinet, "one does not know where any class begins. A bus driver is middle class if he has his own house and sends his children to high school. Money has become more important, family less so."

Several things account for uncertainty about class status. First, the myth of classlessness is still strong. If a Tico's statement that "there are no classes in Costa Rica" is challenged, he or she is likely to retreat to the position that "We are all middle class." We heard this from people in all but the lowest income brackets. Thus 56 percent of the government leaders in Arias's study said they were middle class, although Arias would place only 37 percent of them there.[31] A Puntarenas dockworker interviewed by Miles Richardson and Barbara Bode also insists that he is middle class.

> Although this man may go long periods without any pay and although the only labor he can sell lies in his muscles, he refers to himself as a middle-class person. He first explains that in Costa Rica there are no social classes because, unlike people in Nicaragua and the United States, Costa Ricans are all equal. When the anthropologist presses the issue and points out differences in material possessions and income, he refines the statement to say that Costa Ricans overlook these differences and treat everyone as equal. All have *roce* (from *rozar*, to rub against) with each other. Nothing prevents the rich and the poor from mixing together.[32]

Increased interaction also blurs the lines between upper and middle class. Although the Union Club and the Country Club retain a fairly exclusive upper-class membership, there are many other opportunities for members of the upper-middle class, especially the wealthier contingent, to mingle with their social superiors. These include the Tennis Club, various suburban clubs, and meetings and parties of the powerful business and professional associations, along with their women's auxiliaries. Members of both strata

Many Costa Ricans have several sources of income. This man works as a tailor, barber, and picture frame vendor. (Sylvia Boxley de Sassone)

frequently live in the same neighborhoods, send their children to the same private schools, and spend their money in much the same way.

The new skills demanded by industrialization and urbanization have clouded the distinction between working class and lower-middle class. Despite a widespread disdain for manual labor, this criterion of class is no longer infallible, largely because of the higher wages many laborers command. Skilled workers and taxi drivers, along with store clerks and independent small farmers, are sometimes called working class, sometimes middle class, by themselves as well as others. A taxi driver first called himself middle class, then lower class. Deciding the latter term was unacceptable, he settled on "working class." (We had suggested none of these terms to him.) When occupation and income are not enough to place a person in a certain stratum, education and lifestyle may swing the balance. "Does one live well or not?" says the taxi driver, is the criterion that separates working from middle class.

Like manual labor, dress is no longer an infallible indicator of class status. Clothing is extremely important to working-class urban Costa Ricans, for most of whom such status symbols as comfortable housing and cars are beyond reach. All but the poorest children are dressed in clean garments and polished shoes on Sundays and special occasions. Comments a young American: "Here people dress up even to go to the supermarket. My maid and her kids dress more elegantly than we do." Young upper- and middle-class women, by contrast, have adopted informal dress, often T shirts and jeans, for everyday wear. Upper- and middle-class men, including the president and his ministers, now abandon suit coats on many occasions, wearing instead sport shirts or short-sleeved shirts with neckties.

Many Ticos consider the differences among various sectors of the middle class more important than other class distinctions. The "old" middle class, say some analysts, includes owners of small factories, shops, and service establishments; self-employed professionals; and medium-size farmers. To survive they must be hardworking, efficient, and thrifty.

A second sector is the rapidly-growing bureaucratic middle class. While the labor force as a whole grew about 3.5 percent a year between 1950 and 1970, the number of people on the public payroll grew 7.9 percent a year, and now makes up at least a fifth of the labor force. Although not all public employees are middle class, a very high percentage are teachers, technicians, and office workers or other white-collar workers. Unlike the independent middle class, they tend to measure their progress and prosperity not by what they can save but by what they can consume, and they aspire to the income and life style of the national upper class and the American middle class.

Middle-class salaried employees of the third, private sector lack both the independence of the old middle class and the organized power of public bureaucrats, and are liable to manipulation by their elite employers.

While members of the first sector often complain that they bear the brunt of expense of the welfare state, and those of the third sector share the government employees' emphasis on material consumption, it is the government bureaucrats who, in the opinion of many observers, are less the solid bulwark of the democratic system than a menace to it.

Public employees have tremendous power because they can paralyze many of the nation's essential services, such as health, education, and communications. They are called parasitic and inefficient because they are immune to competition. Through their professional associations and syndicates, they exert strong pressure on government to keep their salaries rising and their benefits increasing. As a result, much of the gain in national income has gone to them, with a disproportionately small share trickling down to the lower class, and least of all to the *campesinos*, whom Arias and others consider "the weakest and most forgotten sector" of the society.[33]

SOCIAL MOBILITY

The growth of the middle class alone shows that there is considerable social mobility in Costa Rica. Many children of working class parents attain middle-class status thanks to the expansion both of schooling and of the public payroll. And many who would otherwise have been domestic servants or farm laborers like their parents have gone up the social ladder a rung or two by taking factory or construction jobs, or by becoming sales clerks, waiters, nurses, teachers, or office workers.

Nor are the ranks of the upper class rigidly closed. Often a professional degree opens the way. Sometimes, too, marriage provides access to a higher status group. Increased physical mobility and the almost complete disappearance of chaperonage mean that young people of different classes mingle quite freely at work and play, in school and university. Their interaction is eased by the deep-seated cultural aversion to putting on airs. Upper-class women are usually expected to marry within their status group, as the husband's status is more crucial than that of the wife. But a number of women of "good family" have married upwardly mobile men, including doctors and bankers, whose parents were lower class or lower-middle class.

Politics has long been a stepping-stone to higher status. Since most high-ranking members of the executive branch (presidents and cabinet ministers) already had upper-class wealth and prestige before they were elected or appointed, Arias believes they are in politics chiefly because they also want power. Legislators, as we have noted, are generally from middle-class backgrounds, and in political positions they seek prestige above all. Rising young lawyers are especially eager to win a seat in the legislature; in their four-year terms they would acquire prestige that would bring them a good clientele. The social mobility afforded by political positions is one reason for the country's stability, in Arias's opinion. No powerful elite blocks political aspirants; once a person has achieved some economic and professional success, acceptance in the political "establishment" follows quite easily.

URBAN-RURAL DIFFERENCES

Urban areas, especially San José, are the centers of wealth, power, and prestige. Most of those at the upper levels of the class system are urbanites; the lower levels are largely made up of country dwellers. Very few of those who attain high public office, Arias found, are of rural origin—only 4 percent of ministers from 1948 to 1974 and 6.3 percent of legislators.[34]

In 1973, 29 percent of urban workers over twelve—and 55 percent of rural workers—received less than ₡400 a month; 57 percent of urban and 83 percent of rural workers received less than ₡700.[35] The great majority of the poor are rural. The director of a social welfare agency finds that 55 percent of the poor are rural *peones* and their families and another 13 percent are small landowners and their families who cannot even scratch a subsistence living from their tiny holdings.[36] A sample study in the early 1970s found that heads of households received an average income of about ₡23,000 in the metropolitan area, while those in peripheral rural areas got only ₡4,250.[37]

Although national leaders seeking votes must court rural leaders, including local government officials and community development workers,[38] middle- and upper-class urban Ticos are ambivalent about their rural compatriots. They may speak of them with somewhat condescending pride as "our *campesinos*," romanticizing their old-fashioned virtues of honesty, hard work, simple living, and hospitality and praising them as "the backbone of the country." At the same time, they chuckle at their crudeness and call them *maiceros* (corn-growers) or *conchos* (hicks).

The range of classes is much wider in the city. In the San José area the cosmopolitan elite hobnobs with foreign diplomats and businessmen, while the poorest live in jerry-built shacks precariously perched on riverbanks and roadsides. Most middle-class jobs are concentrated there, and the middle ranges of the class system are a "sociological salad." There the system of social stratification is most complex, with the greatest social mobility and the most blurring of boundary lines between various levels. Many *campesinos* move to San José in hopes of a higher income, better education for themselves or their children, and a more interesting life. Some find their hopes dashed and add to the ring of urban slums. Others, particularly young people seeking education, find the move essential to "getting ahead"—and few go home again. Even when high schools are established in rural areas, their graduates find few white-collar jobs in their own communities.

STRATIFICATION IN RURAL COMMUNITIES

Possibly because rural communities are smaller, their criteria of class clearer, and mobility lower, they have been studied much more than urban communities. Their patterns of stratification vary. Some communities are almost classless; others are sharply differentiated in various strata; in still others the old two-class system persists. Anthropologist Victor Goldkind found two decades ago that "the biggest gap in social status in the peasant community is between those who own land, or grew up in landowning families, and those who are removed from land ownership by two or more generations."[39] *Campesinos* often told us there are two classes of people—those who own the land and those who work it.

Villages and rural areas made up of family farms have long been the most egalitarian communities in Costa Rica. Among the sixty families of San Juan del Norte observed in 1956, for example, "close kinship ties and near universal property ownership have contributed to make of the village an almost 'classless' society."[40] Similarly, a team of sociologists studying the Turrialba area in 1953 found that family-farm communities had no distinct classes in spite of recognizable differences in social status, and in such communities "paths of communication as well as kinship ties cut across nearly all status distinctions."[41] Peggy Barlett found in 1968 that the people of Pueblo Viejo, Guanacaste, recognized differences in status according to wealth and occupation, but emphasized each person's own achievements rather than the family's status, and did not extend individual rankings to siblings or descendants. "The villagers recognized differences among their standards of living but felt that even the richest among them was still poor, and said many times, 'We are all poor here.' "[42]

On large *haciendas* and plantations, in contrast, a hierarchy guides interaction. The hundred families on a large coffee *hacienda* near Turrialba in 1953, for example, demonstrated a fairly distinct hierarchy, with clearcut statuses agreed upon by local informants. The clearest statuses were the highest, which were closely correlated with occupation. The tiny upper class consisted of the *hacienda* owner or *patrón*, the administrator, and the priest. The middle class was also small; it included the *hacienda* superintendent, the head of the carpentry shop, a chauffeur, a police agent, a teacher, two independent farmers, two sharecroppers, and three foremen. There was less agreement on the comparative ranking of laborers, all of whom were, however, considered lower class.[43] A similarly rigid hierarchy still prevails on banana and sugar plantations and on large cattle ranches.

The core of today's class system in many villages in and near the Central Valley is essentially the traditional paternalism-and-dependency relationship of the *patrón* or employer and his *peones*. Lowest in status and income are landless or almost landless day laborers or *jornaleros*, who, together with more permanently employed *peones*, constitute over half the rural labor force. Many of them work on moderate-size holdings rather than large *haciendas*.

Besides *patrones*, the higher class in a rural village usually includes municipal government officials, the school's director and teachers, the parish priest, and local businessmen. Most of these are found only in the central village of a *cantón*, whose residents all refer to people in outlying hamlets as *gente del campo* or country folk. (They in turn are lumped in that category by residents of larger towns.)

In recent decades the number of rural resident *patrones* has sharply declined, from 13 percent of the rural labor force in 1950 to 0.5 percent in 1973.[44] The *patrones* who remain still have considerable power and prestige. They are often the only persons the average *campesino* cites as the "most important," "most respected," or "most influential" local figures.

Except in remote lowland areas, teachers, municipal officials, and priests have lost some influence and prestige in recent years, as roads and radios have brought many small communities closer to the mainstream of national life. Though many local leaders still use their influence over a community's votes as springboards to posts in national government, local government, never strong, has surrendered many of its functions to the central government, and these leaders have experienced a corresponding decline in status. And although the number of rural high-school students—other potential community leaders—has greatly increased, most eschew community involvement, preferring instead to seek new diversions and a high-prestige, high-income job in the capital after graduation.

As rural communities have become less isolated, class distinctions there have approached the urban pattern. Many rural Ticos send their children to high school and even to a university, thus enhancing their own status in the community while weakening their identification with it. Those with money are now also likely to seek out friends or commercial amusements in a large town, perhaps driving there in their own cars. The wooden or cement-block house of the prosperous landowner is easily distinguishable by its comparatively ornate exterior and its furnishings, reflecting urban middle-class tastes. The *peones*, however, rarely send their children to school beyond sixth grade, and many drop out before completing that. They must remain content with a simple house of adobe or wood and the local *cantina*.

In San Isidro, both the myth of classlessness and the reality of class differences are evident. In the words of a schoolteacher:

> There are no class differences here. There are both rich and poor, but everyone works with his hands, so we are not really too different. The *jefe político* [mayor] cuts the plaza grass by hand. Local teachers, businessmen, and political authorities frequently cultivate a bit of land with their own hands, and women with servants often do housework alongside them. Members of different classes work together on such things as church fairs. There are no separate clubs or other semiprivate diversions, though higher-status villagers predominate in the dance hall. Anyone who thinks he's a *personaje* [V.I.P.] is made fun of.

Like most other Ticos, the teacher seemed unaware of any contradiction in saying almost in the same breath that there are no class differences and that the members of *different classes* do much the same things and work together.

CLASS ATTITUDES

The blurring of class boundaries, the ease of interaction among members of different strata, and the possibilities for upward mobility, we have noted, all work to maintain the myth of classlessness. So do widely shared beliefs and attitudes. Among them is the culture complex that has been dubbed "the middle-class mentality," which is present to some extent in Ticos of all classes.

A faith in schooling as the best means of getting a good job and a good income and thus climbing the social ladder is the strongest element of this outlook. Middle-class Ticos include any academic titles they may possess on name-plates for their front doors and desks and on calling cards. They consider education as intrinsically valuable, and consider people who think only of money *mal educado*, badly educated, particularly if they are lacking in the social graces. Nonetheless they, like lower-status Ticos, see money as the primary determinant of class position; formal education (which supposedly makes one *culto* or cultured) is not so much desirable in itself as it is a means of obtaining a high-income business or professional job, or at least a white-collar sinecure.

Upwardly mobile young members of the urban working class and lower-middle class are still firmly convinced of a second element of the middle-class mentality—the belief that manual labor is degrading. Students would not think of working as waitresses, gardeners, or domestic servants, as many do in some modern societies, to earn their way through the university. Despite appeals in the newspapers, very few pitch in to help harvest coffee. These jobs are very poorly paid, demand long hours, and bring no prestige. A high-school graduate whose mother is a school janitor and whose grand-mother is a domestic servant refused to go to agricultural or vocational school despite his interest in plants and animals. Failing to get into the university, he settled for a secretarial course as a means to a white-collar job in a bank.

A third element of the middle-class mentality is conspicuous consumption to demonstrate success. Many urban middle-class Ticos confess half-jokingly that they like to show off even if they must borrow from loan sharks to pay for a fine car or house, new furniture, or a trip abroad. Though this tendency is not new in the middle class, nor absent in any urban class, it is far more prevalent—especially among the growing ranks of bureaucrats—than it was in the 1940s. It is facilitated by installment plans (though these carry high interest rates) and, often, by the presence of several wage-earners in one family.

"Climbers" try to be seen at fashionable restaurants, discos, and clubs and on flights to Miami. They seek university degrees and foreign schooling as much for prestige as for career-enhancement. A novelist writes of a couple leaving their new car in a parking lot and entering the National Theater with an air of triumph:

> My wife was dressed elegantly. She knows how to dress. I really like a woman who knows how to dress well. The car has air conditioning, a stereo radio, and tape deck. You may ask why air conditioning in a climate of 22°[C]. People don't buy things for their use, but to impress others.[45]

Many poorer Ticos, with similar motives, skimp on food in order to buy stylish clothing.

Despite their penchant for conspicuous consumption, Ticos consider it unseemly to boast about their possessions, neighborhood, or other status symbols. They softpedal their good fortune by saying, "We manage; we have enough for our needs." Anyone who does put on airs is a target for *choteo*, and the disdainful remark "He thinks he's a Popov!"

While almost everyone accepts the basic tenets of the middle-class mental-ity, it finds different expression from one class to another. In the upper class, few admit their elite status, insisting they are middle class even though they may take pride in their ancestry. Few if any Ticos are "idle rich"; the upper class shares the work ethic of the nonbureaucratic segment of the middle class.

Among this latter class, hard work and thrift are still seen as moral virtues. Like many middle-class Americans, its members deny that luck has anything to do with their success. Anyone who really wants to work, they insist, can get ahead. Members of the "old" middle class stress work and thrift more than spending and pull, and feel superior to both the poor and the rich. Said a man in his sixties, successful in both education and politics, whose three sons are all professionals:

> While the scions of most wealthy upper-class families have been spending the capital their ancestors accumulated, without bothering to invest it or educate themselves, many children of peasants and workers have studied to become professionals. Anyone who is poor must be lazy or have a wasteful vice like drinking. Twenty years ago it was not hard to find someone to wash the windows or cut the lawn. Now they demand preposterous pay for their services, and even so it is hard to find anyone to do it, in spite of the unemployment they say exists.

Sharing the middle-class outlook, many workers and peasants have long been averse to collective movements for improving their status. Aside from banana workers and some urban members of the working class, lower-class Costa Ricans, including *campesinos*, have had little "class consciousness." They rarely give the system as a whole either blame or credit for someone's failure or success, but tend to believe that hard work and good luck account for success and bad luck for failure. Like many other Ticos, they tend to overlook socioeconomic conditions that allow and encourage upward mobility in favor of such partly correct individualistic explanations as "He was willing to study hard for years."

Goldkind noted that peasants, far from disdaining manual labor, place a high value on it and think most urban employment—especially office work—is greatly overpaid and is not really work at all. They also place much less emphasis on conspicuous consumption than do villagers and city folk.[46] We found these generalizations still largely true in the 1970s. The old rural values of thrift, hard work, and plain living have not entirely disappeared even among younger *campesinos*, and are especially strong in newly settled areas remote from urban influences.

Like other Ticos, lower-class Costa Ricans respect "educated" people, but see class differences almost entirely in economic terms. "You can do anything with money" is a firm working-class belief, often expressed with bitterness (especially by urban workers) or resignation (especially by *campesinos*). This interpretation of class differences may help working-class Ticos counter middle-class descriptions of them as uncultured, uneducated, and lazy. They see money as essential to acquiring political power or the schooling necessary to a lucrative job, and the luck of being born "rich" as more important than merit in the scheme of things. With luck, too, they may be one of the winners in the weekly national lottery drawing.

Campesinos are more likely than urban workers to feel that economic inequalities are desirable and necessary. One forty-six-year-old *peón* argues, "The world needs both rich and poor. Rich people need the poor to work their land for them, or they'd get nowhere. And poor people wouldn't have work if it weren't for the rich."

A decade ago we often heard pious Ticos say "God made the poor. There are some of every kind, and we must be content." But there are signs of a trend away from this traditional fatalism. Hundreds of workers attend night school to get a high-school diploma that may lead to a better job. Many condemn politicians who promise a better life for the poor but fail to deliver. Fewer are resigned to poverty as God's will. Where urban influence is strong and work is hard to get, the *gamonal* who lives simply and works alongside his *peones* is no longer as highly respected as before. Many *peones* and peasants now see him as a grasping fellow who, by doing manual labor, takes the bread out of some poor family's mouth.

In San Isidro de Heredia we noted the presence of class resentments. Poor people who ask members of the local upper class for favors complain that they are often brushed off with a request to come back tomorrow. Though they respect high-school students for their presumed knowledge, some consider them too cliquish; and, in the words of one young *peón*, "Because those boys can put on a necktie, they think they're *personajes*." Higher-class *isidreños* may be criticized behind their backs for showing off" by buying their clothes at San José's largest and most expensive department store even though they may be cheaper locally. Some are seen as "stingy local capitalists" who either hole their money away or spend it on themselves rather than investing it and creating jobs. Several *peones* digging a grave in the local cemetery pointed to an ornate mausoleum and said that its luxury did not make its occupant any better off than the poor people buried in the ground. They remarked that a rich man who had died recently was buried in an expensive coffin bought "with money that could have helped a poor man."

Easy give-and-take among people of all classes is encouraged by Costa Rican norms and values, but it is by no means as unrestricted as cultural myth would have it. Interaction often proceeds along class lines. At social clubs where the upper and upper-middle classes rub elbows, members of the old elite tend to form cliques. Although *isidreños* say that "everyone talks to everyone else," a high-school student perceives the limits of their social intercourse:

> The upper class invite only members of their own class to weddings and parties. If they have poor relatives—*chatarra* [junk]—there is a problem with invitations; they don't want their San José friends to see them. But the *chatarra* don't want to be humiliated, so they would not accept anyway. The poor invite only people on their own level to weddings. Those in the middle may invite a few rich and a few poor.

The resignation of the poor, the conservatism of those with even a small plot of land, and the complacency and greed of consumption-oriented Ticos with moderate incomes (and, of course, of those who benefit most from the regressive tax system and will do nothing to raise taxes on property and capital gains) are the despair of reform-minded Costa Ricans. Yet most Ticos, to some degree, accept, ignore, or deny their country's inequalities.

MINORITIES AND "RACE"

In Spain and Spanish America, *raza* is perceived as "a cultural tradition which may or may not accompany racial characteristics."[47] The "white" majority of Costa Ricans tend to be aware of both cultural and physical differences between themselves and the most conspicuous minority groups—Indians, blacks of West Indian ancestry, and Chinese. Although they consider themselves tolerant, their tolerance often appears condescending, and there is strong evidence that many consider members of these groups not only different but also inferior. During the Nazi era, in fact, many advocated "racial purity" and discriminatory laws against Jews, blacks, and Chinese. Few people today are inclined toward such extremism, but prejudice persists, and so, to a lesser extent, does discrimination.

Skin color is the racial characteristic to which Ticos are most sensitive. Even before 1850, "whiteness" had become part of the national image propagated by the elite—an image that included political stability and widespread land ownership as well, and by the end of the nineteenth century, also embraced literacy and democracy—all traits that were emphasized as contrasts to neighboring countries. Ticos of the nineteenth and early twentieth centuries equated whiteness with civilization and progress.[48] Pride in whiteness lingers today. Costa Rican passports still include a notation on skin color, and only recently has mention of the people's "whiteness" disappeared from tourist literature. A schoolgirl's patriotic essay, published in a newspaper by her politically ambitious father in 1974, included the sentence "Somos de raza blanca" (We are of the white race).

Many other Central Americans accuse the Ticos of "thinking they're Tarzan's mother"—that is, of feeling superior, in part because their skin is lighter. Many Costa Ricans of Guanacaste province, most of whom resemble their Nicaraguan neighbors rather than *cartagos*, as they call *Meseta*-dwellers, resent what they see as the latter's sense of cultural and racial superiority. One suggested in a letter to the editor of *La Nación* that his province should form a separate nation. "Simply because we have an accent and some words that are different, our skin is a little brown, and we have some Indian features, we are objects of ridicule."[49]

There is, however, no "race problem" of the dimensions found either in the United States or in Latin American countries with a sharp cleavage between a dominant "Ladino" group and the poor Indian masses. A sociologist suggests one reason: "Racial groups of other types are so small that the white majority does not feel the need to discriminate against them."[50] Nonetheless, members of those small minorities do feel the weight of discrimination, both overt and covert.

Most of Costa Rica's 9,000 Indians live as subsistence farmers in scattered villages near the southeastern border.[51] Belonging to six linguistic groups, they preserve their old languages. They see the world as created by God or Sibu, and controlled by good and evil spirits who dwell everywhere. A few shamans still foretell the future, are called on to cure disease, and are believed to control such natural forces as rain.

In many other respects, however, their culture is like that of other poor *campesinos*. They are nominal Catholics, but also listen to Protestant missionaries. Increasingly they speak Spanish, as radios and schools enter their lives. Rifles as well as spears and bows and arrows lean against the walls of their thatch-roofed dwellings.

The white majority long ignored the Indians because they were no "problem." Then a number of things happened within a few years' time to make Indians conscious and resentful of their low status, as well as to rouse others to try to improve it.

In 1945 the government allotted each Indian family sixty hectares (148 acres) for practicing their traditional, ecologically sound system of crop rotation. But many have been wheedled, tricked, or forced into selling their lands for a pittance, while others complain that lands are taken from them by supposedly legal means because they have never been given clear titles. The whites who covet their lands have sometimes set fire to their fields and houses, poisoned their water supply, let animals loose to trample crops, or plied an owner with liquor until he signed a bill of sale. Because of such treatment and the indifference of local authorities, Indians now hold little land.

In the 1960s a newspaper campaign awakened public indignation and spurred attempts to solve the problem. A congressional investigation followed, and a protective organization, the National Commission of Indian Affairs, was formed. Articles and pictures in the daily papers quote Indians as saying, "We are proud to be Indians. But why do whites mistreat us?" And "We do not want to be treated like second- or third-class citizens or as outcasts." Many are quite aware of Costa Rican history, and one chief has been quoted as saying:

> We are ready to declare to the face of Costa Rica that slavery continues here, for the law is for the descendants of Sephardic Jews and not for the sons of the aborigines who have populated the territory for thousands of years. We are Ticos too; the constitutional norms that declare everyone born in Costa Rica to be equal [should] apply to us too.[52]

The congressional investigating committee, reporting that the Indians are miserably poor and exploited and have a high incidence of alcoholism, urged that they be given the rights and guarantees of full citizenship. Various agencies, public and private, have taken steps to improve education, nutrition, and health services and to promote community development. In

March 1976, President Oduber declared the Indian zones under a state of "national emergency," and created five areas totaling almost 110,000 hectares in which non-Indians would not be allowed to rent, lease, or buy land. But when Indians from fifty-four communities met for five days in 1978 to discuss their problems, they declared that the laws to improve their situation had never been enforced.[53]

Some Costa Ricans insist that the Indians be left in peace to practice their ancient cultures. Others argue that only shreds of these cultures remain, and that to keep them isolated, as museum pieces to be visited once in a while, is shameful. One writer believes there is only one decent solution: "to integrate them into our nationality immediately."[54]

BLACKS

Costa Rica's black minority is not a survival from the days of slavery. The black slaves of colonial times were almost completely assimilated by the end of that era; traces of their culture and physiognomy remain strongest in the north Pacific area. Some Afro-Caribbean people came to the Costa Rican shore as early as 1825, intending to stay. They were turtle fishermen and farmers who planted the coast south of Port Limón in coconut palms, marketing the nuts and oil and a few crops. For 150 years they have been nearly self-sufficient.[55]

Most black Costa Ricans, though, are descendants of the West Indians, mostly from Jamaica, who came in the late nineteenth century to work on the Atlantic Railroad, and stayed to work on the new east coast banana plantations. They had expected to return to their native islands with a sizable nest egg. Loyal British subjects in the heyday of the empire, they were content to live quite apart from the "Spaniards," whose language, religion, hygiene, and easy-going work habits they despised.[56]

White Costa Ricans, too, preferred such segregation. Wages in the banana zone, however, were five or six times as high as those in the highlands and work was steady all year round. In the mid-1920s work became scarce in the highlands and the east coast was far more healthful than it had been when the Jamaicans arrived. Many highlanders went to work in Limón, and tension arose between them and the blacks. Ethnic conflict focused on jobs, treatment on the job, and status in the strict hierarchy of United Fruit Company towns. Ticos resented the blacks, believing that they got the supervisory, technical, and clerical jobs, and thus were paid higher wages, simply because they spoke English.[57]

When the banana company abandoned its blight-ridden Atlantic-side plantations and transferred its operations to the Pacific side, it offered to resettle its workers there. But it was forbidden to employ *gente de color*, or "colored" people. President Ricardo Jiménez signed a law to that effect in 1935,[58] arguing that relocation would upset the country's "racial balance" and possibly cause "civil commotion."

West Indian immigrants and their descendants, according to an estimate based on the 1973 census, number perhaps 35,000, about 2 percent of the population. They constitute a third of the population of Limón province, where they work chiefly as independent cacao farmers and banana *peones*. Few are left of the first generation, who formed a distinct cultural group (English-speaking and Protestant), lived according to Jamaican customs, and never dreamed that they might stay on and raise their children in a new land. The government was as little interested in them as they were in becoming assimilated. They sent their children to private schools using Jamaican texts in English.

The first generation of blacks born in Costa Rica had no country, for they were not recognized as British subjects and Costa Rica denied them citizenship. Since the law did not permit them to own land, the small subsistence farms they carved out of the jungle were often taken away by whites with "official" papers in Spanish, a language they could not read. They had, in the early years, made friends with Ticos who came to live in Limón. But more and more Ticos came and displaced them in jobs; banana production declined and English no longer helped in getting employment. As a result, by the 1930s blacks were largely paupers. So many migrated to Panama and the United States to seek wartime employment—half the population of Limón, according to one estimate—that going into the streets of Limón on a Monday morning in the early 1940s was like visiting a cemetery.

Things began to change for the better with the events of 1948. Blacks ignored the government's insistence that they fight on its side, but many joined Figueres, who won their loyalty by speaking English to them, dancing with them, and kissing their babies. They were the group most affected by the change of government. A 1948 decree declared that anyone born in Costa Rica had all the rights of citizenship. From then on blacks began to enter politics, move to San José, attend public schools, and assimilate culturally. The graduating classes of 1957 and 1958 were the first to contain many black university-educated professionals.

But prejudice and discrimination persist. The idea that blacks are not really Ticos is often stated or implied. Many white Costa Ricans think of blacks as stupid and ugly, and consider them good only for sports, music, and work.[59] Shopkeepers address whites as *"don"* or *"señora,"* blacks as *"moreno"* or *"morena."* (*Moreno* means brown, and some blacks resent this euphemism, preferring to be called *negro* or *negra*—black.) Newspaper drawings depicting *limónenses* remind one of caricatures of blacks in the United States four or five decades ago.[60] A congresswoman chiding her colleagues for a disorderly session said it was like a *merienda de negros*, a Negro luncheon party.[61]

Quince Duncan asked fifty high-school students and recent graduates of Jamaican ancestry to write down the main problems of Costa Rican blacks. They cited, above all, poor education. Teachers from outside the black community do nothing to help raise the self-esteem of black children; they never teach black history or culture, evade the issue of cultural differences, and ridicule and punish those who speak English in school. Children often use English as a secret language in school and Spanish at home—but by conventional standards, they speak neither one well.[62] More and more, however, adopt the Spanish language and other elements of Costa Rican culture as they reach their mid-teens. Rather than looking outward to the

Western Caribbean system of black coastal and island societies, of which Limón has long been a part, Costa Rican blacks are increasingly looking inward to Costa Rica and demanding their full rights as citizens.[63]

CHINESE

An 1862 law prohibited immigration by blacks and Orientals, but the ban was lifted to allow cheap labor to be brought in for building the Atlantic railroad, with contract provisions that once the work was done, the workers would receive passage home. Over 600 Chinese laborers came in 1873; they were paid a fifth of the going wage and made to live and work under miserable conditions. After some time the government permitted no more to enter, and many of those who survived were, in effect, sold as household servants to prominent Costa Ricans.

In recent decades Chinese and other Orientals have immigrated quite freely. They are easily absorbed into cosmopolitan San José, but are much more conspicuous in smaller towns, especially in the lowlands, where they sometimes own most of the retail stores, restaurants, hotels, cinemas, and bars. In one lowland town, for example, Chinese own 60 percent of the stores, 90 percent of the bar-restaurants, and both movie theaters.[64] In rural Limón province they act as middlemen, buying and selling cacao and bananas. Many Ticos resent their competition on the grounds that they do not put the money back into the community but save it in order to send for their relatives.[65]

Just as with the blacks, there is a marked difference between the attitudes of immigrant Chinese and their children, and between older and younger white Ticos. There is more prejudice among the elders on both sides, and more voluntary segregation from the Costa Rican "mainstream" among the older Chinese. Young *chinos* are generally more obedient and studious than their Tico schoolmates. Their elders form a tightly knit community with its own social organization. They may not know even basic Spanish after a decade or more of living in the community, and, although they may donate to the school and church, they rarely support other community projects. They take a very conservative stance toward politics or steer clear of it entirely for fear of alienating customers. Although some Ticos fear that "the *chinos* will take over all of Guanacaste," there are an impressive number of successful cross-cultural marriages.[66]

OTHER GROUPS

Little Costa Rica has received migrants from many nations, and most of them have made a comfortable niche for themselves or blended into the society without great visibility or many accompanying problems. Foreigners have contributed in many ways to the economic and social development of Costa Rica,[67] and continue to do so.

If a number of the colonists were Sephardic Jews, their descendants are so thoroughly Tico that the fact is almost exclusively of historical interest. Another group of Sephardic Jews immigrated from Holland about a hundred years ago, and also assimilated quite successfully, entering business and, in the third generation, the professions. "Some remember their grandfathers, some don't, and some don't want to," comments a Costa Rican of more recent immigrant Jewish ancestry.

About 350 families concentrated in the capital now form the highly endogamous Jewish colony, founded by Ashkenazic or Eastern European Jews. The first few *polacos*, as most Costa Ricans call Jews, came in 1928 and 1929. Antisemitism, overt in the 1930s and 1940s, is in little evidence today, and Jews are prominent in the liberal professions, industry and commerce, and, recently, in government and politics.

Beginning in the last century, Germans, Englishmen, and Frenchmen as well as Spaniards were attracted by coffee prosperity. Many became successful coffee planters and exporters, merchants, ranchers, and industrialists; some of them, and many of their children, married Ticos. Germans are now sufficiently numerous and prosperous, in spite of setbacks during World War II, to support a German-language school and church. French influence was especially notable among the upper class during the nineteenth and early twentieth centuries. Although it is no longer essential that anyone with aspirations to high social status speak the language, a French school and a cultural center flourish. Some residential districts of metropolitan San José bear the names of European migrants whose coffee *fincas* gave way to urban development—Rohrmoser and Dent, for example.

The largest category of alien residents in 1980 had come from other Central American countries, especially Nicaragua. Many—up to 100,000 in 1979—were Nicaraguan refugees from Somoza's reign of terror, welcomed by many Ticos despite a traditional distrust of *nicas*. Many other Nicaraguans were smuggled across the border to work idle lands, or have been hired on banana and African palm plantations.

Mexico, Canada, and the United States account for thousands more. Most conspicuous of these are the Americans. Besides the diplomatic and foreign aid missions, Peace Corps volunteers, missionaries, and businessmen, ever greater number of American tourists and retirees have come in recent years. Several private English-language schools and weekly newspapers cater largely to an American clientele. Many signs in San José and other tourist centers are in English. McDonalds, Kentucky Fried Chicken, pizza parlors, and a Playboy hotel have followed the gringos south.

SUMMARY AND CONCLUSION

This discussion of class, race, and ethnicity has demonstrated the interweaving of myth, reality, and change in Costa Rican society. In spite of the high value Ticos place on democracy and equality, their society contains inequalities of many kinds. Conversations about stratification often begin with Ticos denying that a social class structure exists, then switching to an insistence that all Costa Ricans are middle class. From there many go on to make class distinctions from the perspective of their own socioeconomic status: family background, income, education, occupation, and life style. But they continue to emphasize the possibilities for social mobility, supporting their claims by citing rags-to-riches stories, the growth of the middle class, and the blurring of distinctions between classes in an increasingly urban and heterogeneous society. Many of the well-to-do stress the easy interaction of Ticos of all classes, but not the barriers that still prevail in such situations as mate selection and in the relationships of the poor with bureaucratic employees.

Many Ticos, including relatively poor ones, share a "middle-class mentality," which emphasizes luck and pull as well as individual effort, and sacrificing to get ahead as well as spending to show one's success. The bureaucratic sector, with its stress on security, successfully uses pressure groups to maintain high incomes and perquisites for government workers. In fact, the strength of public employees has kept the poor from sharing in many of the social benefits of recent decades. The greatest differences in income—and in class structure and attitudes as well—are found between urban and rural dwellers.

It is likely that the persistent myth of classless democracy not only eases the consciences of "haves" but makes more bearable the lot of many "have-nots." Thus the myth, like the stress on personal dignity, may on the one hand impede change by blocking awareness of reality. But, on the other hand, when such awareness occurs, the myth serves as a goal and promotes attempts to realize it, including government programs that aim to reduce the more glaring inequalities.

Treatment of minorities is also affected by persistent myths—that Costa Rica is relatively advanced because most Ticos are "pure white," that Ticos are tolerant, and that Costa Rica has no "race" problem. The small Indian and black minorities are becoming increasingly vocal, demanding their rights as full citizens, but anxious also to preserve some features of their old cultures and languages. The Chinese are less inclined to share in community and cultural life, yet more inclined to intermarry with other Ticos. All minority groups benefit from the myth of tolerance, for it challenges the white majority to live up to its stated values by helping solve their problems.

A gamonal and his wife in a highland village (Mavis Biesanz)

5

HOUSING, HEALTH, AND EVERYDAY LIVING

In previous chapters we discussed how Costa Ricans are grouped into communities and classes. Now we look more closely at how they live. What is the typical house of a lower-middle-class *Meseta* dweller, for example, or of a poor peasant? How does the family who lives there go about its affairs during an ordinary day? What do Ticos do to prevent and to cure illness? How does the society care for those unable to look after themselves?

HOUSING

The first colonists lived in thatch-roofed huts with dirt floors, much like the aboriginal dwellings. Then, for three centuries, most Costa Rican houses combined Spanish tradition with available materials in a style that harmonized with the natural surroundings and was extremely functional.[1] Skilled artisans were few, and the colonists were too poor to import sophisticated tools and materials; they used what was at hand—mud, clay, grass, vines, wood. For the adobe walls of their single-story houses they mixed mud with grass clippings or sugar cane waste, trampled by oxen and shaped into large sun-dried blocks put together with fresh adobe for mortar. The walls rested on foundations of stone and wood or rose directly from hard-packed earth. Workmen shaped roofing tiles by patting soft clay over their thighs, which meant that their shape varied according to the tile makers' physiques and skills. Doors, window and door frames, and window bars and shutters were made of moisture-resistant wood. Floors were of packed, swept earth, hard woods, or rectangular clay tiles. The walls were usually coated with whitewash with a wide strip of Prussian blue at the base to discourage pecking chickens. A veranda, an open gallery over which the roof extended, usually opened on an interior patio or to the front of the house. There the family and neighbors gathered to talk in the afternoons and to celebrate special occasions.[2]

These earthquake-resistant houses predominated on the *Meseta Central* and in Guanacaste until the turn of this century. Their similarity gave cities and towns a pleasing air of uniformity and harmony. Only a few such dwellings remain. Most Ticos now live in small wooden or cement-block houses, many of them painted in combinations of bright pink, green, turquoise, and blue. Floors are of wood or tiles, the roof of zinc or corrugated iron that rusts with time.

Nearly four-fifths of all dwellings had piped-in water by 1973, while more than two-thirds had electricity. Methods of human waste disposal varied greatly. Of every 100 dwellings, fifteen were connected to a sewer system, thirty had septic tanks, forty-three had privies, and only twelve had no provisions at all.[3] Modernization of water supplies and sewage disposal is proceeding—against resistance in some towns and villages—under an autonomous government institute, with British technical aid.

Yet these statistics mask great regional variation. Few houses of the 14 percent with dirt floors are found on the *Meseta*; most are in lowland areas. While more than a third of the *Meseta's* houses have walls of concrete blocks or bricks, roughly nine out of ten in other areas have wooden walls, and many of the rest are of cane or branches. Electricity, running water, and flush toilets, too, are far more common in the Central Valley than in other areas.[4]

Most Costa Ricans prefer to own rather than rent their homes. Sixty percent had realized this dream in 1973.[5] In urban areas, 53 percent of dwellings are owned by the occupant.[6] While housing projects, subdivisions, and varying land prices make many urban neighborhoods fairly homogeneous in terms of social class, location of urban dwellings is often no indication of class status. Large, expensive houses may stand next to shacks, especially in San José's suburbs and in large towns.

The design and furnishings of Costa Ricans' homes both reflect some features of national culture and indicate their approximate class position. Wooden or cement block walls and plastic curtains divide into rooms the single-story house of the small farmer, skilled city worker, or low-grade white-collar worker. The front door opens on a *sala* (parlor) where guests are entertained. As is common among all social classes, special effort is taken to furnish the *sala* as well as possible, for appearances are important, and this is the only room in the house that any but intimate callers see. Artificial flowers, china figurines, family photos, and cheap souvenirs crowd shelves and adorn a low doily-covered wooden table in the center of the room. Several plastic-covered upholstered chairs and a matching sofa are neatly arranged around the table. The women may make their own clothes on a sewing machine standing in the corner. Religious pictures, school diplomas, family photographs, and gaudy lithographs deck the walls. Farther back and invisible from the *sala* are a kitchen, dining room, bathroom, and one to three bedrooms. While the thick-walled adobe houses have few windows, traditionally shuttered tightly at night and during illness to keep out "harmful" breezes, newer houses of wood or concrete blocks usually have glass windows in each room, frequently covered day and night with plastic curtains or venetian blinds to ensure privacy.

A small electric stove usually dominates Central Valley kitchens, though even there many rural residents still cook with firewood gathered and chopped by the men and boys of the household, stacked in a shed, and burned in a narrow-chimneyed iron stove that stands on a wooden platform. A cupboard or two, some wall shelves, a sink of stone or cement with a cold water tap for washing dishes and clothes, and a wooden table for preparing meals complete the kitchen. In the small dining room are a table, several chairs, and very likely a television set. The couple's bedroom may contain a double bed with a cotton-stuffed or foam rubber mattress and pillows. Two or three older children sometimes share each bed in other rooms; some may sleep in the *sala*. A wooden dresser, a vanity table, a night stand, and perhaps a small rug and table lamp are found in each bedroom. A porcelain lavatory stands outside the bathroom, which may contain only a flush toilet and a cold shower, recently acquired luxuries for many Ticos (and important status symbols among members of the urban lower class). The walls in each room are painted in different pastel colors; green is a favorite in living rooms. At least one overhead light bulb dangles in each room. In rural areas a wooden or tiled porch is adorned with a variety of flowers, ferns, and other plants in tin cans or boxes, and perhaps by a caged songbird or a parrot on a perch. Here the family sit on benches in the evenings and on Sundays to talk and watch neighbors pass. Folk-remedy herbs and vegetables, especially the easily cultivated *chayote* squash, which grows on a climbing vine, are planted behind the house if space permits. A motor scooter or an old car may be parked near the house.

The wealthier residents of urban areas usually live in one-story houses, less often in two-story or split-level ones, with a low tiled or cement front porch, a large, well-kept lawn, a carport or garage and a paved driveway, and perhaps a verdant patio within or behind the house. A high cement wall, crowned with broken glass to discourage burglars, surrounds older upper-class houses, while newer ones may have grill-covered windows, burglar alarms, and a watchdog or two, plus a neighborhood private guard service—an old Spanish tradition. A cement walk leads to the front door, which is complete with nameplate and doorbell.

Living room furniture may be of the beautiful native hardwoods, upholstered in showy materials. Wall-to-wall carpeting is more and more likely to be found in such homes. Family photographs, vases and figurines, pre-Columbian artifacts, reproductions of famous paintings or originals bought on travels or painted by family or friends adorn the room. A dining table and chairs may occupy one end of the room or a separate dining room. In a more informal room the family entertain close friends and watch television or play records. There may also be a library or study. Bedrooms, like parlors, are often ornately furnished. A cliché of upper- and upper-middle-class homes is a scrolled gilt mirror and shelf in the entrance hall. Generalizations

An upper-middle class house *(La Nación)*

about furnishings, however, are increasingly risky as younger couples turn away from mahogany and brocade to simpler things. Completing the layout is a small, sparsely furnished maid's room and bathroom near the kitchen, and a utility room and patio for hanging clothes. The kitchen contains the usual electrical appliances owned by affluent families in the Western world, and the bathroom the usual amenities.[7]

The homes of the heterogeneous middle class range between the two types already described. Some members of this class cling to houses they have lived in all their lives, or since marriage, while others have realized a dream of moving into a new suburban house, whether simple or pretentious. It is far easier to generalize about the life styles of the very rich or the very poor.

The dwelling of a poor urban laborer is generally found in a crowded and unhealthful *tugurio* or slum. It is often part of a rundown building, or it may be a dark, unpainted shack with floors of dirt or broken wooden planks or tiles, and one or two makeshift partitions. Most such homes are as neat and clean as conditions permit. They are likely to have only one bedroom.[8] Several people may sleep in each bed, which may be no more than a set of raised burlap-covered planks. A few small glass windows admit light, while fresh air enters through the open door. Though several people may sleep in the *sala,* it is always partitioned off from the rest of the dwelling with any available material, even if a few wooden chairs are its only furniture. Pictures of saints adorn the walls of the *sala,* together with calendar girls, magazine pictures of luxurious homes and smiling blond babies, and newspaper photos of "society" brides or favorite soccer players. A wooden outhouse, sometimes shared with other families, stands in back. Water is taken from a stream or, in some urban *barrios*, from a municipal tap. Most such dwellings are rented.

Squatters' illegally erected shanties on the fringes of San José and the larger towns are pieced together from boards discarded by sawmills, tin cans, and stray sheets of tin roofing. Many are located near rivers or streams which

A house in the dry Pacific lowlands (Sylvia Boxley de Sassone)

serve as the only source of water, and few are visible to the middle-class motorist or pedestrian on his or her daily rounds. Their occupants cannot pay even the minimal rent of the poorest legal housing.

Campesino houses, as we saw, usually have wooden walls and tin roofs; many have dirt floors. In many such homes at least some of the tools and furniture are still homemade; a stone mortar and pestle may be used for grinding corn, and candles furnish light. Though dirt floors are common in the hot lowlands, most houses there are raised a foot or two off the ground on wooden posts as a protection against dampness, and floored with rough wooden planks. Jamaican immigrants to the marshy lowlands of Limón built houses even higher up on posts to avoid animals and floods and to provide space underneath for a shaded work area and for drying clothes. The wooden boards that separate the various rooms reach about a meter short of the ceiling, allowing air to circulate. Many poor *campesinos*, including Indians, live in windowless one- or two-room houses of *caña* (a kind of slender bamboo) with roofs of grass or palm thatch and dirt floors. *Caña* may be used to partition off rooms and to form, just under the roof, a wide platform for storing food and tools and for sleeping; it is reached by a notched log ladder. The walls of vertical *caña* allow breezes to pass through. Chickens run in and out. Next to the house, a thatched roof supported by four log posts may shelter other belongings.

According to Jorge Sánchez, Minister of the Economy in the Oduber administration, there is a housing deficit of 130,000 units, and one-third of the existing 332,000 dwellings need major improvements. The shortage of

An urban slum (Rodrigo Montenegro)

adequate housing affects over half the population, and is considered one of the country's main problems.

Various agencies—public, subsidized, and private—have attempted since the 1930s to keep up with population growth and the deterioration of buildings, and to remedy the housing shortage. In recent years only 10,000 new homes have been built annually, about half the estimated number needed. Oldest of the surviving public housing agencies is INVU, the National Institute of Housing and Urbanization, which has been building low-cost housing since the 1950s, largely as a means to clear the slums but also for lower-middle-class occupants. From 1958 to 1973, however, it averaged only 900 units a year. Many of INVU's houses are beyond the means of the poor. Middle-class INVU housing, for instance, costs from ₡41,500 to ₡100,000 ($4,860 up to nearly $12,000). One gloomy prediction is that San José will always be ringed by slums because, as soon as some poor families manage to escape shanty towns, others take their place.

INVU projects continue expanding to the south and southwest of San José, and, as land becomes scarce and expensive, INVU now constructs multifamily buildings of two or more stories as well as the usual rows of small adjoining one-story houses with concrete-block walls, concrete floors, and zinc roofs. Each unit in a typical "colony" has a living-dining room, two or three bedrooms, and a bathroom with toilet, shower, and wash basin. Some critics find INVU projects lacking in provisions for recreation, sociability, and esthetic values,[9] while others say private enterprise could have built better houses at a lower cost.

Most Costa Ricans are "morning people." They rise early and go to work and school early because even in the rainy season the morning is almost sure to be clear and sunny, at least on the Pacific side of the central mountains. A cold shower or bath begins the day, and most Ticos are neatly dressed and well groomed. Their unvaried but apparently satisfying diet is built around rice, red or black beans, and tortillas as well as strong black coffee with great quantities of sugar. Jokes a charcoal maker high in the mountains:

> My breakfast consists of coffee and rice and beans; the next day I eat beans and rice, so I won't get bored. Another day I eat *gallo pinto* ["spotted rooster"— beans and rice fried in oil and seasoned with onion, garlic, and salt] to vary my diet. Ah, yes! and tacos with rice and beans![10]

Breakfast and supper are light, the noon meal heavy. Snacks and soda pop or coffee are taken at frequent intervals. Vegetables and fruits are not prominent in the menu, though they are available the year around. Beef and pork are preferred to fish. Sweet pastries and cakes, as well as macaroni and other pastas, round out a typical diet.

Most housewives do just about the same things day after day. But diet and routine do vary according to rural or urban residence and social class.[11]

An electric light or candle is already burning by 5:00 A.M., and often an hour or two earlier, in the kitchen of the rural *peón*, whose wife and older daughters rise early to prepare his breakfast and begin other housework. A bath in a nearby river or a quick sponging with soap and cold water dipped from a metal pail with a gourd begins each day. Older *campesinos* no longer heed their parents' warning that bathing after age forty may prove fatal: "Better earth on body than body in earth." After donning a faded dress and perhaps a sweater, the women light the wood fire to boil a kettle of water. After pouring the water through a cloth bag full of powdered coffee, often prepared from homegrown berries, they sit awhile with a cup of the strong black brew sweetened with several spoonfuls of white sugar or homemade raw sugar syrup. Then they prepare the lunches a child will take to the men for their brief nine o'clock break: store-bought tortillas or white bread, cups of cold black beans and rice, a bottle of *aguadulce* (raw sugar dissolved in hot water), and perhaps some sausage, meat, or eggs.

Rising around five, or earlier if they must walk far,[12] the men slip on their worn shirts and pants, denim aprons, canvas hats, and sheathed machetes. Shoes are often saved for mass and other special occasions, while rubber boots are commonly worn by all members of the family during the rainy season, when roads and trails become extremely muddy. With their sweetened coffee they eat tortillas and sour cream, dry white bread, or perhaps a fried egg with a plate of *gallo pinto*. As they wait on the men, the women nibble their own breakfast.

Up at about six o'clock, the younger children bathe and then eat a similar breakfast, including coffee, which is thought to be nourishing and is even given to babies. Many children between ages six and twelve are in school from 7:00 to 10:00 A.M.; others attend a later session. Children not in school

77

play near the house or run errands while their mother and older sisters make the beds, feed the chickens, and sweep the dirt or plank floor, perhaps using a homemade broom of small branches. The women then wash clothes with cold water and a bar of laundry soap. They rub them in one section of the sink, rinse them in another, then lay them on the grass or bushes or hang them on a barbed-wire fence to whiten in sun and rain for a day or so. In areas without piped water, the nearest stream is used for laundry. Dried clothes are pressed with flatirons heated on the stove, several irons sometimes heating up while the one in use is cooling. Only on Sundays are the women free of laundry chores, for Ticos highly value clean, unwrinkled clothing. When girls are old enough, they wash and iron the blouses of their school uniforms daily, and press the skirts to have them fresh.

Between 10:00 A.M. and noon, the women and children lunch on rice, black beans, fried plantains, bread or tortillas, coffee, and perhaps a bit of milk for the children, purchased from a farmer or vendor on a regular contractual basis. Foods are prepared the same way every day. Soon after midday the men return from their six-hour work shift and take coffee with bread. Though they may sit awhile, they will probably not take a siesta. Nor will the women lie down until they retire for the night, although they will sit down for brief respites. Peggy Barlett found that women in a farm village in Guanacaste worked on an average about 44 percent of the time; men, less than 27 percent.[13]

Should the family have a bit of land, the men may work it during the afternoon.[14] Favored crops for home use and possibly for cash are beans, corn, chayotes, and perhaps coffee or sugar cane. Boys aged eight and up are expected to help if they are not in school. Their sisters may begin household chores and babysitting at about age six. Thirty years ago, a *peón* spent most of his afternoons working his plot or making rude furniture for the house. Fewer *peones* today have any land of their own, and most now buy furniture as well as food. Many spend their afternoons chopping firewood, playing with the children, listening to the radio, or talking with other men at a nearby *cantina* or on a village street corner. Boys and young men devote considerable time to impromptu soccer games.

Women spend the afternoon finishing the day's housework and boiling black beans for the coming day, meanwhile listening to Latin American dance and pop music and Mexican soap operas on the radio. Children run occasional errands to the store on weekdays, though parents buy most necessities on Saturdays at a village *pulpería* or a nearby town market. Everyone has a cup of coffee with bread at about three o'clock. Supper is eaten soon afterward. Often taken with *aguadulce* rather than coffee, supper is otherwise a repetition of lunch. During the coffee harvest, a *Meseta* family may spend its extra money for cheese, sausage, or *olla de carne*, the traditional stew made with beef, yucca, potatoes, corn, plantains, squash, and other vegetables.

After supper the women wash the dishes and put the younger children to bed, sometimes saying a prayer with them. Other family members may have a cup of coffee and listen to the six o'clock news on the radio while the women iron and sew. In areas with electricity, the older children may watch television for an hour or two, at home or with neighbors, while the younger men talk or play soccer with friends. The family may say a Rosary, a vanishing practice even in the countryside. A cup of coffee is taken just before retiring, and most members of the family are asleep by seven or eight, leaving the door ajar for the younger men, who may come in two or three hours later. Coals still glow in the stove, and a watchdog in the yard barks at the occasional passerby.

The daily life of the independent small farmer's family differs only slightly. The farmer and his older sons may exchange labor with kinsmen. They eat lunch with their own families at eleven or twelve o'clock, unless they are working on a distant piece of their often widely scattered holdings. Their meals are likely to include more eggs, meat, milk, and vegetables than those of the landless *peón's* family.

An urban manual worker may rise at five o'clock to be at work by six. His clothing may be somewhat newer than that of the *campesino*, and he will probably wear shoes to work. His breakfast almost invariably includes sweetened coffee with *gallo pinto* and an egg, or white bread with sour cream. Unless he returns for the midday meal he may take some sandwiches or rice and beans along as he boards a crowded bus or his motor scooter and departs for work. His wife has coffee and bread (breakfast is often referred to as "coffee") and rouses the children to wash and dress for school. Her house-work routine varies little from one day to another: making beds, sweeping floors, and washing clothes in a wooden or concrete sink next to the house before hanging them on a line or fence behind the house. Having, in all likelihood, no refrigerator,[15] she finds it necessary to send a child to a nearby *pulpería* for each day's needs. Usually charging these until Saturday and buying in small quantities, she pays more in the course of a month than she would if she paid cash in the municipal market or even the supermarket. The *pulpero* enters each day's expenditures in her little booklet as well as in his own accounts. Lunch consists of rice, beans, and *aguadulce* or coffee, with little or no variation in the menu or the way it is prepared. The older daughters are less likely to help with the housework than are country girls. Housework continues in the afternoon while the children play among them-selves in the house or with neighbor children outside. The male "head of the household" may have left for another job after lunch; many urban males hold two or more jobs despite widespread underemployment.

Urbanites of both sexes and all ages and classes take a few minutes for coffee with bread or pastry at about 9 A.M. and again at 3 P.M. Late in the afternoon the worker may stop for drinks at a favorite *cantina*, then play with the youngest child when he gets home. After a five or six o'clock supper—the menu a repetition of lunch—he may return to the *cantina*. If he stays home he is likely to listen to the radio or watch television while his wife sews, finishes her housework, and chats with the younger children. The older boys are likely to be at night school or talking with friends at a poolhall, street corner, or *cantina*. Older girls, except those in night school, are normally at home. By ten or eleven most of the family are asleep.

Up at 5:30 or 6:00, members of the urban middle class may have a bowl of packaged cereal, an egg, and a glass of fruit juice with their morning bread and coffee. The man, wearing a tie and possibly a suit coat, is off by car or bus to start work at 7:00 or 8:00. Although his wife may have one or two full-time servants, she does some cooking and sewing, which, unlike most manual labor, she does not consider degrading and may even enjoy. She also shops at the supermarket and knows the best places to buy fresh fruits and vegetables in the municipal market.

Noon dinner is the main meal of the day. Most of the family may be present, for the breadwinner usually has a two-hour lunch break and most children attend school only half days. The housewife relies more and more on convenience foods such as dehydrated soups, canned refried black beans, canned vegetables and juices, jams and jellies. Besides the ubiquitous rice and beans, dinner often includes soup, beefsteak, plantains, bread or tortillas, a salad of lettuce and tomatoes, cooked vegetables, eggs, and milk, topped off by fruit and coffee. A brief siesta may follow, though fewer Ticos of any class take siestas than in previous years. Shortly before one or two o'clock, the husband is off to work again. Leaving the younger children with a servant, the mother may go shopping, call on friends, have her hair done at a beauty parlor, or attend a tea or club meeting. Or she may stay at home and watch television, or help younger schoolchildren with their homework. After work her husband, like the urban working-class man, may stop for drinks, though at a more elegant bar. Like men in other classes, he plays briefly with the youngest child when he arrives home.

Supper, served about six, may consist only of sandwiches or leftovers from lunch; middle-class suppers are now much lighter than a few decades ago. Older children, especially boys, may go to the movies in the evening or drop in on a friend, while others watch television or read the papers in the living room. Just before exams, high-school and university students may study much of the night. Ordinarily, however, they do very little studying. In the upper-middle class, the head of the household may entertain business or professional acquaintances at a restaurant or night club, or perhaps at the home bar, a recent innovation among wealthier Ticos. On ordinary nights most family members are asleep by eleven, except perhaps for the older boys, who may be at a dance hall, soda shop, soccer match, or *cantina*, or simply driving around in a car.

The daily life of an upper-class family is in many ways like that of the middle class. Men of this class, however, are more likely to have independent occupations allowing flexible working hours. Upper-class households also include more live-in servants—often a maid for cleaning, a nursemaid, and a cook.[16] A chauffeur and a part-time gardener may also serve the family. Most upper-class women, even those who do not work outside the home, regard servants as necessities, and the "servant problem" has long been a favorite conversational theme; since at least the late nineteenth century the better-off Ticos have lamented that "These days one cannot find an honest, hard-working servant as one could in my mother's day." Thanks to servants, upper-class women spend more time shopping, calling on friends, doing volunteer work, and attending teas, canasta parties, and club meetings than do middle-class women. Men of this class may spend considerable time working with political parties and economic pressure groups, relaxing at their clubs or with their mistresses, and travelling to the United States or elsewhere for business and pleasure.

HEALTH AND LONGEVITY: STATISTICAL TRENDS

Until recent decades, Costa Rican parents were aware of sickness and death as very real and constant threats to themselves and their children. Statistics show a dramatic drop in both, with far better chances for babies to survive to adulthood, and a longer life expectancy.

The death rate dropped from forty-one per 1,000 in 1894 to eighteen fifty years later. The postwar years saw a sharp decline from fourteen in the late 1940s to five in 1978. Life expectancy at birth was about forty years in 1927; it is now seventy years (sixty-eight for men and seventy-two for women)—about on a par with Uruguay, Argentina, and the United States. In 1920, one baby out of every four born alive died before reaching its first birthday; by 1979 this figure had dropped to one in forty-five, a rate of twenty-two per 1,000. Though far above the rate in "developed" countries, this rate is the lowest in Latin America. The death rate of children between the ages of one and four has also dropped sharply—from twelve per 1,000 in 1953 to two in 1974.

This spectacular improvement in the life chances of newborn Costa Ricans can be attributed largely to better control of diarrhea and infectious diseases. Because diarrhea is especially hard to control and prevent, the death rate from diarrhea is often considered an important indicator of a society's level of development. Until 1974 it was the leading cause of infant deaths in Costa Rica. Now prematurity is in first place.

MALNUTRITION

Malnutrition was long a cause of death in itself, and a contributing factor in deaths from other causes, such as diarrhea and measles. Even a few years ago the data on malnutrition were grim, especially in rural areas.[17] "Malnutrition of children from birth to five years on a national level has not fallen below 50 percent in the last 25 years," according to a 1975 study.[18]

At one time, says Dr. Edgar Mohs, director of the Children's Hospital, most Ticos were quite well fed; the beef stew that has become a luxury for the poor was an everyday dish, and the diet was much more varied than it is in most homes today. The shift from peasantry to peonage has meant that many families no longer have land, time, or energy to grow their own grains and vegetables, to raise chickens and pigs, or to keep a cow or two, while a *peón's* wages seldom allow him to feed his family adequately.

Mothers often give a disproportionate amount of food to older children, not knowing that deprivation in the first years causes irreversible damage to brain cells. Urban mothers consider early weaning and bottle feeding convenient, a preference increasingly common among rural mothers as well. Many rural parents skimp on food partly because just fetching it from town once a week is a major chore, says anthropologist Ian Rawson; they may have to walk three or four hours.[19] Often more than half the nutritive value of food is lost because children have parasites that cause diarrhea (85 percent have parasites, according to some estimates). On the national level, low production of basic foods, inefficient marketing, and the high prices resulting from both these factors have also contributed to malnutrition. The preference for highly advertised and prestigious but relatively nonnutritive foods such as refined snacks, soda pop, and baby formula is also blamed as is a lack of interest in growing and eating vegetables and fruits.

Ticos attribute much of the improvement in their health and longevity to modern medicine—to vaccines, prescription drugs, hospitals, doctors, and health education. The picture is not, however, as onesidedly favorable as it might seem. Two prominent doctors working in child health and nutrition question the development model of unlimited growth, of "more of everything," that their country seems to be copying from the United States and Western Europe. Along with improvements in some aspects of health, say Leonard Mata and Edgar Mohs, Ticos in recent years have experienced a marked decline in physical activity, and an increase in the level of anxiety and tension, as well as in obesity, alcoholism, smoking, and narcotics use.

Some doctors see "developed" countries as accountable for much of the problem of Third World malnutrition. The rich countries, they say, refuse to pay adequate prices for agricultural products, and furthermore they export "certain practices, medicines, and substances that undermine the health of our people."[20] Malnutrition, as they see it, is due not so much to lack of food as to ignorance, indifference, poverty, and social injustice.

Whatever its causes, malnutrition has apparently declined markedly in the last several years. Between 1970 and 1976, the number of infant deaths attributed to malnutrition fell by 70 percent.

RURAL HEALTH AND COMMUNITY MEDICINE

The decline in malnutrition and in preventable diseases is undoubtedly due in large part to a remarkable government program. Several government agencies now cooperate to bring health services and preventive medicine to the poor, especially in dispersed rural communities, and two meals a day to all preschool and primary school children and expectant and nursing mothers.

The Program of Rural Health, established in 1970, was built on the existing structure of malaria prevention and control, made obsolete by its own success. Before that year 90 *céntimos* of every *colón* spent on health care went for curative medicine, mostly in communities of over 2,000 inhabitants. The new program is primarily preventive and aimed at the 60 percent living in small communities, and especially at the 31 percent in settlements of fewer than 500 people.

The program began by establishing rural health posts attended by paramedical personnel, and visited regularly by doctors and nurses. The program was given new impetus in 1974 with the passage of a law creating "Family Assistance" to provide the indigent aged with pensions and all needy children with food. Financed by special taxes on sales and payrolls, the measure was originally designed to achieve redistributive justice simply by a transfer of funds, but soon took the form of a many-pronged attack on malnutrition and disease, especially among the rural poor. By 1977 it reached over a half million Ticos in 2,500 communities, in each of which a community development association was formed under DINADECO. The residents themselves are expected to supply the labor and meet much of the cost. The posts are staffed by paramedical personnel given a short but intensive course in vaccination, nutrition, prenatal care, and simple medication. They are expected to visit every home in their area, averaging about 150, every six weeks, to take a health census, and to counsel people on health, hygiene, and family planning. Covering their territory by boat, jeep, motor-cycle, horseback, or on foot, they refer urgent cases to the nearest clinic if the doctor is not due for a routine visit. The drop in deaths from communicable diseases is one indication of the program's success.

Central to the new emphasis on prevention is the nutrition program financed by Family Assistance. School lunchrooms and preschool day care centers provide primary school and preschool children, as well as pregnant women and nursing mothers, with two meals six days a week the year round. By December 1979 there were 2,900 such lunchrooms, serving a fourth of all Ticos and all but 3 percent of primary schools. The constitutional provision that the state is responsible for providing food for indigent children is finally being fulfilled.

This provision and the conviction that deficiencies during the early years result in irreversible damage to the brain, and thus to the quality of the nation's citizenry, are cited to justify the program, which at first was opposed by those hardest hit by the new taxes. But the program does not stop with free meals. For food to be properly absorbed, children must be cured of parasites and prevented from contracting them again. Therefore, other government agencies help communities achieve a good water supply (which also lowers the incidence of hepatitis and typhoid), and provide free latrines for those who sign up to install them. Because many parasites enter through the feet, the Ministry of Education supplies shoes to indigent children. Mothers are taught elementary hygiene and food preparation at the nutrition centers. Teachers are encouraged to organize school gardens. Every school-age child who eats at the nutrition center or school lunchroom must stay in school. Children and mothers who live too far to come daily may fetch powdered milk and protein concentrates.

The nutrition program has generally been accepted, and is now firmly rooted in each community. Each center depends on the community to provide transportation of supplies, maintain the buildings, and pay for assistant cooks and cleaning supplies. Thus its members are encouraged to develop a sense of participation in the program and to feel responsible for its success.

The Ministry of Health is in charge of health posts and the larger health units called *unidades sanitarias,* which offer a basically preventive program in rural communities. In 1974 it also instituted a Community Medicine program to reach poor urban neighborhoods, which are expected to cooperate in establishing and maintaining facilities. Other agencies—those in charge of social security, housing, water supply, and child care—are also coordinated by the Ministry. This program is financed by Family Assistance, as are preschool centers that offer "integral care" to children of working mothers. The staffs of the few centers established since 1975 include teachers and assistants, social workers who also work with family and community, nurses' aides, nutrition workers, cooks, and cleaners.

THE SOCIAL SECURITY SYSTEM

Many Costa Ricans give the social security system (CCSS) most of the credit for improved health and life expectancy. Before it was established in the early 1940s, and for a long time afterward, most medical care was either private or charitable. Hospitals had an air of the old European pattern of convent care and charity. In each provincial capital a Board of Social Protection made up of clergy and laymen administered a hospital financed in large part by lottery tickets. Indigents were treated free of charge, but most lower-class people feared hospitals as places where one went to die.

President Calderón Guardia conceived of social security as a plan to ensure national health standards rather than merely to provide pensions. Doctors, druggists, and employers opposed the plan from the outset, and at each stage of expansion. It started on a small scale, covering salaried workers with less than ₡300 a month income. Little by little the ceiling on salaries was raised, each step accompanied by complaints that private medicine and business would be eliminated by socialization. By 1979 nearly all Ticos were covered by social security, and the CCSS also had taken over all the community hospitals, "to avoid costly duplication of services."

CCSS has been called the strongest formal organization in the country. Not only does it enjoy absolute administrative autonomy, it also has *de facto* legislative power, for all rules and regulations set by its board of directors are mandatory and universal. It is the government's biggest business, with a yearly budget of ₡2.6 billion, and 18,000 employees. Of the country's 1,235 doctors, a thousand work for CCSS.[21]

The system is often criticized as wasteful, expensive, and dehumanized—a massive and impersonal bureaucratic monster that administers deficient medical care, especially in outpatient clinics.

A common complaint is that a seriously ill person is given an appointment weeks or even months away. Acutely ill patients must sit and wait their turn, often for hours. There are no provisions for treating even the dying at home. Many prefer to go to private doctors and pharmacists rather than struggle with red tape and delays, even though they (and their employers) are obligated to pay premiums to CCSS.

Despite these shortcomings, residents of remote areas are especially thankful that health care is reaching them. In 1968, before the rural health plan was established, one of the authors (Richard) visited a settlement on the Osa peninsula and happened to attend the funeral of a small child. She had become ill the day before, and even though the parents went into Golfito on business, they did not take her along because they had no money for a doctor or medicine. Today such cases are rare. A *peón* in a village near Cartago notes the change:

Social Security is not perfect, but it is a lot better than what we had. A sick person once had to be carried into town on a man's back, and then usually had to be taken to the hospital in Cartago. Now a nurse is here all the time, and the doctor comes two mornings a week.

PSYCHOLOGICAL DISTURBANCES AND ALCOHOLISM

Doctors perceive an increase in tension, anxiety, and mental illness in recent decades.[22] The incidence of emotional disturbance is said to be especially high among rural migrants to the city; hoping for a better income and a better life, they are often disappointed, and may eventually contribute to the statistics on prostitution, alcoholism, and suicide.

The reported suicide rate—one attempt per 10,000 persons per year—is about the same as in other Central American countries, and shows little variation by age and social class. One specialist, however, believes it is increasing among young people, and attributes this rise to boredom due to a lack of recreational facilities, and frustration due to a lack of fit between schooling and job opportunities.

A modern 1,400-bed psychiatric hospital in a San José suburb is a self-contained village. Its flexible program treats both full-time inmates and patients who either sleep there and work by day or sleep at home and come for psychological counseling and chemical and occupational therapy. Most Ticos have an aversion to visiting friends and relatives there or admitting that they know anyone there. Many see mental illness as contagious. Yet institutionalization is much more common now than in the past, and communities and families will more often label as problematic and "psychotic" some behavior that was once tolerated, perhaps with amusement.

Health workers consider alcoholism one of the most serious and widespread problems in Costa Rica. Estimates of the number of alcoholics and excessive drinkers vary from 80,000 to 200,000. The director of the National Psychiatric Hospital says that 40 percent of the beds are occupied by alcoholics with mental problems.

A 1972 study reported that sales of alcoholic beverages "have increased more than seven-fold during the last twenty years; they have tripled within the last ten; and have more than doubled in six years."[23] A study of drinking habits by the National Institute on Alcoholism in 1970 found that the lower the level of income and education, the higher the incidence of alcoholism. Most Costa Rican alcoholics are in their twenties, while in other countries the median age is about forty-five.[24]

It is possible that the alcoholism problem, a relatively new one, stems in large part from the disorientation accompanying rapid social and cultural change. Dr. Alberto Zamora, who works with rehabilitation of alcoholics, believes many alcoholics drink to relieve depression, which in turn arises from their frustration in a consumption-oriented society that cannot fulfill their wishes.[25]

Drinking has also become firmly embedded in the culture, part of the social rituals surrounding many leisure-time activities, as well as of the culture complex of *machismo*. Opportunities and pressures to drink exist everywhere. In 1975 there were 9,000 *cantinas*, "more than schools, churches, nutrition centers, high schools, and playing fields" combined.[26] A telegraph operator in a small town says he is not accepted by townsmen because most are heavy drinkers and he does not drink. A highland village priest has noted increased drinking in recent years, especially among women, although they do not go on weekend binges as many men do. Drinking is common even at adolescents' parties. Boys of ten or twelve are often given drinks at parties and wedding receptions. Since heavy drinking is identified with *machismo*, abstinence is sometimes considered a sign of effeminacy. At any social gathering where alcoholic drinks are served (and such occasions are common) the male teetotaler—even if he is a recovering alcoholic—is repeatedly urged to "have just one."

Although the fact that liquor is a substantial source of government revenue has undoubtedly blocked wholehearted efforts to deal with the problem,[27] the Institute on Alcoholism and the rehabilitation center receive government support. There are numerous chapters of Alcoholics Anonymous, and the Salvation Army also has a program. In 1976 police were told to stop arresting and imprisoning drunks; alcoholics were officially recognized as sick rather than criminal and were to be turned over to the Institute instead of jail.

POPULAR MEDICINE

Most Ticos share to some degree what anthropologists call "popular medicine"—a complex of ideas, facilities, and practices regarding the cause and cure of illness, that only partially coincide with those of "orthodox" medical specialists. Practically every Tico diagnoses and prescribes at the drop of a symptom.

Especially in rural areas, Ticos take colds, stomach upsets, and aches and pains more or less for granted, as part of the natural order of things. More serious illnesses are ascribed to God's will (though not as punishment for misdeeds), or to an evil spell worked by a witch in the pay of an enemy. Although they scrub and clean with disinfectants, water, and lemon juice to ward off illness, this practice often stems from belief in countermagic against evildoers rather than in any microbe theory.

Among beliefs regarding the cause of illness is the danger of *aires* or drafts. All sorts of dire consequences can follow careless exposure to the air when one is warm, perspiring, or ill. One hears of people who become paralyzed or blind when their hair was cut and a draft hit their necks or when they took a shower or changed from warm to cool clothing without a proper interval for cooling off, or went outside without a sweater.

Another complex of beliefs relates to "hot" and "cold" substances; a proper diet should not go to either extreme. Along with other Spanish Americans, Costa Ricans hold that some foods are "hot" and irritate the digestive organs, especially the liver; they include coffee, liquor, and pork. "Cool" fruits such as pineapple and watermelon, and doses of Andrews' Liver Salts, counteract the effect of hot substances and refresh the liver. But some foods, such as sardines and to some extent all fish and seafood, are very cold and cause stomachaches; then "hot" camomile tea is indicated.[28]

Body functioning can also be disturbed by a *susto* or emotional shock. The penal code reflects the prevalence of this belief in its prescription of punishment for anyone who shocks another person in delicate health—a pregnant woman, for example.

People of all classes draw on a broad spectrum of cures and healers. Some are supernatural—saints, spirits, and God. Others have empirical referents—doctors, midwives, pharmacists, and persons who give injections in their own homes, catering to many Ticos' belief in the almost miraculous powers of the needle. But before turning to any of them, a Costa Rican is likely to try home remedies, some from the drug store, some from the market or the nearby woods and fields. Almost everyone knows and uses some local herbs: one researcher found the head nurse of a health unit drinking a brew made of papaya leaves "for the liver."[29] Friends, maids, cabdrivers, all will tell one which herbs to get for a cold, an ulcer, arthritis, or almost any other ailment that human flesh is heir to, and how to use them. Another common prescription for a variety of ills—colds, stomach upsets, fatigue—is Alka-Seltzer. We have seen Ticos take a couple of Alka-Seltzer tablets after a good restaurant meal, simply as a precaution against indigestion.

Pharmacists often diagnose and prescribe. There is a long tradition of self-medication in Costa Rica, encouraged by the ease with which patent medicines and even prescription drugs may be obtained. In 1976 the government clamped down on the dispensing of barbiturates and tranquilizers, but many other medications, including most antibiotics and several opiates, were still freely available. The expansion of social security may somewhat discourage this practice, but it continues in part because it is not as time-consuming as getting attention at the local clinic, and because many are convinced that the social security medicines are inferior and that the same drug may be indiscriminately prescribed for many unrelated illnesses. In remote areas the *pulpería* owner acts as a prescribing druggist; he has a license from the Ministry of Health for the pharmaceutical supplies he sells.

Among less orthodox curers are *curanderos* and homeopathic doctors. The latter prescribe tiny amounts of medicines that produce the same symptoms as those from which the patient suffers, on the theory that "like cures like." They say the medicine, not the doctor, does the curing. *Curanderos*, on the other hand, insist that the patient have faith in them, and prescribe herbs and special diets. Though orthodox doctors and their prescriptions are gaining ground, few Ticos rely entirely on modern medicine for diagnosis and healing; they prefer to combine herbs and Alka-Seltzer, prayers and prescriptions, magic and medicine.[30] And they tend to agree that the crucial ingredient is faith, whether in herbs, saints, or doctors.[31]

6

THE FAMILY AND THE LIFE CYCLE

Costa Ricans measure today's family against an idealized picture of the nineteenth-century home as the center of a simple, virtuous life of hard work. Like bees in a hive, says one historian, parents and children constituted unified families that provided the moral base of the society.[1] Sexual relations, Ticos believe, were restricted to marriage, while divorce and desertion were almost unheard of.

Foreign observers note that family ties are still strong and extend to a large circle of relatives. Kinship ties guide and control individual behavior. Most Costa Ricans seem to regard their home as a haven from life's troubles and are slow to invite outsiders to share their family life.

Many families, however, do not fit this description. "Free unions" have always been numerous; some of them are as stable as legal marriages, but many more are not. They account for a large share of "illegitimate" births, which amount to 38 percent of all births.[2] In one out of five births the father is listed as "unknown." Desertion, alcoholism, and abandonment of children are so common that both Church and state have created agencies to help their victims, strengthen existing families, and educate children and young people, especially those contemplating marriage, in sexual and family responsibilities.

SPANISH AND LATIN AMERICAN CULTURAL PATTERNS

Spanish family patterns were not carried intact to the Americas; the long and risky passage across the Atlantic and the hazards of untamed jungles made early exploration and colonization almost entirely a masculine undertaking.

For decades few Spanish women made the crossing, and most *hidalgos* either sought white women from neighboring colonies or cohabited with Indian and black women, taking them both peacefully and by force. Only after three or four generations of miscegenation did Spaniards formally marry "mixed-bloods."

Extended families on their isolated *haciendas* formed in effect small patriarchal societies. Living in widely scattered settlements linked only by mule trails, many of the colonists mated with siblings and other close relatives, according to Sanabria.[3]

Visiting clergymen were as dismayed by adultery and incest as by neglect of Catholic rites, including marriage. Once the clergy's efforts to establish towns around churches had succeeded, it was somewhat easier to enforce Spanish family mores, particularly premarital virginity and wifely chastity. Marriages were frequently arranged by parents, and girls were carefully supervised.

Vestiges of Spanish patterns survive today in the stress on family honor, the strength—albeit diminished—of the extended family, and the definitions of proper sex roles and relationships. Slights against the honor of family members—including deceased ones—may be punished by recourse to law: even if one personally avenges the insult—through assault, for example—he has far less fear of legal reprisal than if he commits a similar act from other motives. The law holds that damage to the reputation of a person (a man's financial probity or a woman's chastity, for example) hurts all his or her relatives. In Spanish tradition, continuity of blood lines, traced through males, is deemed so important that procreation is considered the greatest purpose of marriage and there must be no doubt about who is a child's father. In "respectable" families, therefore, women have been regarded as creatures whose honor and chastity must be protected, even though men have been free to engage in promiscuous relations with women whose reputations did not matter to established family lines.

As in colonial days, extended family groups in Latin America act as units in politics, business, and social affairs. Brothers, uncles, and cousins are expected to help in time of need. When he goes into business, says William R. Lassey, the typical Latin American tends

> not to consider business as an impersonal activity (as an 'economic' man would) directed at maximization of profit, but as an extension of his family's drive for social status. The family has probably supplied his initial financial contacts, his initial job, and the non-family group associations without which it is nearly impossible to get business done. In other words, business appears to have a strong social orientation related to personal ties.[4]

Although the nuclear families that make up an extended family in Costa Rica may be scattered,[5] they usually interact far more closely among themselves than with outsiders. Much of their "social life" consists of Sunday visits to a wide circle of kin and their christening parties, weddings, and funerals. And much of women's conversation, in particular, unravels the relationships, by blood and marriage, of "Fulana" and "Zutana."

The Family Code reflects widely held ideals of mutual aid. It makes spouses responsible for supporting each other as well as their minor or disabled children; children responsible for their parents; siblings, for minor or disabled siblings; and even grandparents and grandchildren, great-grandparents and great-grandchildren, mutually responsible when closer relatives are incapable of providing for them. And, in fact, widowed or impoverished parents or grandparents, siblings, aunts, uncles, or cousins of either spouse often do join the household, sometimes in exchange for domestic services, child care, or financial help. Orphaned nephews and nieces, or relatives who have come to study or work in the area, may also be taken into the home.

The roles and relationships of the sexes are governed by deeply ingrained values, beliefs, and patterns of interaction as well as by legal codes. They cluster in two complexes that are sides of the same coin—*machismo* and *marianismo*.

The myth of *machismo* rests on belief in the natural, inborn superiority of men over women in anything political, economic, or intellectual; the myth of *marianismo*, on belief in the equally natural and inborn moral and spiritual superiority of women. The first justifies male dominance and privilege; the second, female submissiveness and self-denial.

Most Costa Rican women, especially those of middle age and older, are not merely resigned to the pattern of male dominance and female submission, but also rationalize and justify it through *marianismo*, which glorifies "women's infinite capacity for humility and self-sacrifice."[6] Many women take bitter pride in the suffering they endure for the sake of their husbands and children and describe them at length to a sympathetic listener. They often call marriage a cross which it is woman's highest calling to bear and through which she gains virtue in the eyes of God and society. To call a wife and mother *abnegada* or self-sacrificing is to pay her the supreme compliment. Overtly dominant wives are criticized by members of both sexes, who are likely to quote the saying, "The rooster sings, the hen only cackles." "Where the woman is in charge, everything goes to ruin," says a sixty-five-year-old Tica.

From childhood on, culturally defined differences in sex roles are emphasized. A girl is presumed to be, and hence taught to be, more home-bound, weaker, more emotional, more vulnerable, and less intelligent than a boy. A boy is presumed to be, and hence taught to be, more demanding, aggressive, and spoiled, and is freer to do as he wishes. If a woman is not protected in her chastity and her reputation as a virgin or a faithful wife, then she is assumed to be a loose and accessible woman, in the classic Latin virgin/mother/whore complex. In either case she is submissive to one or more males, and her status is defined almost entirely in terms of her relationships with men. An unmarried virgin is a *señorita* or a *muchacha buena* (good girl); if she remains unmarried after about age twenty-five, she is an old maid. A promiscuous "fox" is a *zorra*; a prostitute, a *puta*. Single nonvirgins are *mujeres* or women; the title of *señora* is given married women and common-law wives. No such abundance of terms denotes men's sexual behavior or marital status.[7]

"FREE UNIONS" AND MATRIFOCAL FAMILIES

Married people tend to have higher prestige than those in "free" or consensual unions,[8] though these do not bring strong opprobrium. Although many such pairings are permanent, a woman may be a *compañera* to a succession of men,[9] each of whom may refer to her simply as "my woman," and father one or more of her children. Under law, *compañeras* have all the rights of legally married wives, including social security benefits, except that they may be called on to testify against their "husbands" in criminal cases.

While 46 percent of Costa Ricans over fifteen years of age were legally married in 1973, 8.3 percent lived in free unions, a rate that had not changed since 1950. Most such arrangements are found in rural areas, with by far the highest rates in the lowland provinces, where for every two married couples there is one free union.[10] Such couples are most numerous among the very poor, reflecting the fact that many lower-class men cannot assure their women and children of steady financial support and consequently lack authority and commitment. In many regions, too, it takes hours to get to a priest. Even when it is easy, couples may not have their union solemnized because one or both believe that as long as they do not tie the knot they are happier and more independent. "I can throw him out if he behaves badly or does not provide for the family," say many women.

Female-headed families are also numerous among the poor. While 35 percent of the eighty-two lower-class women in Eugenia López de Piza's

"Queen Bee" family (La Verne Coleman)

sample were part of a nuclear family, and another 13 percent lived in a group of two or more related nuclear families, over half lived in matrifocal or mother-centered families. Nearly a quarter of these were "queen bee families," which are common among poor Costa Ricans. Each includes a grandmother, her daughters, and their children; the women of the middle generation work outside the home and provide economic support while their mother runs the home and looks after their children. Most of these women had been deserted, and the rest had never had an enduring sexual relationship. López de Piza found these homes harmonious, and the women in them said they found a man's presence disruptive.[11]

Such women sometimes have children as a result of brief affairs with middle- or upper-class men. Many Ticos, including some who have achieved middle-class status, freely state that they were *hijos naturales*—born out of wedlock. And more than a few upper-class wives steeped in *marianismo* have tolerated or even encouraged their husbands' recognition of such children, saying that, after all, it is not the fault of the children themselves. When, as occasionally happens, such children are legally recognized, they may share in the estate or receive a good education; they may even be taken into the paternal home, particularly if they were born before the marriage.

FAMILY SIZE

We asked a woman of eighty-eight, married at fourteen, how many children she had had. "I was given twenty-nine, but a lot of them died. Only eight grew up, and now I have seven." Families of seven or more were common until very recently. Then a phenomenon occurred that has attracted the attention of population experts the world over. The crude birth rate dropped from 48 live births per 1,000 in 1960 to 29.5 in 1975. The drop in fertility rate is even more dramatic: in 1960 the average woman who had survived her childbearing years had 7.3 children; in 1975 a similar woman had 3.7.[12] Costa Rica is the only country in Latin America in which the birth rate has fallen so sharply and so rapidly,[13] and in all the world only Taiwan has had a comparable decline.[14]

This sudden drop in the birth rate is especially interesting because cultural ideals long supported large families. Until the 1950s most Ticos felt that a couple ought to accept "all that God sends." Pregnancy was expected to occur in the first year of marriage, and childless or one-child couples were criticized or pitied. *Campesinos* felt that a large family was no economic hardship: "One more child just means adding water to the soup." The labor of each child on the family plot was in fact thought to improve the family's status, for "each child brings a loaf of bread under his arm." Large families were also common among the urban poor, most of whom were ignorant of birth control methods. Even in the upper and middle classes, some of whose members practiced birth control, large families were not unusual. Because infant mortality was high in all classes, a high birth rate ensured that some children in each family would survive childhood hazards.[15]

The 25 percent drop in fecundity between 1960 and 1968 occurred despite Church and state opposition to birth control. For many years anyone

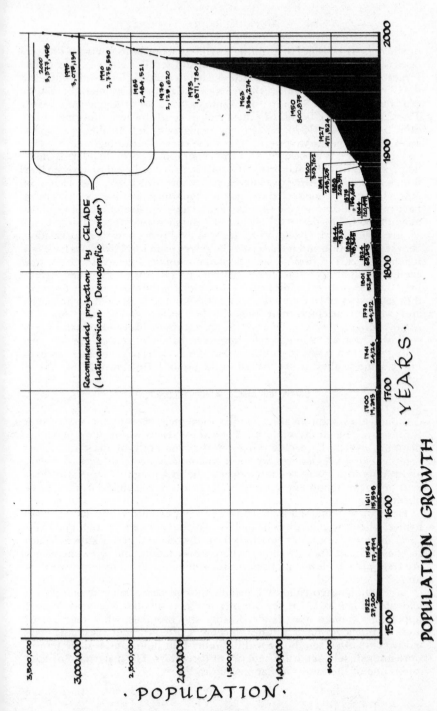

POPULATION GROWTH

· YEARS ·

· POPULATION ·

Recommended projection by CELADE
(Latinamerican Demografic Center)

Year	Population
2000	3,577,466
1985	3,078,139
1970	2,775,580
1965	2,484,521
1970	2,129,620
1975	1,871,780
1963	1,336,274
1950	800,875
1927	471,824
1900	303,162
1891	249,205
1869	229,591
1876	195,084

93

practicing, advertising, or printing anything about birth control—or even discussing it—was subject by law to a prison term of three to ten years. Protestant mission doctors who cautiously introduced "family planning" at the Clínica Bíblica and during their Goodwill Caravan missions to rural areas ran some risks; one doctor, for example, lost a government post. Many Ticos, nonetheless, began to practice birth control when information became available. By 1976, 64 percent of married and cohabiting couples, according to one survey, were using some contraceptive method.[16]

Various trends associated with the general process of "modernization" help explain why the majority of Costa Ricans have chosen to have smaller families, as well as why government policy was reversed.[17] The decline in infant mortality is one such trend; many people no longer feel that they must have many children so that they can expect a reasonable number to survive to adulthood. The desire to "get ahead," and increased opportunities to do so, are often cited; these factors (as well as a proven inverse correlation between education and fertility) may largely explain why birth rates have not fallen as quickly in rural areas, where opportunities for mobility are scarce even for couples with few children. Most Costa Ricans who say they wish to limit the size of their families want a better life for the children they do have; they say it costs an enormous amount to raise and educate children properly, and "we want the children we do have to be educated and healthy." Married urban women over age twenty-five are the most likely to practice birth control. These women generally have their babies while they are still very young and then resort to contraception. Their "level of religiosity," according to some studies, is not related to the use of birth control.[18]

BIRTH, INFANCY, AND CHILDHOOD

Although they want smaller families than their parents did, most Costa Ricans love and desire children. Even those Ticos who believe in family planning usually have children soon after marrying or deciding to live together. First pregnancies are most common between the ages of twenty and twenty-four. Most women welcome the first pregnancy and usually at least one or two more, even though they may say that children are a heavy burden.

Pregnancy, nonetheless, is considered a discomfort and an inconvenience; when a woman gives birth Ticos say she "got well." Except in remote rural areas, most expectant mothers have several medical checkups in health stations or social security clinics, where examinations and a few medicines are free, while middle- and upper-class women usually consult private doctors.

A generation ago childbirth usually took place at home attended by a midwife; as late as 1973, one out of five births still did. Now middle- and upper-class women use private doctors and hospitals, while most births occur in public hospitals and health centers, often without anesthesia. The mothers are often sent home within twenty-four hours and resume housework immediately; some are kept two or three days. The maternal mortality rate is one of the lowest in Latin America.[19]

Boys born in hospitals are circumcised soon after birth. Girls' ears are usually pierced and adorned with tiny golden earrings within a few days after birth. If the infant is taken out, it is warmly dressed, even with a woolen bonnet and shawl, as Ticos believe any draft is dangerous. Neighbors and relatives calling to offer congratulations bring gifts of clothing, toys, soap, and money, or gifts of food to the very poor or to mothers too ill to cook.

A man and a woman, generally a married couple, are asked to serve as godparents, a role far less important today than a half-century ago. They are usually close friends or relatives of one of the parents, but the father's employer is sometimes chosen. Poor couples often prefer affluent god-parents from whom special gifts might be forthcoming on the child's birth-days and other special occasions. Godparents have traditionally taken the child to church to be baptized about a week after birth; many now let several weeks elapse.[20]

The names given the child reflect the fact that, like other Latin Americans, Costa Ricans trace descent through both the male and female lines. One receives both a paternal or first surname and a maternal or second surname. (Children of "unknown fathers" receive only their mother's sur-names.) Women retain their surnames when they marry, both legally and in common reference, but also add *de* (of) with their husband's first surname.

Until several decades ago, a child's first or middle name was often that of the saint on whose day he was born, while some parents preferred to name children after their own favorite saints or relatives or after themselves, modifying male names to fit girls and vice versa. Religious names such as the Spanish versions of Charity, Jesus, and Mary of the Most Holy Trinity were popular. These names are less common today, and "American" names such as Betty, Mary, and Frank are not unusual. Nicknames are popular, as they have been for decades; a nickname acquired in childhood or adolescence often sticks with a Tico for life, sometimes to his discomfiture. Working-class males are particularly likely to receive nicknames from their peers.

Two or three decades ago babies were nursed for eight to ten months, sometimes for several years. Today 20 percent of all new mothers do not breast feed at all, and another 30 percent quit after a week—discouraged, many say, by doctors and nurses. After ten weeks only 9 percent are still nursing their babies. Health authorities initiated a campaign in 1978 urging mothers "not to deny your children the best of all foods."

Mothers believe that bottle feeding should be abandoned only when the child no longer demands it, and children five or six years old are often seen with a bottle or pacifier. At about three months some parents begin to supplement the bottle with bean broth, mashed banana, egg yolk, vegetable purees, and baby cereals. The availability of packaged and canned baby foods has made this a common pattern. Parents may also give vitamin supplements.

Most children are greatly cherished, and parents take their well-being into account when making any major decisions. The availability of schools and health centers weighs heavily in parents' deliberations about a choice of residence, and those who settle in isolated areas often work to bring such services to their community or send their children to live with relatives near a school. Since almost all households have radios, most people are well informed about the need for vaccinations and try to comply with recommendations, especially when there is a threat of an epidemic.

A child's first birthday is a great occasion. *Campesinos* may slaughter a pig and invite relatives and neighbors to celebrate, especially for a first son. Some families pay to have the child's photograph printed in a leading newspaper. Other birthdays are seldom publicized, except for a girl's fifteenth.

Preschool children are much more likely to play with siblings or cousins than with unrelated neighbors. Among the lower classes, a child's older sister and its mother's sisters and cousins often play a major role in its upbringing, especially if the mother works outside the home. Very poor couples, widows, and unwed mothers may give one or more children to the maternal grandparents or a maternal aunt or uncle, who often treat their charges with great affection. Many middle- and upper-class parents entrust paid helpers with child care even if the mother does not work outside the home. Private nursery schools and kindergartens are increasingly popular among more prosperous families. Government kindergartens are used mainly by the lower-middle class. Beginning in 1975, the government established nutrition centers and complete day care centers for children of mothers who work or study. Factory workers usually prefer to leave children with relatives even when their employer is obligated to provide free day care, as are all whose labor force reaches a certain size.

Child-rearing patterns reflect the fact that until quite recently many children died very young, and parents would let them enjoy what might be a brief stay on earth. Until a child's survival seemed certain, discipline was, and is, very rarely applied. Infants and toddlers are allowed much free rein. Their misdeeds are laughed at if not ignored, or at most punished with a gentle scolding or a soft slap on the leg. Crying children are hushed by attempts to distract their attention.

Machismo begins early. A young American woman reports:

> My Tica friend was horrified that my three-year-old son helped clear the table and wash dishes. Her little boy gets anything he asks for; she runs to fetch him a glass of water. She lets her little girl, a year younger, fend for herself. And then she bitches about how spoiled her husband is!

López de Piza found that the eighty-two poor women she interviewed were "demanding of their daughters and tolerant with their sons; they protect their boys. [These are] ideal conditions for *machismo* to arise. As soon as a girl can walk a broom is put in her hand; a boy is sent out to play."[21]

At four or five, the working-class child is no longer pampered. Little sympathy is won by crying, and minor injuries are ignored. Rural children begin running errands at this age, often walking long distances to bring *papá* his nine o'clock lunch. Six-year-olds of both sexes pick coffee with older family members to supplement the family income. Girls of six are expected to help sweep, wash dishes, and care for small brothers and sisters. By age eight or ten they can perform all household tasks, and often do so if the mother works. López de Piza found that most poor women remember their childhood as a difficult time. Many had to drop out of grade school to help at home.

By age eight, rural boys are likely to chop firewood, herd and milk cows, and help their fathers in the fields, using small machetes of their own. Some also help sweep and mop, though after puberty these are usually regarded as exclusively female tasks. Urban children are less helpful. Many children of the upper and middle classes do not help their parents in any way even if, as in many middle-class homes, there is no servant. Girls of all classes, however, may be expected to wait on their brothers of whatever age.

Most Ticos believe that children four years of age and older—especially boys, who are considered more impulsive and disobedient than girls—must be punished for misdeeds. Forty years ago the father was the chief disciplinarian and often used his belt or leather machete sheath to punish a child for disobedience or lack of respect for elders. Middle- and upper-class parents preferred to deny privileges, as they still do, but spankings were not uncommon. A child was expected to address its parents as *señor* and *señora* and was forbidden to walk between two seated adults or to take part in their conversation. Immediate obedience was demanded. Says a sixty-six-year-old San Isidro woman: "A parent would send a child on an errand, spitting on the threshold as the child ran out the door. If the child wasn't back before the saliva dried he got a beating."

Other adults were also expected to discipline children. An eighty-four-year-old peasant woman recalls, "If a child was disrespectful to an adult, even a stranger, that person had the right to strike the child. He might then take the child home to its parents, who would thank him." A fifty-year-old rural school director adds, "The teacher was also expected to punish disrespectful or lazy children. Pranksters or slow learners might be beaten in front of other pupils. Grateful parents might give the teacher a gift such as a chicken." Grownups believed that severe punishment brought moral and spiritual benefits: "Better to go broken to heaven than in one piece to hell."

Though still widely considered an essential ingredient in socializing children, punishment is much less harsh today. Until 1948, Costa Rican law gave the father the exclusive right to punish his children, though mothers often punished them as well. While forbidding excessive punishment, today's Family Code obliges both parents to "correct" their children "in a moderate way." The mother is often the chief disciplinarian and may limit punishment to a scolding or a tug on the ear. One observes much less yelling at children in public and less tugging and slapping than in a typical American shopping center.

In one study of class differences in socialization, Fatima Araujo found that parents of the middle and upper classes punish preschool children by material deprivation and denial of pleasure. Because they envision their children in positions of power and authority, upper-class parents emphasize responsibility, honor, loyalty, and self-esteem. Desirable values for the middle class are occupational success, personal realization, individual independence, honesty, and generosity. Working-class parents expect of their children what society expects of them—obedience, respect, discipline, and honesty. Physical punishment is most common in this class.[22]

Mothers play a much larger role in child-rearing than do fathers. Although an increasing number of mothers work outside the home, the majority still do not. Fathers often work far from home and give their children little attention even when at home. They may play with the children briefly, especially with the youngest, but they consider feeding, cleaning, and dressing children exclusively women's work. Fathers who hope that their children will make progress in school or catechism also depend on their wives and older children to help the younger ones with difficult assignments. Even though the mother holds him up as an authority figure, the father is often absent, and children tend to run to their mothers with their problems, turn over earnings to her, and pay much greater attention to Mother's Day than to Father's Day (which has only recently been celebrated—and commercialized—at all, whereas the streets are crowded with shoppers for weeks before Mother's Day).

The Constitution states that "parents have the same obligations to their children born out of wedlock as to those born within." But enforcement is difficult among the poor. Since 1933 the National Society for the Protection of Children has used threats of imprisonment to induce fathers to provide child support. Its efforts frequently fail, however, and one reason is that many women do not report the father, especially in lowland areas where courts and police are few and where matrifocal families are common.

Even where they are present, lower-class fathers may have little authority over their children. One reason appears to be the children's earning power. Especially in urban areas, mothers may work outside the home and put several children, most often sons, to work shining shoes, begging, or hawking candy, newspapers, or lottery tickets.

YOUTH IN COSTA RICAN SOCIETY

About one Tico out of four is between ten and nineteen years of age. This quarter of the population is far more free than previous generations to choose a mate or a job and to engage in premarital sex. It is better situated, with the expansion of mass education and leisure time, to develop a "youth culture," and is more conscious of its potential as a political pressure group.

Older relatives, including parents, in all industrializing societies are losing authority over youth, often because of beliefs and attitudes that arise from new economic relationships. The chief factor is the separation of the extended family from the process of making a living. Typically—though not always—each nuclear family is expected to provide mainly for itself. The shared work of a family firm or an agricultural estate, with its orderly pattern of inheritance, gives way to the scattering of the family in an ever-widening choice of individual careers.

Costa Rica is no exception. Until recently Costa Rican youths, especially males, often remained subject to their fathers' authority even after marriage. Land ownership was relatively widespread and all children were likely to

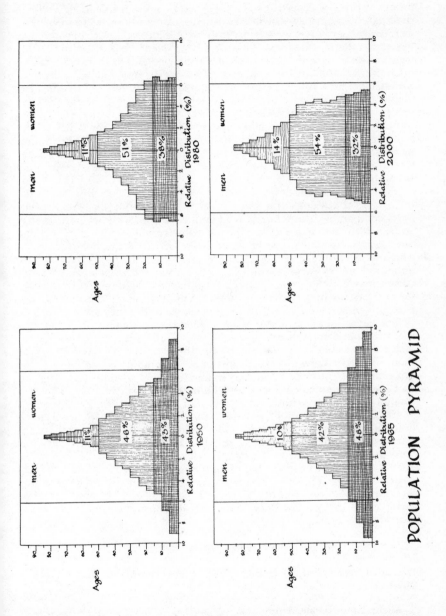

POPULATION PYRAMID

99

inherit. Since few *campesino* youths today can expect a sizable legacy from their parents, who may own little or no land, many seek work in a town or on an *hacienda,* perhaps leaving home to do so. A middle-class urban youth may expect to inherit something, but probably not land, which he would hardly want to work anyway. Upper-class males may be tied to their parents and other kin by hope of inheritance and a position in a family business or professional firm. But even they, like an increasing number of middle-class youths, may now live in urban apartments even when their families live nearby. Fathers and other relatives at most social levels, then, have little or no control over the job choices and opportunities of young men. Girls, whose family statuses are more important to them, are more submissive to their parents and more confined to the home. Though the trend is toward greater freedom, many continue to live at home even when they work, leaving only when they marry.

There are few well-defined rites of passage in a Tico's life. One is the celebration of a middle- or upper-class girl's fifteenth birthday with a special party comparable to a debut. A paid announcement with her portrait may appear in the newspapers, which once reported only upper-class "coming out" parties. No similar transition exists for boys. High-school graduation, which an increasing proportion achieve, and legal maturity at eighteen[23] are minor milestones by comparison. The Civil Code states that a person under fifteen may not enter into contracts or personal obligations. With the consent of parents or guardians, however, one may marry even before age fifteen; without consent young Ticos must wait until they are eighteen.

The beauty of adolescent females is celebrated constantly, in public girl-watching and compliments, "queen" contests, and advertising. Adolescent males are steeped in *machismo.* Their great degree of freedom allows them—and social pressures motivate them—to demonstrate *machismo* on the soccer field, in the bull ring, in traffic, and in sexual relationships. "Effeminate" ways are gossiped about, and homosexuality is generally abhorred, though by no means rare.

In many ways Costa Rica, like other industrializing societies, seems to be losing its emphasis on respect for elders and becoming increasingly youth-oriented. While few youths espouse political beliefs significantly different from their parents', many complain that the country is run by "old men." In 1970 a Ministry of Culture, Youth, and Sports was created, and a bill was passed to lower the voting age from twenty to eighteen. Advertisements increasingly tout the "youthful flavor" or "youthful look" of products. Massage parlors, gyms, and beauty salons cater to men and women who want to look and feel younger.

COURTSHIP AND MARRIAGE

A Peace Corps volunteer in the village of San Antonio de Belén wrote in 1976:

All the Tica girls wanted a gringo *novio* [sweetheart]. To me, it was like being in junior high school again. Girls had to be in by 9 or 10 P.M. We went to movies; we walked around the central square holding hands; we hung out at the ice cream parlor.[24]

Even such dating was not permitted until recently. Until the late 1940s *novios*—no matter how close to marriage—rarely went out together, meeting instead at the girl's house. If a young man's interest in a girl was reciprocated, he asked her father for the *entrada,* permission to call on her at times specified by the father. Visits were seldom allowed more than once a week, and at least one parent stayed in the parlor with the couple. These brief visits were the only chance most couples had to get acquainted. Says a *campesino* married in 1930: "When the *novio* came to call, he and the *novia* could not touch each other except for a brief handshake. If it ever reached her parents' ears that she had even talked to him on the street, she'd get a good beating."

Chaperonage has greatly declined. Young people today have a much greater chance to meet members of the opposite sex. Thousands of young women, even in the countryside, attend coeducational high schools or work in stores and offices where they meet young men, often from other towns. While their mothers had to be home by six o'clock, these women now are often allowed to stay out until midnight, though in rural areas and more traditional urban families, especially of the middle and upper classes, those under eighteen are usually chaperoned at night. (Even the university women we polled believe, three to one, that "women ought to have less liberty than men." Thirty-seven out of the forty males agreed.) Males in their teens and older have for some decades been permitted to go out alone whenever they wish, and even, in some cases, to stay out all night, provided they tell their parents ahead of time.

Most young Ticas believe that to fulfill her destiny as a woman a girl must marry and have children. Although she may have begun to talk about her *novios* at age twelve or thirteen, not until her fifteenth birthday does a girl take friendships with boys very seriously. Pressured by family and friends, she is anxious to marry, as most females do, in her teens or early twenties. Costa Ricans say that a single woman of twenty-five has "missed the train," and girls speak in terms of "catching" or "grabbing" a man. Males feel less pressure, for they have a longer period of eligibility and, as they see it, less to gain by marrying. They are more likely to see *novias* as companions or sexual partners than as prospective wives, but they too usually marry by age twenty-five.[25]

Flirting is a national pastime. A favorite method of flirting or beginning a romance has long been *dando cuerda* (making eyes). A young man shows his interest in a girl by silently and insistently staring at her. If the look is returned and he already knows her, he may invite her to a soda bar or a movie, or ask to walk her home. If they are strangers he may seek a mutual acquaintance to introduce them, though many now consider this unnecessary. If the pair hits it off, he will ask to see her again, perhaps arranging to meet her at a movie or dance and not visiting her home until they have met several times.

The *retreta* or band concert in the park, where boys and girls strolled around the square in opposite directions, long provided opportunities to

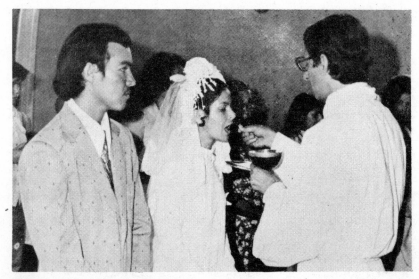

A working class wedding (Sergio Méndez)

look over the opposite sex and choose a *novio*. Courtship today in both town and country most often begins at dances. These may be special "dress-up" occasions such as those sponsored by schools or social service clubs. More often, young people meet at one of the hundreds of dance halls, usually connected to a *cantina*, that have appeared in all but the smallest communities since the 1940s.

It is still not universally acceptable for a "good girl," even chaperoned, to date several boys concurrently, though this seems to be changing rapidly, at least in the capital. If a boy and girl go out together even once, they are generally assumed to be *novios*, but many insist they are simply friends. Though couples seldom have an explicit agreement to become *novios*, they seal an implicit *noviazgo* by exchanging rings, handkerchiefs, or photos. The relationship is no longer tantamount to engagement,[26] but while it lasts each expects the other to see no one else.

Despite girls' frequent and even proud comments that "we Ticas are very jealous," *novias* tend to suppress expression of jealousy, thereby reinforcing *machismo* and setting the pattern for marital interaction. Says a university student:

> The *novia* waits on her boyfriend hand and foot and takes care of him if he is sick. She is not sincere. Whatever he does is well done. If he is unfaithful and tells her, she insists she is not angry. We know the problem, but we are too hypocritical; we already spoil them as *novias*.

Another pattern may have the same consequences in the lower class. Said a nineteen-year-old coffee picker:

My *novio* won't let me go out with anyone else. When I find that *he* has done so, I get very angry. Then he gets drunk and cries, and one of his friends comes to tell me how he is suffering. Then I forgive him."

Teenage girls still tend to hold a romantic view of courtship in which the sweetheart is idealized and the match believed to be predestined. Most middle- and upper-class Ticos claim to marry "for love." By contrast more than half the lower-class women in López de Piza's sample said they married or formed consensual unions in order to escape their parental homes.

Among middle- and upper-class young people, romanticism is to some extent giving way to ideas of companionship and sexual pleasure. Many young people see the *novio* relationship as simply an agreeable pastime, and *novios* are much more easily replaced than a generation ago. Some high-school and university girls want to project a "sexy and liberated" image rather than a romantically feminine one. Says a nineteen-year-old female university student: "They rebel because boys are given so much more freedom, and they go overboard trying to attract attention. They read *Cosmopolitan*, wear transparent blouses and tight pants, go out, smoke, and drink to show how liberated they are."

The trend away from highly romantic conceptions of marriage is reflected—and probably reinforced—by the increased popularity of organizations that attempt to stabilize new and impending marriages. They invite young people, recently married couples, and parents to lectures and discussions by doctors, psychologists, sociologists, and clergymen. Such diverse topics as dating, psychological problems of marriage, family budgets, the physiology of reproduction, birth control, and child raising are covered. One major goal is to make up for the near-total lack of sex education from most parents.[27] The Center of Family Orientation, founded by executive decree in 1968 and financed mainly by the Episcopal Church of England, broadcasts its lectures nationwide. The Christian Family Movement is an international Catholic association with more conservative stands on birth control and other issues. In 1975 the Costa Rican Catholic Church adopted a resolution to require engaged couples to attend short courses given by the Center of Family Integration during five evenings, chiefly to help instill a "sense of responsibility" in both *novios*. Attendance, however, is very low.

Until about sixty years ago, a peasant suitor was required by his *novia's* parents to leave three cartloads of firewood by their doorstep. His parents in turn expected her to grind corn and make *tortillas* to send to his mother. The urban girl had to learn to cook, sew, and adorn the parlor. Her mother showed her handiwork to visitors, especially mothers of possible sons-in-law.

While such tests have passed into folklore, most working-class girls today, asked what qualities they consider most important in a husband, echo their grandparents' attitudes by saying that he should be a good worker and free of any costly "vices." The girls in our university poll, by contrast, rank "hard-working" seventh among twenty-five traits that they would look for in a husband, and "moderation in drinking" ninth. "Liking home life" takes first place. Mothers in all classes, though they have little overt authority in the matter, tell their sons to look for a faithful girl who likes home life, and boys' attitudes regarding the ideal wife reflect this advice.

Mate selection is limited largely to those of "suitable" age, class status, and educational level. In one study, 80 percent of a sample of high-school boys indicated that it was far more important that their families accept a *novia* than that their friends accept her, or that she be interested in getting ahead socially.[28] As in many other stratified societies, parental influence on mate selection is strongest in the upper class. "It's all right with my parents if I love a poor girl or sleep with her," says an upper-class boy, "but I'm afraid I might be disinherited if I married her." Upper-class parents put even stronger pressure on their daughters, for the class status of a married couple depends mostly on the husband's family background, education, and financial status.

Most weddings are preceded by a formal engagement period that lasts two or three months, seldom more than a year. After obtaining the girl's consent, the boy asks for that of her parents. The *novio* and his father or both parents may then arrange to call on the girl's family. Relatives and friends may celebrate the engagement with a small party. The upper- or upper-middle-class girl is given as conspicuous a ring as possible. Her parents may pay for an announcement on the social pages of a newspaper, a practice no longer limited to the upper class. Broken engagements are few, and those that occur afford juicy material for gossip. They are a disgrace for the girl, who then has less chance of finding a desirable husband; little stigma attaches to the man.

In the middle and upper classes, the *novia's* women friends, most of them unmarried, have a tea for her, called the "farewell to being single," a few days before the wedding. After she is married she is likely to see even less of her single friends than will her husband of his, for her new interests and obligations will differ from theirs more widely than do those of single and married men.

The evening before the wedding, close friends and relatives attend a party at the bride's house. Most have brought gifts which are unwrapped and displayed on a table. After drinks and dancing, the *novio* and his cronies, or a hired band may assemble outside to offer the bride-to-be a serenade. Perhaps they will then spend a night on the town of the sort they may often have enjoyed on what the *novio's* friends jokingly call "happier occasions, before he was caught." He is teased about how on the morrow, after "the big step," he must renounce forever the pleasures and liberties of bachelorhood, and is warned about domineering wives and mothers-in-law.

Until the turn of the century weddings were celebrated at home; now most take place in church. The local parish church is the scene of weddings for the poor, but many middle- and upper-class Ticos favor a fashionable and "more elegant" church in a different neighborhood.

An equal number of persons of each sex serve as *padrinos* (in this context, witnesses rather than godparents). They are usually relatives and friends, often of the parents' generation, but many couples seek local and national politicians or rich acquaintances likely to give lavish gifts as well as lend class. In rural areas even the poor invite the mayor, the schoolteacher, and the most prosperous farmers.

The groom waits at the altar with his mother, who is to give him away.

After the guests enter, the *padrinos*—directed by a master of ceremonies at the more elegant weddings—walk down the aisle in pairs, and stand in two rows facing each other along the aisle near the altar. Then come the bridal attendants, the best friend of the groom escorting the bride's best friend, and perhaps other bridesmaids. A small child carries the *arras*, a symbolic dowry of thirteen coins. The bride follows on her father's arm; her white gown and veil provoke loud whispers and head-turning.

After the standard Catholic wedding service, the couple kneels and a long white silken cord (or perhaps a gold chain traditionally used in the bride's family) is draped around their shoulders while the priest blesses their future children.

The wedding party usually attends a reception at the home of the bride's parents or at a dance hall or private club. Drinking and dancing continue for two or three hours, and then the newlyweds depart for a honeymoon that may last several weeks. Even working-class couples often spend a few days at a beach, though some are back at work in a day or two, as their parents were.

RESIDENCE PATTERNS AND FAMILY INTERACTION

Until about fifty years ago a bride often went to live with her husband's family. This was especially common in rural families and the urban upper class. Peasant sons continued to work the family land, while their wives were largely subject to their mother-in-law's authority in household affairs. If a patriarch's land was divided up after his death, relatives and neighbors helped each heir build a new house on his homestead. Siblings and their spouses continued to visit and help each other, and the widow went to live with one of her married children; unmarried children often moved in with married siblings. Because of these extended kinship ties, a single surname still frequently predominates over several square kilometers of rural territory.

If his own family was very poor, the young husband might move in with his bride's family. If she inherited land he usually worked it, though it remained in her name. Some parents wanted their daughters to continue living with them after marriage to help with housework or to care for them.

But many newlyweds would not live under the same roof with either set of parents unless poverty compelled them to, and even then only temporarily. The couple might, however, build a house near one family, most often the husband's, perhaps on family-owned land. Even in comparatively urbanized areas it is still not unusual to find several married siblings, most commonly brothers, sharing their parents' household or living on adjacent lots inherited from a parent or received as a wedding gift.

Today, however, there are far fewer unified family properties in the countryside than there were early in the century. Because of this as well as improved transportation and new job openings throughout the country, many married couples live some distance away from both sets of parents.

Working-class couples living far from their parents typically exchange brief letters with them four or five times a year. They may visit them every six months or as rarely as every three or four years; some visit only when a close relative is seriously ill or dies. When parents live less than an hour's bus ride away, their adult offspring may visit them on Sundays, often taking spouse and children along. Relatives unite for weddings, funerals, and baptisms, and sometimes for Christmas Eve and New Year's Day; even then, however, many members are likely to be absent.

Extended family ties are strongest in the upper class; second and even third cousins are usually recognized. Family pride, as well as nepotism and other forms of economic aid, lend older relatives considerable control over younger ones, as we noted in the case of mate selection. While extended family households are not the norm in the upper class, neither are they uncommon. Households are often larger in the middle class than among the poor, in spite of their having fewer children, for such families are better able to afford servants and to house relatives.[29] Family reunions and other visits among kin are especially frequent in the middle and upper classes.

As in most modernizing countries, paid work is increasingly being entrusted to outsiders. Farmers who can afford hired hands, whether on a permanent or seasonal basis, say, "Relatives take advantage of you. They'd always be taking things, and not expecting to work hard." Similarly, an Heredia artisan building a house for himself and his wife explained why he preferred to hire nonrelatives: "It's easier to dismiss them if you don't like their work, and you don't create hard feelings within the family." Many Ticos now prefer to borrow from banks and other institutions rather than from a relative precisely because the lending institution's rules and regulations let them know exactly where they stand.

In 1935 Jones commented: "Community activities are poorly developed. . . . The family continues almost to monopolize social interests."[30] This was far less true in 1980, especially in the cities. Schools and informal peer groups, television and movies have taken over much of the socialization of children. Family members of different ages and sexes often go their separate ways in the course of a daily routine of work, study, and diversion, and may even take their meals separately because of conflicting schedules. Many students and employed youths, whose evenings are occupied by night school, parties, or dates with friends and *novios*, are seldom at home except for solitary meals and sleep. An increasing number of mothers work outside the home, while many middle- and upper-class women spend hours at teas, card parties, study groups, club meetings, and beauty parlors. Even when all family members happen to be together in the evening, television has largely supplanted conversation and games, and individual prayer has in most cases replaced the family's evening Rosary.[31]

Family members may also attend Sunday mass separately. But other weekend and holiday activities are frequently shared, especially by upper- and middle-class parents and younger children, who go on Sunday picnics, trips to the zoo or amusement park, visits to relatives, and beach outings. With improved transporation such shared activities are perhaps more frequently enjoyed than twenty years ago. While older Ticos of all classes stress the tendency of modernization to reduce family interaction, this has occurred far less than in the United States, judging from repeated comments by American exchange students that, as one put it, "family ties are very strong here; much affection is expressed, and young people [including university students] usually live at home until they marry."[32] Olda Acuña and Carlos Denton hypothesize that Costa Rica's small size, and the fact that higher education and professional opportunities are concentrated in one metropolitan area, make dual-career marriages more viable than in larger countries.[33] These same factors certainly also help maintain nuclear and even extended family ties.

MARITAL RELATIONS AND THE STATUS OF WOMEN

Men and women, according to the 1949 constitution, "enjoy absolute equality." The new Family Code does not repeat this clause, although it reiterates several others, and recent legislation regarding property, family authority, engagement, and other matters has actually reduced women's rights—or made it easier for men to evade their responsibilities—according to a male authority on family law.[34] Yet to the women of many other societies, Costa Rican laws appear—on paper at least—very advanced indeed. Husbands have no legal control over their wives' business affairs. Women can make contracts, take out loans, have credit cards in their own names, and form business corporations on their own. The law also forbids sex discrimination in hiring and salary. Women are entitled to maternity leave and time off for nursing after returning to work. Though acceptance of a sexual double standard prevails in most social situations, no longer is the Tica subject to unfair divorce laws. Until 1974 she could divorce her husband for adultery only if "open and scandalous concubinage" could be proven, while a single act of adultery on her part gave the husband grounds for divorce. Now adultery of any sort serves as grounds for either mate.

Because expertise is at such a premium in many "developing" countries, women who acquire socially useful knowledge and skills are more likely to get prestigious jobs than are their counterparts in industrialized societies. And their work is made easier by the extended family and by servants. Women, many combining a wife-mother role with their studies, now outnumber men in most departments at the universities, and the majority, instructors say, are more highly motivated than their male classmates. Women have entered many professions and careers besides the traditional ones of teaching, social work, nursing, and office work. A few have served as cabinet ministers, ambassadors, legislators, and provincial governors. According to the 1973 census, 48 percent of Costa Rica's pharmacists, 16 percent of dentists, 8 percent of physicians and surgeons, 4 percent of lawyers, and 32 percent of university faculty and administrators were women.

Still, if both a man and a woman are considered for a high-level job, the choice is usually in favor of the man. In lower-level jobs there is a distinct wage differential. Among workers who had not finished sixth grade and received between ₡100 and ₡2,999 a month, the average salary for males in 1973 was ₡452, for females, ₡328.[35] Of those with a sixth-grade education, 36 percent of men and 66 percent of women received less than ₡400 a month.[36]

The proportion of women in the labor force grows steadily. In 1963 only one worker in ten was female; in 1973, roughly one in five. Many husbands are happy to have a working wife, particularly if she is a schoolteacher. But others fear that a working wife reflects on their ability to provide; upper-class men in particular consider it degrading for wives to work. And some husbands fear that their wives will be unfaithful if they work around other men.

With notable exceptions, most Ticas, even among the middle and upper classes, have more limited interests than do the majority of men. A Russian woman married to a Tico agrees with our impression that their thoughts and energies are centered almost exclusively on their children, houses, husbands, and fashions. "They have few cultural interests. Women hardly read newspapers except for the social pages. There is little interest in world events."[37]

Wives are identified mostly in relation to their husbands. Numerous formal associations of women are based on the fact that their husbands happen to share an occupation: wives of lawyers, doctors, journalists, pilots, accountants, and so on form clubs.

"Compared to lower-class women, middle- and upper-class urbanites are at least partly liberated," comments an elderly Tica. "But the wife or *compañera* of an artisan, peasant, or laborer is a housebound slave." Lower-class men find their amusement almost entirely outside the home and talk, albeit desultorily, for hours with other men in *pulperías* and *cantinas* and on street corners. A walk through any village or town after dark, or a glance into a movie theater, reveals a preponderance of males. For many lower-class women, movies and trips to the village or city are memories of girlhood days. She must ask permission of her husband or *compañero* even to visit a relative, and if she goes any distance, he insists that a sister or child go along. When asked why they seldom go anywhere, women of this class reply that there is too much work at home. Many lower-class couples hardly communicate, talking only about the most everyday and immediate matters. Nor do men help with domestic chores even if their wives have other jobs, are ill, or have just given birth. They do not think of housework as work and, in any case, consider it a woman's responsibility. Most men fear that they would be considered effeminate if they helped.[38]

López de Piza found that the lower-class woman is taken for granted, both at home and when she works for pay. All the women in her sample have worked hard since childhood and now feel spent, but they do not consider this an injustice or an abuse. On the contrary, they never talk of their rights, only of their responsibilities. Their main concerns are feeding and clothing their children. Many earn money while at home by taking in laundry and sewing, or preparing food for sale outside the home. But they do not think they are really making an economic contribution, even when they provide the main source of income; they are "just housewives." Having a *real* job means going outside the home.[39]

Middle-class couples, a sociologist found, experienced more satisfaction in their marriages than did lower-class partners and were more likely to confide in each other and somewhat more likely to perceive their acquaintances' marriages as happy.[40] Among young, well-educated couples, where both work or study, men are now likely to share domestic tasks.

While wives in all classes may use the formal *señor* or *usted* to address their husbands, men commonly address their wives with the "familiar" *vos*; in many middle- and upper-class marriages, both say *vos*. Terms of mutual endearment are numerous: "my life," "my heart," and *mijito* or *mijita* (my child). As children come along, the pair may call each other *mamá* and *papá*.

Although middle- and upper-class wives are more free than their lower-status sisters to go out for work and amusement, many accept, without complaint, the philosophy of "the man in the street and the woman at home." Men often appear at parties without their wives; when women go along, they have to be very careful, they say, lest they offend their husbands. A man who notices his wife talking for more than a moment with a male nonrelative may join the two and perhaps tell his wife suddenly that it is time to go home. Widows and divorcees of any class, even in middle age, are often expected to live with parents and other relatives, who carefully guard their reputation for chastity. Young wives whose husbands travel on business are kept under their inlaws' wing; someone invites them for dinner each evening, visits them, and otherwise checks up.

Many women are content with the situation. They "do not see their submissive position as degrading or intolerable as long as the conditions of their life are fairly decent, although they can be bitter and resentful when they are not."[41] They believe women are superior in what is really important—moral and spiritual strength. "Why should we want to be equal to men?" asks one Tica. "Our intrinsic virtues are enough to make us proud."[42] Even those who have "made it" professionally tend to stress the special qualities of women rather than equality with men. A woman dentist says her profession is most appropriate to females because of "their innate delicacy and natural humanitarian and esthetic feeling," while a microbiologist says hers "requires much patience, dedication, carefulness, and above all perception—special characteristics of women."[43] Thus the cult of *marianismo* provides consolation to women, whether they resent or accept their status.

THREATS TO MARITAL SOLIDARITY

Machismo and wives' resentment of it may lead to friction and the breakup of a marriage through desertion, legal separation, or divorce. Fonseca and his associates found the lowest incidence of broken marriages in the upper class and rural samples, and the highest number of separated women among the urban poor.[44]

Desertion is still, as it has been for generations, "the poor man's divorce." The most dependent wives and *compañeras* have long been those most susceptible to desertion; as López de Piza found, they are chiefly uneducated women burdened with many children. A mother of eight tells a familiar story: "Men like a woman who's young looking and free to have fun. My husband started to go with another woman, and finally just moved in with her." Alcoholism and wife-beating (which often go together) are other common factors in the breakup of lower-class unions.

Separation and desertion are far more common than divorce. In 1886 the "liberal generation" established legal provisions for divorce,[45] but for nearly a century the divorce rate was negligible because of restricted legal grounds and the scandal invariably involved. Costa Ricans express dismay over what they interpret as an alarming recent increase in divorce. In 1964 there were 126 divorces; in 1970, 226; in 1977, 1,960.[46]

This sudden jump in the divorce rate followed an easing of restriction in the Family Code in 1974. After a minimum of three years of marriage, for instance, a divorce can be obtained by mutual consent, and it may be decreed in less than a month. This is now the chief grounds for divorce. Most couples involved are in their late twenties or early thirties.

Husbands' infidelity continues to create marital friction. The masculinity of the male celibate and the faithful husband is suspect among his cronies. Men who can afford the time and money establish mistresses in separate houses, though most men's extramarital sex experiences are confined to brothels or to brief affairs with secretaries, shop girls, and domestic servants.

Many women once forgave their husbands' philandering, and some still do, by saying that men's strong sex drive required outlets outside the home, but that they always came back to wife and children. Wives are not and never have been immune to jealousy. But, says a divorcee:

> Women here are very patient and sweet. They get a divorce only when they can't stand it any more. The breaking point now comes sooner than it did before. The money men spend on drink and other women makes them angriest of all. As many women become independent economically they don't have to put up with it.

This growing economic independence, it is widely believed, has also made women vulnerable to changes that female adultery, allegedly rare a generation ago, is much more common today. This belief may be less an expression of fact than of the suspicion and hurt pride with which many men react to the partial emancipation of women. A wealthy businessman who travels a great deal divorced his wife because she objected to staying at home while he was gone; she asked if she could go out with friends, and that was the end of the marriage.

Despite expressions of alarm over its frequency, divorce is no longer the scandal it once was. Divorced women say they are far more accepted by most people than a generation ago, though it is still easier for men to find another spouse and to avoid stigma.[47] Two recent presidents and perennial candidates, both divorced and remarried, were criticized for many political and personal failings, but seldom if ever for their divorces. Today's divorce rate, still low but rising, may reflect this increased tolerance at least as much as it does any increase in marital unhappiness.

La juventud, youth, is brief. Many Ticos feel that a woman's sexual attractiveness fades in her late twenties, while men of this age often regret that they are "too old" for any but a spectator role at soccer games. A male approaching middle age may boast of sexual exploits, just as do adolescents. Yet he is likely to say that a man is old by fifty, and after that, "Every day is a gift." Most Ticos let adult birthdays pass unnoted; higher-status men, however, may observe their fiftieth birthdays with big parties. Women do not care to publicize this date, for it is said of postmenopausal women that *"ella ya jugó"*—she has "finished playing" (the sex game). In fact, women are labeled elderly at age forty. Only on silver and golden wedding anniversaries do most older Ticas acknowledge milestones in their own lives.

Very old people, especially women, may spend much of their time in church, while men gather in parks, *cantinas,* and *pulperías*, where they recall the past and discuss politics and local news. A great many spend most of their time at home listening to the radio or watching television, playing with—or actually babysitting—their grandchildren, or sitting at a window or on the veranda watching passersby. Few clubs or other facilities cater to the elderly, partly because their numbers are relatively small.

While youth is increasingly valued and parental authority has declined, most Costa Ricans still feel an obligation to care for parents who can no longer work—an obligation formalized in the Family Code. Old-age pensions are far from universal and rarely adequate. Most Ticos send money to their aged parents or take them into their homes. The director of one of Costa Rica's homes for the aged, all of which are subsidized by both taxes and private donations, says that most inmates of such homes are still those who need special care because of mental disturbance or gross physical defects or disabilities, but that a growing proportion are now placed there by working daughters or by grown children unwilling to care for them. And a retired schoolmistress complains:

> Thirty years ago it was an honor to care for one's aged parents. Many girls did not marry because their parents needed their help. If a teacher asked the school director for leave because a parent was sick, she got it, and the director often took over her class. Not any more!

Social workers concerned with the problems of the aged say that public officials cite the traditional unity of Latin American families simply as an excuse for evading the problem of providing proper care for the aged. A survey by IMAS, the social welfare institute, found that over 71 percent of those over sixty-five now living with relatives would prefer to be in a home for the elderly. Only 2 percent of the country's 17,000 low-income old people were in such homes in 1975.[48]

Costa Ricans are far more likely to reach old age than in former years. Life expectancy at birth is now estimated at nearly seventy years, and the death rate of five per 1,000 (1979) reflects not only the comparative youth of the population but also improvements in medical care and public health.

When a death occurs, friends and relatives are notified by telephone or wire or by a message read over the radio. Middle- and upper-class families also insert an announcement of their bereavement in the newspapers, but in most cases it comes too late for the funeral, usually held within twenty-four hours, as required by law. Few corpses are embalmed. The open coffin, a wooden box covered with felt or plush for the poor, a metal casket costing several hundred dollars for the wealthy, is usually placed in the family living room for the wake if there is time to hold one; well-to-do families may rent a room in a funeral home.

Wherever possible, a church funeral service is held; then the mourners accompany the hearse or pallbearers to the cemetery. The priest seldom joins the procession. At the cemetery entrance the coffin is lowered to the ground, and all may take a last look at the dead face through a small glass panel in the top. After the coffin is placed in a mausoleum or niche or lowered into a grave, the mourners leave.

In striking contrast to the simplicity and dispatch with which burial takes place are the numerous religious and memorial ceremonies that follow. Friends and business associates of the deceased and the bereaved buy space in the newspapers to express their condolences; the more prominent the person, the more black-bordered boxes in the papers. A Rosary for the departed soul is said at home before a temporary altar banked with flowers every evening for nine days; mourners then chat over liquor and coffee. On the ninth day the Rosary is led by as many as nine professional mourners, depending on the family's means and desire to keep up appearances. An elaborate mass is said at the church, followed by a special meal at home for all who attend. A mass and a Rosary usually mark the date of death each month for a year, followed by a banquet as generous as the family can afford on the first anniversary of death.

In 1943 social anthropologists found that mourning customs had become less strict in the preceding decade:

> Black was traditionally worn two years for a parent, husband, or wife, one year for brothers, sisters, or parents-in-law, three months for an uncle or an aunt, a month and a half for a cousin. If one's parent died, the curtains of the house were kept drawn, pictures and adornments were covered in black for one year, and the family left home only to attend mass. . . . Now, one mourns only about half as long as formerly.[49]

Many men now wear no mourning even for a close relative; women, especially old women, are stricter, and widows sometimes wear black the rest of their lives. Yet women, sometimes still in black, may now attend parties a few weeks after the death. A combination of black and white is called "half mourning" and is a transition to brighter colors.

A Rosary and sometimes a mass are said on each anniversary of death for another decade or two, or until the immediate relatives themselves have died. Old women like to recall, "Next month it will have been thirty-seven years since Fulana died," while relatives and friends may have a poem or eulogy published in the newspaper on the anniversary, perhaps with a picture of the departed and an invitation to a memorial mass. It is against the law to defame the memory of a dead person, and thus the family honor; the spouse, children, siblings, parents, and grandchildren are allowed to bring suit and defend the honor of the family. Every year on November 2, the Day of the Dead, as well as on Mother's Day, August 15, Costa Ricans laden with flowers make pilgrimages to family graves. In many ways the dead continue to be members of Costa Rican society.

Mother's Day, San José Workers' Cemetery (Katherine Lambert)

7
EDUCATION

"Education and only education is the answer to all the problems of Costa Rica," declaimed the keynote speaker at a 1977 convention of teachers. Many Ticos agree that formal education can solve all social ills and bring Costa Rica international prestige as well. Among older Ticos of the middle and upper classes, the highest praise of a person has long been that he or she is "very cultured." Young people of all classes now demand opportunities for schooling, confident that a diploma is the key to a good job and high social status.

Reflecting this faith, the nation invests a large share of its resources in its school system. Nearly a third of the 1978 central government budget—9 percent of Costa Rica's GNP—was earmarked for primary and secondary schools.[1] The formal education system, the largest common enterprise of Costa Ricans, engages about 27 percent of the population as teachers or students.[2]

Even when the budget was much smaller and the percentage of students far lower, Ticos took great pride in their schools. In the last two decades, however, many Costa Ricans have begun to wonder if this faith and pride are justified, and to speak of a "crisis" in education. Even as school attendance from preschool to university has greatly increased, they charge, the quality of teaching and learning has declined. The myth of "more teachers than soldiers"[3] and the boast of the highest literacy rate in Central America, they say, have blinded most Ticos to the system's many defects, and thus kept them from adapting it to the great changes of past decades. At the same time these changes have led them to reject the traditional goals and values of education without developing clear alternatives.[4]

In an effort to understand this feeling of crisis, we shall first see how the myth arose, tracing the virtues and limitations of the educational system in both history and national character.[5] As a university professor of education says, "The Tico self-image and ideal image weigh heavily on education."[6] In the course of this chapter we also deal with the impact on education of other aspects of the social structure—the family, the political system, and inequality of classes and regions. We explore the myth as both blinder and ideal, as obstacle and as goal.

DEVELOPMENT OF THE SCHOOL SYSTEM

Formal education, like most other institutions, was even less developed in isolated and impoverished Costa Rica than in neighboring colonies. Schools were few and books almost nonexistent. The chief aim was to teach Catholic doctrine, although primers, written chiefly by priests, also included lessons in writing and simple arithmetic. Colonial governors were hard pressed to find literate persons to help administer the colony, for few colonists attended any school, and, except for foreign-educated priests, the upper class in general was as ignorant as the rest.[7] When independence was declared there were only six people in Alajuela who could read. One of the few literate laypersons of the late colonial era is described by her grandson:

> My grandmother was a teacher of "first letters," and taught reading with a primer, counting and subtracting with the fingers, and Christian doctrine with a catechism written by a Jesuit of the time of Philip II. She also taught geography. The world for her consisted of Guatemala, Spain, Rome, Jerusalem, and Heaven—neither more nor less.[8]

In 1814 citizens of San José hired Bachiller Rafael Francisco Osejo,[9] a Nicaraguan graduate of the University of León, to serve as rector of their new school, Santo Tomás, and to teach philosophy. After independence was declared late in 1821, Osejo urged that "public instruction is unquestionably the basis of public happiness, and our institutions run a great risk for lack of it." By the end of the year, the founding fathers had begun to establish schools.

Many public officials in the early days of the republic, including the first president, José María Castro, were former teachers and showed great concern for education, believing it to be an instrument for building and guaranteeing democracy. An 1828 law, largely unenforced, made school attendance mandatory for children. The 1869 constitution provided that education should be free, obligatory, and tax-supported. Costa Rica was one of the first nations in the world to make this provision.[10]

Through most of the nineteenth century the great majority of pupils were boys, although a few women taught cooking and sewing—along with the rudiments of literacy and Catholic doctrine—to small groups of girls. Slow learners were often struck with spiked boards or made to kiss their classmates' feet or to kneel on dried corn, a stone in each outstretched hand. "Letters enter with blood," it was said, and "A whipping accomplishes more than a sermon."[11]

In colonial times and the first decades of the republican era those who wanted a university education had to go abroad. Then in 1844 Santo Tomás was given university status, an event viewed by all involved as the greatest in national history—the promise of light and progress. *Colegios* (high schools) were opened in major towns in the 1860s and 1870s.

In 1888, under the "liberal generation," the university was closed except for the law school, on the grounds that it was too tied to the Church and the scholastic tradition and that funds were better spent on the new high schools. Although primary and secondary schooling were indeed upgraded, it became necessary for anyone who aspired to master any field except law to become self-educated (as indeed many Costa Rican intellectuals have been) or to go abroad, which required either official favor or family wealth. Although separate schools of fine arts, pharmacy, education, and agriculture were founded after 1888, no university was established until 1940.

Poverty and illiteracy long hampered the very educational progress that was supposed to eradicate them. Few primary school teachers had much preparation in the subjects they taught, and most of the teacher training institutes opened during the nineteenth century were soon closed for lack of funds. According to one estimate, less than 10 percent of the population in 1864 had attended any school, and 89 percent were illiterate.[12] After that date, school enrollment steadily increased, thanks largely to wealth from coffee exports as well as to the constitutional provision for tuition-free compulsory schooling and to the reforms of the 1880s.

Those who finished secondary school and earned a *bachillerato* were a distinct elite. Their schooling was roughly comparable to two years of college today. The great gap between this elite and the majority, most of whom were either primary school graduates or dropouts, bothered leaders imbued with the ideal of Costa Rica as a democracy of "highly cultured" people.

Education itself is still an article of faith. But for most young Ticos the goals of schooling have changed. The increased need for technical expertise, administrators, and skilled workers has shifted the emphasis away from being *culto*. People whose parents never aspired to higher education now demand it as *the* means to jobs, income, and status. Political leaders try to meet these new demands. The result is a quantitative revolution—mass education.

THE QUANTITATIVE REVOLUTION AND THE QUALITY OF SCHOOLING

A taxi driver who completed only second grade but whose two children are university students represents this revolution. Since the 1940s, the number of schools, students, and teachers—and of *colones* invested in education— have all risen enormously.

In 1943, 11 percent of the population was enrolled in 759 public primary schools; in 1977, 19 percent of a much larger population attended 2,798 public and sixty-seven private primary schools. In 1943, there were only five public *colegios* and several smaller private ones, and only one secondary school student to every twenty in grade school. By contrast, the 1977 figures show 200 public and twenty-six private secondary schools, and a ratio of secondary to primary school students of 8 to 20. Between 1970 and 1974 alone, the number of high schools doubled.

In 1943, the new University of Costa Rica (UCR) enrolled 716 students. By 1968 it had 9,500. Then came the great surge of *colegio* graduates demanding entry, so that the 1970s saw the establishment of the Autonomous National University (UNA), the Technological Institute (ITCR) and several regional university centers. Between 1970 and 1975 the number of university students more than doubled (18,870 to 37,577), reaching 44,000 by 1979.

In 1943, 18 percent of a very small government budget went for schools; in 1978, as we noted, nearly a third of a comparatively huge budget was allotted to schools. From 1965 to 1979, the education budget—apart from building construction—rose from ₡11 million to nearly ₡2.000 million.[13]

What accounts for this quantitative revolution? The growth of population, and especially the baby boom of the 1950s, for one thing.[14] Another is the increase in middle-level jobs demanding a fairly high level of schooling—primarily commercial, industrial, and bureaucratic jobs. As the middle class has grown, so have its aspirations for its children and its demands on government to provide schools. Rural communities have also demanded schools and have helped build them. Many rural people have been attracted to the San José area by hopes of better educational opportunities for their children,[15] and the government has tried to stem the tide by providing schools all over the country. While the six years of primary school have long been obligatory, schooling through the ninth year—including the first three-year cycle of secondary education—is now compulsory for all who entered school since 1973. By law the central government must provide facilities for nine years of schooling in every canton and every population center of 5,000 or more residents. In the 1960s many municipalities were paying students' bus fares to the nearest high school; now they have high schools of their own. And the greater availability of university education motivates many to finish high school.

The dropout problem continues, although the rate has declined over the last three decades. The 1973 census showed that over half of all Costa Ricans age fifteen and older had not completed primary school. In the early 1940s nine out of every ten children who entered first grade dropped out before finishing sixth grade; by 1974 the dropout rate had fallen to 25 percent.[16]

The 1973 census showed that only 5 percent of the labor force had graduated from high school. Dropouts, while declining, remain high: 43 percent of those between ages thirteen and fifteen were not in school in 1979, and 67 percent of those in the sixteen to eighteen-year-old category.

Literacy is a common test of an education system. Census figures show that the literacy rate rose from 66 percent in 1927 to 89 percent in 1973. But these figures take into account only "pure" or "total" illiterates over age ten, and are based on simple tests such as the ability to sign one's name. Thus many "functional illiterates," who may have learned the basic skills in the brief time they attended school but have let them lapse, are classed as literate. Minister of Education Fernando Volio caused a stir in 1974 when he challenged the myth of high literacy, saying that there are at least 400,000 illiterates in the country—over 20 percent of the total population, and 30 percent of those ten and older, rather than the official 11 percent.[17]

Serious questions are also raised about the education of those who stay in school. Mass education, says sociologist Daniel Camacho, has resulted in an academic scene of "classroom cages," teachers by the hour, and students by volume. High-school graduates enter the university unable to read and write acceptably and with such spotty general knowledge that in one class of sixty freshmen, for example, not one had heard of the French Revolution.[18] The quality of most university training is also questioned. Philosopher Constantino Láscaris says the system as a whole provides "twenty years of elementary education."

To what extent are these charges true? How can we account for the present status of the school system? Before seeking answers in the larger society, let us look at what goes on in the classroom—at what is taught and learned there, and by what methods, both in theory and in practice.

CONTENT AND METHODS OF SCHOOLING

Primary Schools. A rural schoolteacher told us in 1968: "The students must memorize all sorts of things that have nothing to do with their lives, and these are not learned in a practical way but almost entirely out of books and lectures." This, in a nutshell, is still the most common criticism of both content and method at all levels of education.

The primary school curriculum is virtually the same as it was forty years ago. Through all six grades of primary school the same subjects are taught, with somewhat different content each year and with some leeway for teachers regarding schedules, materials, and methods. Programs for each subject come from the Ministry of Education, but they are not specific, and the teacher must draw up lesson plans.

The curriculum is identical in town and countryside. Policy-makers often debate this point. The majority believe that different curricula would be discriminatory, and that all Costa Ricans should have the same basic schooling. The high incidence of rural dropouts leads others to question this decision and suggest that the content of schooling is especially remote from everyday life in rural areas.

Methods of teaching accentuate this gap. At all levels mechanical memorization is favored over active participation, investigation, questioning, independent reading and study, and problem solving by the students. "The rote method of getting through the Ministry-imposed syllabus is so ingrained," says an OAS adviser, "that teaching a class is like pushing an 'On' button, then switching it 'Off.' "

Primary school lessons involve mainly writing and memorizing textbook information,[19] often dictated by the teacher and copied into notebooks for lack of enough books to go around. Few field trips or visual aids, except perhaps for charts (often made by the teacher) give concrete meaning to classroom lessons. Even in science classes, experiments and direct observations are few, for not only are most schools too poor to afford much equipment, but teachers often fail to take advantage of local resources. "The other day," said a rural school supervisor, "I sat in on a class when the teacher was drawing a beautiful picture of a cow on the board. The children weren't paying the slightest attention. They were looking at a real cow just outside the window." Homework consists mostly of neatly recopying a lesson dictated in class, and many teachers seem to regard a tidy notebook as evidence that a child has mastered the material. Original compositions are seldom assigned, and then only on specified topics.

Secondary Schools. Until 1964 all secondary school students, except for those in the few separate vocational schools, studied a fixed academic program directed exclusively toward the *bachillerato*, a prerequisite for entering the university. Since then changes have gradually been introduced. While the first three years are still devoted to basic general education, the fourth cycle consists either of two more years of academic courses or three years of "professional" training—in agriculture and animal husbandry, industrial arts, secretarial work, or accounting—in specialized *colegios*.

The great majority of high-school students are still found in academic *colegios*. The academic curriculum is so overloaded that any one subject can be learned only superficially at best. In the seventh to ninth years, thirty-five class periods totalling twenty-four hours a week are devoted to courses in Spanish and other languages, social studies (with emphasis on Costa Rica), mathematics, science, music, religion, plastic arts, education for family life, technology—for example, photography—and some optional or "club" time. With the ninth year, basic general education is completed.

The fourth cycle of academic high schools continues to include languages, social studies, mathematics, and science, plus added courses in philosophy and psychology in the tenth year, and in technology, music, and plastic arts in both the tenth and eleventh years. Two periods of physical education, one of group activities—in which theater is increasingly important—and one of religion round out the week.

This ambitious curriculum belies the frequent assertion that secondary schooling is simply a continuation of primary schooling. But there are not enough trained teachers for so many subjects in so many schools. Materials are lacking. Laboratories are few. The school day is short, and the school year has many interruptions.[20] Students are assigned more and more books; but they are much too expensive for most students, and publishers and bookstores are seldom given enough advance notice to have a supply on hand at the proper time. Students must, therefore, spend many class periods copying lessons dictated from books or, later, seeking them in the library. Experiments, field trips, and original themes are rare. Courses are watered down, summarized, and simplified.

Even more than at the primary level, many administrators and teachers see the development of independent thinking and study habits as a major goal of secondary schools. At present, however, lessons consist mostly of lectures and dictation, and great emphasis is put on memorization. The meager school and public libraries are seldom used except for required reading. "It wasn't so long ago that teachers at the Liceo de Costa Rica (one of the country's oldest *colegios*) would send latecomers to the library as a *punishment*," says one teacher.

Teachers themselves see as the main defect of the school system the fact that they are not allowed to fail students in various subjects on a yearly basis. Under the plan now in effect, students are promoted or failed only at the end of each three-year cycle. Just as a child can get into second grade without knowing how to read and write, so high school students are promoted en masse, despite low grades on their frequent exams.

This picture of secondary schooling as "notes, exams, and jabber," charged a group of high school professors, is reflected in poor preparation for jobs and university courses. How, they ask, can students be expected to handle life problems effectively when year by year they are taught to be "simple repeaters of concepts, definitions, names, and dates," in a system that does not encourage reflection, observation, experiment, and reasoning?[21]

THE SCHOOL IN SOCIAL CONTEXT

The school system is highly centralized. The constitution provides that "public education shall be organized as an integral process, correlated in its various cycles from preschool up through the university." This coordination of various levels is the responsibility of the Ministry of Education in San José. Its control of the school system is both bureaucratic and academic, governing supplies as well as syllabi.

At the top of the hierarchy is the Minister of Education, appointed by each incoming president. While many staff members stay on through changes of administration, a new Minister may replace others with friends or political partisans. He or she heads the Superior Council of Education (CSE), which acts as a board of directors charged not only with making general policy but also with specific decisions on curricula, texts, allocation of funds, teacher qualifications, supervision of teachers, and other technical aspects of education. In practice, Ministers, especially forceful ones, control the program. Their control rests largely on the paternalistic tradition, "in which each subordinate solves his problems in private conversation with the Minister,"[22] a tradition so deeply established that delegation of responsibility will be slow in coming.

Most Ministry employees and all school employees, including teachers and janitors, are civil servants. The civil service system is supposed to free them from political influence and permit appointment strictly on merit. Many Ministry employees and teachers, however, believe the system is *more* politicized than it was before civil service was introduced.

Party politics influences allocation of funds and jobs. Like the Minister and most members of the CSE, the personnel director of the Ministry is a political appointee. Congressmen exert pressure on him or her, as well as on the Minister and other officials, to give jobs to those they prefer.

There are ways of bypassing civil service regulations and giving jobs as political rewards or personal favors. In 1976 delegates from technical schools complained to the Minister and the president's staff that school directors were named according to party affiliation and personal friendship with influential politicians, and that scholarships were given on the same basis. They also charged that high schools had been established in inappropriate places, to repay political debts.

The social class system and the school system have long had a reciprocal influence. Although the founding fathers and numerous administrators throughout Costa Rican history have worked to make education "free, obligatory, and laical," it continues to discriminate in favor of the well-to-do. Each teacher hands out lists of supplies—paper, notebooks, pencils, paints, crayons, books—that students must buy. Uniforms, intended to cut down on display and thus democratize the schools, are often beyond the means of poorer families.

A team of psychologists sees poor nutrition and physical care as the main causes of learning problems.[23] Malnourished children have long drooped in class and even slept at their seats. The recently established nutrition program, according to some teachers, has already eased this problem. It also encourages low-income parents to keep their children in school, for poor farmers and urban single mothers reluctantly took their children—especially boys—out of school after three or four years to help on the farm or in the household, or to earn money in the street. Even before then, the children would miss several weeks during the annual coffee harvest. Although parents are obliged by law to send their children to school, they have rarely been forced to do so. Many teachers sympathized with a family's economic straits, and municipal authorities often tacitly cooperated.

Although fewer poor children drop out of school now, many are alienated by a teacher's higher-class status. "Most elementary teachers are from the working or lower-middle class but aspire to higher status," says a University of Costa Rica sociologist. "When they try to impose their middle-class standards on a working-class or peasant child who can't see what good they are, the child is likely to lose interest in school." On the other hand, teachers are the only models of "proper Tico behavior"—that is, middle-class norms—in many communities, and may thus help promote social mobility among some of their students.

Well-to-do families generally send their children to private elementary and secondary schools, most of which are either religious or foreign-colony oriented. In 1966, 24 percent of high-school students were in private schools; a decade later, the percentage had fallen to 6.5, though absolute numbers were about the same. The Ministry of Education supervises such schools closely to ensure compliance with the standard curriculum. Instruction is generally at a higher level than in public schools, in part because the children can afford to buy supplies and texts and also have a home environment conducive to study. These children are also under pressure from their parents to do well and "get ahead." It is not surprising that a far larger percentage of graduates of private schools than of public schools are admitted to the universities.

Despite the high degree of centralization in education, each school reflects not only a community's socioeconomic level but also the level of cooperation among its adult members. Subsistence farmers in peripheral areas typically meet soon after they settle in a new locality to request help from the government in establishing a school. The government usually gives some help, perhaps sending out a construction expert, while the community may donate locally produced lumber, a building site, labor, and possibly money and supplies. (By contrast, the state usually bears the total cost of more elaborate urban schools, where funds are forthcoming from the Public Works Ministry rather than the education budget.)

When a rural school is opened, all children in the district commonly start out in first grade. In one remote hamlet we visited in 1968 we saw pupils between the ages of seven and seventeen in the first and only grade of the new school. Rural schools, including those with all six grades, are accorded only one teacher until enrollment passes fifty, and one-third of all schools have only one teacher.

Typically, after a school is built, a soccer field follows, *pulperías* are opened, more people settle in the area, and the community usually develops more services. By contrast, where no school exists little social organization is usually evident.

One group of social scientists observed in 1950 that "rural people place high value on education but their standards are lower and their facilities much poorer" than those of urbanites.[24] This is still the case. Not only are money and effort concentrated in the metropolitan region, but schools everywhere are built according to a single plan designed for the highland climate. Thus lowland schools have tin roofs that transmit heat and too little ventilation. Then, too, rural transportation—often along muddy footpaths—may be difficult: many high school students at Ciudad Neily, for

One room school house in a remote area (Katherine Lambert)

example, have to get up at 3 A.M. to get to school by seven. Rural teachers, often of urban or suburban origin, may have little understanding of a community's special problems; and those sent to particularly distant places are generally inexperienced and in many cases uncertified novices, hoping for the earliest possible transfer.

In 1973, total illiterates over age ten constituted 5 percent of the urban and 14 percent of the rural population, with the highest figures in the coastal provinces.[25] A trend toward closing the rural-urban gap is evident from data on completion of primary school. The percentage of those fifteen to nineteen years of age with six years or more of schooling rose from 47 percent urban and 10 percent rural in 1950, to 87 percent urban and 62 percent rural in 1973.

Although they have no special career plans for their children, many of today's urban workers are well aware of the relationship between formal education and jobs, and demand that their children finish at least sixth grade. This pattern is increasingly prevalent in rural homes as well. Many high-school and university students from working-class homes say the chief reason they continued to study was parental insistence. Wanting them to concentrate on schoolwork, many parents demand much less help with farm and household chores than thirty years ago.

Much as many parents value schooling for their children, cultural patterns of child rearing may hinder learning. Says Sira Jaen:

> There is nothing more terrible than having a "good mother." The spoiled child cannot take criticism or correction. He cannot admit that he makes mistakes, or judge his own work and improve it. Girls, even in the university, may cry if corrected. This pattern is so much a part of our way of life that teachers think to "stimulate" a child means only to praise him. They pride themselves on being "tolerant" and "understanding" rather than telling a child he has made a mistake and must correct it. Parents and teachers are afraid of giving children "complexes." They call them *pobrecitos* [poor dears], and mothers, especially, are more likely to worry about their studying too much than too little.[26]

While virtually all Ticos stress the importance of formal education, there is less consensus, even among policy-makers, on its goals—the kind of person and the kind of society they want the school system to help produce. Concern for traditional values is strongest among middle- and upper-class Costa Ricans in their fifties and beyond, who approve of the traditional Latin American curriculum oriented to the university and a professional career. This elitist system has "aspired to one principal objective: a general humanistic cultural training for the 'superior person' destined to assume some sort of authoritative position in the society."[28]

This view of education is seriously questioned by many Ticos who see education as a public investment in the "development" process. A modernizing society needs technicians and specialists of many kinds. And it needs jobs for its ever-growing labor force. Neither need, say critics, is met by a system still geared to producing "cultured" people.

So deep-rooted in middle-class culture is the aversion to anything smacking of manual labor, however, that even when other options are open, most prefer the academic track—not necessarily because they want to be *cultos* but because they want the high social status that white-collar jobs and the professions can bring. Many young people who fail to achieve that status become "resentful social misfits."[28] *Pueblo*, a radical weekly, tells of high-school graduates in Puntarenas whose families have made great sacrifices to educate them, and who now find themselves pushing a broom in a hotel, or a wheelbarrow on a construction job.[29] A year after graduation, of forty-seven graduates in one class in Ciudad Neily, only two had jobs.

Although education is often cited as a tool for social change, analysts of the institution are more inclined to see it as a means of preserving the status quo and of exercising social control. "When teachers' jobs are spelled out by a state bureaucracy, and routine and hierarchy control what they do, they are unlikely to be innovative and creative," says Francisco Gutiérrez, an educational reformer. "Costa Rica has an army of teachers dedicated to keeping things as they are."

Schools are an important agent of indoctrination in patriotism, loyalty, and a strong belief that Costa Rica is the best country in the world and that its government confers all kinds of benefits on the people. In visits to schools, we observed children being told these things, directly and indirectly, through repetition of the national hymn and other patriotic songs praising the "Switzerland of Central America," and through the pledge of allegiance or salute to the flag. The children are told that their nutritious meals and the gifts of school libraries show the peacefulness of the nation and the superiority of its democratic government, especially in comparison to other countries that spend their money on weapons. They hear that other nations look on theirs with admiration and envy.

INNOVATIONS IN SCHOOLING

Each new government, almost ritualistically, announces grandiose plans for "total reform" of education. The Ministry and other agencies continue, meanwhile, to work on a smaller scale, trying to improve the curriculum and teaching methods, as well as to provide more preschool, vocational, and adult education. Rural teachers attend workshops led by advisers in various subject areas. The laboratory school of the University of Costa Rica encourages participation of students in decision-making, as well as independent research and creativity in the arts. A handful of primary and secondary schools, both public and private, have since 1973 experimented with a program of "Total Language" that uses "the massive culture of images and sounds" that is neglected in schools where teachers talk and students listen—the media of music, theater, film, videotape, dance, plastic arts, and tape recordings.

Few Costa Ricans are avid or even habitual readers, and libraries have only recently become important. Students at all levels, increasingly asked to do research, now crowd the National Library and university libraries. The Ministry and private groups have helped establish over a thousand small school and community libraries.

Recess in a school patio (Sylvia Boxley de Sassone)

A small fraction of all preschool children, many of them with working mothers, attend new government-sponsored day care centers, or kindergartens within public primary schools. The uniformed kindergarteners, between twenty and thirty to a group, spend three hours each weekday morning with a female teacher who leads singing, supervises painting and active play, gives lectures, and reads stories—activities intended to develop sensory-motor skills as well as social skills needed in elementary school. By 1985 the Ministry hopes to have half of all preschool children enrolled in such centers, mostly in poor urban neighborhoods and remote rural areas.

Vocational training, now growing in importance, was once a poor relation of the academic system. Early vocational schools were founded by priests in the 1940s and 1950s to help street urchins, and priests still function as teachers and directors in many such schools, which are now supervised by the Ministry. Vocational and technical courses are now offered in addition to academic courses, or in separate "technical" high schools. Not long ago, agricultural schools were so badly equipped that they used only blackboards to teach children how to plant radishes. Today many have their own land—not enough for some large-scale projects, but enough for gardens, bees, rabbits, and fruit trees, and in some cases for cattle.

Fernando Volio considers the decision to institute short courses for secondary school students and graduates one of the most important in recent years. These optional "short careers" emphasize technical and on-the-job training, and may begin either with the tenth year of school or following graduation from high school. The new Colegios Universitarios of Cartago and Alajuela train secretaries and bookkeepers, as well as health workers and many other specialists, for most of whom jobs are waiting.

Despite the utility of such technical schools for the nation's well-being, many students settle for a technical school simply because it is the only one nearby, but keep their sights on professional careers. Thus, a survey of students at one vocational school found boys in a cabinet-making class hoping to study law, civil engineering, chemistry, and architecture, while girls in a sewing class wanted to study medicine, psychology, and biology.

One attempt to make technical training more attractive capitalizes on the Costa Rican respect for titles. The six-year technical high school confers a "professional" *bachillerato*; technical schools beyond high school are called "university schools"; and the title of *profesional de nivel medio* (middle-level professional) has been substituted for *subprofesional*. These names are intended to overcome the taint of manual labor or low status.

An attempt to increase Costa Rica's supply of skilled workers has been undertaken by the semiautonomous National Institute of Apprenticeship, INA, founded in 1965. Its directors recognize the danger of alienation among youth who find no place for themselves in society, and believe the task of preventing it must be undertaken "in a direct and immediate manner based on real necessities."[30] The INA not only teaches the practical skills needed in a modernizing society, but also directs this training toward specific job openings that already exist, after investigating the needs of each business or industry.

Opportunities are numerous for adults to earn primary or secondary diplomas or to take special courses, and many take advantage of them. Any weekday evening one sees hundreds of older teenagers and adults, books and notebooks in hand, going to public schools, business schools, technical schools, language classes. Many of them are factory workers, clerks, and domestic servants; some are housewives.

The Ministry's Department of Adult Education, created in 1970, combined a number of previously unrelated programs. Its director says that "uneducated" adults feel little connection with their society. They must be taught to recognize their own needs and responsibilities so they can participate more fully in programs that affect them. They are taught not only the three Rs, but how government agencies function, how to take advantage of their services, how to understand the language of the news media. Courses are taught by schoolteachers, who get extra pay, and by volunteers, often university students. Classes, frequently quite informal, are often held in factories after the teacher's and students' regular workday.

Two programs take advantage of the widespread ownership of transistor radios. A radio course called *Maestro en Casa* (Teacher in the House) gives instruction in primary grades, using materials the student must fetch weekly and have corrected by a teacher. Upon passing exams, the student is awarded a diploma.

Beamed by radio to all of Central America and Mexico is *Escuela para Todos* (School for Everyone), founded in 1965 by a Costa Rican and her Austrian husband. Its staff answers questions about everything except politics, some by radio, many more by letter, and has built up a library of answers based on information from professors and encyclopedias. Sample questions from the 100,000 the staff received in the program's first decade: Why is the sky blue? How should I fertilize the garden? How can I cure pimples? What can I do to rid a cow of screwworms? "We talk as to a friend who wants to know, not as teacher to pupil," say staff members. The school is now a government "autonomous institution."

FOREIGN INFLUENCES

Although many innovations have been of foreign inspiration, they are often resisted precisely because of this origin, on suspicion of not conforming to "our idiosyncrasy." But foreign influences have affected Costa Rican schools at all levels throughout the nation's history. For generations professionals and professors were trained in Chile, Uruguay, Argentina, and Europe. In the last three decades the United States' influence has been especially great. Hundreds of Costa Ricans have taught in the United States, often returning to teach in their own land, while thousands have studied in American high schools and universities. American professors, educational advisers, and students have also come to Costa Rica in considerable numbers. Many elements of American educational theories and methods have been adopted in Costa Rica, while texts by American authors have been widely used in universities and technical schools.

Since the early nineteenth century, foreigners and Costa Ricans trained abroad have served on high-school and university faculties. Of 2,845 university professors in 1976, 215 were foreigners. Many of these are excellent and highly qualified, and represent a saving for Costa Rica. In times when it may cost $30,000 to train one research scientist, the help of foreign experts will at least offset some of the brain drain of capable and promising Costa Ricans who find better pay and facilities abroad, especially in the United States.

Since World War II a number of European countries have also given grants, loans, and scholarships and sent advisers. The Soviet Union and Rumania give scholarships covering all expenses during study for a graduate degree; there are said to be 400 Costa Rican students in the Soviet Union alone. Some countries aid technical and vocational schools; Taiwan, West Germany, and Great Britain help with agricultural education, and Spain contributes heavily to libraries and educational television, while several countries help INA. UNESCO and OAS specialists work in the Ministry of Education.

In recent years educational leaders have established strong ties with other countries in Central America. The Organization of Central American States publishes many books now used in Costa Rican schools. The High Council of Central American Universities (CSUCA) has become an active proponent of the idea that the university must be in the vanguard of economic development and social reform. CSUCA and the Federation of Central American University Students both arrange student exchanges as well as numerous lectures and workshops among students and professors of isthmian universities.

Although many Ticos welcome foreign influence, they insist that all ideas, methods, and courses be oriented to *la idiosincrásia*—the special problems and values of Costa Rica. In 1978 President Carazo called for an educational plan worked out by Ticos alone, saying foreigners have neither "the vision nor the psychology" for the task.

HIGHER EDUCATION

After going without a university since 1888, Costa Ricans hailed the establishment of the University of Costa Rica in 1940. Despite great resistance, its monopoly was broken three decades later by the establishment of other centers of higher education, including a private university.

UCR, located on an attractive campus in suburban San José, had fewer than 6,000 students in 1965, but four times as many by 1974. In 1972 it was already overcrowded; there was not room for all who met the entrance requirements, and some students complained that they could not take essential courses. Other charges were that the UCR had become too rigidly academic, too tailored to "a certain class," too "elitist," with no opportunities for "the people," and too opposed to change. Soon afterward President Figueres and the PLN-dominated congress decreed the establishment of a new university in Heredia—the Universidad Nacional Autónoma, or UNA—and named as Rector the priest and labor organizer, Padre Benjamín Núñez, who had fought alongside "don Pepe" in 1948. Heredia's Superior Normal School was absorbed into the new UNA as the School of Education when the university opened in 1973 with 1,000 students. The following year UNA had 5,400, and by 1977, 10,000.

Because the rapid growth of both universities strained available facilities and funds, and because of local demands in many areas, "regional centers,"

University of Costa Rica (La Nación)

each affiliated with one university or the other, have been created. These are explained as part of a plan to democratize and decentralize education, and to make it more responsive to the community and region and thus counteract the capital's monopoly of resources, including the talent and abilities of young people from the rest of the country. Through special courses and research projects, it is hoped that the centers will link the universities with specific "development problems" where they arise.

Helping correct the tendency to train unneeded professionals while importing needed ones is the Institute of Technology near Cartago, whose first class was graduated in 1975. TEC offers intermediate levels of technical-professional training. It serves as a bridge between highly skilled labor and university-trained engineers; for example, its construction engineer degree fills the vast gap between construction foreman and civil engineer. Industrial production, industrial maintenance (a most important specialty, since nearly all equipment is imported), electronics, and highway construction are among the subjects in the curriculum. A San Carlos branch contains a school of forestry and agriculture. The program is by no means purely technical; it also includes subjects associated with a liberal arts education. So, too, does the State University at a Distance, founded in 1978, which offers credit courses via television.

The UCR is generally regarded as the best and most prestigious academic center, and high-school graduates usually try first for admission there. Teaching and engineering graduates predominate, with most of the remainder taking degrees in the social sciences, literature, medicine, accounting, agronomy, pharmacy, architecture, dentistry, microbiology, journalism, philosophy, and fine arts. Most degrees are equivalent to a bachelor's degree; only the dental and medical schools offer the doctorate. In any case, foreign doctorates tend to confer more prestige, although the medical school is considered by far the best in Central America. After the *bachillerato* a student may take two or more years of course work and write a thesis that will enable him to put *Lic. (licenciado)* before his name. In recent years the prestige of the *licenciatura* has suffered from the new master's degree, which has higher status. Engineers (who proudly place *Ing.* before their names) study a total of six years.

Despite their constitutionally guaranteed autonomy, universities feel tremendous pressure from would-be students and populist politicians, who insist that everyone who wants to attend should be admitted. It is risky for any politician to oppose this policy. Applicants are selected on the basis of entrance exams and a review of their high-school grades. A month before classes begin, the universities publish lists of those who have been accepted. Those who are left out invariably protest, under the leadership of student association activists; a second list is then published that leaves out very few applicants.

To accommodate all the thousands they admit, the universities must water the soup, hiring many poorly qualified instructors, crowding into inadequate facilities, doing without much needed equipment, and restricting laboratory work. The journalism school of the UCR, for instance, until recently lacked a television set for its courses in television journalism; there was not so much as an Instamatic for the photography course. One full-time professor, two half-time instructors, and others paid by the hour taught the courses.[31] (The situation has improved since then.)

When the first-year general studies courses were instituted in 1957, they were hailed as a means of ensuring well-rounded, "cultured" graduates with a knowledge of the humanities, even in specialized careers. Twenty years later they are being used to remedy the deficiencies of secondary schools and to ensure that all students have more or less the same general knowledge before they specialize.

Just as at lower levels, lectures and memorization characterize university teaching. A third-year student told us that most of his courses were taught "the same way as everything else I've had since first grade." A sociologist studied the teaching methods of 116 UCR professors in 1977 and found that most rely chiefly on lectures, often combined with group discussion and directed reading in texts. A few use laboratories, seminars, research projects, and field work, and a very few offer independent or individualized study.[32]

"Students not only are not accustomed to studying, but they are accustomed to *not* studying," says philosophy professor Roberto Murillo.[33] Though they often complain about excessive homework, they can often get away, as they did in high school, with doing little until just before exams. A Costa Rican professor of anthropology remarks that most students, particularly at UNA, come unprepared to class and even to exams, but always take a swat at it, faking knowledge. Students and professors alike rarely admit that they simply don't know.

UNA authorities have tried to institute more flexible and less bookish methods than those common at UCR, stressing field research and social action (such as union organization and community development) and informal group discussion more than lectures. "Where a biology course in the UCR might be concerned with things like genetics," says a UNA student, "we talk about pollution. In our sociology class we have round-table discussions and lots of arguments, but no exams. We are graded on participation."

A UNA professor of cooperative management tells us that he was about to give some lectures on methods of accounting when his superior told him that accounting is technical, and therefore "not part of the national reality." He resigned.

Both universities try to orient students to this "national reality" in different ways. While all UNA courses are presumably geared to it, the UCR now requires that all students attend an interdisciplinary seminar with that title. In the first semester they study social research methods; in the second, they conduct team research on a specific problem, under the direction of a professor. To graduate they must put in 300 hours of community service. Says a professor, "The idea is to prevent elitism and narrow professionalism and give the student a conception of national and world problems. But most students are very apathetic toward this social action program. It's hard to get them out of their shells. They have not learned to think, to pursue a problem to a conclusion. While the leftists are not so apathetic, they express ideological clichés in a completely automatic way."

Social sensitivity at both universities is often equated with a Marxist orientation and leftist militancy. In recent years the apathy of the majority of students has highlighted the activism of a small number of leftists of various persuasions. Leftists usually win student government elections in which absenteeism runs as high as 80 percent. Banners and billboards advocating leftist causes drape campus buildings, walls, and trees. Some departments at both universities are openly pro-Communist.

Uncritical use of Marxist-Leninist tenets and idioms is especially apparent in the schools of social science, fine arts, and medicine. One introductory sociology instructor used only four sources as texts—works by Marx, Engels, Lenin, and Mao.

Although the UCR has a more positive image among Ticos than the UNA, many upper- and upper-middle-class citizens look with alarm on the Marxism of many professors and students at both universities. Costa Ricans often take events elsewhere in Latin America as warnings, and many point to the history of Latin American universities that became politicized and were finally closed. The idea of the university as primarily an instrument of social change, says a particularly severe critic, "has led to the political university, the revolutionary, anarchic, ideological, erotic, and heterodox university."[34]

Amid charges of elitism and privilege from liberals of the old school and leftists alike, a private university was opened in 1976—the Autonomous Central American University (UACA). Founded by a group of UCR professors who chafed at the power of department heads there, it attracted 375 students to its scattered classrooms the first year, and 3,200 in 1978. It is organized into autonomous colleges on the British plan. Though the tuition is up to three times as much as at the UCR, there are scholarships and loan programs, and a trimester plan with little wasted time. Professors have small classes and considerable freedom in methods; the tutorial system encourages a long, close relationship between students and teachers. A great deal of research and reading is assigned, and reports on assigned themes are presented and discussed in groups. Many of the students are transfers from the big universities, who say they are attracted by UACA's "academic excellence." This image is fostered by the private university's studious atmosphere, thanks to lack of budget problems and political turmoil, and to adequate classroom space that allows enrollment in desired courses. Although some Ticos object that it competes unfairly with public universities, others regard its competition as a healthy stimulant.

THE STATUS OF TEACHERS

In a country that has made education one of its guiding myths, the teacher, naturally enough, is put on a pedestal and often compared to a priest, an apostle, or a sculptor who gives form to something shapeless. Her sacrifice and altruism "make her as sacred as a mother."[35] Politicians, writers, and journalists are lavish with praise. "Unfortunately," says Oscar Arias, "there is a deep chasm between these customary eulogies and the hard reality within which they work."[36]

For decades most teachers have been women, both single and married, and even today 90 percent of elementary school teachers are women. Low salaries have not enabled middle-class men to support families by elementary school teaching, so young male teachers are likely to seek secondary school positions or school directorships after a few years of teaching in primary school.

Salaries. Teachers' salaries have long accounted for well over half of every *colón* spent on education. Salary and placement are based primarily on civil service ranks that reflect training and experience, though placement, as we have seen, is still sometimes affected by political pull. School directors are paid according to experience and the size of their schools. After thirty years a teacher can retire on a pension based on the average of the last five years' pay. Those who work in hardship posts are paid a bonus of from 25 to 100 percent of the basic scale and, if they stay there, can retire after twenty-five years. But even these inducements don't keep many out in the country very long.

Although their unions generally succeed in gaining salary increases that more than offset the effects of inflation, teachers' salaries remain low compared to those of other public employees. While hours are comparatively short and vacation days many, teachers must continue to study until they have a complete certificate, and many buy supplies and even repair buildings out of their own pockets after repeated appeals to the Ministry prove fruitless.

Nonetheless, teachers are often charged with being interested primarily in their short workdays, three-month vacations, and their salaries and prestige—motivations considered normal in most occupations, but beneath the dignity of this calling. Some older teachers allege that few of their younger colleagues are genuinely interested in teaching and that unions have given them a wage earner's mentality. "We talk a lot about the ends of education," says veteran professor Marco Tulio Salazar, "but the chief end of most teachers today seems to be the end of the month."

Teacher Training. About two-thirds of those teaching special subjects and vocational courses in 1977 had not completed the training program for a "title" or certificate. Neither had 42 percent of preschool, almost 20 percent of primary school, and 25 percent of high-school teachers. Some "aspirant" or "authorized" teachers are high-school graduates who have taken posts in rural areas that teachers with titles had turned down.

Despite all its power, the Ministry has no control over the training of teachers. Normal schools have been absorbed by universities, which, being autonomous, can set their own curricula, methods, and standards.

Teacher training curricula, like those in secondary schools, consist of a great many subjects treated only superficially. As in the schools they come from and those in which they will work, the future teachers make few independent observations or experiments, read little, and see few educational films; they spend most of their time memorizing lectures and cramming for exams. Thus the training of new teachers tends to reflect and perpetuate traditional authoritarian patterns of education. When the graduate is abruptly plunged into teaching, with little or no guidance or follow-up training, the easy and natural thing to do is to teach as one was taught.

Teachers' Unions. The nation's 30,000 teachers, organized into pressure groups, "have made more than one president sweat and several ministers tremble."[37] Most teachers are members of ANDE, the National Association of Educators, founded in 1941. Many of its 23,000 members do not like to call this organization a union. When it was suggested in 1960 that ANDE reorganize as a union in order to have more power to improve pay and working conditions, a retired teacher recalls, "nearly everyone, including teachers, rejected the idea on the grounds that unions are communistic, smack of lower-class manual workers, and so on. I am amazed that they have finally unionized; teachers used to be the most cautious and conservative group in the country."[38]

ANDE is still far more conservative than its two rivals. The Association of Professors of Secondary Education, with about 5,000 members, was founded in 1955. The Syndicate of Costa Rican Educators, with 6,000 members (who are also members of ANDE), is so active that rural teachers are often approached by a recruiter long before any representative of the Ministry of Education, even the area supervisor, comes around.

Strikes have often been called or threatened against various measures that affect teachers' status. Most often the issue is salary. But on many occasions in Costa Rican history, teachers have organized massive demonstrations against some unpopular political measure—not necessarily one that would have affected them directly—and they have seemed to the public to personify the civic conscience of a democratic nation. Today even the threat of a strike often swings things their way.

Rural Teachers. Although teachers may be quite young and considered outsiders with urban ways, they are among the most respected people in small communities, especially in isolated rural areas.[39] He or she (about 50 percent of those in "hardship posts" are men) is usually the best-educated person in the community and the only representative of government aside from the school supervisor, who may come by horseback or boat two or three times a year, and perhaps an occasional policeman making the rounds. Rural teachers may be expected to lead prayers, give medical advice and treatment, write or visit public officials requesting favors for the community or for individuals, and play a prominent role in all community activities.[40] They tend to increase Costa Rica's cultural homogeneity by introducing values and norms characteristic of the central highlands, which they have learned in college even if they are not from that region.

Rural teachers' behavior is still carefully watched and controlled by fear of gossip; they are supposed to be models of decorum for local children. "We are like priests," complained a young schoolmistress. "We can drink or smoke, but we'll be much more strongly criticized than most people would be. We can't dress *a la moda* or there'll be a scandal. Tongues start wagging at our slightest misstep, and we have to go to San José for any fun." Male teachers, though to a lesser extent, also chafe at community watchfulness. Largely as a result of such controls, the school is one of the places where Costa Rican cultural ideals are most clearly visible to children.

Partly to escape this vigilance, and partly because adequate housing is lacking, many teachers commute to rural posts daily rather than live near their schools, or at least leave for weekends and holidays.[41] In remote regions, teachers have generally lived with a local family. The government recently undertook to build houses for teachers in such areas. The community is asked to donate the lot and lay the slab foundations, and a totally prefabricated house is erected, complete with furniture, adequate for a family of six. When the first such house was finished in 1976, Minister of Education Volio declared that the program would bind the teachers more closely to the community and allow them to regain much of the leadership they had been losing, as well as sparing a new teacher the difficulty of finding a place to live.

University Professors. University professors in Costa Rica (about a third of whom are women) "form a species of intellectual proletariat," according to one writer who wonders why they stay on when their salaries are so small compared to those of congressmen, ministers, and heads of autonomous institutions. Their rejuvenating contact with youth, he concludes, is the main reason.[42] (Prestige, we suspect, is another.) Nearly half the UCR faculty have other jobs and teach only part time, but a growing number of recent UCR graduates now teach full time at university level.

Low salaries, which lead many university graduates to seek higher incomes elsewhere, even abroad, have kept the general caliber of university teaching rather low. Many professors have little background in their subjects: in 1977, only 10 percent of UNA professors had doctorates; 30 percent were *licenciados*; and the other 60 percent had B.A.s or high-school teaching certificates. An increasing stress on academic degrees, nonetheless, has made it harder for self-educated persons who distinguished themselves in the past to be professors (or even members of professional associations). Comments a professor, "The great journalist José Marín Cañas taught in the School of Journalism. But he did not have a degree, so eventually he was fired and one of his own students was put in his place."

Full-time professors are granted tenure after three years. Rank and salary then depend far less on seniority than on degrees and publications, though no "publish or perish" policy exists and the few scholarly publications are not widely read. Professors lacking tenure may be fired without cause. But academic freedom, professors insist, is generally respected within the universities, and even those without tenure may express unorthodox beliefs without fear of losing their jobs. Most are reluctant to do so, however, because they want to *quedar bien.* After his mild defense of marijuana in the national press in 1969 drew sharp criticism from many quarters, a relatively outspoken philosophy professor promised to be silent; his opinions were called dangerous to immature students.

Such inhibitions, characteristic of Costa Rican society in general, are due in part to the nation's small size. "One feels he is going to be seeing the same people all his life," explains a professor, "so he's usually careful not to offend them, especially if he's in any professional circle, which is sure to be small."

CONCLUSION

If any Costa Rican institution reveals the chasm between myth and reality—and the role myth can play both in lulling people into complacency and in challenging them to improve that reality—it is education.

According to the myth, the nation's school system is the basis of Costa Ricans' cherished democracy, peace, and stability. At the same time it is the road to individual and social progress. The tremendous increase in numbers of schools and students at all levels is a source of national pride. So is what is perceived as the high level of literacy and "culture."

Most of those who would puncture the myth wish these things were all true, but are only too aware of numerous contradictions and qualifications. Only by facing reality, they believe, can their society make the myth come true.

The present system of formal education does help instill widely shared values in children and thus helps preserve the status quo, but it is far less effective in promoting social change, partly because change is viewed as necessarily disruptive and even violent. Only slowly, in the face of a deep-seated preference for "liberal" education and professional white-collar jobs, is the system beginning to produce the technicians and skilled workers needed for economic development.

Formal education is certainly a major route to individual upward mobility. But many students, especially those from poor homes, drop out along the way, so that the system also operates as a screening and sifting process based largely on social class rather than on ability alone, and helps perpetuate the class system.

The quantitative revolution (which has included a reduction of this drop-out rate) is impressive, but resources—buildings, equipment, trained teachers, effective teaching methods, appropriate curricula—have not yet caught up with sheer numbers of students, especially at the high school and university levels. Although there is acute awareness of the need for a qualitative revolution, and some attempts and experiments are directed at just that, the centralized, hierarchical system is so firmly established, and help for the classroom teacher so inadequate, that little change may be anticipated in the near future. Mass education has meant a lowering of academic standards. But other deep-rooted cultural factors also work against academic rigor and intensive work in all fields: the desire to *quedar bien*, which makes criticism appear a personal injury; the tendency to take the word for the fact and the title for the content, and to skimp on actual effort; and the undue influence of political power on the naming of school personnel.

Like all human organizations, the system is open to charges of obsolescence and anachronism when it cannot or does not keep up with inevitable changes. Charges of disruption and radicalism directed at reformers are perhaps also to be expected. While each new administration announces sweeping plans for educational reform, the most likely possibility for fundamental change lies in experimental classrooms and teacher-training programs that will function as a leaven, gradually transforming programs and methods from within. The chief obstacles are the bureaucratic and political structure of which the educational system is firmly a part, and unquestioning belief in the myth itself.

High school students with the Declaration of Independence (Francisco González)

8

RELIGION

Nine out of ten Costa Ricans are at least nominal Catholics, but there are all degrees of belief and practice among them. Most Ticos neither observe nor expect rigid conformity to the rules and doctrines of the Roman Catholic Church as defined by the Vatican and the clergy. Theirs is often described as an "easy" or "lukewarm" Catholicism. They are proud of their tolerance in religion as in other areas, and look down on anything smacking of fanaticism.

The 1949 constitution, like its predecessors, recognizes Roman Catholicism as Costa Rica's national religion and provides for state contributions to the maintenance of "the Church." It also specifically permits "the free exercise within the Republic of other cults not opposed to universal morality or good customs."

Though far weaker and poorer than churches in many other Latin American countries, the Costa Rican Church is, in the absence of an army, the strongest traditional organized institution after the state. In his study of the Church and the labor movement, James Backer concluded that "how the Church reacts to economic, social, and political development can be important if not crucial in relation to the form of development that the Costa Rican society adopts."[1] Development in turn affects many aspects of religious belief and observance. Some practices associated with Catholicism have changed form and others have disappeared altogether. As a result, many believe that "Christianity as a moral and spiritual reality and the Church as a temporal and contemporary institution and structure are in crisis."[2] A veteran priest sees a decline in ethical values as well as in faith, and blames this decline on "the sudden advances of the last twenty years in technology and science that create expectations of creature comforts, such as TV and household appliances, which cannot be satisfied for the masses in an underdeveloped country."[3]

Religious "crises" have often been discerned before, and the influence of the Church has not declined steadily with modernization. It has, on the contrary, experienced ups and downs related to other trends in sociocultural history and to the happenstances of leadership. Even in colonial days religious leaders expressed concern about their flock.

THE COLONIAL PERIOD

Spain regarded the conversion of the Indians to Catholicism and the preservation of the faith among the colonists as an integral part of her mission in the New World, subordinate only to the quest for wealth and empire.[4] Costa Rica's clergy were named by the Crown and trained mostly in the seminaries of Nicaragua, Guatemala, and Mexico. Their early attempts to convert the Indians seldom involved force but were often naïve; for example, they considered the mere sight of a crucifix enough to convert the most stubborn heathen. Later missionaries often helped grow food, taught elementary reading and writing as well as basic Catholic doctrine, and sometimes served as judges. Because of these labors, as well as intermarriage between Indians and Spaniards, and the decreasing size and power of the indigenous population, most of the Indians who lived in the territory at the end of the sixteenth century practiced Catholicism to some degree, as their descendants do today.

In 1711, on a rare pastoral visit to the isolated colony, the Bishop of León was appalled by low mass attendance and irritated by failure to pay tithes. He ordered the colonists to build a chapel in each parish within six months under pain of excommunication, and forbade marriages and burials without prior payment of fees. When he found no change on a visit three years later, he decreed the excommunication of all rebellious and disobedient colonists, but the decree had no effect and was rescinded before long.

THE NINETEENTH CENTURY

Clergymen were very active in politics in the early years of the republic. Five of the nine members of the first governing junta, including the president, were priests. Says Ricardo Blanco Segura, "This is not surprising if we consider that the clergy were the nucleus of the educated elite of the era, as well as those the people most trusted, given the importance of religion in those years."[5] Despite this, and although the first constitution declared Catholicism the state religion, the Church remained poor and subordinate. The Pope did not grant Costa Rica her own bishopric until 1850; meanwhile both León and Rome generally remained aloof from the country's ecclesiastical matters.

The observations of Wagner and Scherzer, devout German Catholics, are

Early eighteenth-century colonial church at Orosi (Luis Ferrero)

especially interesting because some of them still hold true. In 1853 they found that

> the majority of Costa Ricans are good believing Catholics, customarily going to confession at least once a year; their belief is not fervent, however, and they go to church more from hereditary custom than from individual impulse. They are not intolerant, and the rich class is indifferent without caring at all about philosophy. They respect the ignorant and unlettered clergy, but accept neither Jesuits nor the intervention of priests in secular affairs. And above all, they do not want to give much money to the Church.[6]

LIBERALS VS. CATHOLICS

Toward the end of the century, Catholicism was tempered by currents of Freemasonry and liberalism among teachers and political leaders. By the 1880s such ideas—largely a result of foreign travel and the immigration of non-Catholic teachers and businessmen—had influenced most Costa Ricans with any pretensions to being "enlightened" or "modern," and a mild anti-clericalism had appeared. During that decade the government secularized cemeteries, permitted divorce, declared the separation of Church and state, and abolished religious instruction in public schools. In 1884 British-educated President Fernández expelled the Jesuits and denied admission to members of any religious order. When Bishop Thiel protested, he too was briefly exiled. Nonetheless, the state continued to accord the Church a special constitutional status and token subsidies, and one of the inaugural rites for each administration continued to be a ceremony in the Cathedral. And compared to their freethinking leaders, the populace remained staunchly Catholic, and otherwise thrifty *gamonales* donated money to build churches or buy stained glass and imported bells.

The confrontation of Bishop Thiel's Catholic Union Party and the Liberal Party in the early 1890s was the only serious conflict between clerical and secular power in Costa Rican history. But President José Joaquín Rodríguez' electoral manipulations kept the Catholic Party aligned with a weak presidential candidate. Thus, said a later president, he saved the country from "the bloody battles inevitably provoked by a clerical government."[7]

Most of Rodríguez' successors until 1940 were freethinkers, but not overtly anti-Church. Ricardo Jiménez was elected president three times in spite of campaign charges that he was an atheist. After Jiménez's 1909 victory, "the most recalcitrant Catholics felt very much at ease under the presidency of the atheist who knew how to maintain liberalism *a la costarricense,* that is, a balanced liberalism, extremely compliant with all religions and political tendencies."[8]

Anticlericalism among intellectuals and politicians, in turn, declined after President Calderón (1940–1944), a devout Catholic, worked with an intellectual archbishop, Victor Sanabria, as well as with Communist Party founder Manuel Mora, to institute his landmark social reforms. Against strong opposition he repealed the anti-Church laws of 1884, thus including religious education in the curricula of public primary schools and officially permitting Jesuits and orders of monks and nuns to enter the country—policies seldom challenged today.

THE CATHOLIC CHURCH TODAY

Catholicism still permeates Costa Rican culture. Perhaps 2,000 towns and villages are named for saints, and in many the patron saint's fiesta is the high point of the year. Nearly all Costa Ricans are baptized, married, and blessed before interment by Catholic priests. Crucifixes, saints' pictures, and religious calendars are prominent in nearly every home, bus, school, and government office, and in many cars and taxis. Simple shrines are common in public parks and along country roads; crosses mark places where travelers met death. News media give considerable coverage to church events, from Vatican Councils to parish fairs. Editors and columnists in the major newspapers often argue from an openly Catholic viewpoint, and feel no need to explain why. Politicians frequently attack or defend a program by citing papal encyclicals or "Christian principles." Before a new commercial or government building is opened, it is customarily blessed by a priest, as are many private homes, and even new fleets of taxis and buses.

Everyday speech is salted with phrases and proverbs out of Costa Rica's Spanish Catholic tradition. While visitors no longer announce themselves by shouting "Hail Purest Mary!" predictions, hopes, and appointments are still qualified with "God willing." Relatives and friends departing on a journey, or even an errand, are told to go with God, while a common reply to inquiries about one's health is "Fine, thank God." Thanks are often expressed "May God repay you."

Roman Catholicism is still the official religion. Far from abolishing religious education in primary schools, the National Liberation Party extended it to secondary schools. Women's suffrage also strengthened the Church's political position. In 1953 President Ulate knelt to dedicate the Republic to the Sacred Heart of Jesus. Presidents and cabinet ministers attend special masses on Labor Day (May 1) and other occasions. Each government agency has a patron saint, and many public buildings have chapels or shrines built by employees' donations. The Catholic marriage ceremony is the only religious one recognized by the state; non-Catholics who wish to be married by their own clergy must also be wed in a civil ceremony. (The civil ceremony alone is not recognized by the Church.)

In spite of its official status, the Church remains comparatively poor. Its portion of the central government's total budget is less than 0.01 per cent. The government pays the salaries of bishops, professors in Catholic schools, and teachers of religion in public schools, many of whom are priests. Church-owned land, however, is no longer exempt from taxes, and some priests complain that "the state takes away more from the Church than it gives." Local churches are financed almost entirely by their congregations, whose offerings and fund-raising events barely suffice, in most cases, to keep the church open and pay the priest. Parishioners contribute little, just as Wagner and Scherzer noted 125 years ago.

The Church as an organization is small as well as poor. Some 350 priests serve an estimated 1,100 churches. The country is organized into four dioceses, each headed by a bishop. Although the title of Archbishop accorded the Bishop of San José is mostly honorary, his views and personality influence the national church. About seven out of ten priests are diocesan, and are directly subordinate to their bishops. The rest belong to seven foreign religious orders, including Jesuits, and are answerable to the heads of these orders; the bishops' authority over them is limited largely to assignment to certain parishes. Most diocesan priests are Costa Ricans, while almost all "religious" priests, as Ticos call the others, are from Spain, the United States, Germany, and Italy.[9]

There is about one priest for every 5,000 Catholics. While this ratio is high for Latin America, priests complain that their small numbers help account for lukewarm Catholicism. This scarcity is felt most keenly in outlying areas. Some urban churches have more than one pastor, while in some rural areas, one priest must make the rounds of ten or fifteen churches, and Catholics in the remotest areas see a priest only a few times a year.

Although a seminary has trained Costa Rican youths for the priesthood since 1852, it has never attracted many students. Only three priests were graduated from the seven-year course in 1976, and none in 1978. Asked why, the Vicar General said, "The priesthood demands sacrifice, and our youths are not taught to lead lives of sacrifice. Today's worldly life, without spiritual emphasis in the home, explains the lack of dedication."

Nearly a thousand nuns do social work among the poor, run the women's prison, teach school, and work in hospitals. Organized into twenty-six congregations, nuns are far more numerous than in Panama, Nicaragua, and Honduras. About 57 percent are Ticas. A few peripheral communities are served exclusively by nuns, and in some communities where a priest comes only occasionally to perform Sunday mass, nuns baptize, visit homes, teach in primary and secondary school, and give communion. In 1979 the first lay deacons—married men over age thirty-five—were authorized to preach sermons, baptize, and give communion to the sick where priests are lacking.

Although neither rich nor overtly powerful, the Catholic Church has wide influence, both direct and indirect. It reaches many Ticos through sermons, religion classes in schools, catechism classes preceding first communion, radio stations, and the *Eco Católico*, which sells about 11,000 copies a week. Archbishop Sanabria created an Association of Educational Development and Social Action within the Church. One legacy is the vocational school system, originally established to keep shoeshine boys and other street urchins out of trouble. Taken over by the government in 1955, it still includes some priests as directors. A number of private high schools are run by Catholic priests and nuns, and many of their graduates, largely from the upper and upper-middle classes, become the nation's political and economic leaders.

THE CHURCH AND POLITICS

Sanabria was by no means the first Costa Rican clergyman to become involved in partisan politics, nor was he the last. Bishop Thiel and Padre Volio (the same General Volio mentioned in Chapter 2) were politicians as well as social reformers. Padre Benjamín Núñez has been extremely active in the PLN, as Minister of Labor, prime mover behind the party's declaration of social democratic ideology, ambassador to Israel, and labor organizer. Nonetheless, the 1949 constitution retained the provision that "neither clergy nor laymen may make political propaganda of any sort by invoking religious motives or by taking advantage of religious belief."

Clergymen have often disregarded this clause, particularly in relation to communism, and public reaction to their partisanship has been largely adverse. In 1966 some priests issued thinly veiled warnings from the pulpit that the faithful should not vote for "communistically-inclined" Daniel Oduber. In at least one village, when the priest expressed this opinion, many parishioners were so annoyed that they boycotted the patron saint's fiesta. When priests spoke out against the establishment of a Soviet embassy during Figueres' last administration, the President angrily told them to stick to saving souls. Political partisanship by the clergy is generally considered "an abuse of spiritual office."

THE CHURCH AND REFORM

The liturgical and social reforms spelled out under Pope John XXIII and by the 1968 conference of Latin American bishops in Medellín (CELAM) created sharp divisions among the Costa Rican Catholic clergy. Archbishop

Carlos Humberto Rodríguez Quirós, a former monk and a member of the old upper class, never identified himself with the social reformist position of Medellín. In office from 1960 to 1979, he emphasized religious observance, prayer, and ritual so strongly that many priests and laymen found him timid, passive, and anachronistic.

Most clerics who chafed at the former archbishop's conservatism adopted the "liberation theology" position, which combines the social Christian philosophy with nationalism and rejects both communism and economic dependency on industrialized countries. Monseñor Román Arrieta, chief advocate of this position, is now archbishop; as bishop of Tilarán he attracted many supporters, especially for his espousal of agrarian reform— but reform *a la tica*. While he promises to "let fresh air into the Church" and favors the Medellín guidelines for achieving a just society, he wants reforms tailored "to respond to our idiosyncrasy."

A marked contrast in religious and social philosophies between older and younger clergy, evident in the late 1960s, is far less distinct today. A few older priests still see their role as confined to church and rectory, to the redemption of "sinful, corrupt human nature" through "spiritual" means—mainly sermons, sacraments, and wise counsel. But, like most of their younger colleagues—who are more apt to wear jeans than cassocks—they are now likely to preach social justice as well as the traditional message of salvation.

This world view, one that avoids the older distinction between the wicked world and the pure Kingdom of God, is reflected in the Theological Institute of Central America, founded in 1971, and coordinated with the Ecumenical School of the Sciences of Religion at the National University. Priests, nuns, students, and laymen attend its annual courses, taught by university graduates, which emphasize greater community service and awareness of problems as well as participation in their solution. Its director says priests are obligated to arouse a social conscience among their parishioners, and an awareness of social problems as part of the problems of the nation as a whole.

Priests today find considerable support for this approach from their bishops. In late 1979 a collective pastoral letter from all the bishops, called "Evangelization and Social Reality," denounced development limited to the economy and advocated one that embraces political and moral factors, and especially wider participation, education, and respect for human dignity. It stresses the right of labor to organize and strike, and endorses cooperativism and agricultural communities. "In a society that values Christianity there must not be a single human being who lacks the necessary means to satisfy his fundamental needs."

Many priests today work to establish and support cooperatives, craft shops and markets, lay organizations and short courses to improve family life or to teach skills needed in the business world. Some are active in the labor movement, Scouts, reforestation, and agrarian reform.

Priests are still influential in small communities. A community development worker in a small town found that husbands objected to their wives' attending meetings unless the priest announced them from the pulpit. In many rural areas priests are admired for their learning and asked for advice on all manner of personal and community problems. On Sundays they may receive gifts of food, and farmers may bring them the "first fruits" of each harvest.

But even in rural areas, the recent educational attainments of many laypersons have apparently diminished priests' relative influence; priests are less often asked to head local community development associations, antialcoholism campaigns, or even chapters of religious organizations. Better communication with the more secularized and freethinking capital may also help account for the clergy's decline in status, as do growing contact with other countries and increasing cultural diversity within Costa Rica itself.

CATHOLICISM, TICO STYLE: EDUCATION AND OBSERVANCE

"Ticos are good and in a sense even devout Catholics. They observe religious practices as the structure demands," says Padre Alfaro. "But this does not mean the same thing as faith. There is a great lack of conviction and commitment, of living faith. In this sense Ticos are definitely lukewarm Catholics." For over a hundred years observers have noted this easy and nonrestrictive Catholicism. A Venezuelan told us, "In my country, when one says he is a Catholic or a communist, he *really* is. Not here."

Although this relative indifference has often been attributed to "modernization," there has been no consistent trend toward secularization and greater anticlericalism. In some respects, indeed, the Church has gained rather than lost influence since 1940. Catholic doctrine, for instance, has been part of the school curriculum since the Calderón administration. About 80 percent of public elementary schoolchildren receive two catechism lessons a week from state-paid teachers trained in a state institute, or by priests, monks, or nuns. In remote schools the regular teacher assumes this responsibility. Only a note from parents will excuse a child from these lessons, and generally the small minority of Protestant children are the only ones absent. Most children also receive about three months of special catechism in their parish church to prepare for their first confession and communion some time between ages six and nine. Local women instruct the children in groups, and the parish priest periodically reviews their progress.[10] Mothers, and often grandmothers, who have already taught children a few prayers, usually help them memorize the catechism. Still, of the 90 or 95 percent of all Costa Ricans who are baptized in the Catholic Church, only about half go on to their first communion.[11] Parents of those who do not receive the sacrament often explain that they cannot afford the appropriate clothes for their children.

Parents, especially fathers, take little interest in their children's religious instruction after first communion, and, says a children's court judge, religious education is often sterile, cut off from the rest of life.[12] Nonetheless, many, including ministers of education, consider it essential to the formation of "the Costa Rican character."

Since 1965 thousands of adults have attended the Church-sponsored *Cursillos de Cristiandad*. The intensive three-day courses begin with a short retreat for prayer and meditation, and include religious discussions, emotional sermons, doctrinal instruction, and an effort to create ties of love among all involved. They are taught by several thousand lay teachers who go all over the country to teach and to help priests with mass, with personal problems of local Catholics, and with social and economic programs. Many who have attended report that the courses help Catholics to understand and practice their faith, rather than simply going through the motions for reasons of tradition, conformity, or emotion unrelated to knowledge of doctrine.[13]

Many people believe that attendance at mass is greater than it was a few decades ago. A former teacher at the seminary disagrees:

> It seems greater simply because there are many more Costa Ricans! Also, there are many more opportunities to attend; in my village, I say three masses on Sunday and one late Saturday afternoon. But ten years ago I directed a team that surveyed the problem in many communities. They found that on a typical Sunday or other day of obligation, about 25 percent of Catholics attend mass. I do not think it is any different in 1976.[14]

Urbanites attend mass somewhat less often than villagers, in part, perhaps, because the greater anonymity of the city makes it easier to escape social pressures. Many rural districts have a small chapel built by local residents with profits from fairs. Mass may be said there no oftener than once a month. But many walk up to an hour to attend mass in their canton's principal district. And when the priest makes one of his rare visits to the chapel, *campesinos* may arrive from their remote farms several hours before him.

Lowland regions—where, unlike the highlands, few communities are named for saints—have always had comparatively few clerics, though

San Isidro de Heredia church after Sunday Mass (Mavis Biesanz)

Spanish religious orders have recently sent a number of priests to these areas. Mass in some lowland communities is celebrated only once a year if at all. Families and neighbors may pray among themselves, but the priest has apparently never been an important part of lowlanders' religious lives. Even where there are permanent priests and frequent masses, lowlanders attend mass less often than *Meseta*-dwellers.[15] Observes a *Meseta* businessman who has moved to Guanacaste, "On the *Meseta* the first thing people want in a village is a church. In Guanacaste, it's a school."

Women are generally regarded as more "spiritual" than men, and are still in the majority at mass, especially in urban areas. At least since the mid-nineteenth century, the attachment of males to the Church has been so weak that many men, even in the generally devout rural working class, do not enter a church after childhood except in their wedding finery and their burial caskets. Many Ticos report greater participation in church rites among rural and urban men since Sanabria's support of the Labor Code, and even more since the reforms of Vatican II and the *cursillos*.

Elderly people attend mass frequently, often daily when there is a resident priest. Male adolescents and youths are the least likely of any age group to attend at all. Few Costa Ricans other than elderly people and young girls confess or take communion more than once a year, the minimum demanded by the Church, and many men who consider themselves good Catholics never do. Fear of being scolded appears to account for much of the aversion to confession. And many men say confession would be hypocritical, because they would inevitably commit the same sins again before long. "It's better to get your sins forgiven once and for all just before the umbrella folds up [on one's deathbed]," one man remarked.

A generation or two ago, family prayers were commonly said upon arising, grace before each meal, the Angelus at six in the evening, and a Rosary before retiring. Prayer is now mostly an individual matter. When family members do say a prayer together it is normally an evening Rosary, perhaps a weekly rite led by an elderly grandmother, or a special festive one with friends and neighbors invited, on someone's "name day" or the day of a favorite saint, or on February 2, when the Pope blesses all nativity creches.

The marked decline in participation in Holy Week rites is often cited as clear evidence of secularization. In the 1940s, processions were long, solemn, and elaborate. Everything was closed up tight from Wednesday afternoon until Saturday. People stocked up on canned goods and baked bread ahead of time, as markets were closed and strict fasting rules restricted cooking. No cars or buses moved from Wednesday noon of Holy Week until Saturday morning; the few errant drivers were the targets of shouts and even of stones. In many towns and villages, processions still attract numerous spectators, whose colorful clothes are a far cry from the somber black of three decades ago. But for many Ticos, Holy Week is now one long binge. Many urbanites go to the beaches or travel abroad. Businesses may close for the entire week. Cars move freely, though few buses operate on Thursday and Friday. Many older Ticos lament this change, saying Holy Week is almost a carnival now, with drinking and dancing in homes and at beach resorts.

A girl's First Communion

Women have traditionally helped poor families in their parishes through church-connected charities such as the society of San Vicente de Pablo. Men have joined fraternities which pay for the privilege of carrying images in religious processions. The large Church-directed Acción Católica, which was charged with religious education for several decades and accused of being reactionary because of its subordination to the Church, has given way to a number of specialized groups of laymen called "apostolic organizations," chief of which are the Christian Family Movement and the Legion of Mary.

CATHOLICISM, TICO STYLE: BELIEFS AND ATTITUDES

Many Ticos, especially those who have taken short courses and read the Bible, fulfill what they see as their obligations to the Church out of deep faith and commitment. The religious behavior of others is governed by a more personal belief in God, or by a desire for social acceptance, emotional satisfaction, or the fulfillment of wishes for health and material things, by attitudes toward particular priests, by the deeply ingrained insistence of Costa Ricans on freedom to choose what to believe and do, or by several of these.

The range of combinations of belief and doubt, observance and neglect, among Costa Ricans is wide. A Catholic philosopher, Luís Barahona

Jiménez, sees superficial and easy religiosity as part of the Tico life style, in which the predominant note is *la gana*—what one *feels* like doing:

> Only a few people trustingly await the resurrection and the life promised by Christ. For the rest, existence goes along carried by the simple gravity of letting themselves live, or of "going on living," or "getting along" as we hear people say.[16]

Belief in God is far more general than regular religious observance. Until recently few Costa Ricans—even those who rarely if ever attend mass and who question many doctrines—have admitted to disbelief in God. The Catholic majority scorn professed atheists far more than they do Protestants. Just as in many societies it is safer to practice adultery than to advocate it, in Costa Rica it is safer to be silent than to express any doubt about the existence of God the Father and Creator. In San Isidro, declared a twenty-six-year-old high school graduate, "The old women would throw holy water on anyone who did."

Costa Ricans of all social levels, says Barahona, "accept the will of God in such a way that it is pagan fatalism more than Christian resignation."[17] An upper-middle-class woman expresses a common belief: "Nothing happens without the will of God—absolutely nothing." If plans go wrong—if one misses a plane, for example—there is some reason only God knows, and disappointment should be shrugged off. Illness brings out both the faith and fatalism of Ticos. When sickness strikes a person or a member of his or her family, one is likely to make a "promise" of some act to be carried out upon recovery. If death occurs, however, it is due to the will of God. No one dies until his or her appointed time. "When God calls you to die, no one can save you," said a farm overseer, and a *peón* nodded strong agreement.

Some say that the Church has played on their fatalism to encourage *campesinos* not to migrate to the city. According to one political scientist, the priest director of Catholic Action, organized in the 1940s, declared that one of its main goals was to stop the exodus from the countryside that was encouraged by urban wages more than double those of rural *peones*. If to do so priests stressed the will of God, they also appealed to the peasants' self-esteem. "Priests were told to emphasize that agriculture was the root of national wealth, that the poor life of the *campesino* was honest, moral, and preferable to the corrupt life of the capital." Sermons cast scorn on vice-ridden city life and the immorality of the rich, while lauding rural virtues.

Belief in God and acceptance of God's will are not highly correlated with religious practice. Rather, a desire for social acceptance, and its corollary, fear of criticism, account for much religious observance, just as Wagner and Scherzer noted in 1853. Ticos often observe that religion is important "because it makes people behave." Powell's generalization about two rural communities a quarter of a century ago still appears to apply, especially in small towns and villages:

> Possibly more important than the fear of being condemned to hell as a form of social control, are the customs themselves, which exert considerable pressure

on the people to conform, and a number of people adhere to the regulations of the church not so much out of conviction, as for fear of what others will think and say.[18]

He found this social control function of the Church more effective in a settled peasant community than in one where most worked as *peones*.

Social pressures impel many otherwise indifferent Ticos to baptize their children, to help them prepare for first communion, and to observe Catholic wedding and funeral customs. In any social class women, in particular, can lose status by failing to do any of these things. Many men, by contrast, observe a reverse kind of conformity; they are afraid of appearing too devout and being branded as strange and perhaps effeminate, or even hypocritical. Says a sixty-year-old foreman, "I'm suspicious of a man who goes to mass every day; he's probably the biggest sinner of all." At Sunday mass in most churches, about half the men stand at the rear or even just outside the door, while women and children occupy the half-empty pews. Such voluntary segregation is diminishing, however, as men become more involved in church-related activities.

Besides social approval and freedom from criticism, many Ticos seek emotional satisfaction, including a sense of security, in church. In the early 1940s people said they went to mass for "satisfaction," "out of habit," and "to be with God."[19] Three decades later, when we inquired why people went to mass, they were likely to answer "It's a sin not to," and to add that God, while merciful, punishes sins in this life as well as the next. A young rural *peón* told us he attends mass, confesses, and takes communion so he will "be safe in case anything happens to me."

Some seem to find the beauty and ritual of the mass emotionally satisfying, though they may not express this feeling in so many words. Observance rises dramatically after a "mission" or revival featuring emotional, exciting sermons. The recent upsurge of the charismatic movement, called Spiritual Renovation, has a largely emotional basis. Several parishes are centers of charismatic masses, which feature "the gifts of the spirit," speaking in tongues, prophesying, clapping, swaying, and shouting amens and alleluias. Archbishop Rodríguez was wary at first, but early in 1976 he gave priests permission to conduct such services and meet with interested Catholics. At that time some 10,000 Catholics identified themselves with this movement[20] and, as in many countries, it continues to grow and to gain increased acceptance from the Church hierarchy. In 1979 Archbishop Arrieta and President Carazo attended a mass in the National Stadium dedicated to the Holy Spirit.

Personalismo is important in religion as in politics; many say they go to church because they like the priest, or stay away because they do not. The Tico, says Padre Alfaro, accepts a priest not out of sheer faith or respect for his status so much as because he is a *persona*, which means he talks well, expresses himself in a way they can understand and sympathize with, is well informed on national and international affairs, has the interests of the community at heart, and thus commands respect.

But even a respected priest can rarely dictate to Costa Ricans. Says Padre

Alfaro: "In my twenty-nine years as a priest, I have dealt with university students, young people, old people, rich, poor, intellectuals—all kinds. I have never yet found a group that says 'Yes' simply because one is a priest."

So strong is the Costa Rican insistence on freedom that Church doctrines as well as individual priests are subject to question rather than automatic acceptance. Although some Ticos are fervent Catholics who firmly believe every part of the creed and speak proudly of their "blind faith," many more are likely to boast "I am a Catholic, but not a fanatic." Even practicing Catholics may reject some basic doctrines. We met many Ticos who call themselves *muy católicos* but do not believe in hell. Heaven, yes. But most rewards, they say, are here on earth, achieved through morality and conformity. Still others find Catholicism so easy that they believe *"El que peca y reza empata"* (One who sins and prays, balances his accounts). Many say that while the laws of the Church are strict, God is merciful. Ticos who have remarried after divorce may continue to attend mass in spite of the fact that they are not allowed to take communion. Many otherwise *muy católico* Ticos say priests cannot dictate to them how many children they should have. If the *padre* wants me to have more, let *him* feed them," some say. Many Catholics of both sexes express more concern with their direct relationship to God and to other persons than with the wishes of their priests.

CATHOLICISM, TICO STYLE: THE CULT OF THE SAINTS

In keeping with the pragmatic bent of their Catholicism, many Ticos say they pray most often when they want something special. In a crisis, Ticos, like many other Latin Americans, often pray to a favorite saint who they believe has special attributes and powers, sometimes very specific ones—for instance, to help the petitioner conceive a child, find a lost object, or pass an exam. The *santo* may be a canonized saint or, less commonly, some aspect of God such as the Sacred Host or the Sacred Heart of Jesus. Or he or she may be an uncanonized "popular saint" like two deceased Costa Ricans, who many believe have miraculous powers: Marisa died of a brain tumor in 1954 at age twelve in Heredia after she dedicated her suffering to the Lord in return for her father's reconversion from Protestantism. Dr. Ricardo Moreno Cañas was an exceptionally skilled surgeon and kindly physician who was murdered, possibly for political reasons, in 1938. Believers report visions and cures associated with them.

The cult of the saints unites nearly all Catholics, from those who rarely attend mass to those who know that saints, according to Church doctrine, are to be prayed to as intermediaries between their supplicants and God rather than as powerful in their own right. One usually becomes a devotee of a saint recommended by a friend or relative, often a parent. A picture or statue of the saint above one's bed or in a corner of the *sala* and a smaller image on a medallion or card carried on one's person or on the dashboard of a car are believed to bring luck. Some devotees pray before an image of the saint at home or in church, often lighting a candle before it as a "down payment" on a favor desired or as recompense for one granted. If the favor is urgently desired—recovery from an illness, for example—the believer may make a *promesa* or vow—usually not just to "be good" or to give up some vice, but to carry out some devotional act. A woman or girl in distress, for example, may vow to wear the brown robe of the Virgin of Carmen for a certain number of months or years, and to observe the ban on drinking and dancing this promise involves. When a San Isidro youth barely avoided being killed by a truck, he promised his favorite saint he would keep his hair uncut so as to act as Simon the Cyrenian in the following year's Holy Week processions. His shoulder-length locks were (at least in 1968) discordant with his *peón's* garb, but no one teased him. When a child in the same village was wounded in a gun accident, the twelve-year-old boy who had pulled the trigger rushed to the local church to light candles for the victim's recovery, while the sixteen-year-old owner of the gun started the twenty-mile walk to the Cartago Basilica—a common *promesa*—as soon as the boy had been sent to the hospital.

Whatever the favor desired, of whichever saint, nothing will happen unless the petitioner has faith. If the promise does not work, then lack of faith or the fact that one asked too late is to blame.

Acknowledgments of the power of a particular saint are paid for and appear frequently in *La Nación*. During the 1970s an especially popular prayer indicated the growing appeal of the charismatic movement, for it thanked the Holy Ghost and urged devotion to him.

Why is the cult of the saints so strong and widespread? Saints seem closer and more personal than God. Among 373 consecutive citations in the *Eco Católico* noted in a 1942 study, God was specifically thanked only twice. The more "human" a saint, the more devotion he or she appeared to receive.[21] Analysis of citations in the same popular weekly twenty-six years later suggested that this had changed little. Editors, anxious to clarify Catholic doctrine, insist that thanks be worded, for example, "Fulana de Tal gives thanks to Almighty God for a favor granted through the intercession of Saint Martin." But God alone is seldom cited, and one concludes, from listening to Costa Ricans talk, that the *santo* remains the object of greater devotion. God, though frequently described as "the greatest of all," is thought of in terms of power, punishment, and fear rather than His more "human" aspects of love and mercy.

Even those who are aware of the Church doctrine that they should really pray to God, asking the saints only to intercede with Him on their behalf, prefer an intermediary. Says a village woman in her sixties:

> Suppose you ask a favor of the *mandador* [overseer]. He can ask the *patrón* if it's all right, but it's up to the *patrón*. Actually, the Virgin is the best saint to pray to, since she's the Mother of God, and so her Son will listen to her. Don't you, when you lack the desire to do something, go ahead and do it anyway if your mother asks you to?

As this comment illustrates, another source of saint worship may lie in a deep-seated cultural pattern, *la palanca*. Just as Ticos use *palanca* or "pull" to get something mundane accomplished—going to a friend in a government office for a job or a way around bureaucratic red tape, for example,—so they seek a saint who has special "pull" with God.[22]

María Bozzoli de Wille believes that Costa Ricans are not as superstitious as many other Latin Americans, and certainly they are less so than they were a generation or two ago. But many do believe that certain people have "psychic," "magical," or "supernatural" powers for good and evil. The accompanying beliefs and practices are of mixed aboriginal, Spanish, and (in Limón) African origin.

The medico-magic called *curanderismo* (curing) is the main Indian legacy. Their *sukias* (shamans) were chosen very young by older *sukias*, often their own fathers, to be trained in the use of herbs, vines, and chants, each for treating a specific ailment. Many non-Indian *curanderos* still practice their art, based largely on the use of herbs, but also on prayers to saints, canonized or not. "People tell me the *curanderos* know everything and urge me to go to one," says an ulcer patient. "But I am afraid to because the priest would not give me absolution." Diviners who read the future with cards or by palmistry, psychics, and spiritists merge into the amorphous category of *brujos* or witches who specialize in casting evil spells and removing them from clients harmed by other *brujos*.

Witchcraft, like the other practices, is not an integral part of contemporary culture, for there is a great deal of confusion about what to call different kinds of practitioners, and relatively few Ticos have dealt with any. But some communities, notably Escazú, are famed as centers of such phenomena. Bozzoli de Wille and her students studied the village and found that within a radius of no more than ten blocks from the central plaza in each direction were a fortuneteller, six witches (three of each sex), a maker of home remedies, and two "mystics." They have clients from all over the country and even from abroad.[23]

To what extent do Ticos believe in the occult? In this as in other things they tend to be fence-sitters, says Bozzoli de Wille. Just as their speech is heavily qualified with "¿Quien sabe?" "maybe," and "more or less," their consensus on witchcraft is "Probably it's true, probably not." There are things one cannot explain, and the safest policy is "*No creer ni dejar de creer*" (neither believe nor cease to believe). Some believe in a particular kind of witchcraft, others in a different occult practice. Almost anyone can tell you where to find a practitioner for a specific problem, ranging from skin diseases and depression to unrequited love or the desire to harm an enemy or a faithless lover.

Clients of psychics, witches, and *curanderos* come from all walks of life and all social categories, and include many devout Catholics. They often prefer to consult a practitioner outside their home community lest people gossip that they have some problem or want to harm someone. The same person may try several kinds of possible help. "A wife worried because her husband has a concubine may go to a witch, a cartomancer, a spiritist, or a priest, but does not consider all these to be in the same category nor to give the same kind of help," says Bozzoli de Wille. Going to any of the first three is regarded by the Church as a sin requiring confession and absolution.

Evil magic is believed to bring physical or mental illness, financial ruin, and other serious misfortunes. The *aporte*, a buried substance or mixture, is considered the most powerful and dangerous magic of all. Often it is a jar containing

> a disorderly and disagreeable mixture of organic materials from the human body and from food—e.g., hair, blood, bone, meat, semen, feathers, beans, cemetery dirt, cemetery flowers. These things spoil and smell bad. As long as the *aporte* is buried, the harm stays.[24]

Some Ticos routinely exercise preventive "magic" to ward off such evil. They may burn incense in the house on Tuesdays and Fridays, when witches are supposed to be most active. They may place a lithographed prayer to Saint Dimas in the window, asking him to protect the house from "sorcerous women and traitorous men." Because dirt is associated with evil magic, water works as countermagic. If one notices anything unusual around the house, especially near the entrance, one washes the floor at once. A glass of water in the bedroom wards off illness and burglars. Preventive magic may also be carried on the person—certain jewels or medals, crosses or other religious objects, special preparations of herbs and seeds, or papers inscribed with certain formulas. If an enemy has succeeded in casting an evil spell, one may go to a witch for countermagic or ask a priest to exorcise the spell from the house or victim. Like favors from saints or remedies from a *curandero*, countermagic is said to work only if the victim has faith; thus if it fails it is his or her own fault.

The fear of *maleficios* or evil spells reflects the proverbial mutual distrust among Ticos, as it appears to do in many other societies. Of more than 100 clients interviewed, Bozzoli de Wille found that all claimed to be victims rather than aggressors, and that those who take witchcraft most seriously are people who constantly have problems finding work or losing jobs or money or lovers, or have an incurable illness or frequent misfortune. Some go from one practitioner to another and attribute all their problems to evil spells worked by enemies.[25]

Thus they explain failure or misfortune by blaming it on envy.[26] "There are people who will make friends with you just to get an item of clothing, a bit of your hair, or a photo; but you must be careful because it can be used for black magic by a jealous person," says the wife of a prosperous coffee planter in a *Meseta* village.

One can avoid exciting such envy and evil thoughts by being humble, discreet, and modest. Practitioners in turn are controlled to some extent by the belief that if they use their talents for evil ends, they will be punished.

In analyzing the function of such practitioners, Bozzoli de Wille comments:

> the witches' interpretation of *maleficio* may be regarded as an unconscious translation of social and personal disorder as dirt, for which metaphorical cleanliness is then prescribed. Assurance of defense, protection, and prevention will make a person more secure and able to achieve harmony with the surrounding social milieu. Again, "rationally" the witch has condensed a com-

plex personal and social situation into a more compact and simple formula for easier treatment.[27]

Practitioners, then, "reduce anxiety, restore tranquility and cure some psychosomatic ailments."[28]

PROTESTANTISM

From the staid old Episcopal Church, through many proselytizing missions and a Jewish synagogue, right up to today's Krishna Consciousness people and Children of God passing out pamphlets on the street, Costa Rica has more or less tolerated other religions for over a century. Most significantly, it has become a center for training Protestant missionaries for all of Latin America. European and North American Protestants played important roles in commerce, industry, and education from about the time the coffee trade began to flourish.[29] Liberalism and anticlericalism paved the way for the free exercise of alternative religions, but only in recent decades has the number of non-Catholics increased significantly.

The government, as we saw, had to intervene in the burial of a Protestant in the 1830s; about 1850 it provided a "foreigners' cemetery" and promised Protestants support if Catholic clergy or laymen should physically attack them when they built a church. The Church of the Good Shepherd, built in the same spot in downtown San José where an Episcopal congregation still worships, aroused little hostility, because it was not a "mission" or proselytizing church and was meant to serve non-Ticos who had settled in the country. Nor were the Episcopal, Baptist, and Methodist churches of the West Indian immigrants seen as a threat; their members were considered alien and different, but safely isolated in their enclave on the Atlantic.

This tolerance was severely tested when foreigners came to "Christianize" Costa Ricans. Catholic clergy and many laymen fiercely resented the Protestant missionaries, who began to arrive in 1891. Early missionaries, members of the fundamentalist and conservative Central American Mission, "saw the local Catholic population as legitimate objects for conversion, as far from the true Christian faith as tribesmen in the interior of Africa. Latin American Catholicism was condemned as utterly debased and idolatrous.' "[30]

The missionaries' aggressive tactics aroused resentment that erupted in stoning and other incidents. Bishops instructed priests to preach against the dangers of listening to the missionaries, and to strengthen veneration of the Virgin Mary, under attack from the newcomers, by promoting religious festivals.[31] Some priests threatened to excommunicate those who helped the missionaries in any way, such as renting houses to them. Although the government refused to expel them, by 1910 it had prohibited public preaching, advertising of meetings, and establishment of Protestant schools. In 1912 missionaries could claim a total of only 150 baptized converts, fewer than in any other Central American country.

But by 1963, encouraged by Pope John XXIII's reforms and by the conciliatory efforts of local Episcopal priests, the *Eco Católico* had begun to refer to Protestants not as heretics but as "separated brothers." Missionaries in turn now emphasized the virtues of the Protestant position rather than the defects of Catholicism, and most no longer used "Christian" and "Protestant" as synonyms. Catholics and Protestants joined forces in selling Bibles. Priests lectured at the Protestant seminary and language school; missionaries wrote occasional articles for the *Eco Católico*. Catholics and Protestants, clergymen and laymen, joined in social action such as prison reform and the Goodwill Caravans that brought medical, dental, agricultural, and educational aid to poor rural areas, and dispensed information on family planning. While signs (printed by the Catholic Church) saying "We do not accept Protestant propaganda" could be seen in many windows as late as 1969, they are rare today.

In 1974 about 4.6 percent of the population was Protestant, a dramatic growth in numbers in a short time. The increase from 22,800 in 1956 to almost 87,000 in 1974 was far ahead of general population increase.[32]

Like most aspects of social structure and culture, the evangelical movement has felt the impact of nationalism. In the mid-1960s the process of giving preference to Costa Ricans for mission-related jobs began within the Latin American Mission. Although much financial support still comes from the United States and Canada, administration is now based in Latin America. In 1971, the Latin America Mission was restructured to give birth to CLAME, a federation of ministries that represent the former departments of the Mission. The member entities of CLAME, rather than the foreign missionaries, now decide where the money goes and how things are to be run.

Geographic mobility and rapid social change make some Costa Rican Catholics open to conversion. When rural migrants move to San José (which, apart from the West Indians of Limón, has the highest proportion of Protestants), they feel that conversion brings less risk to their status.[33] Converts come mostly from the lower class, whose members, says Clifton Holland, a sociologist and missionary, "feel threatened by the relativity of contemporary life. They look for a sense of security in the modern world, and some find it in the evangelical churches."[34] Few upper-class Ticos become Protestants; they are typically more satisfied with things as they are, and Ticos of any class have a more secure social status as nominal Catholics or freethinkers than they would as Protestants.

Class and migration, however, are only predisposing influences, as is the more tolerant climate of today's culture. An Episcopal pastor believes most converts were probably lukewarm or nominal Catholics, and were repulsed from Catholicism by the impersonality of most churches. Many converts report a greater sense of community in their new congregations than in the Catholic Church. Members worship together frequently, participate more freely in the service, have a voice in making congregational decisions, and develop group solidarity, thanks in part to their small numbers.[35] A pastor, often a licensed lay preacher, is usually present at the frequent services and demonstrates his personal concern for each member of his flock with an appeal that usually stresses the promise of "God's love and happiness" rather than the threat of hell and punishment.[36]

Some Costa Ricans attracted to Protestantism remain fence-sitters because conversion would disrupt many of their social relationships. Some may listen to Protestant radio programs, but if they attend a church, it is the Catholic mass. Others sometimes attend mass, sometimes Protestant services. One of these, an elderly flower vendor, was asked about her religious affiliation. She replied, "I believe in God in heaven and pray to Him." Such fence-sitting often seems to be a way of avoiding possible conflict within the family. But when one member of a family, especially a parent, becomes a Protestant, others commonly follow suit, and are apt to pray together at home far more often than do most Catholic families. Even if other family members do not convert, religious differences seldom cause serious family problems, nor are converts ostracized by Catholic friends. They are, however, likely to see much less of them as they become active in the affairs of their new church, form new attachments there and, very probably, give up drinking—a mainstay of many friendships among Catholic males.

Many converts, and especially their children, rise in socioeconomic status. Says Holland:

> Max Weber's thesis of the Protestant ethic is valid here. Once they are converted, they are more thrifty and responsible, and more conscious of community problems. They drink less, using their money to take care of their children, to feed and educate them better.[37]

In his 1948 study, Norris found smaller class differences among Protestants than among Catholics and saw Protestantism as a vehicle for upward social mobility for these reasons: stress on work, thrift, and perseverance; discouragement of costly "vices" such as drinking, smoking, dancing, and gambling; instilling of action orientation through services in which members of the congregation take much of the initiative—for instance, giving testimonials in church services and prayer meetings; and emphasis on mutual aid among the members of the congregation.[38]

Robert L. Millett sees the greatest impact of Protestant missions on Costa Rica society as follows:

> Contact and competition with Protestants has helped produce the increased Catholic interest in Biblical studies and social action. The main effect of Costa Rican Protestants upon the Catholic Church has probably been to act as something of a catalyst, helping to bring about internal changes without actually participating in them. By offering an increasingly respectable alternative to Catholicism, they have brought about a measure of reexamination and renewal within the Catholic Church. Many leaders of both faiths now admit this privately and some Protestant leaders even concede that their main mission in the future may be to encourage a genuine and deeper Christian commitment among those in the Catholic Church.[39]

CONCLUSION

Their faith may be no less important to the Catholic majority of Ticos than in any past era. If priests complain that "materialism" is now greater than Catholic devotion, it may be countered that Catholicism was never very strong, at least by priests' standards, in Costa Rica. Secular aspects of the religious *turno*, the procession, and even of the mass are still enjoyed by many, though they are perhaps less appreciated today than in the past, when such diversions had fewer rivals. Popular tolerance of the non-Catholic minority and support of ecumenism are generally high, but then religious bigotry was never as pronounced as in many other societies, and Catholic Ticos have long stressed their freedom to believe and practice whatever they wish.

The Catholic Church's adoption of such Protestant practices as Bible study and its increasing commitment to social action may, in fact, have strengthened its position in Costa Rica. Increased literacy and a slowly growing interest in reading and study, moreover, have helped stimulate men's attendance at mass as well as doctrinal study groups involving both sexes. The Catholic Church, though long the official church of Costa Rica, has never been the strong economic and political force that it has been elsewhere in Latin America. But the Church is likely to retain at least a moderate hold over the great majority of Costa Ricans for some time to come. It will thus influence both the direction and the rate of changes in their way of life.

Traditional "Meeting of the Saints" in San Ramón (Miguel Salguero)

9
LEISURE AND THE ARTS

Work and leisure are sharply separated in the minds of Costa Ricans. Except for landowning peasants and creative professionals and artisans, most seem to regard work as an unpleasant though necessary means of earning a living, rather than as good in itself. Nor do Ticos feel compulsive about leisure-time activities, which need not be "constructive" (as many Americans, for example, think they should). They laugh about time they spend aimlessly as *matando la culebra*—killing the snake, a classic explanation banana *peones* once used when irate foremen asked what they had been doing in the jungle.

With a short school day, a two-hour noonday break, and a five-day week (often cut short on Friday afternoons) in many kinds of work, and numerous holidays, as well as unemployment and underemployment, leisure time is abundant for many Costa Ricans, and what to do with it is often a problem. Small-town young people complain most often of boredom, and say their communities are *muy tristes* (very melancholy). On a trip to five small communities in 1977 with Minister of Planning Oscar Arias Sánchez, we noted that one unfailingly urgent request was for recreational and "cultural" facilities—sports grounds, a community hall, a library—"to keep our young people from leaving for the city."

Diversions are usually shared, solitude abhorred. Costa Ricans prefer quiet homes and neighborhoods but enjoy crowds and noise away from home. One of the highest recommendations of a beach resort or night spot is that "everyone goes there." A radio or tape player is taken on every picnic, and juke boxes and orchestras are almost deafening.

RECREATION IN THE PAST

During most of the colonial period and well into the twentieth century, Ticos spent their free time mostly with family members and neighbors, who gathered on wide verandas or around stoves after an early supper to chat and tell stories. Nineteenth-century literature paints a scene of hard work punctuated by wholesome and abundant festivity and merrymaking. Upper class families exchanged invitations to evenings of parlor games, poetry recitals, skits, and singing. On Sundays they often rode out into the country-side on horseback or in oxcarts for a picnic lunch. In January many retired to their *fincas* or took the eight-day oxcart journey down to Puntarenas, where they waited out the dusty months of the highlands' dry season. After the Pacific railroad was completed in 1910, urbanites who could afford only a brief vacation also converged on "the port."

As is still true today, the local *pulpería* (often with a pool table) was the daily social center for village men, who gathered to drink and gossip after work and on Sundays. Their wives were restricted to family and church and occasional neighborly visits in one another's homes or on the street. The week's high point for many *campesinos* was the ride into town to attend

Coffee pickers enjoying a rest period (Mavis Biesanz)

Sunday mass, stroll around, shop for the week's needs, flirt, and chat. Again, the women often stayed home, but they did join in the coffee harvest, which was even more of an occasion for gossip, flirting, and joking than it is now, when so many other diversions are available.

Larger towns boasted a small band of brass and woodwinds. People of all ages and social classes gathered at concerts at the central park on Sunday mornings and several evenings a week; for the young these *retretas* were important occasions for courtship.

Wagner and Scherzer observed that the most "powerful passion of neo-Hispanic people" was gambling, and that men and boys of all social classes gathered to bet on their favorites at the weekly cockfight.[1] Like liquor, tobacco, and fireworks, cockfights were a government monopoly.

Church fairs and annual fiestas, usually on the day of a town's patron saint, were announced by rockets before dawn and concluded with dancing and fireworks after dark. In between there was much eating, drinking, gambling, and bull-baiting, as well as a mass. Religious processions, though generally solemn, also provided a welcome change from daily routine.

As the coffee economy increased the complexity of their society, Ticos' diversions varied according to class, age, and sex. San José remained a large village where few were strangers to one another, but the upper class held exclusive dances, and admission to the performances of touring artists was beyond the means of many *josefinos*. After the National Theater—a "jewel in a mudhole" according to one visitor—was opened in 1897, the elite danced on the orchestra floor, raised to stage level; many girls made their bows to *la sociedad* at these balls.

The upper class could also afford elegant clothing, imported wines, fine horses, foreign travel, and vacation farms. But residents of small towns and villages—encouraged by their priests—scorned the "bad influences" of the capital and praised the sobriety and tranquility of their own lives. Some sighed, then as now, that they were not merely tranquil but *triste*.

As population and occupational specialization increase and transportation improves—in Costa Rica as in other developing societies—identification with community and family tends to decline, and diversions become more abundant, more commercial, more avidly sought, and less easily controlled by family and neighbors. Individual tastes become more decisive, and spectator sports more popular. It becomes relatively easy to escape into the anonymity of other towns and to find cinemas, restaurants, dance spots, clubs, bars, and sports events that fit many tastes and pocketbooks. As women and adolescents gain more liberty, family members increasingly spend their leisure time apart, usually with friends.[2] Television may bring them together for several hours each evening, but affords much less interaction than did the parlor, veranda, and kitchen of yesteryear. By bus, plane, car, and train Ticos travel a great deal both within their country's borders and abroad, often to splurge on toys and Christmas gifts.

Like so many other trends, this one preoccupies many Costa Ricans, who see evidence of mediocrity and moral decay in the way Ticos spend their leisure time. Many—especially young people—seek to "kill time" and engage in a "desperate search" for diversion which, says Enrique Benavides, indicates "a loss of that inner calm that so long characterized the Tico."[3] On the other hand, many Costa Ricans take pride in a recent upsurge in "the fine arts." Encouraged by the government, the universities, and the new Ministry of Culture, Ticos of all classes participate more and more, both creatively and appreciatively, in music, theater, dance, the plastic arts, and literature. Interest in active sports is also growing.

SOCIABILITY AND FRIENDSHIP

Costa Ricans strike many foreign visitors as extremely gracious, sociable, and hospitable. In small towns they hail a passing stranger with an *Adios* or *Buenos días* as well as a friendly, if searching, look. They use the word *amigo* freely, and greet *amigos* with ritual shoulder-patting embraces, inquiries after one's health and that of the family, and promises of invitations to visit.

It comes as somewhat of a surprise, therefore, to hear many Ticos say they neither visit neighbors nor care to cultivate friendships except among relatives. Mario Sancho noted in the 1930s:

> Costa Ricans' sociability is purely formal and is undone as easily as it is formed. . . . It is rare to find cases of neighboring families that maintain close contact. . . . There are many, many families that live next door to one another for years, separated only by walls which allow voices and noises to pass, but that, nonetheless, have no more relations among their members than a friendly greeting.[4]

A number of studies confirm our own impression that most Ticos, amiable as they may act, are extremely wary of intimate friendship, and prefer to remain casual acquaintances. Many say they have no real friends other than kinsmen.[5] "Real friends" are *muy amigos* or *amigos de confianza,* whom one can trust, and usually only such friends are invited to coffee or dinner. Envy, mistrust, and suspicion must be overcome through years of interaction before most Ticos reach this stage. They are especially prevalent among lower-class rural women. Despite their loneliness and boredom, says social psychologist Irma Morales de Flores, *campesinas* rarely visit neighbors except in times of illness or bereavement, when they flock to the afflicted home.[6] But middle-class Ticos also tend to be wary, to doubt the sincerity of compliments and suspect others of hypocrisy.

Much of the reluctance to visit and be visited stems from a fear of being known as a gossip as well as of being gossiped about. Doña Vina, the neighborhood character who goes everywhere, knows all, and tells all with great relish, is a recognizable type personified by a popular radio comedienne. Ticos value privacy as a means of avoiding problems; they fear "what people will say." In all classes, even in San José, "eating people"— gossiping—remains a favorite pastime as well as the major form of social control. Gossip plays an even more dramatic role in small communities, whose residents quote the old Spanish proverb "A small town is a big hell." One woman in her fifties in a *Meseta* village wears a black dress and keeps her hair in two old-fashioned braids hanging down her back. Her children want her to cut her hair and to wear lighter colors. But she fears malicious comments: "Oh, she's looking for a man!" "Oh, look, she's cut her hair! She must think she's a young girl." She even hates to leave the house because, she says, people would peek out from behind the curtains and say "Where do you suppose she's going?"

Friendships formed in high school are among the most lasting. Middle- and upper-class girls, especially, tend to visit in one another's homes and may form cliques that continue to meet after graduation. They may drift apart as they marry and have children, but renew their intimacy once the child-raising years are over.Professional colleagues also form close friend-ships, perhaps because they share more specialized interests and knowledge than do most neighbors and work companions, and often regard their circle as an elite. Informal visiting is perhaps most common among such groups, as are tightly knit cliques that meet frequently for parties and outings.

Despite the superficiality of many friendships, few Costa Ricans enjoy solitude. Both sexes strike up conversations with strangers easily, and the most common icebreaker is a search for mutual acquaintances.

A great deal of socializing goes on outside the home, at service and professional clubs, sports clubs, beaches, and bingo games. Workers chat during coffee breaks—and often during working hours, particularly in government offices. Men of all classes meet with friends or work compan-ions in a bar or cocktail lounge after work.

The *pulpería* is still the traditional rural social center, attracting neighbor-hood men with television, pool tables, juke boxes, and liquor. Those that don't sell *guaro* lose business to the *cantinas* where men sometimes linger for hours, drinking, joking, singing, talking politics and soccer, and occasionally letting loose a high-pitched Mexican-movie-cowboy yell.

Joking is a favorite pastime. Ticos prize quick wit and skill at repartee. Although the emphasis on face-saving and personal dignity makes self-deprecating jokes rare, friends tease each other, while behind-the-back *choteo* or sarcasm belittles those who "think they're superior." Ticos enjoy swapping narrative jokes so much that many have immense repertoires, and joke sessions may go on for hours. Perennial themes are politicians, sex, including the sexual escapades and other misdeeds of priests, parrots' reve-lations of their owners' foibles, and the embarrassing questions asked by a naïve schoolboy named Pepito. Many Ticos also delight in practical jokes. The night after the National Liberation Party won a local election, two San Isidro de Heredia *liberacionistas* entered the *finca* of a friend who had voted for the opposition party, and painted his best horse green and white—their party colors.

FIESTAS, FAIRS, AND OTHER COMMUNITY DIVERSIONS

Crowds and noise abound at the *turnos* (street fairs) that raise money for churches, old age homes, schools, and other causes, and during the annual secular *fiestas cívicas* or *fiestas patronales* honoring a town's patron saint. These fiestas are held in most towns and cities once a year and last several days. In small towns and villages, such events evoke more community spirit than does any other occasion. For weeks in advance committee members may visit local households by truck, asking for and usually receiving a cash contribution, a chicken or steer, a sack of grain, a few eggs, or a bit of *dulce*. Local business-men donate money and labor, and the municipality may donate electricity. Volunteers put up wooden stalls on the plaza in front of the church. Perspir-ing women prepare beef stew, tamales, tripe soup, rice cakes, and other special dishes.

Announced by noisy rockets before dawn, the *turno* normally lasts all weekend. Men, adolescents, and children—all wearing new clothes—are in the majority, for even on these occasions rural women tend to remain at home. Cane liquor, horse shows, mechanical rides, clowns, fireworks, and a greased-pole climbing contest are typical highlights. The local wind ensem-ble, a marimba band, or a combo including guitar, accordion, maracas, and perhaps a violin supplies background music. A neighboring village may send a team for a soccer game. The main money-raisers are raffles, bingo, and lotteries, which attract both sexes, including many children.

Some fairs—notably the popular ten-day *fiestas cívicas* in San José— feature a characteristically Tico form of bull-baiting. Young unarmed men tease a small bull or cow around an improvised ring for a few minutes. Then the animal is lassoed and removed and replaced by another. These *corridas* serve as comedy acts as well as displays of skill or daring, though too much *guaro* or a desire to show off leads some men to risk injury. Nowhere is the animal killed; *machismo* is less often expressed through violence than in many other Spanish-American countries.

Except for a mass and a procession around the plaza when the patron saint is being honored, the *turnos* and *fiestas cívicas* are completely secular. Soccer games, horse parades, band and marimba music, and dancing are seldom missing. Invariably a queen is chosen from among teenagers whose bikini-clad figures have graced the newspapers for days ahead; she is crowned at a special dance. A display of fireworks and a final burst of rockets announce the end of the festivities.

SUNDAYS AND HOLIDAYS

Sunday is the liveliest day in small towns and the quietest in large ones, except at the soccer stadium. Although many Ticos complain that they are bored on Sundays, many others consider it the best day of the week. They dress in their best, attend mass, stroll about, window shop, consume ice cream and other snacks, or watch a soccer game. Parents and children may visit relatives in another community, or go to a swimming resort or the mountains for a picnic lunch. Teenagers may make similar excursions with friends, or attend a dance in the local dance hall (connected to a *cantina*). Others may see a movie.

Fifteen full public holidays were observed in 1979. On most such holidays, all schools, banks, offices, and stores are closed; on some, employees receive full pay. But laws and customs change somewhat from year to year, so that on some holidays not even Ticos themselves are sure what they might be able to accomplish in the way of errands or business.

Secular and religious holidays alike are increasingly an excuse for relaxation or private merrymaking rather than ceremonious public observance. Business and government leaders insist there are still too many for such a poor country. A group that wants a special holiday usually has only to petition the Legislative Assembly, as happened with the Day of the Postal Employee, when almost all post office functions come to a full stop. Each weekday holiday, it is calculated, costs the nation nearly two million dollars in lost production.[7] This "institutionalized vagrancy," as some call it, has been cut down by eliminating some holidays and moving others to the following Sunday.

Any attempt to reduce spending and partying at year's end, however, would probably fail completely. One Tico journalist suspects that Costa Ricans "are more prone to be infected with the Christmas spirit than any other people in the world."[8] Tinsel gewgaws, plastic snowmen and Santa Clauses appear in stores in mid-October, when newspaper ads also begin to tout all kinds of merchandise as Christmas gifts. Early in December, with year-end bonuses in their pockets, shoppers crowd the stores, stopping along the streets to see if a lottery vendor has their desired number for the "fat" Christmas drawing. They swamp the postal system with cards. Children write to the Christ Child asking for presents, many of which will be delivered by his messenger, Santa Claus.

A few days before Christmas the family may decorate a cypress tree. Many insist, however, that the manger scene is the only authentically Costa Rican Christmas decoration. Taking up a corner of the parlor, it is a mixture of secular and religious elements, present and past, admired for its variety and color. On Christmas Eve there is much visiting, drinking, dancing, and gift-giving. At midnight the Christ Child is placed in the manger and the family or adults may attend midnight mass, then celebrate till dawn, going to bed about the time the children get up to see their gifts. Merrymaking is even more boisterous on New Year's Eve.

PARTIES AND DANCES

Many holidays are occasions for parties and dances, which young Ticos, especially, hold on any pretext. Surprise birthday parties are common, as are farewell and welcome home parties, especially among the middle and upper classes. To raise money, schools and clubs hold dances, often including a queen contest.

Young Costa Ricans, even preschoolers, love to dance. Adolescents and young adults flock to small-town dance halls on weekends; discotheques and live bands in larger towns attract crowds even on week nights.

Children's and adolescents' parties, generally held in private homes, are most popular in the middle and upper classes, where youngsters are most likely to belong to an informal clique. Though rock is popular among upper-class youth, who zealously imitate American fashions, most dance music consists of romantic Latin and rhythmic Caribbean tunes.

Adult parties nowadays are more often held in rented halls or club facilities than formerly. Parties and other adult entertainment, especially among married couples, still fit this observation made in the early 1940s:

Most adult social events, especially among the "social" class, have a certain stiffness and formality. Women rise to greet other women who enter, and if they are good friends they kiss each other on the cheek in addition to the usual shoulder-patting embrace. An all-powerful fear of what people will say robs social intercourse of spontaneity.[9]

This reserve, which Jones considered atypical of Latin America,[10] is noticeable in nearly all adult diversions in Costa Rica—until the participants have begun to drink. Only then, for instance, might someone sing. (The few adults who sing while working may be teased as *locos*.) Says a nondrinking Methodist, "Alcohol is the basis of social life in Costa Rica. If you don't drink, you're socially dead." Drinking is firmly associated with fun and celebration and relief from loneliness and boredom. Yet most Ticos do not act exuberant even when they drink.

Many parties are for men or women only. Higher-status women attend teas, showers, luncheons, and canasta and bingo parties. Men of the upper and upper-middle classes attend numerous luncheons and banquets connected with their jobs or service clubs. Even when they go to parties together or gather for visits, men and women in all social classes tend to gravitate to those of their own sex. When conversation does occur in a mixed group, men do most of the talking.

GAMBLING

Games of chance have been popular since colonial days; only their form has changed. Ticos of both sexes enjoy gambling at *turnos* and other public fiestas, although dice games, cards, and roulette have been officially outlawed. Raffles are a favorite way of raising money and encouraging sales. Business firms, clubs, schools, and even private individuals often raffle a car, a watch, or a cash prize, and have little trouble selling tickets. Upper- and middle-class women's enjoyment of poker and canasta is enlivened by the hope of winning a few *colones*. In towns of all sizes, weekend bingo games attract even small children.

As in most Latin American countries, the national lottery is immensely popular, especially with the poor, who part with a few coins every week and splurge on a chance at the big Christmas prize (₡10 million in 1979). When Ticos express a cherished but expensive desire, they often half jokingly add that they will satisfy it "when I win the lottery." They may depend on luck, or they may seek a number that corresponds to their age, the digits of a certain license plate, a dream, or the number they buy week after week; some consult fortune tellers to learn the lucky number.

MOVIES, RADIO, AND TELEVISION

Most Ticos prefer passive, commercialized diversions to active participant ones. For decades they have been avid movie fans; the popular term for children's allowances is "movie money." Most moviegoers are under twenty-five. Groups of boys pack the theaters showing war and crime movies, while couples and groups of girls are more attracted to romantic films. Middle- and upper-class Ticos enjoy American and, occasionally, European movies. Working-class people, less familiar with foreign languages and cultures, and lacking the skill or interest to read subtitles, prefer Mexican and Argentine cinema. A government censorship bureau bans some films and attempts to regulate youngsters' attendance at others that "threaten Christian morals" or "contain crimogenic factors." Their main concern is with scenes of sexual licentiousness, but standards have been relaxed considerably in recent years. Violence, though taboo in Ticos' interpersonal relations, is a great attraction in films, and is not censored. Restrictive admission policies are seldom enforced and are believed to encourage attendance.

Radio is everywhere in Costa Rica. Nearly a hundred stations crowd the air waves. Transistor radios are hung on a convenient place near a *peón's* work spot, and the housewife keeps the radio on all day while she goes about her work and even while she talks with others. Popular music predominates on radio; news, a string of ads, and soap operas fill most other air time.

Television antennae sprout from even the humblest homes. The 1973 census showed that a third of all households had a television set, and the number has climbed sharply since then. Most live programs, usually in color, are soccer games, popular music, giveaway shows, newscasts, and demonstrations of gardening, cooking, and needlework. Politicians campaign via television, officials explain their policies, and charges and countercharges of corruption and other misdeeds fill the small screen. But most viewing time is occupied by old cartoons, movies, and serials from the United States, and Mexican *telenovelas* or soap operas heavy with emotion, melodramatic in plot, and generally as humorless as their United States counterparts.

In the 1940s movies were blamed for the decay of morals and the growing desire for luxuries. Today television is the villain, blamed for everything from the decline in the birth rate to the rise in crime. Imported television films are called "schools for delinquency." In place of what is authentically Costa Rican, say some critics—particularly teachers—imported programs offer ideas and behavior that "do not fit our idiosyncrasy," causing a loss of folklore, popular traditions, initiative, and creativity, and leading to imitation and mediocrity, as well as glorifying deceit, materialism, and violence.[11]

CHILDREN'S AND ADOLESCENTS' DIVERSIONS

Children of all classes play a great deal with siblings until puberty and less often with neighborhood children or schoolmates. Upper- and middle-class urban children are kept indoors most of the time on weekdays until school age, and are generally accompanied by an older sibling or a nursemaid when they go out. Children of other classes tend to play outdoors, in the street if no other place is available. In many rural areas they learn to ride horseback almost as soon as they can walk. Seldom do children of any age play alone. But television accounts for a growing amount of play time. Asked how she handles her six small children, a working-class mother said, "They're no trouble. They watch TV from morning till night."

Little girls enjoy running, playing "house" and "doctor," and playing with dolls, sometimes including small boys in their play. Little boys like to run, kick balls soccer style, and make dams and bridges in gutters and brooks, sometimes allowing girls to join them. They frequently hang around the fringes of older boys' groups, eavesdropping and watching them play. They enjoy imitating cowboys, Zorro, Batman, and other television favorites.

After entering school at age seven, boys and girls play apart, and boys are teased if they play with girls often. Until they reach adolescence, age differences between playmates are often as much as four or five years. School-age girls enjoy jump-rope, jacks, dolls, and *paleta*, a bat-and-ball game. Boys spend much of their playtime kicking a soccer ball around, but seldom play organized games until about age twelve. They also like skateboards, tops, iron hoops (often bicycle wheels), and marbles. In recent years urban children have begun to celebrate Halloween after a fashion; on any evening in late October they make the rounds of neighbors, calling "Halloween! Halloween!" in hopes of candy. Rural boys have long delighted in pilfering fruit from orchards and swimming in rivers and ponds. Many like to hunt birds and small animals. Though many families keep a pet dog, cat, or bird, neither children nor adults lavish affection on them as do many Americans; they reserve cuddling and baby talk for small children.

Poor children have few commercial toys; an older brother may fashion a doll out of a rag or corncob, or a tiny wagon from a scrap of wood. In many communities, local charities distribute toys at Christmas. Boys of the middle and upper classes play with a wide variety of imported toy soccer balls, erector sets, cars, guns, and games; their sisters often have large collections of dolls, dollhouses, and paraphernalia for playing house.

In no class do parents object much if their young offspring play with children of lower-status families. Still, members of play groups tend to come from homes of similar status, based on the associations of neighborhood and school. After puberty, especially for girls, class discrimination in leisure time activity becomes more a matter of parental insistence and gradually of the child's preference as well.

Most Ticos see adolescence as *the* time for having fun, an attitude especially prevalent among the lower class. The poor women interviewed by López de Piza look back on their teen years as the time of dances, movies, community festivals, and the coffee harvest; in their youth they viewed sex as part of recreation. Now, in maturity, they have few such opportunities for enjoyment. Middle- and upper-class Ticos share the conviction that one should have fun in youth, but they also believe both that young people must attend school to get ahead, and that diversion does not end with marriage and parenthood.

The beauty and femininity of teenage girls are constantly celebrated. No fiesta or dance is complete without a "queen" and her "princesses." Like most other Latin American societies, Costa Rica is permeated with awareness of sex—its pleasures, its risks, its relationship to other facets of life. The young female is the focus of this awareness. From early adolescence until well into old age most male Ticos are confirmed girl-watchers, who whistle, call, or murmur compliments (*flores*) that vie with their companions' in originality and wit. Oldtimers say their *flores* were much more imaginative and romantic and less vulgar than today's. Flirting is a national pastime, whether on the street or in the public dance halls that have sprung up even in small towns in the last twenty years. A favorite technique is a long, intense stare.

Social pressures induce many adolescent boys, and increasingly girls, of the middle and upper class to smoke cigarettes, and perhaps two-thirds do so regularly. Advertising in newspapers, on television, and in movie theaters associates certain brands of cigarettes with cosmopolitanism and sophistication.

Marijuana, long smoked by some of the West Indians who settled in Limón and by many men of the *Meseta's* working class,[12] has more recently become popular among middle-class adolescents and young adults of both sexes. So, too, have local hallucinogenic mushrooms. Trafficking in both remains illegal, and is a cause of great concern among older Ticos. But many youngsters who have tried neither hesitate to admit it to their peers.

SPORTS

"Soccer," says a columnist, "is not the sport of Costa Ricans. It is the motor of their existence. Soccer in Costa Rica is escape, pastime, purification, ecstasy, mania, bread, and necessary illusion. And since ours is a people frustrated in many areas, it seeks in soccer the consummation of its longings, the kingdom of happiness, success."[13] Introduced early in the twentieth century, it is played mostly by young working-class males, who have begun kicking a

Impromptu soccer game in a highland village (Mavis Biesanz)

soccer ball around at age two, and spend much of their free time during the next two decades playing with others in any available space. "Middle- and upper-class boys are too soft and pampered to play," a middle-aged team manager told us. Men over twenty-five prefer to watch, insisting they themselves are too old to play.

Soccer has no rival as a spectator diversion. Most Ticos, sober or otherwise, exercise great emotional restraint except when politics and soccer are involved. It is in the somewhat apolitical working class that soccer has the greatest appeal. Political posters rarely adorn the walls of humble homes; pictures of favorite soccer teams often do. A worker may never listen to broadcasts of legislative assembly sessions, but his transistor radio is tuned to major national and international games on Sunday even while he watches another game.

Even the smallest hamlet is likely to have at least one team, whose uniforms and equipment are bought with members' dues or contributions from local businessmen. Teams in the lowest leagues broadcast challenges over the radio, and usually find a taker every Sunday. Spectators of both sexes and all ages crowd the edges of the plaza. Fans cheer loudly and applaud when their team scores and are silent when the opponents do. If their team loses, girls may burst into tears; men may charge unfairness or bad decisions by the referee, and fist fights, even brawls, otherwise rare, may occur. Soccer rivalries arouse more rancor than political disagreements.

The passions aroused by soccer are seen by some as a safety valve, a functional alternative to the violence of more militaristic peoples.[14] But many other sports occupy, collectively, the same amount of space as soccer in the large and popular sports sections of the leading papers and even in *Eco Católico* and the leftist weeklies. Bicycle racing has many working-class fans and participants; boxing and wrestling are favorite spectator sports of men of this class. Most Ticos prefer to fight vicariously, for they pride themselves on their peaceable natures and do not even like to argue, much less fight (although a combination of alcohol and soccer matches or political campaigns may overcome these inhibitions). Even children seldom strike one another. Young working-class males gathered on a street may relieve their boredom by brief impromptu mock boxing, but blows are light and seldom lead to serious fights.

Basketball, volleyball, and tennis are popular among upper- and upper-middle class boys, who often play at their private high schools. Their fathers, even men in their fifties—an age working-class Ticos consider ridiculously advanced even for amateur sports—use the tennis and golf courses of private clubs. Pool has been popular among men of all social levels for over a century, as witnessed by the ubiquitous pool tables, present in fly-specked *pulperías* as well as the exclusive Union Club. Baseball teams are sponsored by large private companies, and there is a large baseball stadium. The sport has long been popular in Limón. Horseracing, auto, motorcycle, and bicycle racing attract some from all social classes, mostly as spectators; polo is played at a horseback riding club. The cockfights once so popular are now much less so; they are also illegal, though sometimes local authorities allow them and levy a tax, presumably for charities.

In the 1850s, Wagner and Scherzer observed that Ticos, especially women, exercised as little as possible, and did not value exercise for its own sake.[15] In the early 1940s, exercise was still generally held to be bad for a woman.[16] In recent decades, however, educational leaders have introduced regular physical exercise in schools, and direct involvement in a variety of sports has climbed for both sexes. The Ministry of Culture, Youth and Sports encourages participation, and has built a popular recreation and sports complex, with an Olympic-sized pool, at the edge of San José. Middle- and upper-class women swim and play tennis and golf at the clubs, and patronize a number of salons for hatha yoga, massage, and exercise, largely for weight reduction. A growing number of young men patronize various schools of martial arts such as karate.

In spite of such efforts, medal-winning runner Rafael Angel Pérez, in a Ministry of Culture film advocating more participation in sports, says most Ticos are "gallery sportsmen," and only about 5 percent regularly exercise or participate. He and other commentators agreed that academics are still stressed in schools at the expense of physical education, and that many teachers and parents regard exercise as *vagabundería*, not as worthwhile as book learning. There is little play space in most school areas, and as yet there are few teachers trained in physical education. A runner training in a small village in 1976 was jailed by local police, who thought he must be crazy.

CLUBS AND ORGANIZATIONS

Much as they dislike solitude, most Costa Ricans are not joiners. In the early 1940s observers found that "the often-remarked individualism of the Costa Rican has kept him from forming many clubs and from doing much to keep them going once they are formed."[17] Since then, voluntary associations have grown considerably in all classes—a common trend in "developing" societies where many new wants arise and where older means of satisfying traditional wants, including the desire for social interaction itself, have become less adequate. Rural high-school boys and working-class youths in larger towns are likely to be members of soccer clubs. Civic clubs for young people include the rapidly growing Boy Scouts. Increasingly popular in rural areas, and encouraged by government and United States advisers, are the 4-S Clubs, similar to 4-H.

Traditional community associations include church and school boards, community development committees, and *Patronatos Escolares* (somewhat like PTAs). In newly settled communities, participation tends to be high, as we noted in Chapter 3. But, as elsewhere, much of the work falls to the same people year after year.

In Costa Rica as in other class-stratified societies, the higher a person's status, the more active he or she is likely to be in voluntary associations. Business and professional men's Rotary and Lions Clubs have many chapters that sponsor dances and civic projects, while professionals use their associations' facilities for wedding receptions and for meeting with colleagues. All these groups have ladies' auxiliaries, whose members meet for tea or chocolate, bingo, and cards, and plan projects to raise funds for charity. Many women's groups do volunteer work in hospitals, orphanages, and nutrition centers.

Although the Union Club and the Costa Rica Country Club continue to be places for the "old families" to meet and dine and dance—and in the latter case to swim, bowl, and play tennis and golf—in recent years many new recreational clubs have been established, with widely varying entrance requirements and dues. Religious and political groups are now popular among middle- and upper-class adults as well as high-school and university students of both sexes, and several literary discussion groups and painting classes are attended largely by women.

Perhaps the greatest joiners are the black residents of Limón. Their branches of the Universal Negro Improvement Association and the Jamaican Burial Scheme Society have long provided social services and recreation; such lodges as the Elks and Foresters also claim many members. Jews and Chinese also have associations based on ethnicity.

THE ARTS

Compared to Latin American countries with large Indian or black populations, Costa Rica is poor in native arts and crafts. Even the elaborately painted wooden oxcart, which has become the symbol of Costa Rica, dates back only to the turn of the century. The wife of a cart maker in San Ramón is said to have designed the first decoration, which quickly caught on. Many painted their own carts, typically in bright colors set off with black and white,

Traditional oxcart laden with firewood (Mavis Biesanz)

in geometric designs and stylized motifs based on flowers, leaves, and vegetables.[18] Such carts are still in use, but jeeps, trucks, and planes have taken over most of their work.

The fine arts as well as crafts, home decoration, and architecture have long reflected what several Ticos call a "kitsch" culture with mediocre standards. They blame this not only on lack of an indigenous heritage but on the fact that Costa Ricans want to possess and show off the products of industrialization. Imitative rather than creative, their tastes, says one writer, are largely shaped by advertising and are evident not only in their possessions—plastic flowers, knickknacks, predictable furnishings—but also in much painting, literature, architecture.[19] The annual crafts fair sponsored by the government offers little but "kitsch."

In a small country where most people want above all to *quedar bien*, criticism is rarely frank, while praise for conventional efforts is lavish. The beliefs that everything foreign is necessarily better and that art can be appreciated only by an elite, the popular suspicion that any man who dedicates himself to art is effeminate, and the unlikelihood of any economic return have also long discouraged interest and excellence in the fine arts.

In recent years, however, the arts have flourished to such a degree that some Ticos speak of "a cultural revolution," one that began, some say, with the establishment of the prolific Editorial Costa Rica as an autonomous but government-subsidized publishing house in 1959.

Changes in the National Symphony Orchestra provide the most dramatic example of the recent growth of the fine arts. Until 1971, a small orchestra played ten or twelve concerts a year; they featured mainly nineteenth-century European classics and attracted two or three hundred listeners. Then President Figueres, who instituted the vigorous Ministry of Culture, Youth, and Sports in 1970, asked, "Why should we have tractors if we lack violins?" Peace Corps worker Gerald Brown, who had revitalized the Bolivian orchestra, was chosen to conduct the new Costa Rican National Symphony. He hired many young foreigners, whose contracts stipulated that each would teach his or her instrument to children and adolescents. Costa Rica has "the only state-subsidized youth orchestra in the western world."[20] In 1978 it performed at the White House and the United Nations. A chorus of a hundred voices, all volunteers, was also established in 1974. Internationally famous soloists often appear with the orchestra. The orchestra often visits small towns, playing in the open air or in a church,[21] and often plays the works of the few Costa Rican composers. These measures have turned nationalist anger at the sudden drastic revamping of the orchestra into pride.

Interest and participation in theater and dance also grew tremendously in the 1970s. In July 1975, for example, thirteen plays opened within two weeks in seven theaters, involving 160 actors. Much of the impetus has come from immigrant Argentine and Chilean playwrights and actors, as well as from the addition of drama to the high school curriculum. Cultural inhibitions that long hampered the growth of dance, such as the attitude toward exercise and display of the body mentioned earlier, are rapidly being over-

Youth symphony orchestra (Francisco González)

come, as seen in growing enrollment in private and university dance classes and a government-sponsored National Dance Company.

Around the turn of the century, everything European—and particularly French—was considered the epitome of culture. This attitude has been slow to change; as late as 1962, when there was no lack of accomplished local sculptors, a foreigner was commissioned to create a statue of Julio Acosta, just as had been done ten years earlier with the statue of León Cortés.

In the late 1920s Costa Rican painters discovered their own landscape and began to develop an art "related to our own land, our customs, and our way of life."[22] For the first time artists sought inspiration in pre-Columbian art and the country's landscapes and houses, and the new school of painters "resorted to an eclecticism of styles to overcome the prevailing academic rigidity."[23] In the late 1950s many artists painted in abstract styles, dismissing that of their elders as an art of *casitas* (little houses).[24]

A government-subsidized House of the Artist has offered free lessons in painting and sculpture since 1951, and many well-known artists got their start there. One means of keeping up artists' morale has long been the formation of groups such as Los Amigos del Arte where artists from various media met to discuss their projects in an informal atmosphere. Even so, public apathy and scorn drove some avant-garde artists into exile. Today, far from rejecting unconventional artists, the universities and the new Museo de Arte Costarricense exhibit work of all kinds, and autonomous institutions as well as private collectors purchase them. The Ministry of Culture sponsors art lessons and art exhibits for all comers on Sundays in city parks.

Until recently, few literate Costa Ricans enjoyed reading. Most recreational reading is still limited to newspapers and magazines, and even these are comparatively scarce outside the *Meseta*. All wide-circulation newspapers are printed in San José. Most emphasize national rather than foreign events, though they include several syndicated columns and cartoons from other countries, and occasional items from American, European, and Latin American papers. Comics, sports news, a horoscope, and a page devoted to news of crimes and accidents are especially popular. Mexican and Spanish *fotonovelas* and romance magazines attract many readers among lower-middle-class women. Among Ticos of different social levels, "women's" magazines (which claim four-fifths of magazine readership nationally) and the Spanish edition of *Reader's Digest* are especially popular.

Book sales and library use indicate an upsurge of more serious reading. Teachers' demands for more outside reading find students turning to their school libraries for research. Since these are closed on Saturdays, however, the National Library is often jammed. The children's library in San José is also well patronized. Only a few other public libraries exist, all understaffed and underfinanced. EDUCA, the Central American university press, constantly gets requests for public libraries through DINADECO, the community development institute, but few communities can raise the ₡800 for the standard 100-volume collection. As First Lady, Marjorie de Oduber, with the aid of the Diplomatic and Foreign Ladies Group, visited widely dispersed communities and donated a small library to some 1,300 schools. The desire to read, then, is apparently growing, and the habit is being formed in childhood.

Publishing was long a risky venture. Traditionally writers paid for printing their own works and often failed to sell enough books to cover the cost. Since Editorial Costa Rica (ECR) printed its first book in 1961, however, it has provided great stimulus to both writing and reading.

Besides EDUCA and ECR, the Ministries of Culture and Education, the universities, and several private firms also publish books, as does UNED, the national "TV University" established in 1978. Newspaper supplements appear at least once a week with poetry, stories, essays, reviews, and interviews with writers. Literature prizes are given annually by the government, *La Nación*, and private organizations. But aside from journalists only a handful of Ticos make a living solely by writing.

Costumbrismo—local color—has been a main ingredient of Costa Rican writing since the 1890s. While poetry has been traditionally flowery and lyrical, concerned with the music of words and with romantic views of nature and love, short stories and novels have largely drawn on local settings. The stories and prose-poems, often in *campesino* dialect, of the great *costumbristas* of the turn of the century depict the ways of different social classes in the developing coffee civilization.

The great literary figures of the early twentieth century were essayists and poets concerned with ideas and their expression in political and social life. Masters of this genre were Roberto Brenes Mesén, the greatest intellectual influence of the 1940s, and his contemporary, Joaquín García Monge, editor of the *Repertório Americano*. Essays continue to be a major form of intellectual and artistic expression, appearing almost daily in newspapers.

The theme of much writing in the 1930s and 1940s was social protest against the exploitation of peasants and *peones* by wealthy landlords and companies. Carlos Luís Fallas's *Mamita Yunái*, which depicts the plight of banana workers, is the best-known example of this genre.[25] Alberto Cañas, a prolific and versatile writer and journalist, complains of the Costa Rican preoccupation with protest: "We are still writing the proletarian literature of the 1930s." But today's authors, while still challenging the "establishment," take a broader view of evolving social and cultural patterns. Cañas himself describes covert political intrigue in a novel whose central character is a congressman. Alfonso Chase, widely considered the best young prose writer, haunts the bars, buses, and red light districts of the capital in search of material for stories depicting the life of today's Ticos in their own settings and their own words. Another outstanding literary figure of Central America, Carmen Naranjo, often dwells on the meaninglessness of modern urban life, especially for the lower-level bureaucrat. Her strong, vivid style is essentially poetic, and her experiments with form often baffle the reader.

With these and a few other exceptions, Costa Rican literature, say several critics, is the most prosaic and anemic of the continent, possibly because life is so peaceful, lacking great goals and struggles. Yet the most traumatic event of the century, the civil strife of 1948, has only recently evoked any fiction or poetry.[26]

Because folklore and folk art are less abundant and less distinctive than in most other Latin American countries, many Costa Ricans believe their country lacks it altogether, or that it is restricted to Guanacaste. Yet many dances, songs, poems, stories, and novels are based on oral traditions with pre-Columbian and African as well as Spanish roots. José Ramírez, former director of the folklore department of the Ministry of Culture, insists that the country is rich in folklore and that the old urban attitude of disdain has changed. There are now a number of folk dancing groups; some have shed the Panamanian and Mexican influence on costumes and repertoires that has long been mixed with authentically Costa Rican art. Emilia Prieto, who first learned folk songs from women working on her father's farm, collects and sings songs from different regions; although fundamentally melancholy, reflecting poverty and oppression, the *campesinos'* songs, she says, relieve the monotony of their lives with some fun.

Although the state has been the chief promoter of the trend toward increased participation in fine arts, and of encouragement of what is "authentically" Costa Rican, it does not try to impose any official esthetic or ideological view. On the contrary, its facilities make it possible for anti-establishment Ticos, especially young people, to express themselves freely. Says Guido Fernández, former director of *La Nación:* "Thus we see a sort of counterculture emerging under the auspices of the government. The fact that young people can express themselves through the arts may help explain why we don't have the political radicalism of other countries."[27]

CONCLUSION

Costa Ricans at leisure reflect both the strength of long-established values and customs and the newer influences that, for good or ill, are shaping their lives. The mythical "average" Tico is sociable but wary of intimacy, jovial but not spontaneous, imitative and passive rather than creative and active, and limited in participant efforts in sports and the arts by his or her fear of criticism for being "different." In some cases, this conformity means adherence to old ways; in others, an effort to be "in the swim." But a new self-conscious emphasis on national values, given impetus by the efforts of innovative and unconventional leaders, has begun to change these patterns and to increase both active and appreciative participation.

A park offers a tranquil oasis in San José (Jorge Ramírez)

10

POLITICS AND GOVERNMENT

"Costa Rica is a breath of fresh air after being in a dark, closed room," said a visitor from neighboring Panama during the campaign preceding the elections of February 5, 1978. "It is like an oasis in the desert of human rights. In Costa Rica liberty is seen, heard, and felt in every moment of existence."[1]

"Costa Rican elections are unique in the world," said observers from the Organization of American States after watching the noisy, colorful campaign and the open and honest voting and tallying of votes.

These are two voices in the chorus of praise for the country's political system. It is hailed as admirable and exceptional not only in comparison to most of Latin America, where few countries now hold free elections, but also to most of the Third World, where one-party states, dictatorships, and military coups are common. It is admired for many other things besides electoral purity. It has no strong military,[2] no guerrillas, no political prisoners. All citizens eighteen and older are required to vote. There is great freedom of expression and assembly. A constitution providing for clear separation of executive, legislative, and judicial powers is highly respected. New office-holders peacefully take over every four years. And in every presidential election but one from 1953 to 1978 the "ins" were ousted, a phenomenon that is usually interpreted as a sure sign of a healthy democracy.

What accounts for Costa Rica's uniqueness? Literacy, the large middle class, the relatively high level of economic development, say some. Others note that democratic procedures and values were apparent long before many Costa Ricans were prosperous or literate or middle class. Many social scientists now reject the thesis that economic development tends to foster democratic institutions[3] and, more specifically, that the economic system of Costa Rica determines its political structure. The reverse is true, insists Stone; Costa Rica's economic system appears to be conditioned by the political system.[4] We would argue that in any society the two systems are too interdependent to allow acceptance of either thesis.

In recent years some political scientists have come to think there is such a thing as too much stability. They suggest that it is really "immobilism," lack of ability to promote fundamental socioeconomic change. They see the much-admired alternation of parties in power as one of several aspects of the political system that work against innovation and badly needed change. Mario Carvajal Herrera, for example, believes a shift every four years from an innovative to a conservative party means that

> instead of four years of change and four years of consolidation it is possible to have two years of change and six years of immobilism. Of four years in government, each party devotes the first year to learning how the system works and the last one to avoiding any action which would be detrimental to the upcoming campaign. . . . In the long run, peaceful Costa Rica may face a violent revolution if the current rate of political change is not increased. . . . There is danger in rising expectations scorned by lack of delivery.[5]

Charles Denton sees little significant change in recent decades and considers the society "immobilist,"[6] while Robert Trudeau goes so far as to suggest that elections "might be thought of as the opium of the people."[7]

In previous chapters we have seen that Costa Rica has undergone many changes since the 1930s, a large number of which Ticos consider progress. We have also seen that serious problems persist and new ones have arisen. "Immobilist" thinkers believe that little or no progress has occurred, and that what might be considered progress has occurred largely *in spite of* the political system, which has failed to attack problems old and new. Throughout this chapter we shall seek the sources of stability in the political system and ask to what extent they result in immobilism and to what extent they meet needs. We consider this search important because in the long run the effectiveness of a system of government is eroded when people lose faith in that effectiveness. This is especially likely in "developing" societies where demands tend to outrun resources, achievements to lag behind expectations and promises, and class conflict to increase. Costa Rica, then, presents a test case of democracy in such a society.

THE STRUCTURE AND SCOPE OF NATIONAL GOVERNMENT

Fresh in the minds of delegates to the convention that drafted the 1949 constitution were the events that had led to the civil strife of 1948. These events made them extremely wary of presidential power, communism, and electoral fraud. The new constitution changed the distribution of power from a highly centralized government headed by a strong president to a decentralized one in which the legislature is considered the leading power, executive decision-making is subject to numerous checks and balances, and elections are supervised and their results decided by an autonomous agency, the Supreme Electoral Tribunal. The constitution reflects the typical Costa Rican attitudes of reserved approval of government and fear of concentrated power, and the belief that "law itself can assure the putting in order of social reality and afford it complete legitimacy."[8]

The constitution provides for a unitary national government in which the seven provinces play only one important role, as electoral districts for the legislature, whose fifty-seven seats are allotted according to population and redistributed after each decennial census if population shifts make it necessary.[9] Within each province seats are allotted according to the proportion of the vote for each party. This proportional representation encourages minor parties to try for congressional seats even when they have no hope of electing a president.

The president is elected for a single four-year term, with no chance of reelection—another precaution against concentration of power. One of the two vice-presidents exercises presidential power when the chief executive is incapacitated or traveling abroad. This power includes command of the Civil Guard, appointment and removal of ministers,[10] and presentation of a detailed annual message to the legislature. The president, who symbolizes national unity, also acts as chief of state on ceremonial occasions. For all other functions he is required to collaborate with the cabinet or the legislature.

Schoolchildren today are taught that the Legislative Assembly rather than the president is the principal power. Diputados are elected for four years and can be reelected only after four more. The legislature has the power to pass, amend, and repeal laws; approve the president's trips out of the country; ratify international agreements; impose taxes; and approve loans from abroad. It checks the executive branch by its power to amend the budget prepared by the Planning Office and submitted by the president, and to appoint the Comptroller General, who checks public expenditures before their release and thus prevents the executive branch from overspending its budget.[11] Approval by a simple majority suffices for all of these measures, but a two-thirds majority is necessary to amend the constitution and to override a presidential veto.[12]

The seventeen magistrates of the highly respected Supreme Court of Justice are chosen by the legislature for staggered eight-year terms. Apparently free of executive control, the Court seems to be fairly independent of congress as well, since magistrates' terms are not concurrent with those of diputados and are automatically renewed every eight years unless the legislature decides otherwise, which seldom happens. The Court names justices of the civil and penal courts in each province as well as a justice of the minor court in some cantons. The legislature has also created special juvenile and administrative courts.[13] A litigant may appeal a decision to a higher court, or the court may transfer the case instead of passing sentence itself. If two successive courts return the same verdict the decision is final.

Little conflict is evident between the judiciary and the other branches of the government. Still, the courts have done much to enforce constitutional checks on presidential power, such as guarantees of freedom of expression, assembly, suffrage, and worship, as well as constitutional prohibitions of *ex post facto* laws, arbitrary arrest, exile, torture, and capital punishment.

The "fourth power," the TSE or Supreme Electoral Tribunal, oversees the formation and functionmg of parties, registration of voters, electoral campaigns, and the actual voting and counting of votes. It interprets any constitutional provisions related to these matters; supervises the civil registry of births, deaths, marriages, and acquisitions of citizenship; and gives out the identification cards necessary for voter registration. Three magistrates are appointed by the Supreme Court for six-year terms, one every two years to minimize partisanship. Two more magistrates are appointed a year before each election.

The 102 autonomous institutions (aside from the eighty municipalities) also reflect a preference for decentralization and for checks and balances of power, as well as for expertise. Each such institution is intended to perform a function once left to private agencies or to central and local government, if it was done at all. Each is a public corporation with its own administration; the constitution provides that it be free of direct control by the central government, thus removing its functions from the realm of political maneuvers. The number of such institutions has grown considerably, especially during Liberación (PLN) administrations. Together, they and other public corporations spend about three out of every five public sector colones.

By any measure, little Costa Rica has big government. Roughly one out of every five people in the labor force—and by some estimates, one out of three—is a public employee. The public sector spends at least 23 percent of the Gross National Product, and possibly twice that amount. The central government budget alone grew from ₡127 million in 1950 to almost five billion colones in 1978, an increase of 15 times per capita.

The government has a finger in almost every pie. Its functions and powers have grown along with its personnel and budget. It is not only the sole legal liquor manufacturer, as it has been since 1852, and the chief banker, as it has been since 1948. It also produces and distributes electricity, provides telephone service, monopolizes the sale of insurance, builds and sells houses, supports symphony orchestras, buys and sells rice and other farm products, builds roads, and promotes development. It spends a far larger share of its budget on health and education than do most other countries. It looks, to some extent, after the welfare of children, the elderly, the indigent and the disabled. It makes itself felt at every turn, not so much in the manner of a police state with the constant presence of the military, but as a bureaucratic giant that must be dealt with in order to own and drive a car, build a shed, buy or sell, employ or be employed.

Is big government effective in providing services to the people and promoting economic development with social justice? That question, more than any other, divides Costa Ricans along party lines.

THE PARTY SYSTEM

Although many Ticos, including adherents to one party or another, distrust politicians and consider politics dirty, many others believe parties play an indispensable role in the society. They see parties as instruments of democracy that raise issues, mobilize voters, and choose leaders.[14] Stone believes they unite Costa Rican society, including its rural communities, as nothing else does. They also, he says, define social classes and, for many individuals, provide an avenue to power and prestige, which in turn may give access to wealth.[15]

Electoral laws help shape the party system. Because it is easy to form a party[16] and because proportional representation makes it possible for small parties to win seats in the legislature, small parties are numerous. Because 40 percent of the vote is necessary to elect a presidential candidate, two large parties usually vie for the presidency. It is very easy to split one's vote because separate ballots are issued for the presidency, the legislature, and the municipal council. Parties that win 5 percent or more of the vote in one election usually reappear four years later because they can claim a share of the campaign fund provided by the government out of the annual budget.

Before 1948, coalitions of extended families among the elite, many of them *cafetaleros*, would informally agree on a candidate to run against the candidate of a similar, rival group, or compromise with their rivals on a candidate. Not until 1889 did candidates feel the need to appeal to the voters themselves by conducting electoral campaigns. In the 1920s and 1930s the first ideological parties appeared—Volio's Reformists and Mora's Communists. The first major party that mingled ideological appeals with personalism was the Republican Party led by the charismatic Dr. Calderón Guardia. The crisis of 1948 resulted in a realignment of political forces and a sharp upturn in voter participation. The increasing complexity of postwar society demanded a new kind of party system.

Founded in 1951, Partido Liberación Nacional has since had a majority in the legislature (until 1978) even when an opposition president has been in office. Its chief opponent, usually more poorly organized and less ideologically based, has typically been a coalition pulled together to back a candidate before each election. Meanwhile, many minor parties have come and gone.

PLN ideology had its roots in the ideas of Haya de la Torre of Peru, head of the Aprista movement, but today it is far more identified with European social democracy and American welfare state liberalism, though with a definitely Tico flavor. PLN is basically reformist rather than revolutionary, favoring social welfare measures that promote health, education, and transportation, but leave the capitalist economy and social structure intact. Often accused of leading the country to state socialism, PLN instead advocates state intervention in a capitalist economy. According to one observer, the party's pragmatic political sense is reflected in the fact that its leaders themselves have been or have become well-to-do businessmen.[17]

Like other social democratic parties in Latin America, PLN depends for power on middle-class professionals and entrepreneurs, and for the bulk of its votes on small farmers and rural *peones*. Besides businessmen, many of its leaders are professionals and intellectuals who set aside some of their clients or university courses for four years to serve in the legislature or the cabinet.

The PLN takes credit for great changes in Costa Rica since 1948, claiming that it has achieved them without sacrificing democratic values. It has, however, been described by at least one political scientist as constructive and innovative when out of office but unable or unwilling, when in power, to implement such measures as substantive land reform and tax reform.[18]

PLN leaders often charge that the continually shifting factions in an opposition coalition have nothing in common but anti-Liberation sentiments and a desire to wrest power from them. Nonetheless, these factions have always supported private enterprise and opposed big spending, deficit financing, and government intervention in the economy. The opposition administrations of Mario Echandi (1958–1962) and José Joaquín Trejos (1966–1970) were times of fiscal reorganization (although in the PLN view, of stagnation).

Costa Ricans, however, tend to vote for the man rather than the party and to play down ideological labels and platforms.[19] "No one knows what the procession will be like until the saint comes out." This tendency helps explain the large number of minor parties.

Such parties, both permanent and evanescent, have won seats in the legislature and on municipal councils. They represent personal ambitions or discontented minorities, usually urban, with varying mixtures of ideology and personalism. Some split off from a major party, protesting its corruption or its control by the old guard who block the aspirations of younger members; this has happened among the Communists as well.

The longest-lived party in Costa Rica, the Communist Vanguardia Popular, was indigenously organized and developed, although it follows the Soviet line and has close ties with Moscow, from which it apparently receives financial support. It has long been tolerated and even respected by many non-Communists as *comunismo criollo*, a native brand identified with social progress and democracy.

Fear of communism because of its role in the strife of the 1940s was reflected in Article 98 of the 1949 constitution, which kept parties alleged to threaten the country's sovereignty off the ballot. The Communists nonetheless continued to recruit members, hold meetings, and publish a weekly newspaper as well as messages in the large dailies. Anti-Communist sentiment, especially among PLN decision-makers, had relaxed so much by the 1970s that full diplomatic relations were established with the Soviet Union in 1973 and Article 98 was repealed in 1975. This change is attributed largely to the image party founder Manuel Mora had begun to project. He had succeeded in depicting the party as more nationalistic and democratic than revolutionary. Mora, described by a conservative columnist as "cultured, studious, mannerly, far from fanaticism and mindless passion,"[20] has gone on record as an "authentic" Costa Rican who believes "the Social Revolution" can be attained by means of law and political compromise, provided Costa Rica does not develop at the expense of her sovereignty.[21]

This moderate stand and the party's collaboration with PLN congressmen, as well as the domination of Mora and his brother over the party, have alienated younger and more militant leftists, who call the Communists the "traditional left" and accuse them of being bourgeois, revisionist, tame, and tired. In turn, Communists dub the tiny but active splinter groups "ultras."

Despite such differences, **Vanguardia Popular** joined forces with the

Socialist Party and the militant Revolutionary Movement of the People in a coalition called *Pueblo Unido*, the United People, for the 1978 election. By 1980 the coalition appeared to be dissolved, though government leaders expressed concern about the increasing militance of Communists, particularly their role in numerous labor strikes.[22]

Although few Ticos might admit it, most parties agree on basic issues and problems though they disagree on solutions and priorities. This is a good thing, says Enrique Benavides; radical differences in theory and basic principles would make a national consensus impossible, and a real crisis, perhaps with violence, inevitable.[23]

The often-voiced fear of one-party government seems to have no basis in a country where parties can form and enter the scene so easily, where presidents of opposing parties typically alternate in power, and where candidates rather than platforms draw votes. Despite the system's stability, election results are seldom foregone conclusions.

CAMPAIGNS AND ELECTIONS

Every four years, voters choose the president and two vice presidents, fifty-seven legislators, and local officials for all the municipalities. Scheduled elections have been interrupted only twice since 1889—in 1917 and 1948—and since 1949 suffrage has gradually been extended to a larger share of the population—women, eighteen-year-olds, illiterates. A million Ticos—about half the populace—were eligible to vote in 1978.

Speculation about who will be the next president begins on inauguration day, Ticos say. Although the electoral code prohibits campaigning until six months before an election, long before then aspirants—many of them incumbent cabinet ministers—send up trial balloons. Some of these self-chosen candidates, goes a Costa Rican joke, think that all one needs to aspire to the presidency is to be a good person—one who has never killed anybody.

Cabinet ministers frequently have presidential hopes. But they must resign in order to campaign because the electoral code includes what may be the strictest laws in the world against political participation by elected and appointed public officials. The president, ministers, congressmen, and even municipal councilmen, teachers, and union leaders may neither run for office nor publicly support any candidate. Harry Kantor, a political scientist who has watched Costa Rica's electoral process for many years, considers these rules undemocratic. In a democracy voters should be able to choose whomever they please, including reelecting presidents and legislators. Then, says Kantor, elections would fulfill their true function by serving as referenda about how well the party in power has managed national affairs.[24]

Minor parties usually form around a candidate, and there is seldom a problem of choice. Major parties long chose their candidates in nominating conventions. In 1977 both major parties held primary elections—PLN in all 409 electoral districts, the Opposition Coalition in a sample of twenty-two. By primary election day in March the field had been narrowed to two precandidates in each party, as others, sensing defeat, dropped out of the race.

Although money alone does not guarantee victory, a well-to-do candidate appears to have an advantage in the primaries, which are not government supported. Campaign funds for the final election, however, come largely from the public till. The 1949 constitution provided that any party that received 10 percent or more of the votes could apply for a proportionate share of the official campaign fund, which consists of 2 percent of the average Central Government budget for the three years preceding the election. In 1971 the legislature reduced the necessary share of votes to 5 percent and provided for advance payment of campaign costs as early as ten months before the election. If a party fails to get 5 percent of the votes, it is legally required to refund the money.

Nelson Chacón Pacheco believes this plan is as immoral as the old way of financing campaigns with deductions from the salaries of public employees. By 1975 the government budget was 37 times as large as in 1950, and 2 percent was an immoderately large sum. Then, too, the fund was designed to cover such costs as voter registration, which is now handled by the Supreme Electoral Tribunal rather than by political parties. Rarely or never has a party that failed to get 5 percent of the votes refunded any money.[25] The plan does not provide for new parties, and it favors the established majority parties. Thus in 1978 large sums were advanced to the 1974 opposition party's heir, but none were available for the new opposition party headed by Rodrigo Carazo—the eventual winner.

Despite the ban on campaigning until six months before an election, campaigns seem to take about two years, and some Ticos complain that the major parties wage endless campaigns. Political propaganda takes up a great deal of space and time in the mass media. Slogans and names are painted in party colors on walls, boulders, roads, and billboards. Party banners float above houses and trees, and wave from cars and bicycles. Although public rallies are permitted only during the last two months of a campaign period, huge "private" meetings are held long before. Lists of supporters appear in

1978 campaign (La Verne Coleman)

the papers. Motorists sound their horns in codes representing their favorites' names. Children amuse themselves on Sundays by standing on sidewalks and roadsides to wave party banners at passersby. Friendships may cool because of political differences, and small-scale fist fights, normally rare, break out in *cantinas* and on streets. Six months before the election the president symbolically turns over the civil guard to the TSE, to be called on in case of any disturbance or violation of the code. (Some demonstrations and brawls had to be broken up with tear gas in 1970 and a few incidents occurred in 1974, but the 1978 campaign was unmarred by violence.)

Campaigns have long tended to stress personalities and emotional slogans. Each candidate tries to convince the electorate that he is the most truly democratic and authentically Costa Rican and, with obvious exceptions, the most sincerely anticommunist. Other "good" words and phrases are peace, patrimony, and civic virtue. "Bad" words include imperialism, dependency, fascism, corruption, violence, unconstitutional, militarism, bureaucracy, and *politiquería*. [26]

The TSE rules on campaign issues if an injured party complains. After Oduber attributed his defeat in 1966 to charges of procommunism, the TSE forbade the use of that charge in any campaign. Late in the 1978 campaign some religious leaders took out full-page ads telling the faithful that communism was not compatible with Catholicism; when Pueblo Unido complained, the TSE forbade further propaganda exploiting religious motives.

With the major parties' tacit but fundamental agreement and the banning of sensitive words and issues and certain kinds of propaganda, personal appeal is all the more important. Candidates try to visit every community at least once. They give speeches and shake hands, smile, ride horses in rural areas. Costa Ricans will overlook a great deal in candidates they like, but will not forgive arrogance. Although major candidates are generally wealthy, no candidate who fails to seem folksy and *humilde* is likely to succeed. One technique of personal appeal is closely identified with Pepe Figueres—*conchovindismo*, the deliberate use of *campesino* idioms and manners to attract rural votes. [27]

Yet seldom do politicians publicly attack another candidate's personal life. Any discussion of sexual habits or family ruptures, for instance, is generally left to word of mouth. Figueres has noted that Costa Ricans may copy a lot of things Americans do, but they would never use sex scandals against their worst enemies.

Election Day, the first Sunday in February every fourth year, is a great public holiday. The TSE has distributed voting materials to some 500 schools that serve as polling places. The members of the local electoral board, whose status is honorary and unpaid but obligatory upon appointment, arrive long before the polls open at 5 A.M. to arrange the tables and improvise a booth for secret voting. A pollwatcher may be present from each party.

Almost all voters try to cast their ballots early. They are ushered into the proper room by teenagers decked out in party colors. Members of the board check each voter's identification card, consult the list to see if he or she is in the proper polling place, and sign the three ballots for president, legislators,

Voting in 1978 campaign (La Verne Coleman)

and municipal officials. Voters dip their thumb in purple ink and place a thumbprint below the picture and colors of their chosen party, fold the ballots and drop each into the proper box, and finally dip an index finger in purple ink to show that they have voted and cannot vote again. Then they are free to join the excited people of all ages honking horns, waving banners, throwing confetti, and buying balloons. Or they may work for their party, perhaps transporting voters to the polls—an important duty because many people vote far from their current place of residence rather than going to the bother of registering a change of address.

Although voting is obligatory, there is no punishment for failure to vote. Absenteeism serves as a form of protest; thus, in long-neglected Limón, a third of the eligible voters stayed away from the polls in 1974.

Though party leaders hold turncoats in scorn, enough Costa Ricans switch colors and enough new voters are added every four years to make the outcome of an election hard to predict. The tendency to switch parties from one election to another, Carvajal believes, is one lasting effect of the 1948 struggle, which many think was caused by the continuation of Calderón's party. Besides blaming the party in power for all the nation's problems, some voters say they switch for fear that too big a margin of victory would make a government less responsive to the people.

A majority of the followers polled by Carvajal think a change every four years is good; an even larger majority of leaders do not. Followers are more satisfied with the system as a whole than are leaders, and identify less completely with parties. They see party (though not personality) differences as so minimal that they can switch colors in successive elections without feeling inconsistent.[28]

Elections reaffirm the pride of Ticos in their unique system. They congratulate themselves on their "civic fiesta" and say that the participation of youngsters and adolescents is an effective way for them to learn about democracy. By inauguration day, campaign-induced resentments among friends and neighbors have all but disappeared, party flags fluttering over buildings have faded, and power peacefully changes hands. Each election further confirms their pride, and each is more peaceful than the last, because, says political scientist Henry Wells, the socializing effect of elections is cumulative.[29]

Elections do not, however, serve as mandates for fundamental social change. By emphasizing emotional issues and personalities and leaving substantive problems to minor parties, the major parties avoid serious cleavages in the electorate and maintain the underlying consensus. Few voters demand greater effectiveness from candidates and parties; most reconfirm the legitimacy of the system by voting as a patriotic duty and accepting the results.

POLITICAL PARTICIPATION AND POLITICAL POWER

According to some accounts of political behavior, Costa Ricans consider voting the only means by which they can and should participate in politics. In general they are portrayed as apathetic, indifferent, and poorly informed.[30]

Carvajal believes, on the contrary, that Ticos not only have a far higher rate of participation in voting than do citizens of most other countries but also that they are about as well informed as those in the United States.[31] Studies by Booth and Seligson found Costa Ricans' level of participation in twenty-one political activities to be somewhat lower than in the United States, Japan, and Austria, but higher than in other Third World nations studied. Modes of participation, aside from voting, include activism in community organizations, asking public officials for personal and group favors, and working for a party, as well as strikes, riots, demonstrations, and squatting. More than 85 percent of a sample of 1,446 heads of families had engaged in at least one of these activities besides voting.[32]

Yet kinds of participation and degrees of power and influence vary greatly by social class as well as by sex, age, and rural or urban residence. The old power elite of *cafetaleros* and wealthy import merchants now shares power with professionals, industrialists, and other businessmen. Some social scientists ascribe to this newly broadened elite a conspiracy to manipulate other groups for their own ends. Trudeau, for example, sees electoral politics as "*at best* a paternalistic device to control the masses (often benignly),"[33] while Romero says "the bourgeoisie divides at the political level . . . to give the dominated class a feeling of a multiparty, participatory, open democracy."[34]

Such generalizations probably ascribe far too much unity and collective rationality to the elite. In Costa Rica the distribution and use of power is more complex. We can examine it from several angles: the power structure within the leading parties, the class origins of those in high government positions, and the power and participation of various categories within the population, such as youth, women, the middle class, *campesinos*, and pressure groups.

PLN was formed as a basically middle-class party to give this long-neglected sector power and opportunity to compete with the old oligarchy. Thus "it attracted many new professionals, small property owners, bureaucrats and educators."[35] Capitalizing on their high party positions and their connections with government corporations and autonomous institutions, a number of the founders, who were idealistic young men in the 1940s, have become *nouveau riche* landowners and businessmen, according to Jorge Romero; he charges they make "a successful and lucrative business of politics."[36]

PLN's chief rival, the continually changing coalition of parties called *La Oposición*, includes more large farmers and cattle ranchers, wealthy businessmen, managers, and executives in private business than does the PLN. It represents the old elite, with some members of the new entrepreneurial elite. Carvajal found opposition leaders to have higher incomes and more foreign education than PLN leaders. They were closer in their attitudes to business and mass media leaders and tended to favor the status quo rather than social reforms they considered leftist.[37]

In his study of formal leadership, *¿Quién Gobierna?* (Who Governs?), Arias noted an initial post–1948 period of conflict between the traditional power elite and the new groups of industrialists, businessmen, and agricultural entrepreneurs. Relations have significantly improved with the alternation of parties in power, which has ensured relative social stability, and with the investment by many old *cafetaleros* in diversified industrial or financial enterprises, which has made it difficult to differentiate between the old and new elite.[38]

Political plums such as good positions in the bureaucracy serve to quiet many dissenters. Some high government posts are especially juicy; their perquisites enable a middle-class bureaucrat to have many things only the wealthiest can otherwise afford: foreign travel, duty-free automobiles, entertainment allowances, and a chance to hobnob with the rich and powerful of many nations.[39]

Faith in the system, general acceptance of it as legitimate, also upholds the power of the elite. Figueres once accused Ticos of being as domesticated as sheep. They prefer to let scandals die, and are not easily aroused to passionate defense of a position or cause; they prefer peace and compromise, and leave most problems to the government.

The governing elite, regardless of party, are overwhelmingly urban, male, well-to-do, educated, and middle or upper class. Analyzing the backgrounds of the 461 ministers, legislators, and Supreme Court justices from 1948 to 1974, Arias found that

> most were already in the upper class when they got their first political post—94 per cent of ministers and 60 per cent of *diputados*. No ministers and only 3 *diputados* came from the lower class. The rest were middle class. Only 4 per cent of ministers and 6.3 per cent of legislators were of rural background.[40]

It is a common belief among middle-class urbanites that peasants in particular are normally politically inert. In comparison to some other groups, they do appear conservative and inactive; certainly the leftists, who lament their unpopularity with peasants, think so. It is a mistake, however, to label them all as apathetic and indifferent. Booth found that they interact frequently and on many levels with community organizations—more so, in fact, than do city dwellers.[41]

But peasants have the least political clout of any category of Costa Ricans. Their relative lack of organization, leadership, and formal education, and their feelings of impotence reinforce one another and help keep them comparatively powerless. Though their votes are eagerly sought, most feel far less interest in politics on the national level than they do in municipal government and community development.

Costa Rican women have, on the whole, far less interest in politics and far less power than men. Most wives follow their husbands' political leanings without question; when they differ, it is cause for comment. Major political groups are directed almost exclusively by men. Parties have women's auxiliaries that usually meet separately.

Yet many women felt and expressed strong convictions of their own long before they had the vote. Women, joined by high school students, marched against the Tinocos in 1918. They have demonstrated for honest elections, against the Soviet embassy, and in favor of a revised Family Code. But they have not organized permanent pressure groups.

From 1974 to 1978 women held about 8 percent of elective municipal posts. Of the twenty-two women (5.5 percent) among the total of 399 *diputados* from 1943 to 1980, five were serving in the assembly in 1980. In recent years a few well-educated upper-middle-class women have been cabinet ministers, ambassadors, and members of the boards of autonomous institutions such as Social Security. President-elect Carazo in 1978 named four women to cabinet-level positions.

Many young Ticos show little interest in politics. In 1974, when eighteen-year-olds could first vote in a presidential election, 25 percent of all absentees would have been eligible to cast their first vote. Most nonvoters, according to statistician Wilburg Jiménez Castro, are between ages eighteen and twenty-nine.

Most young people tend to adopt political leanings compatible with those of their parents. The few young people who are highly politicized belong to the youth wings of the major parties or to extremist groups of right and left. Although young Ticos are not predominantly leftist, most leftists are young.

In recent years a generational struggle has gone on within the major parties. Young people have felt held back by cliques of old men who control opportunities for political positions and who, they claim, regard their parties' youth auxiliaries as mere cheering squads. PLN youth was described in the late 1960s as a gadfly pushing the party leftward and working for internal democracy.[42]

Divisions by "census data" such as class, age, sex, and rural or urban residence are helpful in understanding a political system. But interest groups also influence decision-making. Today's democracy, insists Arias, is a democracy of pressure groups,[43] whose tactics and modes of expression vary from pairs of students spray-painting slogans on walls to formal associations of workers, government employees, and businessmen who make their positions known through the mass media, appear before congressional committees, or present their cases to government agencies. Personal contacts between members of organized groups (especially those of the upper and middle classes) and those in power are easy and frequent in tiny Costa Rica, and these groups need retain no permanent lobbyists. The relative power of such groups is somewhat different from that in other Latin American countries. Most striking are the absence of a strong military, the relative weakness of the Catholic Church, and the comparatively apolitical outlook of students.

Among the most powerful pressure groups are those of businessmen, organized into associations of manufacturers, coffee growers, cattle ranchers, and others. Such groups maintain contact with the president, ministers, and legislators and their relatives and friends, and engulf the mass media with petitions and proclamations. *La Nación,* though generally pro-capital, comments on their power.

> Whenever any legislation is being considered which is related to industry, construction, or agriculture, the activities of the directors of the interest group concerned determine whether the law shall specify one thing or its opposite.[44]

To a lesser extent, associations of such professionals as physicians and lawyers do the same.

Associations of public employees, as we noted in Chapter 4, are also extremely powerful because their members provide basic and strategic services of many kinds. The independent middle class of businessmen and professionals and farmers is weak in comparison, although individual members speak out when state intervention threatens to increase their taxes or otherwise limit their freedom or prosperity.

Autonomous institutions and public corporations also act as pressure groups. In the overlapping maze of agencies, they compete for power and financing and take out full-page ads to convince the public, and perhaps the legislature, that their far-sighted policies are indispensable to national progress. Entire communities also exert pressure. The citizens of Limón occasionally call attention to the sad state of public services by such measures as cancelling the popular October carnival, as they did in 1974. Strikes, blockades of streets or roads, and demonstrations attempt to achieve publicity and to convince the appropriate agencies to aid a neglected community. More conventionally, community leaders present a list of their needs when a president or minister visits them.

Members of the middle and upper classes talk politics a great deal. Some simply repeat the gossip and rumors and the sharp irreverent jokes about political figures and events that spread like wildfire. Says a journalist: "Spies would die of hunger here, because everyone is a spy. We are born gossips and rumor-mongers so electronic spying is superfluous. No one can keep a secret here. Among us everything is known, but we don't know how."[45]

Much political debate is carried on in the newspapers. The history of the press is closely related to that of political parties and to the vicissitudes of politicians and pressure groups that have owned or dominated newspapers. Several daily newspapers and two leftist weeklies are widely read. There is no government interference with what they print, although a government institution may cut down on paid insertions in a paper that displeases those in power. The constitutional guarantee of freedom of expression is observed in Costa Rica far more than in most other countries. The chief limitations on the content of newspapers are the advertisers and the libel laws. Most papers and broadcast media are owned and managed by the business elite, and space and time are very expensive by local standards. Oduber and Figueres both won suits against the leading paper, *La Nación*, for libel.

Today's papers seem rather mild as compared to those that published harsh invective in the 1940s, including strong personal attacks on the president,[46] and aggravated the hostility that led to the events of 1948. Journalists do little research or investigation. Rather, they print news stories that may be extremely biased, and allow supporters of opposing points of view to reply the next day.

HOW NATIONAL GOVERNMENT FUNCTIONS

Government in Costa Rica functions according to two chief sets of guidelines. One set is written in the constitution and in codes and laws. The other consists of cultural values and norms that also guide decision-making and interaction, whether or not they are given explicit written form. One such cultural guideline is fear of monolithic power. Voters' preference for the alternation of parties; the constitutional system of checks on power, especially on that of the president, and of devices intended to balance power among the different branches of government; and rules against the reelection of the president and legislators and against their participation in electoral campaigns all are rooted in distrust of power. Fear of concentration of power was the basis for the 1949 constitution's decentralization of government functions in many autonomous or semiautonomous institutions.

All these measures weigh heavily in favor of stability rather than effectiveness. In many ways they hamper the functioning of government. The 1949 constitution marked a sharp break with the system of a strong president and a legislature subordinate to his wishes. The power of the legislature to go against the president's wishes makes for constant friction, even when the president's party is in the majority.

Rules against reelection and incumbents' campaigning ignore the realities of party politics. They also work against effective government; each term is a learning experience for the president and legislators—and their learning is largely wasted. No legislator can carve out a parliamentary career with four years in office and four years out. These rules may actually encourage corruption. Because the president is a lame duck from the day the tricolor sash is slipped over his shoulders to the day he leaves office, no fear of defeat in the next election enters his calculations. Roads are built conveniently close to the houses and *fincas* of high officials, who shrug off charges of abuse of power with the retort *"Pa' eso tenemos mayoría"* (That's what we have a majority for). Alternation of parties can be costly: the Labor Code provides that almost all the appointed job-holders who leave when a new party comes in are eligible for severance pay.

Extreme decentralization through a multitude of agencies and autonomous institutions has created a snarl of acronyms with overlapping and often duplicated functions, seriously wanting in coordination and efficiency. Responsibility is so diluted that buck-passing is easy and getting something done is slow and difficult. It is hard to find out just who is responsible for making a decision and who is supposed to act on it.

Over the years, however, an unwritten constitution, a way of doing things *a la tica*, has provided means of getting things done in spite of written guidelines. Some of these make government more effective and responsive, while others have negative consequences. Among cultural patterns for getting things done, compromise is still extremely important, as it has been all through Costa Rican history. A tempest may be raging on the surface, with both sides flinging charges and countercharges in mass media and in assembly sessions. Behind the scenes, meanwhile, a transaction is being worked out that saves face for all concerned and keeps the peace. The very freedom to make charges and countercharges is another way of preserving peace; everyone may sound off through the safety valve of free expression.

Another means of keeping the peace, but a less effective or permanent one, is the symbolic solution to a problem. Costa Rica is often called a nation of laws; but many of the laws exist simply as evidence of good intentions. Symbolic solutions satisfy the formalistic, legalistic outlook common among Costa Rican leaders. They study a problem, meet to discuss it in committees, commissions, seminars, and workshops, proclaim the correct solution to it, pass a law or create a new institution, and presto! the problem is considered solved. One example is the continuing problem of the clouds of noxious fumes emitted by buses. In 1972 an executive decree promising a crackdown on vehicles that continued to contaminate the atmosphere was signed by the ministers of health, transport, and public security. It threatened the owners with seizure of their vehicles after a thirty-day grace period. Nothing happened in 1972—nor in any of the subsequent years when stern measures were announced. Annual headlines proclaim that something is going to be done about the problem; and that is the end of it. Solutions remain in the future tense. *Mañana* never comes.

The Tico aversion to planning was noted twenty-five years ago by Eugenio Rodríguez Vega, who said that anyone who thinks grandly in long-range terms is attacked in the name of Costa Rican traditions. Ticos think in terms of the small, the sure, and the stable.[47] Plans are either unrealistically grandiose or narrow and piecemeal.[48] The former are usually filed away; the latter are hastily made when a problem is on the verge of exploding. Instead of a complete overhaul of the anachronistic and grossly inequitable tax system, for example, one specific tax is levied to meet one urgent problem, another when another crisis looms. Most of the work of the

Planning Ministry consists of long-range "diagnoses" of the problems to be faced in a four-year term on the one hand, and on the other of yearly budgets with very specific outlays such as a new health post promised a village on one of the minister's circuits of rural communities.

The old pattern of paternalism persists in government. The president and his ministers listen to complaints and requests and are photographed handing out the first old-age pension checks under a new law, or cutting ribbons to inaugurate new roads or buildings. At all levels of government officials are besieged by people seeking favors. Making such requests, Booth found, is one way many people participate in politics. A cabinet minister, for example, may find long lines of people gathered outside his or her house every morning and noon trying to get the minister's attention for their personal wishes. Such paternalism allows shortcuts through the bureaucratic maze woven by decentralization and humanizes the impersonality of modern institutions. Still, all of these patterns lend weight to charges of "immobilism"—the needlessly slow pace of institutional change. The remedy many now advocate is a return to the day of strong presidents.

THE PRESIDENCY

Costa Rican presidents under the 1949 weak-president constitution have stretched the rules even to the extent of violating the constitution in order to carry out their programs. Those with charisma have often done so with impunity. Those with a hostile majority in the legislature could otherwise have accomplished very little. One presidential tool is the executive decree, which has the force of law although it must not go contrary to existing laws. Such decrees "have a wide range of importance, perhaps as wide as laws."[49] During the Oduber administration (1974–1978) 4,709 executive decrees were issued as compared to 721 laws.[50]

The trend toward a stronger presidency during the 1970s was indicated by a law passed just before Oduber took office in 1974. It provided that the president would name executive presidents to the autonomous institutions, and that they would be responsible to the executive power. It took away the freedom of autonomous institutions to make policy and left them administrative autonomy.

In spite of the many remaining limitations on his power, the president gives direction to national policy through his influence on public opinion and his close ties with the ministries. Through the Ministry of Planning he coordinates state programs (to the extent they are coordinated at all) and allots their budgets. He interacts frequently with international leaders such as other Latin American presidents, European prime ministers and rulers, administrators of international banks, and United States politicians and bureaucrats. His conspicuous position makes him an easy target for merciless criticism. "To be the president of the Republic is like being a woman in a village of gossips; if she goes out, she is looking for men, if she stays home, she is waiting for them."[51]

THE LEGISLATIVE ASSEMBLY

The Legislative Assembly, considered the principal power in the balance outlined in the constitution, plays a large role in distributing the society's resources. It must ratify international agreements and foreign loans negotiated by the executive by a two-thirds majority before they take effect. It also has investigative powers; it can name special committees with access to all government records and the power to require testimony from anyone in the country; reports of such investigations, however, are seldom acted on.[52] Above all, it passes laws. Since the first law was passed on September 6, 1824, establishing the first constitutional congress, the legislature has passed nearly 6,000 more. The process has been speeded up in recent years as the government has assumed a greater role in the economic and social life of the nation. In Figueres's third administration (1970–1974), for example, 859 laws were passed. Some were as far-reaching as the devaluation of the colón, others as routine as approving the budget for each canton.

Each party (actually, its presidential candidate and top party leaders) chooses a slate of *diputados* for each province, putting the strongest candidates at the top of the list. Voters can split the ticket in the sense that they can vote for one party's presidential candidate and another party's congressional candidates, but they must vote for all the *diputados* of their chosen party. A party's percentage of the popular vote for *diputados* in each province determines how many congressmen it may seat. The system of provincial congressmen means that, in theory at least, a *diputado* represents no specific area, especially in large provinces, and somewhat counteracts the strong loyalty to his or her home canton that a *diputado* may feel. It also leaves those in sparsely populated areas underrepresented and makes it possible for a president to have a minority of his party in the assembly.

A few legislators dominate decision-making. These *diputados* usually head their party slates in San José and sometimes in other *Meseta* towns. They are national party leaders and subject matter experts who provide a core of leadership and expertise. They are the main targets of interest-group pressures and often meet informally with members of the executive branch, including the president, to discuss and negotiate impending bills.

Christopher Baker, in a study of the legislature, classifies *diputados* into three categories according to their "effective participation." The key deputies he calls "nationals." They have legal or other professional training, come from a large population center, and introduce and support bills that seek to allocate resources at the national level. The majority are "parochials," who serve primarily as cantonal representatives, trading votes for local projects with colleagues. They include many who lack national political experience, higher education, or specialized training, and are popularly referred to as *maiceros* or hicks. In between are "national-parochials," most of whom have professional training, usually in law, and come almost entirely from outside the major population centers of the Central Valley. They join the "nationals" in effective decision-making on controversial topics.

When it comes to voting on more controversial and partisan issues that obviously affect the whole society, most *diputados* tend to act as trustees of the national welfare rather than as local delegates. But they rarely vote strictly along party lines, as they are often accused of doing—largely, Baker found, because the majority ("parochial" *diputados*) feel they represent cantons rather than parties, and because Costa Rican parties do not have such encompassing programs or commitments that all issues, or even most of them, become enmeshed in the partisan context. The ban on immediate reelection weakens party discipline—as it was meant to. But it may also weaken the interest of *diputados* in establishing a "good" voting record and truly representing their constituents. Many appear to be interested primarily in making contacts that will help their business or professional careers.

Despite its formal position as the sovereign power, the legislature does not command the respect of many Costa Ricans. Ticos believe strongly in the role of an elected or appointed official as public servant, and in free elections and democratic government, but they tend to question politicians' motives. Many stereotype legislators, in particular, as longwinded, partisan quibblers, indifferent to the national welfare and easily corrupted.[53]

Despite what many Costa Ricans consider its shortcomings, as individuals and as an institution, the Legislative Assembly is a major decision-making body. It balances local and national interests, allows minor parties a voice, and works—imperfectly, as do all parliaments—to make many decisions about who gets what, when, and how. It can be no more effective and responsive and democratic than constitutional and cultural guidelines allow it to be. Until these change, only the varying role performance of individual congressmen can enhance the assembly's prestige and effectiveness.

LAW AND ORDER

Ticos complain not only of an increase in crime but also of a lack of police protection. Burglary is so common that rich and poor alike hesitate to leave a house unguarded; the former resort to window grills, locks, alarms, and private guards for protection. In a 1977 survey in the poor neighborhoods of the metropolitan area, a substantial majority of residents expressed satisfaction with schooling, work, housing, and food, but fewer than half were satisfied with "vigilance and security."[54]

Various reasons for the apparent rise in crime have been suggested. It is common to blame foreigners and foreign influence. Official data, in fact, confirm the popular impression that most major crimes are committed by foreigners, especially Nicaraguans and Colombians.[55] Just as they blamed movies for fostering immorality in the 1940s, so Ticos now call television a "school for delinquency." A former dean of the UCR Law School sees more basic causes: the failure of many institutions to keep pace with social change, the progressive separation of law and morality, and corruption at high levels that sets a bad example.[56] Criminologists generally agree that crime rates rise along with such trends as urbanization, secularization, increased physical mobility, and a decline in intimate relationships accompanied by an increase in impersonal, utilitarian relationships.

Aside from special units such as the Presidential Guard, the elite corps of Military Police, detectives, and narcotics squad, security forces consist of two main sectors. The Civil Guard, with almost 4,000 members, has purely police duties in urban areas. Its preventive capacity has increased in recent years, especially in San José, thanks to the fact that policemen walk in pairs, many armed with pistols, and use walkie-talkies for rapid communication, often to call a patrol car. Consequently crimes, especially burglaries, have apparently declined in the central city; but they have increased on the fringes of the metropolitan area where there is less police protection.

Aside from thefts of cattle and crops, and distilling of contraband liquor, crime is low in rural areas. The 3,000 men of the Rural Assistance Guard would have little to do aside from intervening in drunken disputes during the weekend, except that their role as "public servants" is emphasized. They help build schools, health posts, their own police posts, and simple jails, distribute school supplies and election materials, administer first aid, and radio the police helicopter in case of emergency.

Even in the city, most police recruits are *campesinos*, and half are illiterate. Pay is far too low to attract better-trained men or to keep recruits long. Turnover is 10 percent a month.

Despite complaints about inadequate police protection, neither the public nor its leaders apparently want to abolish the two main causes of the system's defects. One is the firing of thousands of police personnel, including the highest authorities, with each change of administration. This custom endangers efficiency and continuity in state services, says Julio Suñol, and results in a waste of money, knowledge, experience, and training.[57] For some time after each change of government there is a lack of policemen; following the 1978 election, for example, there were only seventeen policemen in the Alajuela post, normally manned by 100. An even more fundamental reason for the lack of a career police force and an efficient system is the fear of militarism that brands any attempt at modernizing the police as militarization. Year after year the legislature denies a salary raise consistent with improving the caliber of the police.

The judicial and penal systems have also come in for criticism—prisons as infrahuman, courts as slow and faulty. Reform in both was stimulated by Enrique Benavides, a lawyer and journalist who investigated and wrote about a flagrant miscarriage of justice that resulted in three men serving fifteen years of a life sentence under miserable conditions before he proved them innocent.[58] Many prisoners have been held a year or two for crimes punishable by as little as a month in jail.

A significant reform that speeds the judicial process was instituted in 1975, when public hearings with all parties present replaced the old system under which the judge was investigator, prosecutor, and defender as well as judge, and arrived at his decisions in the privacy of his chambers. Unlikely to change very much or very soon is class discrimination in imprisonment and sentencing. The poor are much more likely to be arrested than the well-to-do, partly because the police feel a sense of inferiority toward those of higher socioeconomic status and are afraid they will use their pull to punish anyone who dares arrest them. Much white-collar crime, especially tax evasion, is not considered really "criminal" and, even when known, is rarely punished. On the rare occasions when a prominent person is arrested, his name may be withheld from the press and he is given preferential treatment in prison. A 1967 study of penitentiary inmates found that only five of the 840 prisoners could be considered members of the upper or middle class.[59] The poor also complain that the rich can put up bail (and maybe skip the country), pay good lawyers, and buy witnesses. "Justice is for the rich," they say, echoed by a popular humorist's verses: "The law stretches or shrinks, depending on whom it applies to; this happens the world over, but more so in Costa Rica." Except for the last phrase, few serious observers of the system would disagree.

AUTONOMOUS INSTITUTIONS AND STATE ENTERPRISES

As striking a consequence of post–1948 decentralization as a stronger legislature and the Supreme Electoral Tribunal is the rise of the autonomous institutions. By the 1960s it was clear that their autonomy hampered their effectiveness by minimizing accountability and coordination. In a compromise between centralization and decentralization many large *autónomos* now have a director appointed by each incoming president, and are required to coordinate plans with the Office of Planning and the Council of Government (the president and his cabinet). Yet some, such as the Social Security Institute, continue to make their own regulations and agreements with other agencies concerning matters that many think should be decided by the legislature. There is also a tendency to expand an *autónomo's* functions beyond its original purpose. As one example, the National Production Council (CNP), formed in 1949, was to be the technical, social, and financial promoter of agriculture, partly through a system of price supports. It soon assumed regulatory functions and before long was actively interventionist. Eventually it became a business enterprise participating in the market economy by buying and selling agricultural products. Its directors claimed this would regulate supply and demand, prevent speculation by middlemen, and ensure that the public could buy staples at a reasonable price. Finally, it also became an industrial producer, marketing cooking oil and other products under its own label.[60]

Have the *autónomos* helped to achieve social goals in nonpolitical ways as originally intended? Some apparenlty have, to an extent. Social Security (CCSS), for all its flaws, deserves much of the credit for the improvement in the general level of health; ICE, for spreading the communications network ever farther and developing water resources for power and irrigation; INA, for annually training hundreds of workers in marketable skills. But in general, critics say, the *autónomos* have become too large, too numerous, and too wasteful in their duplicated and uncoordinated efforts.[61] The lack of clearly allocated responsibility hampers decision-making and action, and invites inefficiency, partly because, according to economist Eduardo Lizano Fait, there is no mechanism comparable to the profit motive for measuring results. Since a government *autónomo* took over the Atlantic railroad, critics say, service is slower than in the more leisurely days around the turn of the century; a loaded freight car takes ten days or more to get from Limón to San José (an eight-hour run) and no one seems to know where it is at any given time.[62] Blame for such defects is often aimed at a wider target than any one *autónomo*—the public bureaucracy as a whole.

BUREAUCRACY

More than 60,000 employees, including teachers, are paid from the central government budget and over 60,000 more are employed by *autónomos* and public corporations. In 1950 these groups formed 5 percent of the labor force; in 1978, at least 20 percent—one of the highest rates of government employment in the world.

These public employees are the most secure, the best paid,[63] the most highly unionized, and the most powerful of salaried workers. The Labor Code protects 95 percent of all public employees, guaranteeing them certain compensations if they are fired on any basis other than gross incompetence. If an incoming president replaces a number of key decision-makers, severance pay can run into the millions.[64]

Almost all central government workers are covered by the civil service system. This system, in effect since 1953, was designed to replace political patronage with a merit system. The intent of the law was to cover decentralized institutions as well, but this was never carried out. The spoils system, though much weakened, dies hard. There are still ways, even in the central government, of finding the post for the person rather than the person for the post. To be sure, the days are gone when a new president could replace all opposition employees with his own supporters. But new jobs can be created, and there are ways around civil service procedural requirements. The opposition cannot make much political capital out of the fact that the "ins" practice the spoils system. To attract support, they themselves must make it clear that supporters will be rewarded.

Dissenters, as we noted earlier, are often effectively silenced with political posts. Likewise, thousands of high-school and university graduates looking for white-collar jobs have nowhere to go but government service; this keeps them from protesting against the system and thus promotes at least temporary social tranquility. It is often said that "The State is a cow with a thousand teats and everyone wants a teat to suck." A humorist adds, "A baby who suckles does not bite."[65]

While the bureaucracy thus dampens potential social protest, its great size and power have other consequences as well. The supposedly neutral bureaucracy has become the largest pressure group in the country, and one of the strongest. It is hard to control; its insatiable demands for higher pay, shorter hours, and greater fringe benefits are accompanied by stated or implied threats to strike and thus shut off important services. Electrical workers, nurses, and even doctors, as well as teachers and office workers, often threaten to strike and sometimes do so.

The bureaucratic middle class is often called a bottleneck; its voracity eats up so much of the social benefits provided by the government that many of these never reach the poor. It is, as we have seen, the most consumption-oriented group in the society. Because it does not produce wealth in the way farmers and industrialists do, these groups consider it parasitic. During a crucial stage of economic development, the president of Uruguay compared the pay windows of public institutions to sharks about to devour all of the nation's production. Costa Rican leaders are very much aware that they may be contributing to this form of "social suicide."

The public may not be aware of such dangers, but they complain constantly that services in government offices and facilities are slow, inefficient, and rendered with indifference and even discourtesy. Residents of outlying provinces often have to spend time and money in San José to get simple matters attended to. A teacher's appointment must be processed through eight agencies. The authors once spent a month getting a routine auto permit that required seventeen trips to nine different agencies. Often one office after another disclaims responsibility and sends the supplicant to still another. "Come back tomorrow" is a standard request. As in other Latin American countries, this situation has given rise to a new occupation, that of *despachante*. For a fee, he waits in line, makes all the necessary trips, gathers the needed papers and signatures, and makes his living from patience and knowledge of the ropes. And, as we have noted, in Costa Rica, as in many other societies, red tape is also cut by the right political affiliation, pull, high social status, and (less frequently and flagrantly than in many other countries) bribes.

The waste of the taxpayer's money in such a system is often irritatingly visible, not only in the mazes one must learn to run but also in the fact that many employees seem to have nothing to do. Ronald Fernández Pinto believes that the cost, depersonalization, and inefficiency of government agencies "erode the confidence of the public in the capacity of the government to process and fulfill its demands" and thus also erode its legitimacy.[66] Alienation is especially common, he believes, among the rural population, who are aware that the urban middle class monopolizes the bureaucracy's jobs and services.

GOVERNMENT INCOME AND EXPENDITURES

In 1950 the total costs of the central government were ₡127 million. Twenty years later they came to nearly a billion colones, and the 1978 budget was ₡4.7 billion. ₡5.4 billion more was earmarked for decentralized institutions. The public sector thus accounts for somewhat more than half the total GNP of some ₡16 billion.

Taxes and contributions such as social security premiums now amount to about 22 percent of the GNP as compared to 14.4 percent as recently as 1972. Most tax revenues—some estimates range from 75 to 90 percent—come from direct taxes on production and consumption. Since everyone pays the same percentage of sales tax and import duties on purchases, the system is a highly regressive one, falling hardest on those least able to pay, those who must spend a higher percentage of their incomes on taxable items.

Producers and employers must pay social security premiums, corporate income taxes, and payroll taxes. Personal income and property, on the other hand, get off so lightly that in this sense, at least, Costa Rica cannot claim to be highly "socialized." Since the property tax was first imposed in 1956 it has been only about 0.3 percent. This encourages people to build luxurious houses rather than invest in productive enterprises. Few Ticos are subject to personal income tax; about 45,000 paid in 1975. Revenue is reduced, some say, by legal loopholes and deducations and by the ease of tax evasion in a country where white-collar crime is largely ignored.

Even when tax revenues are high, during a coffee boom for example, expenditures outrun them. (A large deficit is so typical of the annual budget that President Oduber said it is as normal as a rainy day.) Besides the revenues earmarked for specific purposes, a large share of income is allotted by law to certain ministries or other institutions. Economists see fiscal policy as a weak spot in an otherwise healthy economy.[67] And many Ticos are concerned about the large debts to foreign banks and agencies that their government has contracted to meet its expenses.

LOCAL GOVERNMENT AND COMMUNITY DEVELOPMENT

In the early 1800s municipal councils were so strong that President Carrillo felt he had to eliminate them as sources of dissent and even subversion in order to achieve national unity.[68]

By the late 1860s national unity and central government were secure enough that local government posed no such danger. The constitution of 1869 provided that each canton would be a municipality where councilmen would name the board of education, since municipalities were made responsible for providing free and obligatory education.

Today each of the eighty cantons has its own municipal council, elected every four years along with the president and the legislature. Each council names a municipal executive as a sort of city manager. The Supreme Electoral Tribunal determines the size of the council (from five to nine voting members) on the basis of the canton's population. Each district in the canton chooses a delegate to represent its interests who has a voice in council meetings but not a vote.

In the past three decades municipalities have steadily lost jurisdiction. As education has become more centralized the town school board has less to say about policy. In most municipalities electricity and water and sewage are now taken care of by national *autónomos*. The social security system has absorbed community hospitals once run by local boards. Central ministries provide police protection. Municipal autonomy is limited to such services as garbage collection, public lighting, and upkeep of streets—functions often poorly performed, as the many potholes even in San José's streets attest.

Scanty resources are usually blamed for this ineffectiveness. In 1975 half of all municipalities had budgets of less than one million colones and only seven spent more than five million colones.[69] Municipal revenues come from such diverse sources as a levy on the slaughter of pigs, stamps for legal papers, and permits to erect buildings, hold serenades, and sell liquor. To get anything of importance done the municipality depends on specific appropriations voted into the government budget by the legislature. Party politics strongly affects such allotments. It helps if a provincial congressman feels identified with the canton and if the majority of councilmen belong to his party. When the president or ministers come around, councilmen and other community leaders present appeals for funds to help with specific projects.

It is often charged that party politics keeps the quality of municipal councils low. Party leaders distribute council seats on the election slate as political favors, usually keeping in mind possible influence over voters.[70] They tend to regard municipal ballots as relatively unimportant and are not particularly concerned with the qualifications of candidates other than their partisanship.

In long-established communities, the same families have dominated local politics and hence local government generation after generation.[71] This may be an additional reason, besides greater social equality and more urgent needs, why there is more cooperation on community projects in newly settled communities.

Proponents of stronger municipal government oppose the "urban imperialism" that allows San José to dominate the country, but recognize the inefficiency and unrepresentativeness of most local governments. The main attempts to solve these problems are the activities of IFAM, the Municipal Promotion and Advisory Institute, and DINADECO, the institute for promoting and coordinating community development associations. The first is aimed primarily at the municipal government; the second bypasses it but does not eliminate the necessity of working with it.

The stated aim of IFAM is to coordinate various agencies that promote rural industry and regional development, and thus increase rural employment. It provides technical advice and credit to municipal governments but, in order to preserve their autonomy, participation is voluntary.

One IFAM study found that there is a strong predisposition among members of a community to work together, but that the municipal government does not tap it. Most community projects were found to originate with groups of residents, while some are suggested by individuals, and the smallest number of all originate with the municipal council.[72] DINADECO claims to try to make the most of any initiative and willingness to cooperate. Its leaders say they want to abolish the prevalent notion that everything must come from the top and to promote "grass roots" collective action.

Ten years after the Law of National Development was passed in 1967, DINADECO was supervising 900 local community development associations, which had built houses, roads, bridges, parks, churches, and schools and provided electricity and a potable water supply in many communities. It works with other government institutions such as the Family Assistance program, but depends largely on local initiative.[73] Its effectiveness is somewhat limited by the uncooperativeness of many local councilmen, who see their power and prestige threatened when national politicians bypass them and seek support among community development leaders.[74]

Costa Rica's foreign policy has hinged chiefly on economic considerations. In discussions of whether or not diplomatic ties with a given nation should be strengthened, ideological, military, and cultural considerations are normally subordinated to the question of whether Costa Rica would stand to gain much by trade with that country, and the congressional Committee on Financial Affairs is a major source of decisions on foreign policy.

In recent years both the scope and nature of diplomatic relations have widened. Costa Rica has become a moral power on the international scene, believes Gonzalo Facio, who served as Foreign Minister from 1970 to 1978. Because of its unusual political system, its representatives are listened to with respect in such international forums as the United Nations when they speak out for human rights and national sovereignty. These same considerations halted the process of establishing normal relations with Cuba when that nation's troops entered action in Africa. "If they could go in there, they could come in here," Facio said.[75]

The moral power of Costa Rica is reflected in the establishment there of the InterAmerican Court of Human Rights in 1979, which will consider alleged infringements of human rights through member states and the InterAmerican Human Rights Commission. Prospects are good for the establishment of a Peace University, sponsored by the United Nations, which would offer postgraduate courses in such issues as energy, human rights, ecology, and the quality of life.

In 1970 Costa Rica had diplomatic connections with thirty-six countries, and in 1979, with ninety-six. Among additions since 1970 are countries in the Soviet bloc, including the Soviet Union. Many Costa Ricans strongly opposed the opening of the Soviet embassy in 1972. President Figueres pointed out that the Soviets had begun buying Costa Rica coffee during his predecessor's administration, and that the thaw in the cold war and the policy of detente adopted by the United States indicated that the time had come for diplomatic relations.

Costa Rica's relations with the United States are in many ways her closest foreign ties, even closer than those she once maintained with France and England. All Ticos acknowledge their country's economic dependence on the United States for trade and loans, though many lament it and especially deplore the "cultural domination" that has led to Americanization of many aspects of life.

"We are more and more alone," Figueres once commented on the decline of democracy in Latin America. Costa Rica is the only country that, by its own definition, has no army. Its small reserve of volunteers receives part-time military training from volunteer instructors. "The reserve has always existed," the Vice-Minister of Public Security told us. "Any citizen can join. But it is active only in emergencies like the Nicaraguan crisis." When we asked him about the vulnerability of a country without military defenses, he answered, "Keeping peace and freedom within the country is more important than any fearful attempts to prevent invasions and attacks. We have hardly any enemies. One of our best defenses is having no defense." These words echo those of Oduber's Minister of Public Security: "Can you imagine the international reaction if a nation that is voluntarily defenseless were attacked by a militarized one? It would be a shame impossible to erase. Our very vulnerability makes us strong."[76]

Costa Rica tends to identify somewhat more with the few remaining Latin American countries with regular elections than with military dictatorships. This self-described "Central American Switzerland" also seeks common cause with small nations. Costa Rica has joined various efforts to organize for economic power, such as those of coffee and banana exporters, the Latin American Economic System, and, in particular, the Central American Common Market.

Although abundant lip service has long been given to the idea of Central American union, integration—still limited mostly to trade and some educational and "cultural" exchange—falls far short of political union in a Patria Grande, and Costa Rica has been especially slow to participate fully in the Common Market. Costa Ricans feel set apart from the rest of Central America by their political system, their greater wealth, and their comparative "whiteness," literacy, and cultural homogeneity.[77]

A newer trend points to the cooperation of Caribbean countries around what they call "our sea." With Venezuela, Colombia, Mexico, and other Central American countries, Costa Rica has agreed to work toward sovereignty of the area's "resources and destinies." Leaders of these countries hope that by forming multinational corporations among themselves, and supporting a merchant marine and perhaps an air cargo fleet, they can promote their economic independence of the big industrial powers.

Costa Rica has tried hard to maintain peace with her neighbors. Only twice since independence have large numbers of Costa Rican troops invaded foreign soil: to repel William Walker in 1856, and to contest the border with Panama in 1921. Although it was among the first countries to declare war on Japan after Pearl Harbor, Costa Rica sent only token troops to the front during World War II, and very few Costa Ricans took part in the 1965 Organization of American States invasion of the Dominican Republic. All of Costa Rica's other military actions were fought on its own territory. Most of these were civil wars or skirmishes. Occasionally trouble with Nicaragua has flared up. The OAS supported Costa Rica in 1955 when Nicaraguan President Anastasio Somoza, a friend of Calderón and bitter personal and ideological enemy of Figueres, abetted an invasion by Calderonistas and Nicaraguan soldiers; Costa Rican youths flocked to join, and turned them back under air cover provided by the OAS.

During the 1978–1979 civil war in Nicaragua, the Costa Rican government, in the eyes of many Ticos, abandoned its traditional policy of non-intervention in the affairs of other countries, and gave various kinds of support to anti-Somoza forces besides the traditional practice of granting asylum to political exiles and refugees, of whom at least 75,000 came. In November 1978 it severed diplomatic relations with the Somoza government and expropriated Somoza's *latifundio* in Guanacaste. Some Costa Ricans severely criticized the government for violating neutrality; they objected to the fact that Sandinist forces were allowed to train in the northern jungles near the border and that many Ticos helped and fought with the Sandinists. The provisional junta met in San José and after Somoza fell in July 1979 Costa Rican officials escorted them to Managua. Despite criticism, it was evident that the Costa Rican people were jubilant over the victory of the revolutionaries, for they had nourished hatred for Somoza for many years. Relations with the new government were cordial.

NATIONALISM A LA TICA

The things that unify all Costa Ricans and set them apart from non-Ticos foster a sense of nationalism. But it is nationalism *a la tica*—relatively mild and moderate, defensive rather than aggressive. It is tempered by their proverbial hospitality, tolerance, and love of peace as well as by their desire to *quedar bien*, which includes a desire to make a favorable impression upon people of other nations.

The flag, the national seal, and the national anthem are parts of many ceremonies, in school and elsewhere, and the criminal code provides for prison sentences and fines for anyone who shows contempt or publicly reviles any one of them. But more evident than these things as symbols of nationalist feelings are cherished myths—the democratic myth in particular. A national folklore has grown up around the belief that Costa Rica is a unique and peerless society with honest elections, individual liberty, and no social class divisions.

Costa Ricans often explain what they do by saying "Ticos are like that." A sense of national identity is apparent among all classes and in nearly all regions.[78] Improved transportation and communication, the mass media, more widespread enrollment in the public education system, and the expansion of other government influences weaken localism and foster this sense of identity. It may also increase as Costa Ricans are exposed more and more to foreign people and cultures and thus become more aware of their own distinctive way of life.

"Big Macs" and the widespread use of such expressions as "O.K." indicate to some Costa Ricans the increasing "cultural domination" by the United States, which, they think, corrupts the mother tongue and competes with the creative efforts of Ticos themselves. Many problems and shortcomings are blamed on foreigners or foreign influences. The degradation of the quality of life and morals so commonly bewailed is laid at the door of cultural domination through television, advertising, and consumerism in general. Foreign professors are accused of poisoning the minds of students with theories that do not "fit the national reality." A candidate for the presidency insisted, "All the bad things we have are imported." Even President Oduber said, "When I have to confront crime, vagrancy, bribery, strikes, etc., I see much of the result of importing foreign values." Though he had studied in both Canada and France, he once declared, "From our students who went to other countries to be 'educated,' we received the love of easy money and the idea of living well without working."[79]

CONCLUSION: LEGITIMACY AND EFFECTIVENESS

Costa Rica's democratic system has often been said to be "in crisis," and expressions of alarm were frequent in the 1970s. Their tranquil liberal democracy is in danger, some say, of being replaced by some other system, perhaps going the way of Uruguay, Argentina, or Chile. They see warning signs in what they regard as the government's lack of effectiveness—of rapid solutions to problems and prompt answers to needs and demands—and in an erosion of its legitimacy, which many attribute to political corruption.

Such critics often ignore the strides the society has made in such areas as health, communications, transportation, and agricultural production, not to mention such arguable indices of a better life as economic growth and increasing per capita income. Some argue that the "basic structural changes" they say the society needs can be achieved only through a revolution followed by a strong central government able to make rapid decisions and take drastic measures.

Still others, including political leaders and many writers and social observers, suggest specific reforms. They frequently suggest longer terms for the president and congressmen, shorter campaigns, lower campaign costs, and a reduction of the bureaucracy. In more general terms, they insist that there should be clearer lines of responsibility in government and especially in the bureaucracy, a clearer balance of powers among the branches of government, greatly improved local government, and controls over the decentralized institutions that would somehow still preserve their autonomy.

Many such changes would require a change in the constitution. Frustrated ever since the 1949 Constitutional Convention, which included only four *figueristas*, threw out the "liberationist" draft, PLN leaders have pressured the legislature to call a constitutional congress to draw up a new constitution. They point out that the constitution of 1949 is essentially a revision of that of 1869, that it was drafted by an unrepresentative assembly traumatized by the events of the 1940s into an irrational fear of presidential power, and that it is far too detailed and inflexible to be amended successfully, for a change in one of its 197 articles would in many cases require a series of changes in others. Only in a new constitution, they insist, could major changes in the relationships of the various powers and the decentralized institutions be spelled out, and clearer lines of responsibility drawn.

Opponents of a new constitution, including the College of Lawyers, consider it a costly and dangerous undertaking; calling a constitutional congess automatically robs the constitution in force, as well as the current administration, of legitimacy. They insist that the proper time for drafting a new constitution is a serious break in the political order such as the 1948 civil war. Advocates declare that, on the contrary, the best time to draft a new constitution is precisely when there is no crisis and there is great consensus on the basic features of the social and political order.

Though some Ticos consider their breed of democracy overly "bourgeois,"[80] the vast majority believe they have the best system they know of, and they want to keep it honest and in working order. A *pulpero* in a *Meseta* village, expressing a distinction we heard time and again, told journalist Miguel Salguero that he does not believe politicians' promises, but also said, "Of course I am satisfied with the regimen we live under. I think it is the best, because there is freedom for everyone."[81] We noted that even such harsh critics of the system as Communists say Costa Rica allows great "*libertad*."

The Costa Ricans' habit of compromise and their basic consensus on important values and norms make debate both possible and fruitful. Though sometimes acrimonious, this continuing dialogue allows the airing of differences and the free play of ideas, and "keeps the blood from reaching the river."

To some extent their democratic system may be seen as a self-fulfilling prophecy. Ticos believe their system is democratic, and therefore they work to make it so. To the degree that the system ameliorates poverty and allows more participation by such groups as women, youth, and *campesinos*, its legitimacy will be even greater than it is today. The cure for imperfect democracy, says a young political leader, is more and better democracy.

Entrance to the Supreme Court Building (Francisco González)

11

CHANGE A LA TICA: SUMMARY AND CONCLUSION

Many changes have occurred in Costa Rica in the past four decades. Instead of 800,000 Costa Ricans, there are now over two million. A far higher proportion live in cities, wear shoes, and go to school. Per capita income has climbed from less than $200 to over $1,500 a year. Economic growth has been steady. Women are having fewer babies, and these babies have about as long a life expectancy as those born in the United States. International roads and air routes have ended centuries of relative isolation. Roads and inter-urban buses, television and radio bring people, things, news, and ideas to all parts of the country.

Most Ticos accept these changes as signs of progress. Yet they are not sure they are any better as people or as a society, and some think they are worse. They prefer that social change occur *a la tica*—in harmony with their treasured way of life. They look at what has happened in other societies and draw lessons about their own, choosing some patterns and policies and rejecting or trying to avoid others. Other societies serve as scapegoats as well as reference groups. Problems and unwanted changes are often blamed on foreign influence and foreign exploitation that threaten the Costa Rican way of life and "the national patrimony."

Despite what they see as recent progress in some areas of their lives, and in part because of other rapid social changes that have accompanied or followed the ones we listed, many Costa Ricans feel that the quality of life has deteriorated. Today's society comes off badly in nostalgic comparisons with some past golden age, often the time of "don Cleto" and "don Ricardo." Then, say old-timers, people were vigorous, self-reliant, and honorable. A man offered a hair of his mustache as a pledge of his word of honor. People worked hard, saved carefully, and spent nonworking hours in church or in wholesome diversions. Everyone from the erudite president to the humble *peón* displayed exquisite manners and great dignity. Authority was respected and crime virtually unknown. Life was more wholesome, simple, peaceful, and orderly.

Now, by contrast, many lament that the "nation of brothers" has split into conflicting groups, and that everything is worse than it was in their grand-parents' generation: people are not as courteous, moral, honest, or self-reliant. They are materialistic, lazy, and wasteful. There is chaos and disor-der in the cities, and disregard for authority and order everywhere. Real patriotism has declined and the country is being sold and surrendered to foreigners. The society's dearest values and traditions are being neglected and destroyed.

This pessimistic view of social change extends to almost all aspects of life, except purely material ones. (Everybody appreciates electricity and hot water!) Today's institutions, beset with problems, are compared to an ideal-ized picture of the way they used to be and to the myths that many still take for granted.

THE FAMILY

The large, united, hard-working family of yesteryear, say tradition-oriented Ticos, has given way to a small nuclear one in which each member goes his or her own way. Government and commerce have taken over from the family such functions as recreation and care of the aged. Not only do they socialize children through schools and the mass media, they even provide many with food and clothing. Divorce, illegitimacy, desertion of spouses and aban-donment of children, and the increase in gainful employment of women outside the home—all these are taken as signs of a severe breakdown in the family.

Despite such fears, the Costa Rican family, in comparison to families in many other rapidly changing societies, continues to be strong and united, especially among land-owning farmers and the middle and upper classes. The home serves as a haven from the outside world and cushions the shock of rapid social change.

EDUCATION

The divergence of myth and reality and the dual function of myth as both blinder and beacon are nowhere more apparent than in education. The myth of "more teachers than soldiers" has enabled a large and still-growing share of the central government budget to be spent on schooling. But recent statistics on illiteracy, school dropouts, and the level of schooling of the labor force have revealed great inequality in educational opportunities; and further blows to pride come from denunciations of the low quality of teaching and learning. Attacks on the myth disturb many Costa Ricans, but also move educational policy-makers to analyze the system's defects and to search for means of achieving a qualitative revolution to complement the quantitative one.

RELIGION

Many Ticos speak of a crisis in Costa Rican Catholicism, both in adherence to the Catholic faith and in the Church as an institution. A crisis, however, implies the danger of decline from a strong position, whereas in Costa Rica the Church has always been comparatively weak and poor as an institution and, for most Ticos, observance has been relatively easy, worship perfunctory, and faith lukewarm. Catholicism *a la tica* has always involved a tendency to pick and choose among articles of belief as well as patterns of observance, and to question priests' authority.

A strong case might be made that faith is deeper now than it was a generation or two ago because of "short courses," the charismatic movement, the competition and example of deeply committed and activist Protestants, and the influence of Vatican II and CELAM. Younger priests tend to believe that if there is a crisis it is due to the traditional idea that their proper role is limited to saving souls for the hereafter; many of them see their proper place in such movements as agrarian reform. Today's political leaders, whose ideas are reflected in the constitution and the public school curriculum, consider religion an important social institution and regard the Catholic faith and religious observance as essential to the Costa Rican way of life.

LEISURE-TIME ACTIVITIES

The way Costa Ricans spend their leisure time, many believe, indicates the decay of morals that has been both cause and effect of the decline they see in home, school, and church. Older Ticos recall wholesome gatherings to sing, picnic, play games, talk, and listen to music. In the 1940s they were already blaming movies for eroding morals by instilling a desire for luxury and idleness. Now they blame television for that and much more, including lessons in crime. They also blame growing materialism on the advertising that supports a capitalist consumer society, and other social changes for the decline of neighborliness and of friendship (although it appears that intimate interaction has long been confined almost entirely to the extended family). Interest in participatory sports and the fine arts, on the other hand, has increased enormously, especially during the 1970s.

THE ECONOMY

Economic crises are daily newspaper fare in democratic countries where the government is closely involved in economic decisions and where party differences are mainly disagreements on economic policy. In today's interdependent world every nation is dependent on international trade. Those nations that are heavily dependent on the export of one or two chief crops or raw materials have little power to affect the terms of that trade. These things are all true of Costa Rica.

Several socioeconomic myths persist: that Costa Rica is a classless society, that it is a "small country of small landowners," and that it is blessed with inexhaustible resources of fertile soil, abundant forests, pure air, and water. Each of these myths is true only in a limited sense, and only in comparison to many other Third World countries, especially those in Latin America that serve Costa Ricans as bases for comparison.

That Costa Rica is a classless society is an enduring myth in two senses of the word: a complex of values and beliefs that conditions their behavior and their view of their society, and a demonstrable falsehood. In spite of economic growth and rising per capita income, great inequality persists, and a third of all Ticos are poor by Costa Rican standards. The middle class is divided into a relatively independent and productive group of professionals and small businessmen and a largely parasitic and unproductive bureaucratic group that has managed to benefit far more from economic advances than have the poor. And Costa Ricans' pride in their "racial" homogeneity and "whiteness" is being challenged by increasingly vocal and demanding minority groups, especially Indians and blacks, who insist that they have never received a fair share of the nation's social and economic resources.

The myth of Costa Rica as a rural democracy of small landowners can be disproved by statistics showing that most farmers have tiny plots of land or none at all, while a large share of land belongs to a relatively few *latifundistas*. But in comparison to many other countries, it does have a large agricultural middle class of independent farmers with medium-sized holdings that give them a decent living. The myth increases land hunger among the poor and stimulates policy-makers to discourage the retention of large holdings and to provide peasants with their own land, supported by advice, credit, and cooperation.

The economy wastes resources partly because of the myth—based on the small population and simple technology of fifty years ago—that they are inexhaustible. Slash-and-burn agriculture continues, cutting of forests has been speeded up, streams, air, and ocean polluted. The long-range plan to substitute hydroelectric power for petroleum and thus make the country more self-sufficient proceeds, but with serious setbacks.

A new myth—that industrialization is the main key to development—guided economic policy during the 1950s and 1960s. But the inflation and food crisis of the 1970s induced policy-makers to encourage food production and make the nation self-sufficient in basic grains.

POLITICS AND GOVERNMENT

Economic crises are usually political ones as well. Political battle lines are largely drawn according to convictions about the government's proper role in the economy. The National Liberation Party, which has dominated politics since the early 1950s, has been largely responsible for a trend toward welfarism, government intervention, and deficit spending. When in power, the PLN's opposition concentrates on fiscal and monetary policy and consolidates the social reforms of the PLN. Aside from these differences there is a broad consensus on national goals, based on the society's dearest and most powerful guiding myth—that of democracy.

Most Costa Ricans firmly believe that democracy is the best possible political system and place a high value on liberty and on honest elections. Almost all Ticos believe that their society comes closer than any other in the world to achieving electoral democracy. Even those who criticize the system as a "bourgeois" democracy—entrusting too much power to the governing elite and the middle class—still hold up democracy as the ideal. Government leaders defend many programs as enhancing "economic" or "social" democracy. One approach is that of distributive justice, reallocating the society's wealth by ensuring everyone of health services, for instance, or providing free meals for children and nursing and expectant mothers—over a quarter of the population in 1979. Another approach that has recently caught hold is to redistribute the means of production through cooperatives, land reform programs, and profit-sharing plans. The tax system, nonetheless, remains almost entirely regressive.

Democracy is regarded as a great treasure in perpetual danger of being destroyed or lost. This attitude gives rise to a seemingly permanent crisis in politics and government. During the long and expensive electoral campaigns the various parties depict election day as a day of judgment on which the wrong choice would spell doom. Social observers and critics, including journalists, intellectuals, and political leaders, constantly view this or that development with alarm. The tension is contagious unless one realizes that it partakes of a hypochondriac's preoccupation with symptoms, real or imaginary, and a rather superstitious feeling that sufficient worry will fend off a real crisis. On the other hand, one also thinks of the saying "The price of liberty is eternal vigilance."

This sense of impending doom was apparent in the 1970s as Costa Ricans measured events and trends by two yardsticks: a cyclical view of their history, and the recent decline of democracy in other Latin American nations, particularly Uruguay and Chile. Some profess to see in their country's history a pattern of regular cycles, each of which ended with the resolution of a crisis that had been building up for years. These cycles are usually described as thirty years long, corresponding to a generation. A writer told us in 1975; "Everything that happened in the 1940s has happened in the last two years, except one thing. When the women march, watch out!" Another said, "All that's lacking for an explosion is electoral fraud." The fateful year was supposed to be 1978, and events were presumably leading up to a dramatic and perhaps violent showdown. As it happened, violence actually declined, and the 1978 election appeared to be a peaceful resolution of conflict.

Costa Ricans often discern parallels between events in their own country and those that led to revolution, one-party government, or the death of democracy—or all three—elsewhere in Latin America, especially in Uruguay. They also ponder lessons that might be drawn from these parallels to help them halt a similar train of events in their own country and prevent a disastrous outcome.

Uruguay, which like Costa Rica was once called "the Switzerland of America," is often thought of as a mirror image of Costa Rica. It was long hailed as 'a model democracy, with a high literacy rate and an educated citizenry. Then, under pressure from striking workers and vote-seeking politicians, the government began to pay increasingly heavy social benefits and to support a disproportionately large bureaucracy. The productive sector proved unable to pay increasingly high taxes and salaries, and spiraling inflation led to demands for greater benefits and higher wages. Production finally broke down. The economy went under, and democracy with it. A military dictatorship took over in 1973. Parallels in Costa Rica include not only a large bureaucracy, extensive social benefits, and deficit spending, but also the overly rapid growth of the capital city, welfare provisions financed by payroll taxes, a strong Marxist influence in unions and universities, a shift from private and charity hospitals to a universalized social security system, and recurrent conflicts of physicians and surgeons with that system.

An economist[1] points out fallacies in the "Uruguayization" analogy: Uruguay was far more dependent on a single export (livestock products) than is Costa Rica, and one that demands little labor. It resorted to an expanded bureaucracy as the easiest way to provide jobs. Bureaucrats were retired early on high pensions; private employees demanded and got the same privilege, but the pension system was seriously underfinanced. By contrast, Costa Rica has a far more diversified, productive, and successful economy. From 1964 to 1971, according to his analysis, Costa Rica had far greater economic growth in terms of both GNP and per capita income; investment grew nearly 12 percent while that in Uruguay declined over 3 percent; central government revenues declined in Uruguay, but multiplied more than four times over in Costa Rica; food production hardly increased in Uruguay while it nearly doubled in Costa Rica—in fact, it declined per capita in Uruguay but grew 31 percent per capita in Costa Rica; and the consumer price index—the handiest measure of inflation—increased from 61 to 4,408 in Uruguay between 1960 and 1971 but only from 92 to 120 in Costa Rica. Finally, he points out that Uruguay spends nearly 3 percent of its GNP on its armed forces, exceeded in Latin America only by Peru, whereas Costa Rica has no military budget.

Misleading though it may be, the Uruguayan analogy may help alert Costa Ricans to the dangers of various alternative policies, particularly to the expansion of bureaucracy. Similarly, from Mexico they have learned what *not* to do in agrarian reform as well as the dangers of one-party government, from Cuba the danger of allowing an excess of foreign investment, from Chile the penalties for politicizing the social security system, and from all of Latin America, the perils of a strong military.

What Costa Ricans do want is a sense of control over their own destiny. The feeling of powerlessness in the face of world events is common enough among citizens of highly industrialized countries. In this tiny country it is even more understandable. To some extent it is relieved by attempts to defend the national heritage against foreign influence and to create a stronger feeling of national unity and identity.

Costa Ricans often remind one another that one small country in a big and interdependent world is restricted in what it can do to guide even domestic social change. Wars, business cycles, technological discoveries, and changes in supplies of food and energy elsewhere affect Costa Rica for good or ill.

Four major problems, increasingly recognized, are the poverty of one-third of all Costa Ricans, the need to prevent overconcentration of population in the metropolitan region, the pressure of a growing population for employment, and the need to protect and conserve soil, woodland, water, and pure air.

Some steps are being taken to solve these problems. Agroindustry is being developed to create jobs in dispersed locations. Development of water power is expected to free the country from much of its dependence on petroleum, encourage new industries and crops, and eventually provide a surplus of electricity for export (to Nicaragua first, as now planned). Technical education is rapidly developing, and the methods and content of general education at all levels are under scrutiny. Community development programs are beginning to improve the quality of life in long-neglected areas. Cooperatives and roads are easing the problems of agricultural production and marketing. International cooperation is reducing dependency. Health and nutrition programs may be seen as an attempt to improve the quality of human resources in the long run and as a holding action to prevent alienation of the poor in the short run. Still in the future are other programs such as tax reform and greater rewards for production.

Businessmen and industrialists have strongly opposed some of these programs, and the proper mix of private enterprise and government intervention in the economy is a recurring point of political conflict. While conservatives cite the dangers of big government, radicals criticize many programs as palliative, piecemeal reformism.

On the whole, however, there is a broad basic consensus about goals and means—and this consensus is one of the great strengths of the society. Through long-accepted patterns of negotiation, dialogue, and compromise, policy-makers usually arrive at decisions that alienate no large sector of the population. They have used the same pattern to recover lands from the multinational banana corporations and to incorporate the banana industry into the economy, thus reducing the nation's dependency and reasserting its sovereignty.

The process of arriving at consensus and compromise on any one issue is slow, but most Costa Ricans regard it as the best and perhaps the only way to work within the democratic system and to preserve individual freedoms while making social changes. Leaders emphasize the need for planning at the same time as they recognize the need for flexibility, expressed in the popular saying "*El camino se hace andando*" (We make the road as we travel). They counsel patience; development is a slow process in which it is impossible to skip any of the necessary stages, though there is no one model of development suited to all societies. They remind their countrymen that the process of development is not automatic or spontaneously generated, but requires conscious, deliberate, systematic effort. They stress the importance, in fact the inescapable necessity, of development along lines other than strictly economic ones. And they note that it is impossible to avoid making mistakes.

The image of their society as uniquely democratic is in some respects a self-fulfilling prophecy. Costa Ricans believe they have a democratic system and therefore they act as if they did and as if it must be preserved. As one Tico put it, "If we believe deeply enough we are the fortresses of our institutions." Every four years elections reaffirm their faith, and at the new president's inauguration representatives of scores of other nations come to do them honor, and thus validate their system in their own eyes. During a presidential term, legitimacy may appear to be eroded as people speak of crises and dangers and the ineffectiveness of the government. Then they work out many of their fears and anxieties in the electoral process, and once again proudly state that the way their democracy functions is a lesson for the world.

Change *a la tica,* then, is to some extent selective modernization conditioned by Costa Ricans' self-image and nationalist sentiments. In his inaugural address on May 8, 1974, Daniel Oduber stated the principles of that selectivity:

> Our authentically Costa Rican culture can and should absorb and assimilate new contributions, whether generated within it by adaptation to new circumstances or by assimilating those that come from other latitudes; but we can never allow a design for Costa Rican society that is not conceived within the essential elements of our authentic historic nature. This is a fundamental fact and a necessary point of departure for every political action and every government proposal. . . . I propose to the Costa Rican people that, without ignoring the wider world of which we are a part and without repudiating lessons from other societies, we should orient the national task on the basis of what we are, of our own idiosyncrasy, and build the country with our own cultural patrimony.

Four years later, in his inaugural address, Rodrigo Carazo called Costa Rica "an oasis of peace in the world". His successor, Luis Alberto Monge, is faced with many problems in keeping it peaceful amid the violence of Central America and the sharp decline in the national economy.

12

TOWARD THE YEAR 2000

(Update, October 1987)

As the final decade of the twentieth century draws near, the problem of guiding change "a la tica" grows ever more challenging. Central American turmoil, serious economic problems, charges of political corruption — all these threaten the peace, democracy, and social justice that are at the heart of the Costa Rican way of life.

Despite parallels with Uruguayan history, leaders no longer speak of "Uruguayization" as a real possibility. What they have done in the 1980s, particularly during the administration of Oscar Arias Sánchez, which began in May, 1986, is to discuss the pros and cons of the path followed since the watershed year of 1948. They question the validity of long-accepted myths, debate options, and, as always, seek to preserve what is valid in their myths and most cherished among their values.

What they do not question is the legitimacy of the system itself. They rely, as they traditionally have done, on dialogue, compromise, peaceful solutions to problems. No longer can these solutions remain largely symbolic. The crisis is real and the demand for real solutions is urgent.

THE ECONOMY: CRISIS AND RECOVERY

The 1980s saw a sharp slump in the economy, followed by steady gradual improvement and serious consideration of new policies.

1981 and 1982 were the most difficult years in Costa Rica's economy in the last half century.[1] From 1950 to 1980 economic growth averaged more than 6% a year. Then the economy shrank; in 1981 by -4.6% (negative growth), in 1982 by -6.9%. In 1982 inflation reached 82%. Per capita income was reduced by 15% and the average salary lost 42% of its buying power.

The colon, which had long remained steady at 8.54 to the dollar, was devalued in 1980 and began to fluctuate freely and chaotically. The cost of imports skyrocketed and it became ever harder to repay foreign obligations. Businesses were threatened with bankruptcy. Unemployment and underemployment doubled. Increasing numbers of Ticos lived in hardship and poverty.[2].

What brought on this severe crisis? A basic factor, says Juan Diego Trejos of the Institute of Economic Research at the University of Costa Rica, is an outworn model of economic development — "import substitution."[3] For over 25 years, one government after another encouraged industrialization on the theory that domestic production would reduce dependency on foreign markets. But industries demanded great quantities of imported raw materials and machinery, and as the balance of trade worsened the country grew more rather than less dependent.

The worldwide recession of 1978-82, a rise in oil prices, and a drop in coffee prices all contributed to the crisis. So did regional political chaos, which discouraged investment and trade. The Central American Common Market had provided buyers for Costa Rica's industrial products. Revolution and civil war played havoc with this market. As its neighbors defaulted on their debts to Costa Rica, it became the first country on the isthmus (aside from Nicaragua) to suffer a sharp economic downturn.

The main reason the crisis loomed as insurmountably disastrous was the gigantic foreign debt. In the 1970s international banks, prodigal with petrodollars, loaned enormous amounts of money at fluctuating interest rates. Autonomous public institutions not subject to budgetary controls such as the Legislative Assembly wields over the central government were especially eager to borrow money. Costa Rica's public foreign debt tripled between 1979 and 1982 and reached nearly $4 billion in the mid-eighties — one of the highest per capita debts in the world. At the same time, international creditor banks sought repayment and imposed much stiffer terms for new loans. Their interest rates, which had been about 6 or 7%, rose to 15%. Just to pay interest took a huge bite out of export dollars; in 1981-2 service on the debt would have taken 75% of income from exports. Rather than pay, Costa Rica defaulted and asked for renegotiation.

The Carazo administration (1978-82), says Trejos, lacked a coherent and effective fiscal and monetary policy. Its erratic, uncertain measures aggravated the crisis. Although government spending increased significantly, the administration refused or failed to increase its revenues by raising charges for publicly provided goods and services — an unpopular measure taken by the next administration.[4]

In 1982 Costa Ricans gave PLN presidential candidate Luis Alberto Monge 60% of their votes in the biggest landslide in three decades. The new administration sought to stabilize and reactivate the faltering economy, and the consequent upturn was almost as sharp as the downturn had been. Inflation fell to 11% in 1983. Economic growth returned to the plus side, totalling 9% in 1983 and 1984. The government rescued businesses on the verge of bankruptcy and pegged salaries to the cost of basic foods. Unemployment declined and buying power began to increase.

These gains were due in large part to generous foreign aid, especially from the United States. In the first three years of the Monge administration U.S. aid reached a total of $643 million, as compared with $67 million in 1978-81. The United States also persuaded international banks to be more flexible and less severe toward Costa Rica. Obviously, this aid has not been disinterested; it has come from a government very aware of its geopolitical interests in the region, and very eager to keep Costa Rica a showcase for democracy and anti-Communism.

During the Arias administration (as of October 1987) economic recovery and growth have been slow but steady. Inflation has been kept below 20%. Private investors, many from the United States and Canada, have responded to special incentives to produce and export non-traditional products such as apparel, electrical parts, processed foods, and fresh fruit, flowers, and ornamental plants.

The government's economic strategy is promoted, even demanded, by international banks and foreign aid agencies. They insist that the government reduce protectionist measures such as farm subsidies and encourage the private sector in banking as well as industry and agriculture.

Debate continues over the proper roles of the private and public sectors, of market forces versus government intervention. In his role as director of the Central Bank, pressured by the International Monetary Fund and AID, economist Eduardo Lizano Fait espouses the neoliberal theory of the free market. Somewhat surprisingly, campesinos — small subsistence farmers — are among his most vociferous antagonists.

The PLN administration of Daniel Oduber (1974-78) encouraged farmers to produce enough corn, rice, and beans to make the country self-sufficient in these staples; they were given easy credit and a sure market through the National Production Council, which also sold to consumers at subsidized prices. Now the government wants farmers to produce non-traditional products while staples are imported from countries that produce them more cheaply.

Campesinos march in protest, carrying banners with such slogans as "We eat beans, not flowers." They insist that the country's food supply must not be left to the mercy of foreign producers in this uncertain world. Why are these proverbially stubborn individualists, long resistant to organization, suddenly demonstrating?

Largely because their dissatisfaction has been fanned into unrest and public action by militant leftists, mostly students, who lost their favorite field of action when the banana industry underwent great changes. No longer are thousands of laborers employed by "the big three." The symbol of Yankee imperialism long after "Mamita Yunai" was no longer a greedy exploiter, the banana industry is now the very mixture of public support and private enterprise, of "solidarismo" rather than "sindicalismo" that many economists see as an ideal pattern. After United Fruit closed down its operations on the Pacific slope — partly because of strikes, partly because the Atlantic side offers easier access to Europe and the eastern United States — banana workers formed cooperatives on land donated by the company, or joined other profit-sharing enterprises. The big three now buy from such independent and organized producers, and Costa Rica continues to rank second only to Ecuador in its share of the export market.

Many see tax reform as essential to true economic recovery. In 1986 the tax burden totalled nearly a quarter of Gross Domestic Product. 70% of this revenue came from indirect taxes on sales, consumption, and foreign trade, only 14% from income tax. Interest groups strongly resist a less regressive plan that would increase taxes on property, income, and profits. The legislature drags its feet on such tax bills, and the government must resort to higher utility rates and social security premiums. The middle and lower classes feel the squeeze.

Rejecting the old model of import substitution and uncertain about reliance on free market forces, the administration has been studying the model of ''sustained development'' suggested several years ago by the United Nations. At its heart is conservation and careful exploitation of natural resources. It is hoped that Costa Rica may one day serve as a model for the rest of Latin America, if not the entire Third World.[5]

Forests now cover only 8% of the nation's territory. At present rates of destruction they will have vanished long before 2000 A.D. Rain forests evolved over fifty million years fall prey in minutes to the chain saw and the match. Though Costa Rica has won international recognition for its numerous national parks and reserves, these show up on a map as small scattered patches in a barren waste of one-crop farms and cattle ranches. (Ironically, the average Tico eats much less beef than he did a decade or two ago; most beef goes to fast-food franchises in the United States.) As the forest disappears, water shortages become more acute. The conservation program may soon find nothing left to conserve.

POLITICS, GOVERNMENT, AND INTERNATIONAL RELATIONS

In a general way, party differences have followed the lines of the debate over the proper roles of public and private sectors in the economy. PLN has long championed a strong role for government, a nationalized banking system and social welfare programs. The opposition is usually a coalition of pro-business pressure groups, now represented by the Partido Unidad Social Cristiana. But these lines are blurred by the pressures of administration. Not only does the opposition when in power rarely tamper with the basic mix of public and private roles evolved over three decades, but the PLN is split over this very question.

Besides restructuring the economy, domestic priorities set by the Arias administration include constructing 80,000 housing units and creating enough jobs to keep up with the pressure of a growing population. Its inescapable foreign policy priorities are set by its proximity to Nicaragua.

Costa Ricans cheered the triumph of the Sandinista revolutionaries in 1979. But they soon grew anxious about having as their neighbor a Marxist state with ties to the Soviet Union and Cuba, and many supported Reagan's hard line. The boundary is jungly and difficult to patrol. Occasional border incidents, usually brief clashes or exchanges of rifle fire, have occurred, and residents of northern areas are uneasy. Elsewhere it is hard to remember, much of the time, that Nicaragua is not somewhere in Patagonia. Although Central American refugees may number 150,000 or more, most are isolated in the camps where they subsist on help from the United Nations and the Costa Rican government.

Many Ticos were lukewarm about Monge's Declaration of Neutrality in 1983. But they supported and applauded Arias' peace initiative in 1987, and were enormously proud when he was awarded the Nobel Peace Prize. (As we go to press, the

Campesinos protest new economic policies. (Judy Mc Clard. *Revista Aportes*).

Nobel Peace Prize winner, President Oscar Arias Sánchez. (Oficina de Prensa, Casa Presidencial).

other Central American nations are slowly implementing some of the Arias Plan's conditions for peace, democratization, and human rights. Challenged by Arias' insistence that Central Americans are capable of solving their own problems and should be left free to do so, and by international support for his effort, the Reagan administration awaits the November 7 deadline without much apparent faith in fulfillment of the plan's terms.)

The University for Peace reinforces Costa Rica's image as a champion of peace and human rights. Proposed to the United Nations by President Carazo, the university serves as a center to promote the teaching of peace in universities and other institutions around the world. Although its financial support is precarious, it is gaining international prestige thanks in large part to its indefatigable and peripatetic Rector, Tapio Varis of Finland.

POPULATION TRENDS

The population of Costa Rica is still young, still growing at a moderately high rate, still largely rural. But trends show that it is aging, and increasingly urban, and that its growth may be slowing down.

At a growth rate of only 2% a year, populations double in 32 years. Costa Rica grows about 2.5% a year.

About 2,800,000 people lived in Costa Rica in 1987. Demographers predict there will be 3,374,000 in 1995. The birth rate fell from 48 per 1000 population in 1950-55, one of the highest in the world, to 29.5 in 1975. It rose again in the 1980s and stands at about 31. This rise may reflect several passing phenomena: the coming to childbearing age of large numbers of females, economic recovery, and the strong stance of President Carazo and his Minister of Public Health against birth control, abortion and sterilization. More problematic is the increase in births to mothers age 15 to 19.

Demographers find reasons to believe that the birth rate and population growth will decline in the near future. About 7 out of 10 married women and common-law wives practice some form of birth control; among women in their thirties and forties the number is greater. The consequences are more clearly seen in fecundity figures than in the crude birth rate. The average number of children born to women of childbearing age was 6.7 in 1950-55, 3.7 in 1975-80, and an estimated 3.3 for 1985-90.[6]

Low death rates also contribute to population growth. Infant mortality, at 19 per 1000 live births, is the lowest in Latin America. Together with the moderately high birth rate, low infant mortality contributes to making the Costa Rica of the 1980s a predominantly young country. Nearly half — 47% — are under age 20; 36.5% under 15.

At the same time, the proportion of old people increases. Life expectancy at birth is comparable to that of developed countries, at 73.7 years. The death rate now stands at 4 per 1000 — one of the lowest in the world. In 1985 those age 65 and over comprised 4.2% of the population, and in 1995 they will be 5%. Since 55 is a common retirement age, it is obvious that those in the middle decades of the life span support large numbers of young and old.

The 1984 census found one Tico out of three living a different canton from that of his birth, as compared to one out of seven in 1973. Cityward migration is in large part responsible for this phenomenal change. Urban areas grow considerably faster than the general population — 3.2% a year. The 1984 census found half the Ticos living in urban centers or their periphery. But 40% still live in scattered rural dwellings, and only 10% in "rural concentrated" areas, villages or hamlets with some features of urban life.

EDUCATION

Among the unusually capable ministers in the Arias cabinet, the Minister of Education, Francisco Antonio Pacheco, is particularly notable. In a short time, and with a meager budget, he has initiated numerous changes — mostly down-to-earth, common-sense ones that demand little money and are aimed primarily at improving the quality of schooling.

1984 census figures show 93% of Ticos over age ten as literate. This figure, comparatively high for the Third World, is open to question. Census takers asked only, "Can you read and write?" Functional illiteracy is harder to measure. One indication is that only those with three years of schooling are really literate, and even in the mid-1980s, 16% dropped out in their second year.

Pacheco insists that the school system must not only form good, literate, honest citizens, but create a labor force adequate to the demands of modern life, aware of the value of time, "capable of solving unforeseen problems, imaginative, critical, but also well-informed."[7] Schools must impart knowledge to give Ticos a firm base of "cultural literacy." (On Independence Day 1987, reporters for *La Nacion* asked 50 people on the street from what country Costa Rica gained independence. Only four answered "Spain.") As we noted in the chapter on education, schools have long failed to teach reasoning and problem-solving, now stated as a firm goal of the system. And they have wasted that irreplaceable resource — time.

The most obvious way to improve education is to spend more time on classroom lessons. For a great many students, the school year was down to 130 days. In 1987 the school calendar was up to 178 days; and they are used to greater advantage by cutting down on ceremonial observances and celebrations, and school time spent on teacher seminars and even picking up pay checks.

In 1986 students at the end of each cycle — third, sixth, ninth, and eleventh years — took exams in math and Spanish. Pacheco calls the results "disastrous." Most grades fell below the 50% necessary for promotion (at least in theory; most students have long been passed on rather routinely to the next cycle). Exams in science and social studies are being given as we go to press. Such exams may eventually serve as a basis for promotion.

On the one hand, the ministry has established computer centers, each of which serves a number of schools, and has begun to meet the needs of gifted children. On the other, it is paying special attention to one-room schools in dispersed rural settlements; though they have only 9% of students, they comprise 45% of all schools. Most are in deplorably inadequate buildings; few have electricity or running water. Helped by funds and advice from AID and the Peace Corps,.

members of rural communities are encouraged to rebuild such schools or construct new ones with their own labor. Their teachers attend special workshops. Printing presses now turn out thousands of pamphlets and workbooks to supply basic classroom materials.

With more rigorous control of the content of schooling, more time in the classroom, higher standards for promotion, and greater involvement of parents, Pacheco believes that Ticos feel a new pride and interest in the quality of schooling — the necessary next step after the quantitative revolution of past decades.

Any observations on changes in other institutions since 1979 must remain largely impressionistic. Is the strong extended family deteriorating? Are significant numbers of Ticos turning to Protestant denominations? Some think so, but there are no firm data to support such conclusions. Observations suggest that participation in active sports and leisure-time and creative activities such as the plastic arts, theater, dance, and music continues to increase.

We reiterate our firmest conclusion: that the Costa Ricans continue to have faith in their system of peace, democracy, and freedom, and to rely on dialogue, compromise, and free elections to arrive at consensus and at solutions to their problems.

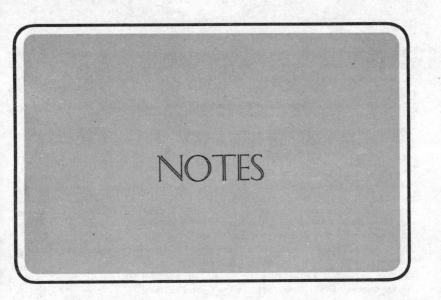

NOTES

CHAPTER ONE

[1] Alexander F. Skutch, *A Naturalist in Costa Rica* (Gainesville: University of Florida Press, 1971), pp. 7–8. See also Chapter 17 for descriptions of the various ecological zones.

[2] For descriptions of the various ecological zones see L. R. Holdridge, *Life Zone Ecology*, rev. ed. (San José: Tropical Science Center, 1967), p. 2.

[3] Carolyn Hall, *El Café y el Desarrollo Histórico-Geográfico de Costa Rica* (San José: ECR and UNA, 1976), p. 17. We follow her delineation of topography in most respects.

[4] Interviews with Ron Liesman and Bill Burger, botanists, Field Museum of Natural History, Chicago, San José, January 1970. Also telephone interview with Joseph Tosi, Tropical Science Center, July 26, 1976.

[5] Mario A. Boza, with Alexander Bonilla, *Los Parques Nacionales de Costa Rica* (Madrid: Instituto de la Caza Fotográfica y Ciencias de la Naturaleza, 1978). This exceptional volume includes excellent color photographs. A smaller inexpensive version is also available.

[6] Among such folkways are the daily bath, place names and foods, including pejibaye, corn, and yuca.

[7] Miguel Gómez, "Crecimiento de la Población de Costa Rica," in *Cuarto Seminario Nacional de la Demografía* (San José: Dirección General de Estadística y Censos, 1968), pp. 138–166.

[8] See his "Cultural Components of Central America," *American Anthropologist,* Vol. 58 (1956), pp. 881–907.

[9] Eugenio Rodríguez Vega, "Debe y Haber del Hombre Costarricense," *Revista de la Universidad de Costa Rica,* No. 10 (Nov. 1954).

[10] Interview with María Bozzoli de Wille, April 29, 1976.

[11] Constantino Láscaris, *El Costarricense* (San José: EDUCA, 1975), pp. 112–115.

[12]Abelardo Bonilla, "Abel y Cain en el ser Histórico de la Nación Costarricense," in Luís Ferrero, ed., *Ensayistas Costarricenses* (San José: Lehmann, 1971), p. 281.

[13]Carmen Naranjo, *Cinco Temas en Busca de un Pensador* (San José: Ministerio de Cultura, 1977), p. 70.

[14]Carlos Monge Alfaro, *Geografía Social y Humana de Costa Rica* (San José: Imprenta Universitaria, 1942), p. 10.

[15]Eugenio Rodríguez Vega, *Apúntes para una Sociología Costarricense* (San José: EUNED, 1977), p. 61. Original UCR edition was published in 1953.

[16]*Ibid.*, p. 126.

[17]Naranjo, *Cinco Temas* . . ., p. 105.

[18]Wagner and Scherzer observed in 1853: "One cannot trust in the promises and contracts of a Costa Rican. This is the most characteristic trait of his nature. Punctuality and conscientious keeping of one's word are extremely rare." *La República de Costa Rica en la América Central* (San José: Ministerio de Cultura, 1974), Vol. I, pp. 211–212. Modern observers say that rural Ticos are far more reliable in these respects than urban Ticos.

[19]Peggy Barlett, *The Use of Time in a Costa Rican Village: Description and Preliminary Interpretation of Data from Pueblo Viejo* (San José: ACM, 1969), pp. 68–69.

[20]Enrique Benavides, "La Columna," *La Nación,* November 7, 1975.

[21]*Codigo Criminal,* Titulo II, Art. 145, "Delitos Contra El Honor."

[22]*Excelsior,* September 23, 1975.

[23]Carlos Monge Alfaro, *Historia de Costa Rica,* 13th ed. (San José: Trejos, 1974), p. 177.

[24]*Excelsior,* September 23, 1975.

CHAPTER TWO

[1]Michael J. Snarskis, "La Vertiente Atlántica de Costa Rica," *Vínculos, Revista de Antropología del Museo Nacional de Costa Rica,* Vol. 2, No. 1 (1976), pp. 101–114.

[2]Carlos Aguilar, *Guayabo de Turrialba: Arqueología de un Sitio Indígena Prehistórico* (San José: ECR, 1972).

[3]Luís Ferrero, *Costa Rica Precolombina* (San José: ECR, 1975), pp. 50–58. Much of this section draws on this source. Archeological evidence indicates that humans may have appeared in Costa Rica about 10,000 years ago, although some recent finds in Nicaragua suggest a far earlier date. See also Doris Stone, *Pre-Columbian Man Finds Central America: The Archeological Bridge* (Cambridge, Mass.: Peabody Museum Press, 1972), pp. 19–20; and Ricardo Quesada López-Calleja, *Costa Rica: La Frontera sur de Mesoamerica* (San José: Instituto Costarricense de Turismo, 1975).

[4]Carlos Monge Alfaro, *Historia de Costa Rica,* 14th ed. (San José: Trejos, 1976), p. 158.

[5]Two different interpretations of this alignment are those of (1) Samuel Stone, who sees the residents of San José—rebellious contrabandists in the colonial era—as having a different life style from the traditionalists of Cartago and Heredia: *La Dinastía de los Conquistadores: La Crisis del Poder en la Costa Rica Contemporanea* (San José: EDUCA, 1975), pp. 251–256; and (2) Rodolfo Cerdas Cruz, who sees Cartago and Heredia as the nucleus of a conservative agricultural-export bloc and San José and Alajuela as interested in commerce and imports; the first wanted simply to replace colonial government with that of the vested interests created in the old regime, while the latter wanted a change to a liberal democratic regime; *La Crisis de la Democrácia Liberal en Costa Rica* (San José: EDUCA, 1972), pp. 28–29.

[6]Where two surnames are given, the first is the paternal one, often used alone.

[7]Monge, *Historia* . . ., p. 192.

[8]Stone, *La Dinastía* . . ., p. 39.

[9]Monge, *Historia* . . ., p. 204.

[10]Clinton Rollins, *William Walker* (Managua, 1945), quoted in Enrique Guier, *William Walker* (San José: Lehmann, 1971).

[11]Samuel Stone, "Sobre la Clase Dirigente y la Sociedad Nacional, " *Revista de Ciencias Sociales,* University of Costa Rica, No. 11 (April 1976), pp. 41–69.

[12]Watt Stewart, *Keith and Costa Rica* (Albuquerque: University of New Mexico Press, 1964).

[13]Daniel Camacho Monge, *Lecciones de Organización Económica y Social de Costa Rica* (Ciudad Universitaria "Rodrigo Facio": UCR, 1967), p. 99.

[14]José Luís Vega Carballo, "La Evolución Agroeconómica de Costa Rica: Un Intento de Periodización y Síntesis (1560–1930)," *Revista de Costa Rica,* Ministerio de Cultura, Juventud, y Deportes, No. 9 (April 1975), pp. 19–70.

[15]A *generation* is "a group of persons with a common historical experience that influences their behavior and ideology, giving them similar attitudes toward the political, social and economic aspects of life." Mario Carvajal, "Ideologías en la Política Costarricense y sus Resultados Electorales," *Revista de Ciencias Sociales,* UCR, No. 7 (April 1973), pp. 7–20.

[16]Marina Volio, *Jorge Volio y el Partido Reformista* (San José: ECR, 1974).

[17]Alberto F. Cañas, *Los Ocho Años* (San José: Editorial Liberación Nacional, 1955), p. 11.

[18]See John Biesanz and Mavis Biesanz, *Costa Rican Life* (New York: Columbia University Press, 1944), for descriptions of these problems as they existed in 1942–1943; and John Patrick Bell, *Crisis in Costa Rica* (Austin: University of Texas Press, 1971), Ch. 2, "The Social Question."

[19]No Costa Rican has yet written a nonpartisan and comprehensive history of the decade. Most historical accounts have been written from the point of view of the "victors"—that is, the Partido Liberación Nacional, whose leader, José Figueres, sparked the civil disturbances of 1948, headed the governing junta that ruled for a year and a half, and was twice elected president. For a dispassionate and well-written account, see Bell, *Crisis in Costa Rica.*

[20]Bell, *op. cit.,* p. 46.

[21]Bell, *op. cit.,* p. 45.

[22]Figueres was not, however, one of the powerful *cafetaleros* of the old elite.

[23]Bell, *op. cit.,* p. 103.

[24]Bell, *op. cit.,* p. 143.

[25]This judgment has been corroborated in a number of personal interviews, including several with Corina Rodríguez. See also Bell, *op. cit.,* p. 158.

[26]This clause was repealed in 1975.

[27]This clause was later changed to provide that presidents can serve only one term. It did not apply to ex-presidents who had served before the amendment was passed; thus Figueres and Mario Echandi ran again in 1970.

[28]Controversy was stirred up again in 1974, when a pro-Calderón account of the conflict, Miguel Acuña's *El 48* (San José: Lehmann, 1974) appeared. Many agreed with Oscar Bakit that "it is not simple to write the history of living people who, out of vanity, self-interest, or pure imagination, have constructed pedestals and have stained honor on one side and the other." See his "Sobre un Libro Polémico," *La Nación,* August 21, 1975. See also bitter attacks on Acuña's book by Alberto Cañas in *Excelsior,* and Cañas's own account, *Los Ocho Años.* Caution about writing contemporary history is especially common in tiny Costa Rica, where people want so much to *quedar bien.* For example, Carlos Monge Alfaro's history text, used in schools for many years and constantly revised, allots in its 1976 edition only sixteen pages to the years from 1920 to 1974, and controversial statements are carefully avoided. By contrast, Monge devotes fifty-eight pages to the years from 1821 to 1876.

[29]Bell, *op. cit.,* p. 161.

[30]Bell, *op. cit.,* p. 160.

[31]Stone, *La Dinastía . . .,* pp. 328–329.

[32] Argentine sociologist José Luís de Imaz took his colleagues to task for ignoring other theories and regarding dependency theory as *the* all-embracing explanation of Latin American social problems. "Adiós a la Teoría de la Dependéncia?" Eleventh Latin American Sociological Congress, San José, July 1974. See also C. Richard Bath and Dilmus D. James, "Dependency Analysis of Latin America: Some Criticisms, Some Suggestions," *Latin American Research Review*, Vol. XI, No. 3 (1976), p. 3–54.

[33] Rodrigo Facio, *Estudio Sobre la Economía Costarricense* (San José: Editorial Surco, 1941, reissued by ECR, 1972). For other statements of dependency theory see Daniel Camacho, *La Dominación Cultural en el Subdesarrollo*, 2nd ed. (San José: ECR, 1974), pp. 11–12; José Luís Vega Carballo, *Etapas y Procesos de la Evolución Histórico-Cultural de Costa Rica* (San José: CSUCA, Serie Documentos e Investigaciones, 1972); and by the same author, "Reflexiones en Torno al 'Estudio Sobre la Economía Costarricense' de Rodrigo Facio," *Estudios Sociales Centroamericanos*, Año II (Enero-Abril 1973), pp. 145–156; and Edelberto Torres Rivas, *Interpretación del Desarrollo Social Centroamericano* (San José: EDUCA, 1971).

CHAPTER THREE

[1] John A. Booth, *Características Sociográficas de las Regiones Periféricas de Costa Rica* (San José: IFAM/AITEC, 1974), pp. 37, 39. Though 44 percent of all those sampled were engaged in farming and cattle raising (as compared to 36 percent of respondents to the 1973 census), only 9 percent in the SJMA sample were farmers, as compared to 60 percent in the Atlantic Slope, 65 percent in the South Pacific, 72 percent in the North Pacific, and 90 percent in the Northern Plains.

[2] As we shall see in Chapter 8, however, these are usually inferior in many respects to urban schools.

[3] See Carolyn Hall, *El Café y el Desarrollo Histórico-Geográfico de Costa Rica* (San José: ECR, 1976), pp. 22–24, 72.

[4] Fernando Zumbado, "Perspectivas del Desarrollo Regional y Urbano: 1," in *La Costa Rica del Año 2000* (San José: Ministerio de Cultura, Juventud, y Deportes, 1977), pp. 151–185.

[5] *Ibid.*

[6] Agricultural economists often distinguish between two kinds of large landholders— *latifundistas*, usually absentee owners whose holdings consist largely of idle or underused land held for speculation, and *hacendados*, whose *haciendas* are large farms or ranches used for raising crops or cattle.

[7] Mitchell A. Seligson, "Unconventional Political Participation: Cynicism, Powerlessness, and the Latin American Peasant," in Mitchell A. Seligson and John A. Booth, eds., *Political Participation in Latin America*, Vol. 2: *Politics and the Poor* (New York: Holmes & Meier, 1980).

[8] Mitchell A. Seligson, *Peasants of Costa Rica and the Development of Agrarian Capitalism* (Madison: University of Wisconsin Press, 1980).

[9] The administrative center of a canton, with few exceptions, is classified as an urban district: some districts that are not administrative centers are also classed as urban. The urban-rural distinction is based on the presence or absence of such features as streets, blocks, sidewalks, water supply, electric light, and other "urban services."

[10] Carlos Joaquín Saenz, "Population Growth, Progress, and Opportunities on the Land," Ph.D. Dissertation, University of Wisconsin, 1969, pp. 51–54.

[11] Victor Goldkind, "Sociocultural Contrasts in Rural and Urban Settlement Types in Costa Rica," *Rural Sociology*, Vol. 26 (December 1961), pp. 365–380.

[12] María Eugenia Bozzoli de Wille, "Aspectos de la Diferencia Rural-Urbana en el Area Metropolitana." Paper presented at the annual meeting of the American Anthropological Association, New Orleans, November 20–23, 1969. Courtesy of the author.

[13]In such sparsely-settled areas as Osa canton on the southern Pacific coast, the traveler on foot or horseback is expected to stop at each house, fill people in on the latest news, and glean any news they may have to pass on.

[14]Luís Barahona Jiménez, *Manuel de Jesús Jiménez* (San José: Ministerio de Cultura, 1976), pp. 157–158.

[15]Tito Prudencio Quirós R., "Estudio Sobre Relaciones Vecinales en un Barrio Urbano de San José," University of Costa Rica, unpublished thesis, 1967.

[16]Eugenia López de Piza, *How Costa Rican Women of Low Economic Class Face Economic and Sex Discrimination*, University of Costa Rica study, 1977. Courtesy of the author.

[17]Chester Lloyd Jones, *Costa Rica and Civilization in the Caribbean* (Madison: University of Wisconsin Studies in the Social Sciences and History, 1935), No. 23, p. 126.

[18]Interview with Mireya de Padilla, director of DINADECO, April 12, 1977.

[19]Peggy Barlett, *The Use of Time in a Costa Rican Village* (San José: ACM, 1969).

[20]John A. Booth, Miguel Mondol Velázquez, and Alvaro Hernández Carvajal, *Una Tipología de Comunidades de Costa Rica* (San José: DINADECO-AITEC, 1974).

[21]Booth, *Características Sociográficas*, p. 28.

CHAPTER FOUR

[1]Enrique Benavides, *La Nación*, August 7, 1975.

[2]Samuel Stone, *La Dinastía de los Conquistadores: La Crisis del Poder en la Costa Rica Contemporánea* (San José: EDUCA, 1975), p. 73.

[3]Any attempt to subdivide the human species into races on genetic grounds can only be arbitrary, using some genetic criteria and ignoring other, often overlapping, criteria. Moreover, many commonly used criteria, such as skin color, vary continuously; that is, there are any number of shades of "light" and "dark" skin. Still, since "race" is a concept that Costa Ricans use, we will also use it, with the understanding that the word "blacks," for example, refers to those persons labeled as "black" in Costa Rican usage.

[4]Bernardo August Thiel, "Monografía de la Población de la República de Costa Rica durante el Siglo XIX," *Revista de Costa Rica en el Siglo XIX*, San José, 1902. Cited in Stone, *La Dinastía*, p. 55.

[5]Carlos Meléndez, *Juan Vázquez de Coronado* (San José: ECR, 1965), pp. 42–43.

[6]Stone, *La Dinastía*, pp. 26, 189, 251–252. Daniel Oduber Quirós and Rodrigo Carazo Odio, who had not been elected when Stone was writing his book, bring the total to thirty-five. We feel, however, that Stone overemphasizes the dominance of these families *as families*. After sixteen or more generations it seems highly questionable that, as he claims on page 200, members of the middle class have no kinship ties with the upper class. The fact that many of those holding economic or political power, or upper-class status—perhaps even two or all three of these Weberian dimensions of class—are not aware of their "noble descent" also appears to make the thesis worth investigating further, as Stone himself suggests. It has also been pointed out that tracing from past to present uncovers so many collateral blood lines that the thesis becomes a bit threadbare. "A genealogist who goes back far enough can always, if he wants to, find a 'conquistador,'" says Constantino Láscaris (*La Nación*, November 27, 1975). This Spanish intellectual was struck soon after his arrival in Costa Rica by the impression that almost all Costa Ricans are relatives. Noting that both Communist writer Carlos Luis Fallas and President Orlich (1966–1970) were descendants of the "great families," he examined the genealogies more closely, only to find that collateral rather than direct lines had been used as evidence. Despite these reservations, we agree with the majority of Costa Rican reviewers that *La Dinastía* is the outstanding work of historical sociology on this country to appear thus far.

[7]Some black slaves were brought from Panama through trade during the early years, and

numbered around 200 all through the colonial period. John Norman Riismandel, "Costa Rica: Self-Image, Land Tenure and Agrarian Reform, 1940–1965," Ph.D. Dissertation, University of Maryland, 1972, p. 24.

[8]Antonio de Acosta Arévalo, for example,who settled in 1659, had 15,000 cacao trees, giving him an annual income of 6,450 pesos, as well as a fleet of ships. The leading families gave between 3,000 and 6,000 pesos as their daughters' dowries. These were real riches in a time when a teacher got 25 pesos a year per four students, a priest's annual salary was 111 pesos, and a black slave cost 165 pesos.

[9]Victor Sanabria Martínez, *Genealogías de Cartago Hasta 1850*, Vol. I, 1957. 1st edition, 1949. Reprinted in part in *Población de Costa Rica y Origenes de los Costarricenses* (San José: Editorial Costa Rica, 1977), pp. 115–214. Creoles were officially listed as Spaniards.

[10]Lowell Gudmundson Kristjanson, *Estratificación Socio-Racial y Económica de Costa Rica: 1700–1850* (San José: EUNED, 1978).

[11]Stone, *La Dinastía*, p. 258.

[12]See, for example, Monge, *Geografía Social*, p. 20. Also Daniel Camacho, *Lecciones de Organización Económica y Social de Costa Rica* (San José: Editorial Costa Rica, 1967), p. 129.

[13]Carolyn Hall, *El Café y el Desarrollo Histórico-Geográfico de Costa Rica* (San José: ECR, 1976), pp. 88, 110. Sixty percent of the 32,353 farms were no larger than five hectares. The larger holdings are generally outside the *Meseta*.

[14]Carolyn Hall, *El Café y el Desarrollo*, p. 51.

[15]Stone, *La Dinastía*, pp. 100, 365.

[16]Samuel Stone, "Inversiones Industriales en Costa Rica," *Revista de Ciencias Sociales*, No. 7 (April 1973), pp. 67–89.

[17]Stone, *La Dinastía*, p. 195.

[18]See Hall, *El Café y el Desarrollo*, p. 53, for names and sources; also the biographical sketch of Julio Sánchez Lépiz (1862–1934) in *La Nación*, September 13, 1976, p. 2B.

[19]John Biesanz and Mavis Biesanz, *Costa Rican Life* (New York: Columbia University Press, 1944), pp. 22–23.

[20]Biesanz and Biesanz, *Costa Rican Life*, Ch. 2, "Class and Everyday Living," pp. 19–24.

[21]Stone, *La Dinastía*, p. 106.

[22]Biesanz and Biesanz, *op. cit.*, pp 19–24.

[23]John Patrick Bell, *Crisis in Costa Rica: The 1948 Revolution* (Austin: University of Texas Press 1971), p. 8.

[24]Juan Bosch, *Apúntes para una Interpretación de la História Costarricense* (San José: Editorial Murua Carrillo, 1963), p. 32.

[25]Stone, *La Dinastía*, p. 241. Italics added.

[26]Oscar Arias Sánchez, *¿Quién Gobierna en Costa Rica?* (San José, EDUCA, 1976).

[27]Eugenio Fonseca-Tortós, Gonzalo Adis-Castro, Francisco Amador-Sánchez, Rafael Hernández-Ureña, and Pierre Thomas-Claudet, *Estratificación Social y Planificación Familiar: Aspecto Descriptivos: Costa Rica*, monograph (University of Costa Rica: Centro de Estudios Sociales y de Población, 1970).

[28]*Censos Nacionales de 1973: Población*, Vol. II, Table 55, p. 244.

[29]A member of the Quirós family published a spoof on his ancestry. See Otto Jiménez, pen name "Ocho-ji-kiros," *Arbol Criollo* (San José: Editorial Irazú, 1964).

[30]Fonseca-Tortós et al. *op. cit.*

[31]Arias, *¿Quién Gobierna?*, pp. 79–85.

[32]Miles Richardson and Barbara Bode, *Popular Medicine in Puntarenas, Costa Rica: Urban and*

Societal Features (New Orleans: Tulane University, Middle American Research Institute, 1971), p. 256.

[33]Oscar Arias Sánchez, *Grupos de Presión en Costa Rica* (San José: ECR, 1971), pp. 117–118.

[34]Arias, *¿Quién Gobierna?*, p. 103.

[35]*Censos Nacionales de 1973: Población*, Vol. II, Table 55, p. 244.

[36]Interview with Padre Armando Alfaro, head of IMAS (Instituto Mixto de Ayuda Social).

[37]John A. Booth, *Características Sociográficas de las Regiones Periféricas de Costa Rica* (San José: IFAM [Instituto de Fomento y Asesoría Municipal], 1974), p. 16.

[38]Stone, "Sobre la Clase Dirigente y la Sociedad Nacional," *Revista de Ciencias Sociales*, UCR, No. 11 (April 1976), p. 41–69.

[39]Victor Goldkind, "Sociocultural Contrasts in Rural and Urban Settlement Types in Costa Rica," *Rural Sociology*, Vol. 26 (1961), pp. 365–380.

[40]M. Alers-Montalvo, "Cultural Change in a Costa Rican Village," *Human Organization*, Vol. 15, No. 4 (Winter 1956), pp. 2–7.

[41]Charles P. Loomis et al., eds, *Turrialba: Social Systems and the Introduction of Change* (Glencoe, Ill.: The Free Press, 1953). See especially Chapter 2, "The Setting of the Study," by Paul C. Morrison, Charles P. Loomis, Sakari Sariola, Juvenal Valerio, and Julio A. Morales. The quote is from p. 62.

[42]Peggy Barlett, *The Use of Time in a Costa Rican Village* (San José: ACM, 1969), p. 62.

[43]Loomis et al., *Turrialba*, Ch. 1, "General Introduction," p. 4.

[44]University of Costa Rica, Instituto de Investigaciones Sociales, *La Población de Costa Rica* (San José: UCR, 1976), p. 126.

[45]Adapted from Quince Duncan, *Los Cuatro Espejos* (San José: ECR, 1973), pp. 11–19.

[46]Goldkind, "Sociocultural Contrasts. . . ."

[47]Roy Simon Bryce LaPorte, "Social Relations and Cultural Persistence (or Change) Among Jamaicans in a Rural Area of Costa Rica," Ph.D. Dissertation, University of Puerto Rico, 1962; summary by Bozzoli, in *El Negro en Costa Rica: Antología*, Carlos Meléndez and Quince Duncan eds. (San José: ECR, 1974), p. 202.

[48]John Norman Riismandel, "Costa Rica: Self-Image, Land Tenure and Agrarian Reform, 1940–1965," Ph.D. Dissertation, University of Maryland, 1972, pp. 84, 102, 106.

[49]B. Torres V., *La Nación*, September 27, 1975.

[50]Camacho, *op. cit.*, p. 59. Also Alex Curling, in a 1969 interview, stated: "There is more resentment against the Negro where there are more Negroes."

[51]María Eugenia Bozzoli de Wille, *Localidades Indígenas Costarricenses* (San José: EDUCA, 1975). About 200 Guatusos live in the north.

[52]*La Nación*, June 4, 1976, p. 6A.

[53]Yehudi Monestel, "Costa Rica: Odds and Ends," *The Tico Times*, May 5, 12, and 19, 1978, p. 2.

[54]Enrique Obregón, "Este Día," *Excelsior*, December 27, 1975.

[55]Paula Palmer, *"What Happen": A Folk-History of Costa Rica's Talamanca Coast* (San José: Ecudesarrollos, 1977).

[56]Quince Duncan, "El Negro Antillano: Inmigración y Presencia," in Duncan and Meléndez, *El Negro en Costa Rica*, pp. 85–89. Much of this section draws on this book. See also Michael D. Olien, "The Negro in Costa Rica: The Ethnohistory of an Ethnic Minority in a Complex Society," Ph.D. Dissertation, University of Oregon, 1965.

[57]Jeffrey J. Casey, "La Mano de Obra en la Industria Bananera: Limón entre 1880 y 1940." Paper presented at the Semanario Centroamericano de Historia Económica y Social, Ciudad Universitario Rodrigo Facio, April 21–23, 1977.

[58]Meléndez, "Aspectos Sobre la Inmigración Jamaicana," in Duncan and Meléndez, *op. cit.*, p. 78. The law appears in *Colección de Leyes y Decretos,* p. 490, listed as Article 5, Par. 3, Law 31, December 10, 1934. Repealed in 1949. (Both laws took effect the year following their signing.)

[59]Duncan, *Los Cuatro Espejos,* pp. 25, 75.

[60]See, for example, *La Nación,* January 17, 1975, p. 3B.

[61]*Excelsior,* September 11, 1975.

[62]A professor of modern languages at the University of Costa Rica says that the "creole" speech of Limón is not a dialect but a new language; most of its vocabulary is English, but its structure and grammar have their roots in West Africa. Fernando Wright Murray, "Un Análisis Sintáctico del Habla Criollo en Limón," *Revista de Filosofía y Lingüística,* UCR, No. 2 (October 1976).

[63]Duncan and Meléndez, *op. cit.,* pp. 124–126. See also discussions of bilingual education, such as that by Clarence Byfield, *La Nación,* September 16, 1974, and reports of the Seminar on "The Situation of the Black in Costa Rica," January 1978.

[64]Vickie Lee Erickson, *Old Lives for New: An Ethnographic Change-Adaptation Study of the Chino Population in Cañas, Costa Rica* (San José: ACM, 1975.)

[65]*Ibid.*

[66]*Ibid.*

[67]See Luís Felípe González Flores, *História de la influéncia Extranjera in el Desenvolvimiento Educacional y Científico de Costa Rica* (San José: ECR, 1978). Originally published in 1921. See also Anita Gregório Murchie, *Imported Spices: Anglo-American Settlers in Costa Rica in the Nineteenth Century* (San José: Ministry of Culture, Youth, and Sports, 1981).

CHAPTER FIVE

[1]Manuel E. Gutiérrez A., *La Casa de Adobes Costarricense* (San José: UCR, 1972).

[2]Gutiérrez, *La Casa de Adobes,* p. 21.

[3]Dirección General de Estadísticas y Censo, *Vivienda,* 1973, p. 235.

[4]John A. Booth, *Características Sociográficas de las Regiones Periféricas de Costa Rica* (San José: IFAM/AITEC, 1974), pp. 20–21 and Tables 5 and 6.

[5]Rentals are increasing, especially in the San José area. Twenty-three percent of all Ticos rented a house, apartment, or bedroom in 1973. Many of the remaining 17 percent were *hacienda* laborers who had rent-free use of a dwelling as part of their pay.

[6]Survey by the Department of Economic Studies, Central Bank, as reported in *La Nación,* December 3, 1974.

[7]In 1973 electric washers were found in 20 percent of Costa Rican dwellings, refrigerators in 29 percent, floor polishers in 16 percent, and water heaters in 12 percent. *Vivienda,* p. 357.

[8]In 1973, 28.3 percent of dwellings had one bedroom as compared to 44.5 percent a decade earlier. *Vivienda,* Table 23.

[9]While Sakari Sariola found in the 1950s that slum dwellers who moved to INVU housing had more comforts and a greater feeling of security than prior to the move (*The Process of Urbanization in the Metropolitan Area of San José, Costa Rica* [U.S. Technical Assistance Administration, 1958]p. 92), a study of one housing project, Colonia 15 de Setiembre, indicts INVU for poor planning from the human point of view. No provision was made for a school or for easy social interaction among neighbors; shops were lacking; transportation to potential jobs was very poor, and upkeep was deficient. "The strict sense of order and rigidity which the grid-form imposes on this site is confining. Rows of these standardized dwellings stretch consecutively over land which might otherwise provide a dynamism and attractiveness to its inhabitants. . . . The prevailing *tugurio* attitude of avoiding commitment to a larger collective unit than the im-

mediate familial circle was perpetuated." There was "extreme social disorganization" for lack of institutions to orient and integrate the residents. Ira Kurz, *La Colonia 15 de Setiembre: A Societal and Physical Overview of a Costa Rican Planned Community* (San José: ACM, July 1970). Judging from disastrous experiences with highrise public housing in the United States, we wonder if the multifamily housing will be any better.

[10]Miguel Salguero, "Así Vivimos los Ticos," *La Nación,* March 30, 1972, p. 23.

[11]The reader should bear in mind that the following descriptions of typical daily routine in each major social class could be qualified endlessly, for any such composite sketch must ignore some of the variations within each class. One important trend ignored in our descriptions, the increasing employment of women outside of the home, will be discussed in Chapter Six.

[12]In contrast with several other countries, most rural *peones* in Costa Rica, even men who are steadily employed, do not live on their employers' land, though there are *haciendas* where large numbers of tenant laborers are dependent on the *patrón* for most goods and services.

[13]Peggy Barlett, *The Use of Time in a Costa Rican Village* (San José: ACM, 1969), p. 26.

[14]In the study of peripheral and central areas, 16 percent of heads of families sampled worked as day laborers or *peones* for someone else and also cultivated their own land; in the peripheral regions the percentage was 20.1. See Booth, *Características Sociográficas,* p. 18.

[15]The 1973 census listed 30 percent of dwelling units as equipped with refrigerators. *Vivienda,* p. 357.

[16]In 1977 there were 60,000 domestic servants; the number declines each year as industrial jobs beckon. *La Nación,* March 1, 1977.

[17]Largely because of this, in 1974, cantons comprised of more than 75 percent rural residents had an infant mortality rate of 57; those that had fewer than 35 percent rural had a rate of 30. *Excelsior,* July 13, 1976.

Equally significant, the death rate in the first two years of life is 50 percent higher in rural than in urban areas. It was 125 per 1,000 for children of mothers with no schooling and 33 per 1,000 for those whose mothers had ten years or more of schooling, as noted in a 1968–1969 study by Hugo Behm of CELADE, the Latin American Demographic Center, reported in *La Nación,* December 30, 1975.

[18]*Programa de Nutrición,* Documento de Antecedentes (San José: US/AID, December 1975), p. 11.

[19]Víctor Valverde, Ian Rawson, Jaime Serra, Olger Barboza, and William Vargas, *Evaluación Nutricional del Cantón de San Ramón* (San José: UCR, Facultad de Medicina, 1974).

[20]Dra. María Gabriela Stein de Guzmán and Dra. Delsa Rangel de Solís, "La Contribución de la Mujer a la Solución de los Problemas de la Salud y Nutrición in Centroamérica." Paper read at meeting of the Association of University Women in El Salvador, 1975. Courtesy DELFI library.

[21]The World Health Organization has set a standard of 10 doctors per 10,000 residents. Costa Rica had 4.1 per 10,000 in 1969, 6.2 in 1974. Ministry of Health, *Algunos Indicadores de Salud,* 1976. The UCR Medical School expects the figure of 10 per 10,000 to be reached by 1983. Doctors are heavily concentrated in the San José area. *La Nación,* September 16, 1977.

[22]Leonardo J. Mata and Edgar Mohs, "Cambios Culturales y Nutricionales en Costa Rica," *Boletín Médico del Hospital Infantil,* Vol. 33, No. 3 (May-June 1976), pp. 579–593.

[23]Linda L. Bishop, "Alcoholism and the Alcoholic in Costa Rica: An Attitudinal Study," Costa Rican Development Studies Program, mimeograph (1972). Courtesy of National Institute on Alcoholism.

[24]Survey data provided the authors by the National Institute of Alcoholism.

[25]Quoted in the *San José News,* April 22, 1977.

[26]Magaly Cersósimo, "Conciéncia de la Miséria Humana," *La Nación,* December 19, 1975, p. 6B.

[27]Dairymen complained in November 1977 that the National Liquor Factory—one of the oldest government monopolies—had priority in purchasing sugar cane syrup and there was a serious shortage of it for cattle feed.

[28]Miles Richardson and Barbara Bode, *Popular Medicine in Puntarenas, Costa Rica: Urban and Societal Features* (New Orleans: Tulane University, Middle American Research Institute, 1971), p. 263.

[29]Whiteford, *Health in Atenas* (San José: ACM, 1967), pp. 40–41.

[30]See Richardson and Bode, *Popular Medicine in Puntarenas*, p. 271.

[31]Marian Fry, *Herbal Medicine in San Isidro de el General* (San José: ACM, 1971).

CHAPTER SIX

[1]Carlos Monge Alfaro, *Geografía Social y Humana* (San José: Imprenta Universitaria, 1942), p. 23.

[2]The "illegitimacy" rate increased from 23 percent of all births in 1963 to 28 percent in 1969 and 33.6 percent in 1973. However, this rise does not reflect an increase in the number of unmarried couples living together, but rather the increase in legally married women's practice of birth control. *Población*, p. 242.

[3]Víctor Sanabria Martínez, *Genealogías de Cartago Hasta 1850*, Vol. I, 1957, republished in *Población de Costa Rica y Origenes de los Costarricenses* (San José: Editorial Costa Rica, 1977), pp. 155–214. Investigating the origins of Cartago families, he also found that creoles were "licentious" with black slaves.

[4]William R. Lassey, "Communication, Risk, and Investment Decision-Making in Costa Rica," Ph.D. Dissertation, Michigan State University, 1967.

[5]A Costa Rican extended family has no culturally defined boundaries, either, since a Tico, like an American, considers the parents and siblings of both of his own parents to be relatives, but his relatives on one side may not consider those on the other "side" to be their own relatives. Moreover, the degree of interaction and affection between two cousins, for instance, often determines whether or not they consider each other to be relatives.

[6]Evelyn P. Stevens, "*Marianismo:* The Other Face of *Machismo* in Latin America," in *Female and Male in Latin America: Essays,* Ann Pescatello, ed. (Pittsburgh: University of Pittsburgh Press, 1973), pp. 89–101.

[7]Carol Polsky, *Women in Limbo* (San José: ACM, 1972).

[8]Tallying with our own observations is a study of an *hacienda* in the Turrialba region, which showed that being married conferred greater prestige than being "*juntado*" or "joined," and that bachelors ranked lower than married men. Charles P. Loomis et al., eds., *Turrialba: Social Systems and the Introduction of Change* (Glencoe, Ill.: The Free Press, 1953), p. 54. Fonseca and his coworkers found no free unions among their upper-class sample, but increasing numbers as one descended the social scale, with more in the slums than in rural areas. The urban poor had the greatest numbers of single men. Eugenio Fonseca-Tortós et al., *Estratificación Social y Planificación Familiar: Aspectos Descriptivos: Costa Rica,* monograph (University of Costa Rica: Centro de Estudios Sociales y de Población, 1970.)

[9]About one-third of the eighty-two lower-class women in López de Piza's sample had lived with more than one man. Eugenia López de Piza, *How Costa Rican Women of Low Economic Class Face Economic and Sex Discrimination* (San José: UCR, 1977).

[10]The 1973 census shows 28.1 percent of inhabitants of San José province married and only 2.5 percent in free unions. By contrast, the figures for the lowland provinces are: Guanacaste, 19.7 percent married, 10.3 percent cohabiting; Limón, 19.3 percent married, 12 percent cohabiting; Puntarenas, 20.6 percent married, 10.3 percent cohabiting. (Note that these percentages are

based on total population.) *Población,* Vol. I, p. 112, Table 21. Comparisons with 1950 and 1963 for those fifteen and older are in *Algunas Cifras de los Censos Nacionales de Población 1973–1963–1950,* OFIPLAN, "Planidatos," No. 1 (August 1975), pp. 36–37; see also the University of Costa Rican publications.

[11]López de Piza, *How Costa Rican Women . . .,* pp. 73, 151.

[12]Countries of low fecundity include Uruguay (2.9 children), the United States (1.9), the U.S.S.R. (2.4), Sweden (1.9) and Japan (2).

[13]From 1960 to 1972 Honduras's birth rate remained constant at 44; that of El Salvador dropped from 48 to 41; Nicaragua, 43 to 37; Guatemala, 47 to 43; and Panama, 40 to 37 in 1972 and 33 in 1973. SIECA, p. 80, Table 38.

[14]The main sources of data for this section include Luís Rosero B., *Impacto del Programa Oficial de Planificación Familiar en la Fecundidad, Costa Rica, 1960–1982* (San José: Comité Nacional de Población, March 1978); Luís Rosero B., *Dinámica Demográfica, Planificación Familiar y Política de Población en Costa Rica* (San José: Comité Nacional de Población, June 1978); National Population Committee, *Costa Rican National Family Planning and Sexual Education Program—1978–1982* (February 1978); and the two-volume report of the Sexto Seminario de Demografía: Informe, December 6–7, 1978.

[15]John Biesanz and Mavis Biesanz, *Costa Rican Life* (New York: Columbia University Press, 1944), pp. 74–75.

[16]Dirección General de Estadística y Censo, *Informe de la Encuesta Nacional de Fecundidad, 1978.*

[17]The 1974 Family Code describes the goals of marriage as "a shared life and mutal aid"—not mentioning procreation as did the 1949 constitution. And a highly successful government Family Planning and Sex Education program has existed since 1969. Between 1960 and 1975 the fertility of women between fifteen and nineteen years of age declined only 10 percent; for ages twenty–twenty-four, it fell by 42 percent; and for ages thirty-five–thirty-nine, 60 percent. Average fecundity fell 50 percent for all women twenty-five years and older.

[18]Rosero, *Impacto,* p. 37., and Alberto González Quiraga, "Attitudes Toward Family Planning in Turrialba," report based on a master's thesis at the Interamerican Institute of Agricultural Sciences. On p. 7 González notes: "Although 82.5 percent interpreted the church position as demanding many children (or as many as might be born), willingness to abide by this interpretation was stated by only 21.7 percent."

[19]*Revista de Excelsior,* February 16, 1975. In 1953, 2.17 mothers died per 1,000 live births; in 1972, 1.01; in 1976, 0.20.

[20]A child's parents and godparents are *compadres* to each other and traditionally have a moral obligation of mutual help and respect. But the institution of *compadrazgo* or coparenthood, apparently never as strong as in many other Latin American countries, is on the wane. Many younger Ticos regard it as a vestige from the past, enduring beyond the religious ritual only in such forms of etiquette as occasionally buying beer for a *compadre,* helping each other with the harvest, and sharing meat when a pig is killed.

[21]López de Piza, *How Costa Rican Women . . .*

[22]María de Fátima Araujo Ribeiro, "Procesos de Socialización Primaria en las Diferentes Clases Sociales del Area Metropolitana de San Jose" Lic. Thesis, University of Costa Rica, 1976.

[23]Legal adulthood is reached at age eighteen or at marriage, whichever comes first.

[24]Rafael Tammariello, *San José News,* May 14, 1976.

[25]Nearly half of all brides are between fifteen and nineteen, a third from twenty to twenty-four; the median age is twenty-one. Half the bridegrooms are twenty to twenty-four, a fourth are twenty-five to twenty-nine; the median age is twenty-four.

[26]Girls and their parents in all classes still strongly prefer *novios* whose visits do more than just "warm the spot." If after a year or so the *novio* has not yet spoken of marriage, the girl herself is

likely to ask him to "vacate the spot" unless he intends to marry her, thus in effect proposing marriage to him. In this practice, and in the fact that Ticos refer to a *novio's* parents as *suegros* (parents-in-law), we see vestiges of the traditional view of *noviazgo* as oriented toward marriage.

[27]Yolanda Mendoza, Centro de Orientación Familiar,*Quinto Seminario Nacional de la Demografía: Conocimientos y Opiniones en Materia de Educación Sexual de Adolescentes en el Area Metropolitana de San José,* September 1970.

[28]Daniel Goldrich, "Peasants' Sons in City Schools: An Inquiry into the Politics of Urbanization in Panama and Costa Rica," *Human Organization,* Vol. 23 (Winter 1964), pp. 238–333.

[29]Robert Williamson, "Variables of Middle and Lower Classes in San Salvador and San José." *Social Forces,* Vol. 41, No. 2 (December 1962), pp. 195–207.

[30]Chester Lloyd Jones, *Costa Rica and Civilization in the Caribbean* (New York: Russell & Russell, 1967), p. 126. First published in 1935.

[31]The Christian Family Movement sees this "fragmentation" of families as a social evil. *La Nación,* August 18, 1974, p. 4C.

[32]See, for example, *La Nación,* August 23, 1975, p. 16A.

[33]Olda M. Acuña B. and Carlos F. Denton L., *La Familia en Costa Rica* (San José: Ministerio de Cultura, Juventud, y Deportes e IDESPO, 1979), pp. 87–88.

[34]Eladio Vargas, "Comentarios al Código de la Familia," *La Nación,* August 15, 1974.

[35]*La Nación,* June 24, 1976.

[36]Dirección General de Estadística y Censo, *Población,* Vol. II, Table 69.

[37]As reported by Inés de Montero, *Revista de Excelsior,* March 23, 1975, p. 10.

[38]These fears, although real, may be unrealistic. A San Isidro man, occasionally employed in cultivating and harvesting coffee, made no secret of doing housework and babysitting while his wife taught school. He was kidded somewhat by other men, but seemed to be well-liked, and his "masculinity" was not seriously doubted.

[39]López de Piza, *How Costa Rican Women* . . . See also pp. 133 and 155–156 of *La Mujer.*

[40]Williamson, "Variables of Middle and Lower Classes." Among middle-class respondents, 79 percent said they would marry the same person if they had their lives to live over, while 54.2 percent of those in the lower class said so. Only 8.4 percent of middle-class respondents had had one or more separations, compared to 14.4 percent of those in the lower class.

[41]Polsky, *Women in Limbo,* p.

[42]Liana G. de Odio, "A Propósito del Año de la Mujer," *La Nación,* July 11, 1975.

[43]"La Mujer Que Trabaja," *La Nación,* August 11, 1974, special supplement.

[44]Fonseca et al., *Estratificación Social.*

[45]In a number of nations, including Colombia, divorce is still impossible.

[46]The divorce rate is still low compared to that of many other countries. One way of looking at the situation is that only 423 of the 240,068 married couples listed in the 1973 census were divorced that year. In the United States there were 4.4 divorces per 1,000 population in 1973; in Costa Rica, 0.226 per 1,000. In 1977 the rate had risen to about 1.02 per 1,000.

[47]The 1973 census lists 3,512 divorced women and 1,557 divorced men. One provision of the Family Code reflects the traditional emphasis on establishing paternity. A widowed or divorced woman may not remarry until 300 days after the final dissolution of her previous marriage unless she has given birth during that period or obtains officially acceptable medical proof that she is not pregnant.

[48]Dr. Charles J. Parrish, *Población en la Tercera Edad* (Heredia: IDESPO, 1978), No. 17, Table A-16, p. 39.

[49]John Biesanz and Mavis Biesanz, *Costa Rican Life,* pp. 105–160.

CHAPTER SEVEN

Ministry of Public Education (hereafter MEP), Bulletin, January 1978, *Costos, Gastos, e Indicadores Económicos de la Educación Pública en Costa Rica*, 1976–1978, Table 7. About 20 percent of the much larger 1979 budget went for schooling.

[2]MEP, *Matrícula Inicial Oficial por Nivel de Enseñanza*, 1970–1977, Table 13. Of these, 1.3 percent attend night school.

[3]This "myth" is literally true, but many Costa Rican critics use the phrase to mean an overweening pride in the nation's educational system.

[4]See, for example, Carlos Monge Alfaro, *La Educación como un Reto* (San José: UCR, Serie Cuadernos Universitarios, 1963), No. 17. See also section on education in *La Costa Rica del Año 2000* (San José: Ministerio de Cultura, Juventud, y Deportes, 1977).

[5]See Carlos Monge Alfaro and Francisco Rivas, *La Educación: Fragua de una Democrácia* (San José: UCR, 1978).

[6]Interview with Sira Jaen, January 18, 1978.

[7]Luís Felipe González Flores, *História del Desarrollo de la Educación Pública en Costa Rica*, Vol. 1 (San José: Imprenta Nacional, 1945), p. 4.

[8]Manuel Echeverria, "Medio Siglo Atrás," in Lilia Ramos, *Júbilo y Pena del Recuerdo* (San José: ECR, 1965), p. 259.

[9]See Chester Zelaya, *El Bachiller Osejo* (San José: ECR, 1971).

[10]United States laws to that effect were passed in 1870–1920; Chile, 1920; Uruguay, 1934. Colombia provided for free education in 1945 but did not make it obligatory. Guillermo Malavassi, "La Educación en Costa Rica," *Revista Filosófica de la Universidad de Costa Rica*, No. 10 (1972), p. 61.

[11]Joaquín García Monge, "El Moto," in *Obras Escogidas* (San José: EDUCA, 1974), pp. 401–440.

[12]González Flores, *História del Desarrollo de la Educación*, p. 32.

[13]MEP, *Costos*, Table 1, and data from MEP Department of Statistics, courtesy Marielos Mazariegos, September 7, 1979.

[14]The sharp decline in the birth rate in the 1960s was reflected in the fact that enrollment in primary schools fell each year between 1976 and 1979; at the same time, enrollment in high schools rose considerably.

[15]Sakari Sariola, *The Process of Urbanization in the Metropolitan Area of San José, Costa Rica* (San José: UN Technical Assistance Administration, 1958). He found schooling the main motive for their shift to San José. Twenty years later, we found, it remains important.

[16]MEP, *Indicadores Educativos*, 1970–1980, March 1974.

[17]Figures on dropouts suggest that he is correct. According to the 1973 census, 22 percent of persons age fifteen and older had attended school for only three years or less. This was, however, a marked improvement from 60 percent in 1950 and 52 percent in 1963.

[18]Alberto F. Cañas, "Chisporroteos," *Excelsior*, November 5, 1975.

[19]Wagner and Scherzer noted in the 1850s:

It seems that the system of instruction here places special importance on memorization; the knowledge of numerous dates and facts serves as a measure of the capacity and knowledge of a pupil. This is why pupils being examined, generally the best in school and selected by the teachers, recited their answers without feeling or thinking, with the speed of a buzzsaw. . . . Never had we heard such excess of detail and trivia; the professors asked, for instance, "How many railroad tracks does Paris have? In which directions do they run? How many times per day do trains go over the tracks?"

Moritz Wagner and Carl Scherzer, *La República de Costa Rica en la America Central*, Vol. I, (San José: Ministry of Culture, 1974), pp. 143–144.

[20]A century ago students spent five full hours a day in classes, and had only a month's vacation. Now the school year of 210 scheduled teaching days between March and November has many interruptions besides Holy Week and two weeks of midyear vacation in July, and perhaps only 175 days are spent in school. The same occurs with the 164-day university schedule; one professor estimated that 57 percent of scheduled class time was missed because of holidays, meetings, and elections.

[21]*Excelsior,* June 27, 1976.

[22]George R. Waggoner and Barbara Ashton Waggoner, *Education in Central America* (Washington, D.C.: U.S Department of Health, Education and Welfare, Office of Education, Bureau of Research, June 1969).

[23]UCR Instituto de Investigaciones Sociológicas, reported in *La Nación,* May 18 and September 26, 1977. Twenty-seven percent of a sample of SJMA first graders were found to have learning problems; 6 percent had severe ones.

[24]Eduardo Arze Loureira and Roy A. Clifford, "Educational Systems," Ch. 10 in Charles Loomis et. al., *Turrialba: Social Systems and the Introduction of Change* (Glencoe, Ill.: The Free Press, 1953), p. 181.

[25]The difference is even more striking if we compare the percentages of those between the ages of twenty and twenty-four who had completed eleven years or more of schooling. In 1963, 18 percent of urban and only 3 percent of rural Ticos had had at least eleven years of schooling; in 1973, the figures were 20 and 6 percent respectively.

[26]Interview with Sira Jaen, January 18, 1978.

[27]John F. Helwig, "A Definitive Study of the Status of Costa Rican Public School Teachers," Master's Thesis, The American University, 1968.

[28]Rafael Cortés Chacón, *Panorama de 95 Años de Educación Gratuita y Obligatória* (San José: UCR, 1966).

[29]Campolibre del *Pueblo,* December 13–20, 1976.

[30]Mario Posla, *La Formación del Hombre para un Puesto de Trabajo,* mimeograph (San José: INA, 1973).

[31]Guido Fernández, *La Nación,* September 9, 1976.

[32]Study by Lcda. Fátima Araujo, reported in *La Nación,* September 17, 1977.

[33]Roberto Murillo, interview, January 23, 1978.

[34]Enrique Benavides, "La Columna," *La Nación,* September 7, 1977.

[35]Fernando Volio, quoted in *La Nación,* February 26, 1977.

[36]Oscar Arias Sánchez, "El Maestro, Guía para el Hombre Nuevo," *La Nación,* September 5, 1977, p. 15A.

[37]Lidiette B. de Charpentier, "Sistema Educativo del País se ha Centrado en Maestros," *La Nación,* February 5, 1979.

[38]Emilia Prieto, interview, January 18, 1969.

[39]See *Talia Rojas, Maestra Rural; Autobiografia* (San José: Lehmann, 1974).

[40]In the Osa peninsula in 1968, we saw the rural teacher wash and dress a young man's ax wound every few days. Since rural health posts have proliferated, however, the school's first-aid kit is no longer the only medical facility.

[41]Writing in 1917, Carlos Gagini noted that many urban teachers went to their rural schools as if into daily exile. They looked down on the *conchos* (hicks), who in turn made fun of the *señorita* who did not even know in which month beans are planted. *EOS,* No. 25 (March 1917), p. 56.

[42]Roberto Murillo, "Gracias y Desgracias del Profesor Universitario," *La Nación,* August 1, 1974.

CHAPTER EIGHT

[1]James Backer, *La Iglesia y el Sindicalismo en Costa Rica* (San José: ECR, 1974), p. 11. Despite some good material, internal evidence as well as checking of facts makes us doubtful of this book's overall reliability.

[2]Mario Segura Vargas, *La Nación*, March 27, 1975.

[3]Interview with Padre Armando Alfaro, May 6, 1976.

[4]Much of this section draws on Ricardo Blanco Segura, *Históría Eclesiastica de Costa Rica: Del Descubrimiento a la Erección de la Diócesis (1502–1850)* (San José: ECR, 1965), especially Chapter 2.

[5]Ricardo Blanco Segura, "Intervención de la Iglesia en la Independencia de Costa Rica," *Revista de Costa Rica*, No. 5 (1974), pp. 79–96.

[6]Moritz Wagner and Carl Scherzer, *La República de Costa Rica en la América Central* (San José: Ministry of Culture, 1974), pp. 199, 201, 211, 251, 253.

[7]Carlos Monge Alfaro, *Históría de Costa Rica*, 14th ed. (San José: Trejos, 1976), p. 241, quoting Rafael Iglesias.

[8]Mario Alberto Jiménez, *Obras Completas* (San José: ECR, 1963), Vol. I, p. 35.

[9]This rough estimate of the number of churches was given us by Vicar General Carlos Galvez Córdoba on May 20, 1976. He listed 366 priests; other sources report 343.

[10]Of some 1,800 catechism teachers in 1971, 3 percent were trained in the Instituto Pedagógico de la Religión, whose main function is training classroom teachers of religion, while 66 percent took short courses and 24 percent were trained by the parish priest. *Análisis Catequético Centro-americano*, Centro Coordinador de Pastoral Catequética para America Central, 1971, courtesy Padre Carlos Balma Alfaro.

[11]A Census Bureau survey of 881 families in 1966–1967 found that 55 percent of children over age fifteen had not made their first communion.

[12]Interview with Lic. María Eugenia Vargas, 1968.

[13]Interview with philosopher Claudio Gutiérrez, University of Costa Rica, January 15, 1969.

[14]Interview with Padre Armando Alfaro, May 6, 1976. Padre Carlos Balma, a member of the survey team in 1966, agrees. See Carlos Balma et al., "Encuesta Socioreligiosa: Barrio La Cruz. San José," mimeograph, February 1967, courtesy Padre Balma.

[15]A priest in Puntarenas province estimates that only 15 percent of adults living within walking distance of his church, the only one for miles around, ever attend mass. Another Puntarenas priest estimates that 7 percent of adults in his parish attend. By contrast, of a sample of 1,500 adults allegedly representative of the country's entire adult population, except for the most inaccessible rural people, 95 percent were Catholics, and of these 69.5 percent had attended at least once in the previous month.

[16]Luís Barahona Jiménez, "Cristianismo a la Tica," *El Gran Incógnito* (San José: ECR, 1975), pp. 146–150.

[17]*Ibid.*

[18]Reed Madsen Powell, "A Comparative Sociological Analysis of San Juan Sur, A Peasant Community, and Atirro, an Hacienda Community Located in Costa Rica," Ph.D. Dissertation, Michigan State College of Agriculture and Applied Science, 1951, p. 227.

[19]John Biesanz and Mavis Biesanz, *Costa Rican Life* (New York: Columbia University Press, 1944), p. 208.

[20]*La Nación*, June 12, 1976, p. 4A.

[21]Biesanz and Biesanz, *Costa Rican Life*, pp. 210–211.

[22]Interview with Padre Armando Alfaro, May 6, 1976.

²³María Bozzoli de Wille, "No Creer ni Dejar de Creer," *Revista de Costa Rica,* No. 1 (November 1971), pp. 35–84. Escazú was called San Miguel in the report, on which much of this section is based.

²⁴María Bozzoli de Wille, " 'Maleficio': A Rational Principle Behind an Irrational Practice," unpublished paper, University of Georgia, 1974, courtesy of the author.

²⁵*Ibid.*

²⁶Bozzoli de Wille, "No Creer."

²⁷Bozzoli de Wille, "Maleficio."

²⁸Bozzoli de Wille, "No Creer."

²⁹Wilton M. Nelson, *A History of Protestantism in Costa Rica* (Lucknow, India: Lucknow Publishing House, U. P., 1963), p. 15. Condensed version of Ph.D. Dissertation, Princeton Seminary.

³⁰Richard L. Millett, "Protestant-Catholic Relations in Costa Rica," *Journal of Church and State,* Vol. 12, No. 1 (Winter 1970), p. 41–57.

³¹Víctor Sanabria Martínez, *Bernardo Augusto Thiel, Segundo Obispo de Costa Rica* (San José: Lehmann, 1941), pp. 470–471.

³²Interviews with Clifton Holland, May 6 and August 23, 1976. See also his "A Profile of Evangelical Churches in Costa Rica," *In-Depth Evangelism Around the World,* Vol. 2, No. 4 (San José: Indepth, January-March 1975), pp. 59–64.

³³Conversely, many black Protestants in Limón now take their children to the Catholic Church to be baptized, believing that their paths through schooling and employment will be smoother if they are registered as Catholics.

³⁴Interview with Clifton Holland, August 23, 1976. See also Paul Pretiz, "An In-Depth Study: What Brings People to Christ?" *Latin American Evangelist* (May-June 1976), pp. 4–5.

³⁵Interview with Padre José Carlo, February 1969.

³⁶Paul Pretiz, "Report on the Study of Influences in Conversion: Limón Section," mimeograph, 1975, courtesy of Clifton Holland. In a sense this study is not representative, for it includes many converts who were never even nominal Catholics.

³⁷Interview, August 23, 1976.

³⁸Thomas L. Norris, "Religious Systems," in Charles Loomis *et al., Turrialba: Social Systems and the Introduction of Change* (Glencoe, Ill.: The Free Press, 1953), Ch. VIII, pp. 167–168.

³⁹Millett, "Protestant-Catholic Relations."

CHAPTER NINE

¹Moritz Wagner and Carl Scherzer, *La República de Costa Rica en la America Central* (San José: Ministry of Culture, 1974), p. 110.

²In recent decades, however, a steep rise in burglaries has made families unwilling to leave even a locked house unattended. In a family without servants, women and adolescents are the members most often obliged to guard the house while others are out.

³Enrique Benavides, "La Columna," *La Nación,* April 20, 1976. Alfonso Chase often writes on this theme.

⁴Mario Sancho, *Memorias* (San José: ECR, 1961), p. 39.

⁵In his 1962 study, Williamson found that 77 percent of his middle-class and 88 percent of lower-class respondents prefer diversions with relatives and family members to those with friends. Robert Williamson, "Some Variables of Middle and Lower Class in Two Central American Cities," *Social Forces,* Vol. 41 (December 1962), pp. 195–207.

⁶Also, Tito Prudencio Quirós R., "Estudio Sobre Relaciones Vecinales de un Barrio Urbano de San José" Lic. Thesis, UCR, 1967, p. 41.

[7]*La Nación*, July 30, 1974. Many of the same government and business leaders who have protested the economic drain of excessive holidays have led a trend to abolish the two-hour midday siesta closing (which in San José results in four daily rush hours), and an increasing number of agencies and stores are abandoning the custom.

[8]Yehudi Monestel, *The Tico Times*, December 13, 1974 and December 19, 1975.

[9]John Biesanz and Mavis Biesanz, *Costa Rican Life* (New York: Columbia University Press, 1944), pp. 192–193.

[10]Chester Lloyd Jones, *Costa Rica and Civilization in the Caribbean*, p. 129.

[11]SEC (Costa Rican Teachers Syndicate) leaders, quoted in *La Nación*, May 31, 1974.

[12]William E. Carter, Wilmer J. Coggins, and Paul L. Doughty, *Chronic Cannabis Use in Costa Rica* (Gainesville: University of Florida and National Institute on Drug Abuse, 1976), pp. 111–112.

[13]"Do-Re-Mi," *La República*, October 27, 1975.

[14]José Marín Cañas, *La Nación*, July 11, 1974.

[15]Wagner and Scherzer, *La República de Costa Rica*, p. 130.

[16]Biesanz and Biesanz, *Costa Rican Life*, p. 200.

[17]*Ibid.*, p. 178.

[18]See Constantino Láscaris and Guillermo Malavassi, *La Carreta Costarricense* (San José: Ministry of Culture, Youth, and Sports, 1975), and J. Ramirez Saízar, *Folclor Costarricense* (San José: Editorial "Imprenta Nacional," 1979).

[19]See Francisco Gutiérrez, "El Kitsch como Lenguaje," *Excelsior*, April 24, 1975; Alfonso Chase, "Notas Sobre el Kitsch," and Orlando García Valverde, "Not a Matter of Taste," both in *Excelsior*, May 4, 1975.

[20]*The Tico Times*, September 24, 1976.

[21]Minister of Culture Guido Saenz once received in his office five *campesinos* from a village on the slopes of Irazú, asking him to send the orchestra there. When he agreed, one of the group produced a sack of beets, apologizing for the humble gift. After the concert, for which the whole village turned out, they returned to thank Saenz with a sack of onions.

[22]Ricardo Ulloa Barrenechea, *Pintores de Costa Rica* (San José: ECR, 1974), p. 13.

[23]Luis Ferrero, *La Escultura en Costa Rica* (San José: ECR, 1973), p. 104.

[24]At least two of these painters, Fausto Pacheco and Margarita Bertheau, are now much admired, years after their death.

[25]Others include Fallas's *Gentes y Gentecillas;* Adolfo Herrera García's *Juan Varela;* Fabián Dobles's *Ese que Llaman Pueblo* and *El Sitio de las Abras;* Joaquín Gutiérrez's *Puerto Limón* and *Murámonos, Federica;* Carmen Lyra's *Bananos y Hombres;* and Luisa González's *Aras del Suelo.*

[26]An outstanding novel of the era and its aftermath is Julieta Pinto's *El Eco de los Pasos* (Desamparados: Mesén Editores, 1979).

[27]Guido Fernández, talk to seminar on Costa Rican culture, June 1976.

CHAPTER TEN

[1]Juan Carlos Voloj Pereira, "Como Ve a Costa Rica un Panameño," *La Nación*, January 16, 1978.

[2]There is no navy, air force, or artillery. Yet the frequent assertion that "We have no army" is belied by the existence of a volunteer reserve, and by the training many officers of both the Civil Guard and the National Guard receive on U.S. military posts.

[3]Richard R. Fagen, "Studying Latin American Politics: Some Implications of a Dependéncia Approach," *Latin American Research Review*, Vol. XII, No. 2 (1977), pp. 3–26; Hugh Montgom-

ery Clark, "Economic Development and the Culture of Modern Democracy: A Study of Developmental Processes Among Costa Rican Students," Ph.D. Dissertation, Michigan State University, 1972. See also León Pacheco "¿Quién Gobierna en Costa Rica?" *La Nación*, December 14, 1976.

[4]Samuel Stone, "Sobre la Clase Dirigente y la Sociedad Nacional," *Revista de Ciencias Sociales*, UCR, No. 11 (April, 1976), pp. 4–69.

[5]Mario Carvajal Herrera, "Political Attitudes and Political Change in Costa Rica: A Comparison of the Attitudes of Leaders and Followers with Respect to Regime Values and Party Identification," Ph.D. Dissertation, University of Kansas, 1972, pp. 5, 7, 52.

[6]Charles Denton, *Patterns of Costa Rican Politics* (Boston: Allyn & Bacon, 1971), especially pp. 105–107.

[7]Robert Hervey Trudeau, "Costa Rican Voting: Its SocioEconomic Correlates," Ph.D. Dissertation, University of North Carolina at Chapel Hill, 1971.

[8]Ronald Fernández Pinto, "Estabilidad y Subdesarrollo: Un Análisis Preliminar de la Burocrácia en Costa Rica," *Revista de Ciencias Sociales*, UCR, No. 11 (April 1976), pp. 17–40.

[9]For the 1978 election, for instance, the migration away from Cartago and Guanacaste provinces reflected in the 1973 census resulted in a loss of one congressional seat for each, which went to Limón and Heredia.

[10]In 1979 the Ministries included Economy, Industry, and Commerce; Finance; Public Works and Transportation; Health; Foreign Relations; Agriculture and Livestock; Culture, Youth, and Sports; Labor and Social Security; Public Education; Interior (to join the former ministries of Public Security and Government); the Presidency (an office of liaison and information for the ministries, autonomous institutions, and independent but government-owned entities); the National Office of Planning, whose director has ministerial status; and the Ministry of Justice.

[11]To minimize political influence, the Comptroller is named in the middle of a presidential term and holds office for eight years, often being reappointed time after time.

[12]Other exclusive powers of the assembly, seldom or never exercised thus far, are that of impeaching the president or other high officials; deciding when the president is incapacitated and calling for his legal replacement; authorizing the president to declare war and make peace; creating new courts; censuring cabinet ministers (which does not automatically deprive one of office, but would probably lead to his or her dismissal by the president); and suspending certain individual rights for up to thirty days.

[13]Cases against any government agency or branch of government are tried in such courts.

[14]Robert D. Tomasek, "Costa Rica," Ch. 4 in Ben C. Burnett and Kenneth F. Johnson, eds., *Political Forces in Latin America* (New York: Wadworth Publishing Co., Inc., 1968); Carvajal, *op. cit.;* and Oscar Arias Sánchez, "Un Horizonte que se Abre," *La Nación*, January 26, 1977.

[15]Stone, *op. cit.*

[16]To apply for legal recognition, at least six months before an election a party must submit the names of at least 3,000 registered voters, with a description of the party's hierarchical structure that demonstrates its democratic and representative nature. A party may also be certified only on the local or provincial level. In 1978, eight parties had presidential candidates and thirteen did not.

[17]Jorge Enrique Romero Pérez, *La Social Democracia en Costa Rica* (San José: Trejos, 1977), pp. 12, 131, 185, 218–219.

[18]Suzanne Bodenheimer, "The Social Democratic Ideology in Latin America: The Case of Costa Rica's Partido Liberación Nacional," *Caribbean Studies*, Vol. 10, No. 23 (19   ), pp. 49–96.

[19]Only 9 percent of political scientist Mario Carvajal's sample of "followers" name or imply ideological reasons for their electoral choices.

[20]José Marín Cañas, "La Eséncia del Comunismo Criollo," *La Nación*, December 21, 1974.

[21] Enrique Benavides, *Nuestro Pensamiento Político en sus Fuentes* (San José: Trejos, 1975), pp. 15–32.

[22] At the opposite pole of opinion from these leftist parties is the MCRL, the Free Costa Rica Movement, an ultrarightist paramilitary group. Not registered as a political party, it regularly publishes attacks on communism and on any measures it interprets as procommunist. Seen as extremist by most Ticos, the MCRL remains small.

[23] Enrique Benavides, *La Nación*, April 4, 1977.

[24] Harry Kantor, "Campaign Calmer than Earlier Years," *San José News*, January 31, 1976.

[25] Nelson Chacón Pacheco, *Reseña de Nuestras Leyes Electorales* (San José: Lil, 1975). See section on "Deuda Política," pp. 292–316.

[26] *Politiquería:* cheap political activity, corruption, self-interest, politics for its own sake, as defined by Dorothy Elizabeth McBride Stetson, "Elite Political Culture in Costa Rica," Ph.D. Dissertation, Vanderbilt University, 1968.

[27] Romero, *op. cit.,* p. 73.

[28] Carvajal, *op. cit.,* p. 197.

[29] Henry Wells, interview, January 1970. See also Henry Wells, "The 1970 Election in Costa Rica," *World Affairs* (June 1970), pp. 13–28; and Harry Kantor, *The Costa Rican Election of 1953: A Case Study* (Gainesville: University of Florida Press, 1958).

[30] Denton, *op. cit.,* pp. 90–91; Suzanne T. Post and Susan K. Jackson, *Political Efficacy in Two Rural Costa Rican Towns* (San José: ACM, 1971).

[31] Denton, *op. cit.* About 60 percent of his sample knew, for instance, who was president of the legislature, about the same as for a similar question in the United States.

[32] Mitchell A. Seligson and John A. Booth, "Structure and Levels of Political Participacion in Costa Rica: Comparing Peasants with City Dwellers," Ch. 6 of Seligson and Booth, eds., *Political Participation in Latin America, Vol. 2: Politics and the Poor* (New York and London: Holmes & Meier, 1979), pp. 62–75; John A. Booth, "A Replication: Modes of Political Participation in Costa Rica," *Western Political Quarterly*, (December 1976), pp. 627–633; and John A. Booth, "Democracy and Citizen Action in Costa Rica: The Modes and Correlates of Popular Participation in Politics," Ph.D. Dissertation, University of Texas at Austin, 1975.

[33] *Op. cit.,* p. 192.

[34] *Op. cit.,* pp. 170–171.

[35] Oscar Arias Sánchez, *¿Quién Gobierna en Costa Rica? Un Estudio de Liderazgo Formal en Costa Rica* (San José: EDUCA, 1976), p. 52.

[36] Romero, *op. cit.,* p. 170.

[37] *Op. cit.,* p. 160.

[38] *Op. cit.,* p. 138.

[39] Francisco Escobar, "Un País Anestesiado?" *Excelsior*, August 24, 1975. See also Denton, *op. cit.,* p. 92.

[40] Ministers form an elite within the power elite. Three out of four had held only high national positions; they did not work their way up. Over half had never held public office before. While most ministers already have wealth and prestige and seek power, many *diputados* seek the power and prestige that will win them wealth and upper-class status.

Supreme Court justices are the most likely to have come from the lower class; 17 percent report that their fathers were workers or peasants. They get a later start because justices have to be at least thirty-five years old with a minimum of ten years of law practice, whereas congressmen need to be only twenty-one. Relatively few judges come from the upper class. Middle-class lawyers prefer the security of a judgeship to the risk of political position or private practice; they lack the upper-class contacts and friendships that pave the way in both fields.

[41]Booth, *Democracy and Citizen Action.* . . . See also his "Political Participation in Latin America," *Latin American Research Review,* Vol. XIV, No. 3 (1979), p. 38.

[42]Bodenheimer, *op. cit.,* and José Luís Vega Carballo, interview, 1969.

[43]Oscar Arias Sánchez, *Grupos de Presión en Costa Rica* (San José: ECR, 1971), p. 115.

[44]Editorial, *La Nación,* July 15, 1968.

[45]Benavides, *La Nación,* October 9, 1974. See also Constantino Láscaris, *El Costarricense,* p. 229.

[46]Bell, *op. cit.,* p. 114; also Biesanz and Biesanz, *op. cit.,* pp. 239–240.

[47]*Op. cit.*

[48]Láscaris, *op. cit.,* pp. 465–469.

[49]J. Mijeski, "The Executive-Legislative Policy Process in Costa Rica," Ph.D. Dissertation, University of North Carolina at Chapel Hill, 1971.

[50]Telephone interview with archivist of the Legislative Assembly, July 6, 1978.

[51]Minúsculos, "Notas Intrascendentes," *Excelsior,* April 26, 1976.

[52]Christopher E. Baker, "The Costa Rican Legislative Assembly: A Preliminary Evaluation of the Decisional Function," in Weston A. Agor, ed., *Latin American Legislatures: Their Role and Influence* (New York: Praeger, 1971). Also interviews with the author. We are inclined to see these committees as a further example of symbolic solutions. (A strong similarity, in this respect, can be found in U.S. presidential commissions on sundry social ills.)

[53]A typically critical editorial in *La Nación,* July 20, 1975, supported by our interviews with many Costa Ricans.

[54]Miguel Gómez B., Vera V. Bermúdez M., and José A. Calvo C., *Informe General de la Encuesta en Zonas Marginales del Area Metropolitana de San José—1977* (San José: Oficina de Información: Unidad de Opinión Pública, March 1977), p. 87.

[55]Enrique Montealegre, Vice-Minister of Public Security, personal interview, San José, October 18, 1979.

[56]Eduardo Ortíz O., in *La Nación,* September 9, 1975, cites strikes declared illegal by the Labor Court but permitted by the legislature; mass evictions of squatters; laws passed to "resolve" pending cases before they came to court; unsolved brutal murders; large-scale smuggling facilitated by bribery of public employees; abuse of public funds, and "a public that watchs all of this in silence."

[57]Julio Suñol, "¿Quiénes, Cuándo y Cómo lo Van a Hacer?" *La Nación,* August 5, 1978.

[58]Enrique Benavides, *El Crimen de Colima,* 3rd ed. (San José: Editorial Costa Rica, 1977).

[59]Padre José Carlo, Iglesia del Buen Pastor, "Encuesta Sobre Datos en Archivos del Consejo Superior de Defensa Social: Penitenciaría Central. July 17–August 23, 1967" (unpublished).

[60]Other corporation-like *autónomos* are RECOPE, the recently nationalized oil refinery; CODESA, the Costa Rican Development Corporation, with investments in 1978 in seventeen enterprises; and INS, the insurance monopoly.

[61]See Denton, *op. cit.,* p. 42, and Fernández, *op. cit.,* for example.

[62]*La Nación,* July 27, 1975, and Hugh de Pass, interview, 1976.

[63]Technicians and specialists are not paid as well as in private enterprise, and government has a hard time keeping them. But most public office workers draw considerably higher salaries than in the private sector.

[64]"La burocrácia," *Gentes y Paisajes,* No. 18 (July 16–22, 1976), p. 3. It was estimated that if Carazo upon his inauguration in 1978 replaced only those whom he could legally replace, severance costs would amount to some 50 to 100 million colones.

[65]S. Gallo, "Picotazos," *La Nación,* September 12, 1976.

[66]Ronald Fernández Pinto, "Estabilidad y Subdesarrollo: Un Análisis Preliminar de la Burocrácia en Costa Rica," *Revista de Ciencias Sociales,* UCR, No. 11 (April 1976), pp. 17–40.

[67]"Semi-annual Economic Trends Report," Economic/Commercial Section, U.S. Embassy, December 16, 1977, mimeograph.

[68]Carlos Meléndez, "Trayectoria Histórica del Municipio Costarricense" (San José: IFAM, mimeograph, n.d.).

[69]Justo Aguilar Fong and Luís Enrique Li Avellan, study for UCR Centro de Investigación y Capacitación en Administración Publica, 1976.

[70]Perhaps in large part because of such a spoils system, municipalities typically spend 80 percent of their budges in administrative costs, according to one community development director (IOZ).

[71]Stone, "Sobre la Clase Dirigente. . .," p. 57.

[72]IFAM/AITEC, El Desarrollo Rural en Costa Rica, June 1976, p. 161.

[73]Carazo placed it under the Ministry of Human Promotion, formerly the Ministry of Culture, Youth, and Sports.

[74]Mireya de Padilla, director, DINADECO, interview, April 13, 1977.

[75]Eduardo Ulibarri, "Facio: Ocho Años Hacia una Política Universal," La Nación, April 13, 1978.

[76]Stephen Schmidt, "Understaffed and Underfinanced, Costa Rica's Cop Corps Works Hard at Keeping Nation Peaceful," The Tico Times, January 16, 1976.

[77]James Calvin Billick, "Costa Rican Perspectives and the Central American Common Market: A Case Study in International Integration," Ph.D. Dissertation, University of Pittsburgh, 1969.

[78]One still hears the word Tico, however, used to mean "them" as opposed to "us" among rural Limón blacks, and among some Indians.

[79]The Tico Times, November 28, 1975.

[80]Chester Zelaya, Oscar Aguilar Bulgarelli, Daniel Camacho, Rodolfo Cerdas, and Jacobo Schifter, Democrácia en Costa Rica? 5 Opiniones Polémicas (San José: Universidad Estatal a Distáncia, 1977).

[81]Miguel Salguero, "Asï Vivimos los Ticos," La Nación, July 13, 1972.

CHAPTER ELEVEN

[1]Interview with a U.S. economist working in Costa Rica, April 15, 1977. Because of his position he prefers not to be named.

CHAPTER TWELVE

1. Jorge Rovira Mas and Juan Diego Trejos, "El curso de la crisis en Costa Rica y las opciones de la política económica en el segundo lustro de los años ochenta," Ciencias Económicas, San José, Editorial de la Universidad de Costa Rica, Vol. V. No. 2, 1985. Also interview with Juan Diego Trejos, Sept. 30, 1987. Other data from Gail Dresner of CINDE and Bonnie Lincoln of the United States Embassy.

2. Ibid.

3. Ibid.

4. Ibid.

5. Interview with Maria Bozzoli de Wille, Sept. 25, 1987.

6. Population data from 1984 census; from Asociación Demográfica Costarricense, Mortalidad y Fecundidad en Costa Rica, March 1984; from ADC's Encuesta de Fecundidad y Salud, EFES 86, June, 1986, courtesy of Paul Granados. Other data from Domingo Primante of CELADE.

7. This section is based on Francisco Antonio Pacheco, "Panorama de la educación costarricense en el primer año de labores," and Ministerio de Educación Pública, Memoria - 1986. Data supplied by Jovita Hernández.

INDEX

Acosta, Tomás de, 17
Acuña, Olda, 107
Age roles:
  aging, 82, 111–12, 169
  children and youth, 95–101, 166–68
  pressure to marry, 101
Agrarian reform (*See* Land reform)
Agriculture:
  agroindustry, 213
  employment in, 30, 36–37
  methods, 38, 210
  place in economy, 30
  regional differences in, 218
Alajuela, town of, 18, 43, 44
Alcohol, use of, 79, 85–86, 165
Alfaro, Armando, 149, 150
Alienation, 126, 198
Amigos del Arte, Los, 173
Animal life, 6
Anti-clericalism (*See* Roman Catholic
  clergy)
Araujo, Fatima, 97
Arévalo, Antonio de Acosta, 220
Argentina, 127, 172, 205
Arias, Oscar, 52, 54, 55, 131, 158, 188,
  189–90
Army (*See* Military)
Arrieta, Román, 143, 149
Arts and crafts, 171–76
Association of Professors of Secondary
  Education (APSE), 133
Atlantic Railroad, 20, 51, 197
Autonomous Central American
  University (UACA), 131
Autonomous institutions, 28, 180, 193,
  197–98, 200
  Caja Costarricense de Seguro Social
   (CCSS), 84–85

Backer, James, 137
Baker, Christopher, 194–95
Balance of trade, 31
Banana industry, 20, 21, 31, 51
Baptism, 95
Barahona Jiménez, Luís, 147–48

Barlett, Peggy, 78
Beef cattle, 31, 35, 37
Bell, John Patrick, 24, 28, 29, 217
Benavides, Enrique, 160–61, 183, 196
Bertheau, Margarita, 231
Birth, 94–95
Birth control (*See* Population)
Blacks, 46, 66–68, 155, 171, 210, 221,
  222, 230
Blanco Segura, Ricardo, 138
Bode, Barbara, 55
Booth, John A., 187
Bozzoli de Wille, María Eugenia, 39,
  152–54
Brain drain, 127
Brenes Mesén, Roberto, 175
Britain, 19, 20, 127
Brown, Gerald, 172
Bureaucracy, government, 56–57, 188,
  198–99, 234

Cacao, 48, 220
Caja Costarricense de Seguro Social (*See*
  Autonomous institutions; Social
  security)
Calderón Guardia, Rafael Angel, 23–29,
  84, 140, 181, 186
Camacho, Daniel, 118
Campesinos:
  alienation of, 57, 198
  class-consciousness of, 62–63
  daily routine, 77–79
  friendship, 161
  housing, 75
  leisure, 159–60
  politics and government, 185, 189
  urbanites' attitudes toward, 58
  See also Agriculture; Peones;
   Urban-rural distinctions
Canada, 69, 155
Cañas, Alberto, 175
Cañas, José Marín, 134
Carazo Odio, Rodrigo, 127, 149, 184,
  189, 214, 219
Caribbean countries, cooperation with,
  203

Carrillo, Braulio, 18–19, 200
Cartago, 16–18, 42, 44, 48–49
Castro, José María, 19, 115
Catholicism (See Roman Catholic clergy; Roman Catholicism)
Catholic Union Party, 21, 140
Cattle ranching (See Beef cattle)
Center of Family Integration, 103
Center for the Study of National Problems, 24
Central America, Costa Rica compared to, 8
Central America, Costa Rica's geographic position within (map), 2
Central America, Costa Rica's ties with, 18–19 31-32, 127, 203
Central American Common Market, 31, 203
Central Plateau (See Central Valley)
Central Valley, 4, 5 (map)
    coffee cultivation in, 19
    population concentration in, 14, 37
    social class distinctions, 50
    Spanish colonial settlement, 16–17
Chacón Pacheco, Nelson, 184
Chase, Alfonso, 175
Children:
    formal education, 114–25
    rearing of, 94–98, 106, 123
    recreation, 166–67
    religious training, 144
Chile, 23, 127, 172, 205, 211, 212
Chinese, 8, 20, 68
Christian Family Movement, 103, 147
Church (See Roman Catholic clergy; Roman Catholicism)
Citizenship, 28
Civil Guard, 196, 231
Civil Service system, 28, 120–21, 198
Civil war of 1948, 23–29, 217
Class (See Social class)
Climate, 4, 6
Coffee:
    agricultural policies and, 34
    cultural mystique of, 31, 35
    early cultivation, 18–19
    political power and, 19–21, 49–50, 181
Colombia, 203

Colonial era, 16–18
    education, 115–16
    family, 88–89
    race and social class, 48–49, 219, 220
    Roman Catholic Church, 138
Columbus, Christopher, 15
Communication, 39–40, 219
    See also Language; Literature; Mass media; Newspapers; Radio; Television
Communism, 23, 24, 28, 52, 131, 142, 182–83, 185, 233
    See also Political parties: Vanguardia Popular
Communities:
    boundaries of as determined by consensus, 38
    cooperation within, 44, 46, 60, 122
    development, 122, 201
    identification with, 11, 33, 45, 46, 60, 160, 204
    rural-urban comparison, 39
Compadrazgo (coparenthood), 225
Compromise, as cultural value, 10, 28, 192, 206, 213
Constitution of 1949, 28, 98, 137, 142, 177, 178, 182, 184, 185, 204, 205
Cooperatives, 211, 213
Coronado, Juan Vázquez de, 16, 51
Cortés, León, 23, 24, 25
Courts, 179, 196–97, 232
    See also Superior Electoral Tribunal; Supreme Court
Courtship, 100–103, 225–26
Crime and corrections (See Social control)
Cuba, 202, 212
Cultural homogeneity, 7–8, 213
    and centralized educational system, 120, 121, 133
Curanderos, 87, 152
Cursillos de Cristiandad, 144–45

Daily routine, 77–81
Day care, 96, 125
Death:
    attitudes toward, 11

mourning, 112–13
See also Health: life expectancy
Deforestation, 31, 35, 210
Democracy, 9, 21–25, 27–29, 177, 181,
183–87, 206, 211
Denton, Carlos (Charles), 107, 178
Dependency, economic, 30, 200, 209–10,
212, 213, 218
Development, 29
export crops, 19–21
governmental effectiveness, 178
growth of voluntary associations, 170
ideological debate concerning, 13,
123, 213–14
Roman Catholic Church and, 137–38,
143
See also Industrialization
Diet (See Nutrition)
DINADECO, 46, 83, 174, 201
Diputados (See Legislature)
"Discovery" and conquest, 15–16, 219
Divorce (See Marriage)
Drama, 172
Drugs, 87, 168
See also Alcohol, use of
Duncan, Quince, 67

Echandi, Mario, 11, 182
Economy, vii, 30–32, 197–201, 209–13
See also Agriculture; Development;
Employment; Energy;
Industrialization
Ecumenism, 154–55
Editorial Costa Rica, 172, 174
EDUCA, 174
Education, formal:
adult, 126–27, 129
compulsory, 115, 117, 121
cultural homogeneity and, 118, 133
cultural value, 9–10, 114, 117
curriculum, 118–19, 121, 123, 124,
126, 130, 132
enrollment, 116–17, 128–29
expenditures on, 114, 227
foreign aid and influence, 127–28
history, 21, 115–18, 128–29, 200, 227,
228

industrialization and, 117, 123
literacy, 115, 116, 117–18, 123
migration and, 95, 117, 122, 227
myth of classlessness and, 47
patriotism and, 124
political influences on, 120–21
preprimary, 121
primary, 118–19
private schools, 121
reform of, 124
religion and, 140
secondary, 119–20
sex roles and, 115
social class and, 83, 121–24
social control and, 124
social mobility and, 57, 60, 114, 116,
121, 123, 124
teaching methods, 118–20, 130–31
universities, 128–31, 134–35
vocational, 125–26, 129, 142
See also Teachers
El Salvador, vii
Elderly (See Age roles)
Electricity, 72, 210, 213
Employment:
agriculture, 30, 36–37
government, 56–57, 198–99
industry, 30
part-time, 79
services, 30, 198–99
underemployment and
unemployment, 36–37
Energy, vii, 6, 31, 72, 210, 213
Equality, as cultural value, 9
See also Democracy; Social class
Esquivel, Ascensión, 22
Europe:
cultural influence of, 51, 82, 127, 173
exports to, 49
immigration from, 50, 69

Face-saving, 12
Facio, Gonzalo, 202
Facio, Rodrigo, 30
Fallas, Carlos Luís, 31, 175, 219
Family:
childrearing, 94–98, 106

Family (*cont.*)
  compared with other Latin American
    countries, 89
  cultural value, 9, 88–89
  descent traced through males, 89, 226
  extended, 89, 95–96, 98, 105–6, 224
  grandparents, 90, 92, 96, 111
  illegitimacy, 88, 89, 92, 224
  interaction, 89, 106, 159, 230
  leisure and, 159–60
  parental authority, 97–100
  "queen bee" families, 91–92
  size of, 92–94
  Spanish influences, 88–89
  See also Courtship; Family Assistance;
    Family Code; Marriage; Sex roles;
    Women
Family Assistance, 82, 83, 84
Family Code, 89–90, 107, 110, 225, 226
Fatalism, 11, 148
Fernández, Guido, 175
Fernández, Próspero, 139
Figueres, José ("Pepe"), 25–29, 67, 128,
  142, 172, 185, 191, 202
Fonseca, Eugenio, 54, 109
Food (*See* Agriculture; Nutrition)
Foreign policy, 202–4
France, 49, 50, 51, 69, 173
Freemasonry, 139
Friendship, 9, 161–62, 230

Gamonales, 51, 63, 140
García Monge, Joaquín, 175
Germany, 49, 50, 69, 127
Godparents, 95
Goldkind, Victor, 38, 44, 58, 62
González Flores, Alfredo, 22
González, Gil, 15
González Víquez, Cleto, 22, 23, 207
Government, local, 59–60, 200–1, 235
Government, national:
  described in constitution, 178–79
  functioning of, 191–93
  income and expenditures, 199–200
  ministries, 232–33
  stability vs. effectiveness and
    legitimacy, 178, 180, 191, 193, 199,
    205–6

structure and scope, 179–80
  See also Autonomous institutions;
    Bureaucracy; government; Courts;
    Legislature; Presidency; Military;
    Taxes; Upper class
Green Revolution, 37
Guanacaste, 18, 19, 45, 64, 68, 175
Guardia, Tomás, 20–21
Guatemala, 18, 25, 27, 138
Gudmundson, Lowell, 48
Gutiérrez, Francisco, 124

Health:
  alcoholism, 85–86
  government programs, 82–85, 94–95
  life expectancy, 81, 92, 110–11, 223
  malnutrition, 81–82
  mental health, 85
  popular medicine, 86–87
  rural, 81–85, 223
Heredia, town of, 37, 42, 44, 49, 128
Herrera, Mario Carvajal, 178, 186, 187,
  188
Holland, Clifton, 155, 176
Homosexuality, 100
Housing:
  design and furnishings, 71–76
  ownership, 72
  public, 76, 222–23
  shortage, 75–76
  social class and, 72–76
Iglesias, Rafael, 21
Immigration:
  Argentineans and Chileans, 172
  Chinese, 68
  Europeans, 50
  Jews, 68–69
  Nicaraguans, 69
  population growth, 8
  Protestants, in nineteenth century,
    139
  Salvadoreans, vii
  United States, 69
  West Indians, 20, 66
Income, per capita, 207
Independence, from Spain, 18

Indians, 48, 65–66, 138, 175, 210
Individualism as cultural value, 10
Industrialization, effects of, 23, 30
  age roles, 100
  class distinctions, 52, 56, 223
  education, 117, 123
  employment, 30
  family, 94, 98, 100, 106
  time-consciousness, 13
Instituto Mixto de Ayuda Social (IMAS), 111
Interamerican Court of Human Rights, 202

Jaen, Sira, 123
Jiménez Castro, Wilburg, 189
Jiménez, Ricardo, 22, 23, 51, 66, 140, 207
Jones, Chester Lloyd, 46, 106, 165

Kantor, Harry, 183
Keith, Minor Cooper, 20
Kindergartens, 125
Kinship (See Family)

Labor Code (See Labor relations)
Labor relations:
  Labor Code, 23–24, 192, 198
  paternalism, 49–50
  unions, 23, 31, 132, 133
Labor unions (See Labor relations)
La Nación, 174, 190, 191
Land distribution, 7, 35–37, 58, 210, 212, 220
Land reform, 24, 210
Land use:
  deforestation, 31, 35, 210
  optimal, 34–35
  population pressure and, 35
Language, 7, 8, 66–67
Láscaris, Constantino, 118
Lassey, William R., 89
Latin America, Costa Rica compared to rest of:
  arts and crafts, 171
  domination by capital city, 40

  economy, 30
  family, 89
  government and politics, 28, 177, 202, 211
  infant mortality, 81
  pressure groups, 190
  racial distinctions, 64
  Roman Catholicism, 137
  school curriculum, 123
  social class system, 47, 52, 210
  universities, 131
Law:
  attitudes toward, 11, 66, 179, 192, 195, 233
  career, 21, 50, 57, 116, 233
  Legislative Assembly and, 194
  See also Courts; Legislature; Social control
Legislative Assembly (See Legislature)
Legislature:
  early republican era, 18, 19
  election of members, 194–95
  principal power, 28, 194
  social class origins of members, 52–53
  structure and functions, 20, 179, 194–95, 232
Leisure, 158–76
  boredom and, 85, 158, 160, 163, 165, 169
  children's and adolescents' diversions, 166–68
  Christmas, 164
  clubs and organizations, 170
  dancing, 160, 164
  drinking, 85, 165
  fairs, 160, 162–63
  family and, 159, 160
  flirting, 101, 167–68
  free time, 158, 163–64
  gambling, 165
  Holy Week, 146
  joking, 162
  mass media, 165–66
  parties, 164–65
  sharply distinguished from work, 158
  siesta, decline of, 80, 231
  social class and, 159, 166–70
  social interaction and, 158, 159, 170
  sports, 168–70

Liberal Party, 140
Liberia, 43
Libraries, 124, 174
Life expectancy (*See* Health)
Limón Province, 21, 46, 66, 75, 169, 171, 186, 230, 235
Limón, town of, 43, 190
Literacy (*See* Education, formal)
Literature, 174–75
Localism (*See* Communities, identification with)
López de Piza, Eugenia, 42, 91–92, 96, 97, 103, 109, 167
Lower class, 54
    marriage and family, 91–92, 96–98, 103, 108, 110
    neighborhood solidarity of, 42
    See also Peones; Poverty

Marijuana, 168
Marisa, 150
Marriage:
    age at, 225
    attitudes toward, 89, 101, 103
    common-law ("free unions"), 91, 224
    described in Family Code, 225
    desertion and separation, 109–10
    divorce, 107, 109–10
    marital relations and sex roles, 107–9
    mate selection, 48–49, 52, 57, 89, 104
    residence patterns, 105
    social mobility and, 53, 58, 59, 61, 224
    weddings, 104–5
Marxism, 131
    See also Communism
Mass media, 40, 47, 165–66, 174
    See also Literature; Newspapers; Radio; Television
Mata, Leonard, 82
Meseta Central (*See* Central Valley)
Mestizos, 7
Mexico, 18, 69, 78, 138, 166, 203, 212
Middle class:
    Civil war of 1948 and, 52, 53
    daily routine, 79–80
    democracy and, 177–78
    friendship, 162

housing, 72–74
marriage and family, 92, 96, 97, 100, 101, 103, 104, 106, 108, 109
National Liberation Party and, 188
occupations, 53
"old" and "new" compared, 50, 52, 56, 190, 199
values of ("middle-class mentality"), 60–62
Migration, internal, 37–38, 42, 227
Military, 48, 177, 190, 202–3, 212, 231
Millett, Robert, 156
Ministry of Culture, Youth and Sports, 161, 170, 172, 173, 174, 175
Ministry of Education, 83, 118, 120, 121, 124, 125, 133
Ministry of Health, 83–84, 87
Ministry of Human Promotion (*See* Ministry of Culture, Youth and Sports)
Ministry of Planning, 179, 192–93
Modernization (*See* Industrialization)
Mohs, Edgar, 81, 82
Monge Alfaro, Carlos, 17
Mora Fernández, Juan, 18
Mora, Juan Rafael, 19, 20
Mora , Manuel, 23, 24, 27, 140, 181, 182
Morales de Flores, Irma, 161
Morazán, Francisco, 19
Moreno Cañas, Ricardo, 150
Movies, 165–66
Movimiento Costa Rica Libre, 233
Multinational corporations, 30
Municipal Promotion and Advisory Institute (IFAM), 201
Murillo, Roberto, 130
Museo de Arte Costarricense, 173
Music, 164, 166, 172, 175

Names, 95
Naranjo, Carmen, 175
National Association of Educators (ANDE), 133
National Institute of Apprenticeship (INA), 126, 127
National Institute of Housing and Urbanization (INVU), 76, 222

Nationalism, 20, 124, 127–28, 155, 204, 207, 212
National Liberation Party (PLN) (See Political parties)
National Parks, 6
National Production Council (CNP), 197
National Republican Party (See Political parties)
National self-image, 1, 7, 8–13, 203, 204, 207–11, 214
National Symphony Orchestra, 172
Neighborhoods, 42, 44, 45, 46
Newspapers, 39–40, 174, 191
Nicaragua, 9, 17, 18, 19, 27, 29, 49, 64, 69, 138, 203, 213
Norris, Thomas L., 156
Nuñez, Benjamin, 27, 128, 142
Nutrition, 77–83
   of infants, 95

Occultism and witchcraft, 152–54
Oduber, Daniel, 47, 142, 185, 191, 193, 200, 204, 214, 219
Oduber, Marjorie de, 174
Old age (See Age roles)
Organization of American States, 29, 203
Orlich, Francisco, 219
Osejo, Rafael Francisco, 115
Oxcart, painted, 171–72

Pacheco, Fausto, 231
Pacific Railroad, 21, 159
Pact of the Caribbean, 25
Painting and sculpture, 173
Panama, 49, 203, 219
Peace, 202–4
   colonial poverty, 17–18
   cultural value, 9, 10, 124, 166, 169, 192
   desire for social approval, 46, 134, 172, 204
Peasants (See Campesinos)
Peones:
   daily routine, 77–79
   early coffee boom, 49
   majority of "lower class," 54, 59
   poverty, 58, 60, 63, 81
   relations with employers, 50, 51, 223
Pérez, Rafael Angel, 170
Personalism:
   business, 89
   employment, 11, 89
   in government and politics, 11, 13, 181, 182, 193
   religion, 149, 151
Pharmacists, 87
Philip II, 16
Physicians, 83, 84, 85, 87, 223
Picado, Teodoro, 24, 27
Pinto, Julieta, 231
Pinto, Ronald Fernández, 201
Planning, government (See Ministry of Planning)
Play, children's, 96
Police, 86, 195–96
Political participation, 187–91
Political parties, 180–83, 201, 235
   minor, 179, 182–84
   National Liberation Party (PLN), 29, 52, 128, 141, 180, 181, 182, 188, 189, 210–11, 217
   National Republican Party, 24, 181–82
   Vanguardia Popular, 24, 182
Pope John XXIII, 142, 154
Population:
   age distribution (graph), 99
   birth control, 92, 94, 224
   changes in birth and death rates, 32, 81, 92
   fertility, 92, 225
   geographic distribution, 34, 37
   growth, 7, 23, 35, 76, 92, 93 (graph), 94, 207
Poverty:
   colonial, 17–18
   neighborhood solidarity, 42
   peones, 37, 54, 58, 60, 63, 81
   redistributive justice, 82, 210
   regional inequalities, 33–34
Powell, Reed Madsen, 149–50
Precolumbian inhabitants, 14–15, 216
Pregnancy, 94
Presidency, 18–29, 179, 191, 193
Press, freedom of, 25, 191

Pressure groups, 189–91
  bureaucracy, government, 190, 198
  business, 190
  compared to other Latin American
    countries, 190
  labor unions, 23, 31, 132, 133
  teachers, 133
  women, 22, 25, 189
  youth, 22, 98, 189
Prieto, Emilia, 175
Protestantism, 154–56
Public Health (See Health)
Puntarenas, town of, 43, 159

Quirós, Tito Prudencio, 42

Race:
  cultural perceptions of, 64, 219
  intermixtures (amalgamation), 48–49,
    89, 224
  prejudice and discrimination, 64–68
  pride in "whiteness," 64, 210
Radio, 40, 78, 96, 126, 166
Ramírez, José, 175
Rawson, Ian, 81
Recreation (See Leisure)
Religion (See Ecumenism; Occultism and
  witchcraft; Protestantism, Roman
  Catholic clergy; Roman Catholicism;
  Saints)
Richardson, Miles, 55
Rodríguez, José Joaquín, 21, 140
Rodríguez Quirós, Carlos Humberto,
  143, 149
Rodríguez Vega, Eugenio, 11
Roman Catholic clergy:
  anticlericalism, 21, 139, 144, 154
  foreigners among, 141
  ideological divisions, 142–43
  Jesuits, 139, 140, 141
  nuns, 141–42
  organization, 141
  political influence, 21, 138, 139, 142,
    185
  prestige of, 143–44, 149–50
  size and geographic distribution, 141,
    145–46

social activism, 143
  training of, 141
Roman Catholicism:
  charismatic movement, 149
  colonial era, 17, 138
  "development," 137–38
  education for family life, 103
  financing of Church, 141
  importance of, to Catholic majority,
    10, 137, 138–39, 140, 144, 145–51,
    225
  in nineteenth century, 138–40
  official national religion, 137, 138,
    140, 141
  public schools' curriculum, 140, 144,
    229
  saints, 150–51
  social acceptability, 155, 230
  See also Roman Catholic clergy
Romero, Jorge, 187, 188
Rumania, Costa Ricans studying in, 127
Rural Assistance Guard, 196

Saints (See Roman Catholicism)
Salazar, Marco Tulio, 132
Salguero, Miguel, 206
Salvadoreans, vii
Sanabria, Victor, 23, 49, 89, 140, 141,
  146
Sánchez, Jorge, 75
Sancho, Mario, 161
Sandinists, 203–4
San José, 40–42
  domination of country by, 43, 174, 201
  founding, 49, 50
  migration to, 37, 117
  slums and public housing, 76
  social class structure, 51, 52, 57, 58, 60
Santamaría, Juan, 20
Santo Tomás University, 21, 115, 116
Schools (See Education, formal;
  Teachers)
Seligson, Mitchell, 187
Servants, 48, 80, 107, 223
Sewage disposal, 72
Sex, 89, 90, 100, 101, 103, 110, 167, 185
Sex roles:
  aging, 111
  childrearing, 96, 97, 98, 100

courtship, 100–103
daily routine, 77–81
defined by law, 107
employment, 107–8
leisure, 108, 165, 166–67, 170–71
machismo, 9, 85, 86, 90, 96, 100, 102, 106, 163
marianismo, 90, 109
marriage, 101, 108–9
religion, 144, 146, 147, 149
Slavery, colonial, 48, 219–20, 224
Soccer, 45, 46, 78, 168–69
Social change, 7, 29–32, 205, 207–14
Social class:
 colonial, 48–49
 housing, 72–76
 income distribution, 53
 industrialization, 52, 56, 223
 interclass interaction, 50, 51, 55, 59, 167
 law enforcement, 197–98
 leisure, 159, 166–69
 lifestyles, 50, 51, 55–56, 60
 literature, 194, 195
 marriage and family, 48–49, 57, 94, 96–99, 102–6
 myth of classlessness, 47, 48, 52, 54, 55, 60, 64, 69–70
 occupations, 53, 56–57
 since 1948 civil war, 52–57
 social mobility, 50, 52, 53, 57, 58, 59, 61, 223
 urban-rural comparison, 57–60
 See also Lower class; Middle class; Peones; Poverty; Upper class; Working class
Social control:
 childrearing, 96–98
 courts, 179–80
 crime and corrections, 195–97, 230, 234
 desire for social approval, 10–11, 46, 134–35, 172, 217
 education, 124
 employment in government bureaucracy, 198
 recreation, 160
 Roman Catholicism, 137–50
 See also Law; Military; Police

Social Mobility (*See* Social class)
Social security, 23, 84–85, 87, 91, 200
Soil, 6, 31, 34, 35
Somoza Debayle, Anastasio, 203–4
Somoza García, Anastasio, 27, 29
Soto, Bernardo, 22
Soviet Union, 24, 127, 182, 202
Spain:
 cultural heritage of, 10
 discovery and colonization by, 16–18, 48
 educational aid from, 127
 religious mission in colonial era, 138
Sports (*See* Leisure)
Squatters, 37, 74–75
Stone, Samuel, 47, 48, 49, 50, 52, 178, 181
Suñol, Julio, 196
Superior Council of Education, 120
Supreme Court, 179
Supreme Electoral Tribunal (TSE), 25, 27, 28, 179, 180, 184, 185, 200
Syndicate of Costa Rican Educators, 133

Taxes, 22, 30, 64, 82–83, 192, 199–200, 211
Teachers:
 as a political force, 22, 133
 as role models, 121, 133–34
 rural, 133–34
 social class, backgrounds and attitudes of, 121, 133
 status of, 131–34
 training of, 116, 124, 132–33
 unions, 132, 133
 universities, 134–35
Television, 40, 78–79, 160, 166, 167, 195
Theological Institute of Central America, 143
Thiel, Bishop, 21, 139, 140, 142
Third World, Costa Rica compared to, 6–7, 30, 82, 177, 187, 210
Ticos, alleged origin of term, 1
Tinoco, Federico and Joaquín, 22–23
Total Language program, 124
Towns, 42–44
Trade, balance of, 31
Transportation, 17, 39, 159, 160, 197

Trejos, José Joaquín, 182
Trudeau, Robert, 178, 187

Ulate, Otilio, 25, 27, 28, 29, 141
Unemployment (*See* Employment)
Unions (*See* Labor relations)
United Brands (*See* United Fruit Company)
United Fruit Company, 51, 52, 66
United Nations, 202
United States, influence of:
  cultural, 69, 82, 166, 202, 204
  educational, 127
  economic, 30, 31, 154, 202
  immigration, 69
  military, 231
  political, 27
  religious, 141, 154, 202
Universities, 128–31, 134–35
  See also Santo Tomás University
Upper class, 48–54, 219, 220
  daily routine, 80–81
  friendship, 162
  government, 19, 20, 21, 49, 50, 181, 188
  housing, 73–74
  marriage and family, 92, 96, 97, 100, 101, 103, 104, 106, 108, 109
  pride in ancestry, 48, 54, 62
  recreation, 159, 160
Urbanization, 37
Urban-rural distinctions:
  communities, 33–46
  education, 118, 122–23, 228
  housing, health, and daily routine, 73–85
  politics and government, 188–89, 194
  religion, 145
  social class, 57–58, 60
Uruguay, 127, 199, 205, 211–12

Values, cultural, 9–13, 207–11
Vázquez de Coronado, Juan, 16, 51
Vega Rodríguez, Eugenio, 192
Vegetation, 6, 34
  See also Deforestation
Venezuela, 203
Vesco, Robert, 54
Villages and hamlets, 44–46
Volio, Fernando, 118, 125, 134
Volio, Jorge, 23, 142, 181

Wagner, Moritz, and Carl Scherzer, 138–39, 141, 148, 160, 170, 227
Walker, William, 19, 20
Water supply, 72
Welfare state, 29, 30, 181
West Indians (*See* Blacks)
Witchcraft (*See* Occultism and witchcraft)
Women:
  colonial era, 48
  education, 107, 132
  heads of households, 91–92
  housework, 77–79
  migration to urban centers, 38
  political force, 22, 25, 141, 189
  recreation, 160, 170–71
  religion, 144, 146
  sexuality of, 89
  See also Sex roles
Work, attitudes toward, 50, 61, 62, 63, 123–24, 158
Working class, 50, 51, 53–54
  daily routine, 77–79
  housing, 72–75
  income distribution, 54
  occupations, 50, 54

Youth, 98, 100, 160, 175–76, 189

Zumbado, Fernando, 34–35